# THE QUAKE

# THE QUAKE

Richard Laymon

St. Martin's Press
New York

Library of Congress Cataloging-in-Publication Data

Laymon, Richard.
The quake / Richard Laymon.
p.      cm.
"A Thomas Dunne book."
ISBN 0-312-13150-X
I. Title.
PS3562.A9555Q24    1995
813'.54—dc20      95-5317    CIP

First published in Great Britain by Headline Book Publishing

First U.S. Edition: May 1995
10 9 8 7 6 5 4 3 2 1

This book is dedicated
to
Mike Bailey

The sort of editor that writers hope for
but rarely find

Thanks, Mike

# THE QUAKE

# ONE

Twenty minutes before the quake hit, Stanley Banks was standing at his living room window. Though he held the sports section of the *L.A. Times* at chest level, he only pretended to read it. He pretended, every weekday morning, to read it.

In case Mother should happen to wheel herself into the room and spy him stationed by the window.

Usually, she remained in the kitchen sipping coffee and sucking cigarettes and listening to the radio.

But sometimes she put in surprise appearances, and the newspaper made a good diversion.

By now, she knew that Stanley was in the habit of standing at the window to take advantage of the morning light while he studied the front page of the sports section.

That was what he had told her often enough.

It wasn't the truth, of course.

In truth, he stood there to watch the sidewalk.

He was watching it, now, over the top edge of the newspaper.

He hoped he hadn't missed her.

He glanced at his wristwatch. Eight o'clock on the nose. She ought to be running past the house within the next five minutes.

'Stanley!' his mother called. 'Stanley! Be a dear and fetch me some matches.'

Stanley felt his throat tighten.

'Just a minute,' he called.

'Do as you're asked, please.'

*I'm gonna miss her!*

Maybe not. Maybe not, if I hurry.

He slapped the newspaper onto the end table, then strode across the small living room to the fireplace, grabbed a handful of matchbooks from a wicker basket on the mantel and hurried through the dining room to the kitchen. He tossed them onto the table in front of his mother. They hit the surface hard, bouncing and scattering. One matchbook skidded off the edge and dropped to the floor beside her wheelchair.

Stanley whirled around. He managed only a single step of his escape before a harsh voice demanded, 'Stop right there.'

'Muh-therrrr.'

'Look at me when I speak to you.'

'Yes, ma'am.' Stanley faced her.

Alma Banks, squinting at him through her pink-framed glasses, jabbed a Virginia Slims between her lips and fired a match. She sucked its flame to the tip of her cigarette. She inhaled, then blew twin gray funnels out her nostrils.

'I asked you for matches, young man. Not for a display of temper.'

'I'm sorry. If you just could've waited for a couple of minutes . . .'

'Your time is so precious that you can't afford to do a small errand for your own mother?'

'No,' he said. 'I'm sorry.'

*I'm going to miss her!*

'Matches. That was all I asked for. Matches. Do I ask so much of you? You're a grown man. You're *thirty-two* years old. You live in my home. You eat my food. Is it so much to ask you to do a little something for me once in a blue moon? Is it?'

'No. I'm sorry. Can I go now?'

'*May* you go now?'

'May I? Please?'

'Go.' A flap of her hand kicked the smoke cloud coiling and twisting away from her face.

'Thank you, Mother.' He headed for the living room, forcing himself not to rush. 'I'll be back to do the dishes in a few minutes. I just want to finish the sports section.'

'You and your sports section. It isn't going to vanish, you know.' She wasn't letting up, but she wasn't following him. Her wheelchair remained silent. She was apparently content to pursue him with her voice. 'Your precious sports page isn't going to go up in a puff of smoke, do you know that? It won't go anywhere.'

He was already at the window.

'But it can't wait two minutes while you find your mother some matches?'

'I *got* you the matches,' he called.

'You threw them at me, that's what you did.'

'I'm sorry.'

'You *should* be.'

He checked his wristwatch. Three minutes past eight.

*If I've missed her . . .*

'I won't always be around, you know,' Alma reminded him.

Time for her to start pouring on the waterworks.

Stanley almost felt like crying, himself. He'd missed his chance for today, been cheated out of it by the selfish whims of . . .

And then she appeared.

Stanley thought, *My God*.

No matter how many times he saw her, no matter where, no matter what she might be wearing, a glimpse of Sheila Banner never failed to slam Stanley in the heart and suck out his breath and raise his penis.

'Oh, Sheila,' he whispered.

She came into view from beyond the oleanders at the left side of the lawn, long legs striding out, arms swinging at her sides with relaxed grace. Her white shoes and socks were so bright they flashed like sunlit snow. Her tawny legs gleamed, alive with shifting curves of muscle. They were bare all the way up to the golden trim of her shorts.

The royal blue shorts shimmered and flowed around Sheila as she ran. Stanley could *feel* how they caressed her. Slick as oil. Sliding over her thighs and buttocks, rubbing silken and warm between her legs.

She wore an old, faded blue T-shirt. Big and loose, it fluttered and flapped around her. Its chest shifted up and down with the jouncing of her breasts. From their steady rhythm, Stanley could tell that she was wearing a bra.

She never ran without one.

Stanley actually glimpsed her bra when her right arm cocked back. Its side showed near the bottom of the T-shirt's armhole. It was white this morning.

The hole gaped enough so that he could see a lot of the bra.

Stanley wished she was not wearing it. Then he would be able to see most of her breast through the armhole. And the way her shirt was cut off at the waist, the way it hung down from her breasts, he would be able to look up from underneath and see them both. Their smooth round undersides . . .

Sure, he thought. If I'm lying on the sidewalk.

After noting that today, as always, she wore a bra, Stanley lifted his gaze to her face. A glorious face. At once smooth and hard, delicate and powerful, silk and granite, innocent and sophisticated. But altogether beautiful, the face of a movie queen and a warrior goddess melded into one stunning, incredible Sheila Banner.

Hair like a thick banner of gold flowed behind Sheila, and was the last Stanley saw of her when she ran past the bushes at the far side of the driveway.

Trembling, he took a deep breath.

Then he retrieved his sports section and stepped over to his armchair in the corner of the room. After sitting down, he pushed himself against the back of the chair so that it reclined and the footrest swung up. He raised the newspaper and stared at it.

3

He imagined himself going after Sheila.

Running out to the sidewalk after she passed, and following. At a discreet distance, of course.

It wouldn't be against the law.

Why *don't* I? he asked himself. Why don't I really *do* it instead of just sitting here and dreaming about it?

She'd be bound to notice me.

So what?

Plenty of so what. She sees Stan the Man, all six foot two inches of him, all two hundred and eighty pounds of him, all red and sweaty and lumbering after her, she isn't going to be exactly overwhelmed with ardor. She'll be disgusted or scared, one or the other. Or both.

And maybe she sees which house I came out of, so she changes her route and that's the last time she ever runs by.

And maybe she realizes it's *my* house behind her backyard fence, and maybe she starts to worry about what else I might be up to . . . So maybe she starts being more careful about shutting the curtains, more careful about what she does in the yard. Warns the girl about me, too.

Lovely girl. Not in the same league as her mother, though.

To Stanley's way of thinking, *nobody* was. Sheila Banner formed a league of one.

He wished he had photos of her. He didn't dare sneak pictures of her with his good Minolta, though. He would have to send the film out to get it developed. People at the processing lab would see it. They might suspect something. For that matter, one of them might be a *friend* of hers.

Stanley just couldn't risk it.

He used to have a Polaroid camera. He'd bought it shortly after moving back into Mother's house, ten months ago. Because he just *had* to have photographs of the incredible woman who ran past the window each morning – who *lived* directly behind him.

He'd made the mistake of showing the new camera to Mother. Showing it to her before he'd even had a chance to use it.

She'd turned it this way and that, inspecting it. Then she'd narrowed her eyes at him. 'Do you suspect, for one minute, that I don't know what this is for?'

He'd blushed hot.

'What are you talking about?' he'd blurted.

'As if you didn't know. And who *is* it that you plan to take your dirty pictures of? Me?'

'No!' he'd cried out.

And watched Mother hurl the Polaroid. It struck the fireplace bricks. Bits of plastic and glass flew like shrapnel. The demolished camera bounced forward a couple of feet, dropped, and crashed to the tiles of the outer hearth.

'I won't have it,' she had informed him. 'Not in my home. Not now. Not ever. I'm ashamed of you.'

Remembering the fate of his Polaroid, Stanley let out a sigh.

I'm such a gutless wonder, he thought.

I could've bought a new Polaroid the next day. I could buy one *today*, for that matter.

*What Mother doesn't know won't hurt her.*

*But if she catches me . . .*

*If she catches me.*

Stanley wished he had the guts to ignore that little refrain. *If she catches me*. Oh, the things he would've done if not for that. The things he would've seen. The wonderful opportunities . . .

He was thirty-two years old, and he felt as if he had missed his life.

Missed it because there had always been a woman watching over him like a prison guard. First Mother, then his wife Thelma, and now Mother again.

I shouldn't have moved in here, he told himself. *Stupid stupid stupid!*

After Thelma's death, however, Mother had begged him to come and live with her. It hadn't seemed like a bad idea at the time. For one thing, Mother possessed a considerable amount of wealth and a little stucco house valued at nearly $400,000. For another thing, Stanley's job had perished with Thelma.

Thelma was the only woman who had ever cared about him. So in spite of her age and size and face, he'd married her two weeks after his high school graduation. At that time, she had already been a fairly successful author of children's books, making enough money for both of them. With no need to find a job, Stanley had gone to work for his wife, answering her fan letters, handling such chores as photocopying and mailing manuscripts, and so on. He'd been her secretary, really. And not a very good one.

With her death, Stanley's prospects of finding a halfway decent job seemed remote. He doubted that he would be able to get by on her royalties.

So he'd agreed to move in with Mother.

And he'd missed his chance for freedom.

He had been like a prisoner whose guard had dropped dead while on duty, leaving his cell unlocked. He could've fled. All it would've required was an ounce of guts. But instead, he'd waited like a model prisoner for the new guard to show up.

*But the cell has a great view*, he told himself, and grinned.

*Sheila.*

*I would've missed out on her.*

5

Stanley checked his wristwatch.

Seventeen minutes past eight.

Sheila would've been back inside her house for some time, by now. With all his meandering thoughts, Stanley had neglected his habit of tracking her movements with his imagination.

He considered pretending he hadn't missed out. He'd done that before, though, and it just wasn't the same. The thrill was to picture her at the *same moment* as her actions: finishing her run, taking out her house key . . .

Oh where, oh where had she kept it this morning? Tucked in a sock? Nothing so mundane as that. No no no. Slipped beneath the waistband of her panties, perhaps. Or maybe she'd kept it safe inside a cup of her bra where it had made an imprint of itself on her breast. So many places where the key might hide, a warm secret pressed to her skin. Places where she would need to delve with long fingers to . . .

*Quit it*, he told himself. *You missed all that. You've gotta catch up and make it simultaneous.*

By now, she had probably finished stripping off her sweaty clothes.

Stanley *loved* to picture that. How she started with a shoe, usually balancing on one leg while she raised the other, bent over slightly and clutched the shoe with . . .

*Catch up, damn it!*

*Yes. Right. What's she doing now? At this very instant?*

Stanley looked at his wristwatch.

Eight-nineteen.

Probably she was already standing under the shower, its hot spray splashing her naked body. Or perhaps she was sprawled out in her bathtub.

Stanley didn't know whether she preferred showers or baths.

Being such an athlete, Sheila was just the sort to prefer showers. But her more feminine and sensual side would relish lounging in a tub full of hot water.

So she did both, the choice depending on her mood.

On *my* mood, Stanley corrected himself.

This seemed like a shower day.

After folding the sports section and resting it on his lap, Stanley shut his eyes. And saw the shower doors through swirling twists of steam. They were sliding doors of clear glass. In spite of the steam, they were not fogged up. He could see through them as if they weren't there at all.

He could see Sheila standing beneath the nozzle, her back to the spray, her head tilted back, her elbows high as she pushed her fingers through her soaked hair. Her face gleamed with water. Shiny rivulets streamed down her breasts, which trembled ever so slightly with the motion of her

6

arms. Drops like liquid diamonds gathered at the tips of her nipples and fell, one by one . . .

Stanley's chair jerked beneath him. In that instant, he thought that Mother had somehow caught wind of his dirty daydream and rammed him with her wheelchair. *Caught you, you filthy pervert!*

By the time he got his eyes open, however, he knew that Mother had nothing to do with the alarming jolt.

Because she wasn't in the room, and the room itself was juddering with such rough quickness that it blurred.

Beside him, the lamp pitched over.

He battered his newspaper aside and leaned forward, dropping the footrest. As he shoved himself out of the chair, he shouted, 'Earthquake!'

Of course, Mother already knew that.

Stanley could hear her scream over the sound of his own voice, the roar of the quake, the clamor of the front window shattering and the noises of things all over the house crashing to the floor.

A falling chunk struck his shoulder when he was halfway to the front door. Plaster?

*The ceiling!*

*I've gotta get out of here!*

He reached out and grabbed the doorknob, turned it and pulled. Only when the door refused to swing open did he remember that he needed to unfasten the dead bolt. He let go of the knob and tried to nip the brass turner between his thumb and forefinger. It dodged him as if it didn't want to get caught.

'Bastard!' he yelled.

Then he pinched it. He gave it a quick twist. A lurch of the house tried to hurl him backward. He grabbed the doorknob just in time, saving himself from a tumble.

'Stanley!' his mother squealed. 'Help me! Help me!'

He looked past his shoulder.

And here came Mother, hunched over and wheeling in from the dining room like a contender making a sprint for the finish line. Clods and slabs of plaster dropped all around her as the ceiling broke apart. White dust sifted down on her.

'Stanley!' she shrieked.

'I've gotta get the door open!'

He turned the knob, yanked. The door flew toward him. He had neglected to unhook the guard chain, but didn't notice his oversight until the chain and uprooted jamb plate lashed his brow.

He staggered backward, swinging the door with him. His grip on the knob began steering him sideways toward the demolished window, so he let go. His own weight shoved him back across the floor. The chair stopped him. It reclined, popped up its footrest, scooted with the impact and pounded the wall behind it.

*Right back where I started!*

Stanley hugged his head with both arms and screamed.

And watched his mother.

He stopped screaming.

Because, after all, this was serious but it was also pretty funny. Funny how he'd gotten thrown right back into his chair. And *really* funny how Mother had quit her bee-line for the door (maybe because the route was blocked with ceiling rubble?) and was wheeling herself around in frantic circles. She was no longer screaming, either. And she had ceased calling for assistance from Stanley.

Hunkered down and working her push rims like crazy, she circled and shouted, circled and shouted, 'Oh my oh my oh my oh my!'

A piece of ceiling plaster the size of a dinner plate dropped straight down in front of her. Either blessed with a good portion of luck or sensing the danger, she halted her wheelchair just in time. The plaster smacked the floor at her feet. 'Oh my oh my oh . . .'

'Hey, Ma!' Stanley yelled. 'The sky is falling!'

She didn't seem to hear him.

As if somebody had heard him, however, the house collapsed. Not all of it, though.

The part that collapsed did not include the living room.

From his reclined easy chair, Stanley only *saw* the cave-in that happened just beyond the dining room archway. A big cave-in that smashed the table flat against the floor and disintegrated the chairs and buried it all under a pile of plaster and wood and stucco. Through the thick fog of dust, Stanley saw sunlight shining down on the heaped debris.

He muttered, 'Holy fucking shit.'

He thought, I'd better get my butt out of here pronto.

He pictured himself making a detour on his way to the door. Scooping Mother out of her wheelchair and running with her, dodging this way and that as sundered support beams slammed down. Getting out the door and clear of the house even as the rest of it crashed down.

*Quit thinking about it and DO it!*

*But what if I leave her?*

*What if I leave her and the house falls down?*

*Wouldn't that be a fucking pity?*

*Let's just get my own ass out of here – and quick!*

As he leaned forward and shoved his heels against the footrest, the quake stopped.

The end of the roar left a great silence.

Mixed in with the silence were quiet sounds. Stanley heard the house creaking as its motions subsided. He heard the distant *wow-wow-wow* of car and house alarms. Somewhere far off, dogs were barking.

His mother's wheelchair was silent. So was her voice.

He looked at her.

She sat motionless, still hunkered over, head down, hands still clutching the push rims of her wheelchair.

'Mother?' Stanley asked.

She didn't move.

'Mother, are you all right?'

Stanley raised himself out of the chair.

'Mother?'

She lifted her head. White powder and flakes drifted off her hair and shoulders as she sat up. Her pink-framed glasses hung crooked on her face. She straightened them. She blinked at Stanley. Her chin was trembling. Spittle had dribbled down from her mouth, cutting moist streaks through the plaster dust.

In a shaky, piping voice, she said, 'It's over?'

'It's over,' Stanley told her.

He went to her.

'What ever will we do now?'

'Nothing to worry about,' Stanley said.

He crouched beside her wheelchair and picked up a chunk of plaster the size of a flagstone. He hefted it overhead.

He could see by the look in her eyes that she suddenly knew what was coming.

'Stanley!' She cringed away and started to bring up an arm.

The good, heavy slab of plaster broke in half when it struck the top of her head. It made a *thuck*. She made an '*Hunh!*' Her glasses hopped down to the tip of her nose, but didn't fall off.

Stanley held on to half the plaster slab. The other half fell, bounced off Mother's right shoulder and dropped to the floor.

She sat very still for a moment.

Stanley raised his slab.

While he considered whether or not to hit her again, her head slumped down. Slowly, she leaned forward. Her glasses fell. They punched her skirt, making a narrow valley between her thighs.

She leaned farther and farther as if hoping to peer down over her knees and find something wonderful hidden beneath her chair.

Stanley stepped back and watched.

She leaned so far forward that her knuckles brushed the debris on the floor. Then her rump lifted off the wheelchair seat. Her head thumped the floor. She did a clumsy, crooked somersault that showed off more of her gray pantyhose than Stanley cared to see. Her legs came down straight

9

and fast. The heels of her shoes exploded glass shards from the demolished window. She bucked as if trying to sit up, then dropped down again and lay still.

Stanley gave her hip a tap with the toe of his moccasin.

'Mother? Mother, are you all right?'

She didn't stir. She didn't answer.

He gave her a good solid kick. The blow shook her, wobbled her head. Stanley saw blood trickling out of her ear.

'That's a bad sign,' he said, and couldn't help but laugh.

Then his laughing stopped.

What killed it was the thought that Sheila Banner might be ruined, crushed beneath the rubble of her home.

# TWO

One minute before the quake hit, Clint Banner yawned and glanced at his empty coffee mug.

It was emblazoned with a portrait of John Wayne as Rooster Cogburn from *True Grit*. A birthday present from his daughter Barbara, who liked to insist that Clint looked 'exactly like Hondo.' She hadn't been able to find a mug with Hondo on it, however, so she'd settled for Cogburn. 'I know you don't look like *that*,' she'd said, making a face. To which Clint had responded, trying to mimic Duke's cadence and voice, 'Give me a couple more years and an eyepatch, little lady.'

He yawned again.

It was eight-nineteen on Friday morning. He had been up since four-thirty, his gimmick for beating the system. Jump out of bed, dress in the bathroom so you don't wake Sheila, and hit the road by a quarter to five for a forty-minute drive through the dark. A drive that would take you twice as long if you slept to a reasonable hour like six. Arriving so early, you had the offices to yourself for a few hours. That was nice. And you got to leave before two, ahead of the afternoon rush. Plenty of advantages.

Took a lot out of you, though.

Another yawn, then Clint picked up his empty mug, slid back his chair, and sidestepped clear of his desk. He planned to get a refill. But he only took one step.

He almost had time to wonder what that *roar* was.

But in an instant he knew what it was. Not an eighteen-wheeler or a freight train cannon-balling toward the building. Not a Boeing 747 about to take down the wall.

The roar came out of nowhere and before Clint could quite find time to wonder what it might be he knew it was a quake because it hit.

It sounded like a quake. It felt like a quake. This was Southern California, land of quakes, so it probably wasn't a 747 crashing into the building. It wasn't a tornado inside the office with him. It wasn't the shock wave from a comet or a nuclear warhead striking ground zero a mile away; they might feel and sound a lot like this, but this was an earthquake.

First it roared.

Then it hurled a body block against Clint.

He staggered sideways, but kept his feet.

A quake had never hit him so hard before.

A *good one*, he thought. *A really good one. Maybe a six-point. Maybe bigger.*

Time for it to fade away now.

It didn't fade.

It grew.

It shook the window blinds so hard they clattered and jumped. It splintered windows. It killed the fluorescent lights. It wobbled the walls. It clawed acoustical tiles off the ceiling. It cluttered the air with the flying debris of papers, case files, pens, Rolodexes, staplers. Drawers of desks and file cabinets leaped open. Computer keyboards and monitors slid and dropped. Chairs on wheels raced across the wild floor.

Clint thought, *My God, it's the Big One! This is it!*

He wondered if this was his day to die.

*Just stand your ground*, he told himself. *It'll go away.*

Standing his ground was not easy. The office floor bucked and jumped. The carpet had *waves* in it – combers two feet high that raced for the wall.

*Impossible*, he thought.

He was seeing·it, though – floor surf.

Clint pranced and stayed up.

And thought, *It's a race. Which calls it quits first, the quake or the building?*

*If the quake wins, I'm dead meat.*

He began his dash for the stairway. Knees pumping high, arms overhead. Dodging, jumping.

*Get the fuck outa here!*

As he ran, he recalled his years of glib wisdom. His quake cracks. 'When your number's up,' pause for effect, 'it's an eight-point-five.' A little Richter scale humor. Or his favorite bit: 'No call to be afraid of earthquakes. A quake is completely harmless, never hurt anyone.' Pause for effect. 'It's the *shit that falls on your head* that'll kill you!'

Or taking a dive down the stairway, he suddenly thought.

At the top of the stairs, he reached for the handrail and missed. He reached again. This time, he caught the wooden rail. But it was jerked out of his grip.

*No holding on.*

The stairwell looked like a narrow tunnel. A steep one. A funhouse slide into a pit. It juddered and twitched down to where the light from above faded. The landing and door were somewhere below in the darkness.

Don't try it, Clint told himself. Wait till the shaking stops!

*Sure thing.*

He bounded down the stairs, leaping, taking two at a time, slapping the walls to help his balance.

Like sprinting down a mountainside, an avalanche on your tail. You'll probably take a headfirst dive, but it's worth the risk. Speed's the trick. Staying in front so you don't get buried, crushed. Staying in front, no matter what.

*Gotta get outa this place!*

Through the roar of the quake, he heard his own yell.

It occurred to him that a fellow with more panache might shout 'Geronimo!' in such straits.

But all Clint yelled on his stampede down the stairwell was, 'YAHHHHHHHH!!!'

At the bottom, he crashed against a wall. He bounced off, fell against the stairs, scurried up and pawed the shuddering door until he found its handle. He levered the handle down. He pushed. Light from the foyer stung his eyes.

He rushed out of the stairwell, dashed across the reception area, flung himself against the front door, threw it open and ran outside into the morning sunlight.

The earth still shook. The quake still roared.

*My God*, Clint thought, *it's never going to stop!*

Covering his head with both arms, he raced into the street.

Into the middle of the street, away from falling glass and walls that might crumble.

He whirled around. The two-story building that housed the law offices of Haversham & Dumont, his employers, appeared to bounce and shimmy. Clint knew it couldn't possibly be jumping about so much without disintegrating. *It's jumping, but not as much as I am*, he thought.

He glanced up and down the street.

Saw several cars.

Couldn't tell for sure whether they were approaching or parked.

Probably just parked, he thought. Nobody would keep on driving through all this.

The cars were being tossed about like skiffs on a rough sea. And seemed to shriek with panic, their alarms set off by the quake.

A sound like the rip of tough fabric made Clint snap his head forward. He muttered, 'Jesus!' Moments before, the front of the office building had been intact except for several shattered windows. Now, it looked as if an oak tree had blasted its way through the stucco wall.

*Got out of there just in the nick of time.*

A horn blared. Its noise melded with the car alarms and the roar of the quake and a legion of other noises – a chaos of shatters and clashes and

13

slams and sirens – so that Clint was only vaguely aware of the horn. The blare was like a sight glimpsed in his peripheral vision. Something barely noticed, vaguely troubling.

Until it wailed in his ears and he turned his head and saw a red Toyota pickup truck torpedoing at him through the road surf.

He yelled, 'SHIT!' and dived for the curb.

Airborne, he thought he'd done a halfway decent job of leaping clear. The bastard wouldn't kill him, probably just clip off both his feet at the ankles.

But he felt no pain until he landed. The pavement scorched his hands and knees, slammed his chest, knocked his breath out. For a moment, he felt as if he were sliding across a cheese grater. Then he stopped skidding. He thought, *Bastard*! and raised his head, wanting to shout at the crazy asshole behind the wheel of the Toyota. But he had no breath for shouting.

The asshole had painted out some of the big white letters on his tailgate. Changing the brand name to TOY.

Clint realized that he had actually been able to read the word TOY.

The word TOY was not a vibrating, pounding blur.

*The quake's stopped!*

Clint thought, *Thank God!*

Then he thought, *Oh my God!* because the red TOY hadn't slowed down for the cross-street any more than it had slowed down for him, and this time there wasn't a man in its way but a gray BMW rushing into the intersection from the left.

Just short of the crosswalk, the TOY cut hard to the right.

Maybe the driver thought he had cleared the curb at the corner. Maybe he figured a bounce over the curb would be better than getting broadsided by the BMW. But hadn't he noticed the power pole? Maybe he'd figured it would snap like a toothpick when he hit it, and he would speed merrily on his way.

The pole did snap.

But the driver didn't speed through a quick spray of splinters.

The pole didn't burst into splinters at all.

Instead, its stump bludgeoned its way through the front of the TOY.

The TOY stopped very fast.

Clint couldn't see what happened to the driver.

But the man in the passenger seat blasted headfirst through the windshield. He wore a blue baseball cap, a plaid shirt, and jeans. Obviously, he had not worn a seatbelt.

He soared over the TOY's crumpled hood. The crown of his baseballcap looked smashed flat. The bill of the cap dangled by one corner and flapped like a fractured wing. His blue jeans were at knee level as he shot past the collapsing power pole. They slipped lower, hobbling his ankles as he glided down for a landing on the far side of the corner.

The BMW, brakes shrieking, intercepted him.

He hit the passenger window headfirst.

The window burst.

His head went through it. The rest of his body didn't. The rest of his body snapped sideways and slammed the back door of the car, then dropped away. It tumbled and flopped, headless, as the BMW skidded to a halt and the power pole finished its downsweep and finally crashed against the street.

The TOY, its dented roof supporting one end of the pole, looked like a cheap metal parody of the Passion – a Jesus on wheels that had broken down on the way to Calvary.

Snapped lines, alive with juice, whipped and crackled high above the crossbeams.

Clint got to his feet fast, ready to bolt if any of the wires should try for him.

The way they leaped and sprang about, no telling . . .

The lines died. They went limp, sagged in midair, and dropped toward the pavement.

*It's over*, Clint thought. *Over. And I'm still here.*

He took a deep breath. He looked around.

Nothing was shaking any more. Most of the buildings along the street were still standing, but two on the next block had collapsed, piling the southbound lane with rubble.

No cars seemed to be moving.

*I made it*, he thought. *The Big One's over, and I'm still here. A few scratches, that's all.*

He glanced at the scuffed heels of his hands. Then at the torn knees of his trousers.

*No big deal.*

*No problem at all with the quake, it was the Toyota that damn near creamed me.*

He pictured himself saying that to Sheila and Barbara. It was the sort of crack they would expect from him, and he would have to remember to lay it on them when they all sat around and told each other their stories . . .

*What if they're not okay?*

*They were in it, too, you dumb shit. A quake that strong . . . But maybe it wasn't so bad over on the west side. They're more than thirty miles.*

*Maybe it was worse.*

*For all you know, Sheila or Barbara might be . . .*

He didn't allow himself to think the word, but he pictured them dead.

Sheila at home, Barbara at school. Both of them crushed and bloody and dead.

Clint swung his eyes to the ejected TOY passenger, glimpsed a smear of red between the shoulders, noticed that the pants had disappeared entirely, along with both the shoes, and looked away fast to avoid seeing more.

*They might be like him.*

*No. They're all right. They're fine.*

*I'VE GOT TO GET HOME. NOW. RIGHT NOW!*

Clint ducked slightly. Close to the ground, the building had open spaces like long narrow windows. He ran his eyes along them until he spotted his old Ford Granada. Just the roof and windshield were visible.

His car looked fine.

So did the parking lot. Nothing had collapsed in there.

He was glad to see no other cars. He'd *assumed* nobody else had arrived at work by the time the quake hit, but he hadn't been absolutely certain. Several people who often showed up around eight-thirty worked on the ground floor, and he didn't always hear them arrive.

They're probably stuck in traffic somewhere.

*Traffic's gonna be a bear. I'd better stay off the freeways, take sidestreets.*

He raced for the parking lot entrance. As he ran, he dug the keys from his pocket.

He scurried down a short slope of driveway, stopped at the side of the rolldown security gate, and found the key to activate it. His hand shook badly. He used his other hand to help guide the key into the slot. He twisted the key.

Nothing happened.

'Come on come on come on.'

He twisted the key again.

With a quiet hum and metallic clatters and rattles, the gate should be lifting clear of the driveway.

There was no hum.

The gate didn't stir.

Clint looked over his shoulder at the intersection. The traffic signals weren't red, yellow or green. They showed no light at all.

He twitched the key, trying to *make* it work. Even though he knew it wouldn't.

Not with the power down.

He could get to his car easily enough. But the gate barred the only way out.

Bash through it?

*Oh, sure.*

16

'Movie crap,' he muttered. *This is real life, and you don't crash through a gate like that and speed merrily on your way. Even if you're lucky enough to live through the crash, your car bites the dust. No way.*

If he disabled his car with a stunt like that, it wouldn't get him home. And that was all that mattered to Clint at the moment.

He had to get home. Had to make sure Sheila was okay. And Barbara. Again, he pictured them crushed.

*A quake never hurt anyone – it's the shit that falls on you!*

Please, God, let them be all right.

Clint jerked his key from the slot. He kicked the gate.

*Damn it!*

His car was fine! His car was in great shape, safe and sound, just waiting to speed him home.

But useless! Trapped inside a goddamn parking lot!

Jailed.

What do I do now? he wondered. Start walking?

He climbed to the crest of the driveway. He scanned the cars scattered along the curbs. Though alarms still blared, nobody had come along to check on them.

Steal one?

How about a little grand-theft auto?

Hell, Clint didn't know how to *go about* stealing one. You pull the ignition? You cross some wires?

Sure thing.

Like which wires?

He frowned at the TOY pickup. He could take that and nobody was likely to make a fuss. It even, certainly, had the key in its ignition. But from the looks of the thing, it was as dead as its passenger, as dead as the driver who was inside somewhere out of sight beneath the smashed-down roof.

The BMW still sat in its lane just to the right of the intersection.

*All right!*

Bending over slightly, Clint could see the driver. A woman. She was sitting motionless, her head turned toward the passenger window. Clint thought she was staring at him.

I'm a witness, he thought. She probably wants to get my name and stuff.

He raised a hand at the woman. Then he hurried toward her. His legs felt weak and spongy. His head buzzed.

Too much action, he thought. Too much everything. But I'm still here. And so is she.

He almost called, 'Don't leave,' but stopped himself. He didn't want to give her any ideas.

She wasn't moving, though. Just staring.

Staring, but not at me, Clint realized as he neared her car. Her gaze was aimed lower. At the passenger seat.

Clint suddenly knew why.

'It's all right,' he said.

She didn't respond. She just kept gazing as if entranced by the sight of her odd companion.

A curl of brown hair draped her brow. Otherwise, she looked neat and prim in her white blouse and her matching gray jacket and skirt.

Clint guessed she'd been on her way to an office job.

She wore very little makeup. And needed very little. Too young and too pretty to require much help. Early twenties?

'It's all right,' he said again. 'It wasn't your fault. I saw the whole thing. You won't be in any sort of trouble. Okay?'

She didn't respond.

*Okay, shit, here goes nothing.*

Clint stepped forward fast.

The head was on the passenger seat. It still wore its baseball cap, but the cap had lost its bill completely, and was no longer Dodger blue. The head lay face up. It was as red as the baseball cap. It was staring at the ceiling, its stump of a neck aimed at the young woman.

*No wonder she's freaked,* Clint thought.

He grabbed the door handle and pulled, but the door was locked. Instead of wasting time trying to get the gal to unlock it, he reached through the broken window and found the lock switch. He flicked it, withdrew his arm, swung the door open wide, and suddenly surprised himself by stopping.

He'd thought he would just sweep the head off the seat, let if fall to the street.

He couldn't do it, though.

This wasn't garbage. It wasn't a spoiled sandwich or a dirty napkin. It was the head of a man who had been alive a few minutes ago.

A man who probably had a family and friends, a job, who was a Dodger fan, who maybe liked to take his kids to the stadium and eat hot dogs under the sunlight . . . Whose crime was being in the passenger seat of a guy who must've panicked when the quake hit.

Clint lifted the head gently by both sides of its face. It was slippery. It was heavier than he'd expected.

He stepped backward with it and carried it well in front of him so blood wouldn't get on his clothes. He took it to the body sprawled on the pavement. He set it down there, neck to neck, and had a sudden urge to fasten it on somehow – tape it or strap it or . . .

*I've gotta get home!*

The head rolled a little when he let go. Only an inch or so. Not far enough to matter.

Rising from his crouch, Clint spotted the dead man's blue jeans near the middle of the intersection. He hurried over to them and picked them up. They seemed clean. He used them to wipe the blood off his hands, then hurried with them to the BMW.

The driver met his eyes. She frowned.

*So she's not catatonic. Is that good news or bad?*

'It's all right,' Clint said. 'I'll just clean up this mess for you.'

She nodded.

He leaned inside the car and did his best to mop the blood off the seat cover. When it looked fairly clean, he tossed away the jeans and swung himself into the car and sat down.

He pulled the door shut.

'I'm Clint Banner,' he said, forcing his voice to sound calm. 'What's your name?'

She blinked a few times, frowned. Her lips moved, but no words came out.

'Your name?'

'Mary,' she whispered. 'Davis.'

'Were you on your way to work, Mary?'

A nod, barely perceptible.

'What do you do?'

'I'm a secretary. With an advertising firm.'

'Advertising.'

Her head bobbed, more pronounced this time.

'Okay, if that's your job, there won't be any work today. Do you understand? We've had a major quake. You don't need to go in to work. What you need to do is go home.' He glanced at her hands. They were clutching her thighs, fingers spread and pressing hard into the gray fabric of her skirt. She wore rings on both hands, but no engagement ring or wedding band. 'Do you have family?'

More bobbing.

'In L.A?'

'Chicago.'

'Then you don't need to worry about them. What you need to do, Mary, is get yourself safely home. Do you understand?'

'I . . . I don't know.'

'Where do you live?'

'Santa Monica.'

'Great!' The word burst out, and Mary flinched. 'Great,' Clint said again, speaking more softly. 'Look, I'll help you. I need to get home to my wife and daughter, and my car's . . . no good. I'm over in West L.A.

It won't even be out of your way. All I need is for you to get me over the hills. And I'll help you. It might be a tough trip. A lot of traffic between here and there . . . traffic signals down . . . roads'll probably be blocked in places . . . no telling what we might run into. We can help each other. Okay?'

'What about my accident?'

'Don't worry about it.'

'But . . . that's hit-and-run.'

'Not today,' Clint said. 'You probably couldn't report this mess if you wanted to. And even if the phones *are* working, the police have business a lot more urgent than this.'

'I . . . I ought to *try* and report it.'

Clint put his hand on her shoulder. He squeezed firmly, but not hard enough to hurt her. 'We can't waste the time, Mary. Do you want to get home today?'

'Yes.'

'So do I. I want to get home so bad it hurts. So what we've gotta do is leave right now, and leave hard and fast. Do you want me to do the driving?'

'I . . . yeah, maybe so.'

# THREE

When the quake hit, the Chevy Nova rocked and swerved left and veered across the center line.

Barbara Banner's stomach gave a sick lurch.

Behind her, Heather squealed while Earl yelled 'Hey!' and Pete muttered, 'What the . . . ?'

'Brakes!' gasped Mr Wellen, slapping the dash with both hands.

Barbara was already jamming her foot down on the brake pedal as she wrenched the wheel to the right. The car cut back into its proper lane, then nosed too far to the right and headed for the tail of a parked Wagoneer.

'You're over-correcting, Bar . . . Stop!'

'I *am* stopped!' she shouted back at her driver's ed teacher.

'Y'are not!' Earl yelled.

Barbara knew that she had stopped the car – braked it to a halt only an instant after it had taken the odd turn toward the Wagoneer. But it kept on shuddering and jerking and twisting its way closer to the Jeep's rear bumper.

'Look out!' Wellen scooted himself across the seat, grabbed the wheel with one hand, flung his left leg sideways, and stomped his shoe down hard on top of Barbara's foot.

'OW!'

He shoved against her foot as if trying to crush it into the brake pedal.

Barbara shot her elbow into his ribs.

Now I've done it, she thought. Oh, my God. What do they do to you for hitting a teacher?

But at least he quit mashing her foot.

'It's a quake!' Pete said. He sounded excited, like the only kid in class to come up with the answer to a teacher's trick question.

'No kidding,' Earl said.

A quake! Clenching the wheel, keeping her sore foot pressed to the brake pedal, Barbara for the first time looked beyond the nearby threats to the school car. She saw a stucco apartment building a short distance ahead and off to the right. It was a two-story building. Instead of a lawn, it had pavement sloping down to parking spaces beneath the ground floor.

21

The whole structure, the pavement below it, and the cars parked inside a few of its nooks, shook as if Barbara were watching through the viewfinder of a camera held by someone in the midst of a grand mal seizure.

She was looking directly at one of its high windows when the glass exploded and a woman came out backward. An old woman with wispy white hair. Wearing a peach-colored terri robe that matched the stucco wall, a color that camouflaged her so that she was nearly invisible except for her head and small hands and bare white legs that kicked frantically at the sky.

'Everybody down!' Mr Wellen ordered.

The old woman dropped out of sight, rump first, scrabbling with both hands as if trying to claw a rung of air.

The wall of the next-door apartment building began to crumble. It was just sloughing down when Mr Wellen grabbed Barbara's upper arm. Clutching it, he fumbled at her hip.

'What're you . . . ?'

She looked down. The safety harness, suddenly retracting, whipped its buckle at her face. She flung her head back. The buckle missed. Then Wellen was pulling her by the arm, dragging her from behind the wheel toward his side of the car. Then he was clambering onto her. Sitting on her lap. Squirming off. Scooting under the wheel. Taking the wheel with one hand, shifting to reverse with the other, and backing away from the Wagoneer's bumper.

'What're you doing?' Pete shouted from the rear.

'Getting us outa here!'

The car lunged forward, shoving Barbara back against the seat.

'Wait till the *quake* stops!' Earl yelled.

Wellen gunned it, speeding up Bedford, the Nova shaking and bouncing and swerving from side to side. A jaunt to the left skidded it toward the side of a parked Plumber John truck. Heather screamed. Barbara clutched the dashboard. Wellen fought the wheel, recovered, and swung them clear with inches to spare.

During the next few seconds, Barbara glimpsed apartment buildings on both sides of the street break apart as if struck by huge wrecking balls. Walls exploded. Roofs crashed down. One building only lost its front wall, while the next collapsed entirely, the next two appeared to be intact and the one after those dropped its north half to the ground while its south half remained standing.

This is really it, Barbara thought. This is the Big One.

She pictured her mother ducking and covering her head as their house on Swanson Street came down on top of her.

No! No, she'll be all right.

Maybe she's not even in the house. Maybe she's out watering the yard, or . . .

*Please let her be all right. And Dad.*

*Dad's so far away, he might not even be getting this where he is. Or maybe just a little tremble.*

'You ought to stop, Mr Wellen,' Pete advised. 'It isn't safe to be driving . . .'

'You'll kill us all!' Earl yelled.

, 'Shut your face, Jones! I know what I'm doing. I'm the teacher around here, right?'

'Doesn't mean you're right.'

'Shut up.'

Barbara released her grip on the dashboard, snatched down the passenger seat harness, swept its belts across her chest and lap, and felt for the buckle slot. Felt for it because she didn't dare look away from the destruction all around them.

*The whole world's falling down!*

But not on us, she told herself. Not so far, anyway.

Even the walls that toppled toward the road were too far away to reach them.

As long as nothing falls on us, we'll be okay.

And she heard her father. Kidding around, as usual. *An earthquake never hurt anyone. An earthquake's harmless. It's the shit that falls on your head that'll kill you.*

Or your driver's ed teacher freaking out and creaming you in a head-on . . .

She thrust the metal tongue into the buckle's slot, heard and felt it lock into place.

*If he crashes now . . .*

A bowling ball sailed down from high on the right and whunked the hood.

Can't be, Barbara thought. Not a bowling ball.

*But it is.*

She saw its finger holes, its pretty purple marbling . . .

It bounced, leaving a big dent in the hood, and the speeding car rushed at the airborne ball. In front of Wellen's face, the windshield dissolved into frosty chunks. Bits of it flew at him. Barbara expected the ball to come in. But it bounced off and fell away, leaving a hole no larger than an orange in the safety glass.

Wellen kept on driving.

'You okay?' Barbara yelled. And realized that her voice seemed strangely loud, that it seemed so loud because the roar was gone. Not only the roar, but the rough shudders and . . .

'I think it's stopped,' Pete said.

'Yes!' Earl blurted. '*All right, sports fans!*'

Heather was crying.

Barbara looked back at her. The girl seemed very small and fragile between Earl and Pete. She was hunched over, hugging her belly, head down, the sides of her face draped by long brown hair. Her shoulders hitched up and down as she sobbed.

'You okay?' Barbara asked.

Heather shook her head. The shrouds of hair swayed.

'We're all right,' Barbara told her. 'We made it. The quake's over.'

The car swung hard to the right. Barbara was thrust sideways toward Wellen, but the chest belt stopped her. In the rear, Pete caught hold of the door handle to keep himself upright. Heather fell across Earl's lap.

He cast his eyes down at her. Wrinkled his nose. Said, 'Hey, get off the merchandise,' and shoved her away with his forearm.

'Take it easy,' Pete said.

'Gettin' her cooties on me.'

'I'm sorry,' Heather murmured.

'Everybody knock it off back there,' Wellen commanded. 'Just knock it off!'

Heather, sitting up straight, leaned away from Earl. Which pressed her right side against Pete. She glanced at Pete as if asking permission. He nodded. Then he slipped his arm across her shoulders. His hand cupped her left shoulder, gave it a squeeze.

And Barbara felt an ache deep inside her. Something like longing or regret. Which made no sense. She didn't even *know* Pete, just from driver's ed.

No sense at all. But it hurt a little, anyway, to see him holding Heather. So Barbara turned forward. She settled back into her seat.

What's wrong with Wellen? she wondered.

Hunched over the wheel, he was peering forward through the hole in the windshield. Barbara could only see his right eye. But it looked bulgy and wild. His red face glistened with sweat. He was gasping for breath. His lips were skinned back, baring his teeth.

It scared her to look at him.

So she looked forward.

Beyond the windshield, a wide road. Blocked here and there by stopped cars. Bordered not by apartment houses but by parking meters, shops, banks, businesses of all sorts – most in shambles. People stumbling about as if dazed.

We're sure not on Bedford anymore, Barbara thought.

No, of course not. That right turn we made . . .

She spotted the Shell station.

24

*Our* Shell station? she wondered. The one with Heinz who called the Granada 'your junk'?

Must be.

So we're on Pico, Barbara thought. And this is La Cienega just ahead.

Familiar territory. At least it would have been familiar if so much of it didn't look as if it had been leveled by bombs.

Barbara spotted the post office beyond the intersection, far ahead and off to the left.

*We're going the wrong way!*

'Mr Wellen?'

He didn't repond. Nor did he slow down as they rushed into La Cienega. Car horns blared.

A Porsche bore in from the side, straight at Barbara.

'Look out!' Barbara yelled.

'Oh, Jeez!' Pete blurted.

The Porche missed, passing behind them.

*Somebody's not obeying the . . .*

The traffic signals at the far corners of the intersection were dark, dead.

*No lights, and he's taking us . . .*

*You're supposed to stop and wait your turn!*

'Wellen!' Earl shouted.

A moment later, they shot clear of La Cienega untouched.

'Stop the car!' Pete snapped.

Wellen picked up speed, weaving from lane to lane.

Heading east on Pico.

East.

Barbara jerked her head around to glance at the others. 'He's taking us the wrong way!'

Earl reached over the seatback. He smacked Wellen on the shoulder. 'Hey! Turn us around!'

'Don't touch me again, punk,' Wellen said.

'Mr Wellen,' Barbara said. 'Please! You've got to turn us around and take us back to school. We need to get *home*. Please.'

'I'll get you back to school,' he said, still hunched forward and peering through the windshield's hole. 'Just everybody quit your whining. I've gotta check up on my kid.'

'Your kid?'

'Yeah, my kid. My daughter.' His head jerked toward Barbara. A quick, fierce, hateful glare. Then he turned again to his windshield hole. 'Nobody stops me. Don't even think about it.'

'Oh, great,' Earl muttered. 'Terrific. So where the hell are you dragging us, you lunatic?'

'Shut your face,' Wellen said.

'Where *is* your daughter?' Barbara asked, trying to sound kind and sympathetic.

'Saint Joan's.'

'What?'

'Saint Joan's.'

'What's that, a church?' Pete asked.

'A school,' Wellen said. 'A Catholic girl's school.' He glanced again at Barbara. This time, his eyes didn't seem quite so mean.

'What grade is she in?'

'She's not in any grade. She's a teacher. Ninth grade English.'

At Fairfax, he slowed down only a bit. He drove onto a sidewalk to get past a line-up of waiting cars, bounced down from the curb, hit the brakes to avoid broadsiding a pickup truck, then gunned the engine and sprinted for the other side as cars in the way swerved and honked.

When Barbara could breathe again, she asked, 'How far away *is* that high school where your daughter works?'

'We'll be there pretty soon.'

'We won't get there at all if you kill us!' Pete yelled.

A tear was sliding down Wellen's face, alongside his nose.

'It'll be all right,' Barbara told him.

'It's such an old school,' he said. 'I think it's been reinforced to meet earthquake standards, but . . . Dear God, look at all this. How could Saint Joan's possibly still be standing after . . .' He shook his head. He was weeping outright, his face streaming.

'We're all worried about our families,' Barbara told him. 'They've gotta be worried about us, too.'

*If they're not dead.*

*Don't even think about that. Mom and Dad are fine. They've gotta be.*

'Your daughter's probably just fine,' she said.

'I don't know, I don't know.'

'Where *is* her school?'

He sniffed. 'On Pico.'

'Where on Pico?'

'Normandie.'

'*Normandie!*' Earl cried out. '*That's downtown!* That's *miles* from here.'

'I'll drive you back to Rancho Heights. Just as soon as I've picked up Katherine.'

'You won't be *able* to drive us back,' Pete said. 'Look at the traffic in that direction.'

'I'll get you back. Don't worry.'

'Just let us off here,' Barbara said. 'Just stop and let us out. We can walk back.'

Sobbing, Wellen shook his head. 'Can't stop. We're almost there.'

'Almost there, my butt,' Earl said. 'STOP THE CAR!' As he shouted, he leaned forward and swatted the side of Wellen's head. A hard smack. The car lurched to the left. Into the path of a gray Mazda.

Barbara braced against the dash. She squeezed her eyes shut.

Instead of a collision, she felt a sudden jerk to the right.

She looked, saw they were back in their own lane, safe for the moment, and glimpsed Earl's hand coming toward her about to launch another strike at Wellen.

She grabbed Earl's wrist. 'Don't! Leave him alone! You wanta make him crash?'

'Let go of me!' Earl wrenched his arm from her grip. But he didn't swing at Wellen. Instead, glaring at Barbara, he sank back into his seat. 'I could *make* him stop, you know.'

'I know. You're *so* tough.'

'You wanta see how tough I am, just keep it up.'

'Oh, I'm scared to death.'

'Everybody shut up!' Wellen shouted.

'If you don't like it,' Barbara snapped at him, 'stop the car and let us out.'

'I'll let you out when I'm good and ready, young lady. I'm still the teacher around here. I'm still in charge. So everybody sit still and keep your mouths shut. Is that understood? And as for you, Jones, you can look forward to criminal charges for assault and battery when all this is over.'

'Oh yeah?'

'Yeah.'

Ahead, both eastbound lanes were blocked by stopped cars.

Wellen didn't slow down.

'Hey,' Barbara said. And cried out, 'NO!' as he poured on the gas. 'Stop it! Are you nuts?'

He cut to the left and they sped alongside the line of halted cars, straight toward the front of an oncoming RTD bus.

# FOUR

'These'll come right down, *right* down,' Stanley muttered as he sidestepped between two of his mother's rose bushes. He hated them. He hated all of her rose bushes. They stood at the cinderblock wall like sentinels posted to keep him away.

Though they couldn't keep him away, they never failed to draw his blood.

No matter how often he trimmed back their thorny branches, no matter how much care he took to suck in his stomach and lift his arms above their reach as he eased through, their thorns always found him.

He'd paid with stinging wounds for his many trips to the wall.

Now, a nettle pricked the back of his shoulder. As he tried to escape it, another nicked his thigh. Both barbs snagged his pajamas and wouldn't let go.

Stanley almost wished he'd left his bathrobe on; its thick nap would've given him some protection from the thorns. But he'd left his robe in the house.

After all, why *should* he wear it? The morning was warm and luscious. Mother was hardly in any position to complain about his attire. *Nobody* was likely to complain, considering the circumstances.

Hell, the *house* had fallen down. What could they expect Stanley to wear, a tux?

He was glad he'd left the robe behind. He enjoyed being outside dressed in nothing except his moccasins and pajamas. He liked how the pajamas drifted lightly against his skin, caressing him. And he liked it that they were so thin; any woman he might meet would be able to see quite a lot of him through the lightweight fabric.

The heavy robe might have saved him from a few scratches, but it would've smothered him, hidden him.

After plucking his pajamas free of the thorns, he made it to the wall.

He braced his hands against the cinderblocks, leaned forward and lifted himself on tiptoes to see Sheila's house.

He moaned.

Beyond the lawn, beyond the concrete patio, the house was down.

It looked as if it had been kicked apart and stomped by a giant.

All that remained was a mess of junk corralled by broken walls – a litter heap of splintered wood, tattered patches of roofing asphalt, red tiles, crumbled stucco and plaster and sheetrock, tendrils of pipe jutting up here and there, a few wires leading to nowhere.

Maybe Sheila wasn't inside when it went down, Stanley told himself. Anything could've happened. Maybe she'd decided to run an extra mile or two. Maybe she'd gone on an errand.

Maybe she *was* inside, but she's still alive.

*And if I save her, she'll be so grateful to me that . . .*

If she was inside the house when it fell, she *has* to be dead.

Stanley squeezed his eyes shut. 'She's not dead,' he whispered. 'She's not. She's just fine, and I'm gonna save her.'

Opening his eyes, he clapped his hands down on top of the wall and jumped. He shoved himself higher, belly and groin and thighs scraping against the rough blocks. Elbows locked, he flung a leg up sideways and hooked the top with his foot. Seconds later, he was standing upright on the wall.

Nothing to it!

Should've done it months ago! Should've climbed right over the wall and enjoyed some close-up views.

But he'd never dared. Afraid of being caught.

By Mother. Or by Sheila's husband.

So he had never done more than peer over its top. At night after Mother had gone to bed. During the day, those occasional times when Mother was away from the house without him.

He'd seen a lot, but never enough. Never near enough.

From now on, there would be no Mother in his way. He could do whatever he pleased.

But now it was too late. The quake had seen to that.

It just isn't fair, Stanley thought.

From his height above the wall, he could see that the houses on both sides of Sheila's place still stood. They had broken windows, some cracks in the walls, and they might've sustained some serious damage beyond Stanley's view. But they hadn't collapsed.

*Why her place?*

Nobody even *lived* in the house to the left. It had been vacant for two months, a FOR SALE sign in the front yard. And the young couple who lived in the house to the right both held full-time jobs. So they probably weren't even home when the quake struck.

Nobody home at two out of three. The quake had dropped the only house with a person in it.

*Not just any person. Sheila.*

*My Sheila.*

29

Stanley leaped. In midair, he realized he should've lowered himself down from the wall instead of jumping. But it was a bit late for that.

His feet pounded the ground. Pain shot up both his legs. He stumbled forward, leaving one moccasin behind, and fell. He landed on his knees, dived from there, and skidded headfirst over the grass.

The grass felt thick and soft and very wet. Stanley lay motionless on it for a few seconds, then got slowly to his feet. The front of his pajamas clung to him. Where the pale blue fabric adhered to his skin, it looked nearly transparent.

He went back for his moccasin, slipped his foot into it, then headed for the ruin of Sheila's house.

The sunlight on the concrete patio made him squint. The patio looked fine. Normal. Just the same as always. There was the Weber grill that often sent such wonderful aromas into the evening. There was the picnic table, a flower pot in its center, a long bench on either side. There was the lounger with its faded, green cushion.

Four times during the past few weeks, he had gazed over the wall and found Sheila stretched out on this very lounger. She had worn a skimpy white bikini. She'd rubbed her skin with oil, but hadn't been able to reach the middle of her back.

Only twice had he seen the daughter come out to sunbathe. Her bikini was orange. Compared to Sheila, she looked scrawny. Skin and bones. Cute, but not in the same league as her mother.

*As if anybody could be.*

Only last Wednesday, Louise Thayer had taken Mother to a bridge party and Stanley had visited the wall. Peering over the top, he'd spied Sheila sprawled bellydown on the lounger. She wore a baseball cap and sunglasses. She read a book. Her bikini top was untied, leaving her bare and glossy all the way down her back. A small white triangle draped the middle of her rump. A white cord crossed her hip. Except for that cord, her side was nothing but sleek skin all the way down from her shoulder to her foot.

Stanley had gazed at her, aching.

She's got to move sooner or later, he'd thought. She'll get up. And maybe she'll be careless about her top. Maybe she'll lift herself up, and it'll stay down there on the cushion.

Maybe she'll even turn over onto her back without it!

Yes!

She might! She just might!

And Stanley had suddenly remembered the binoculars in his bedroom closet.

He couldn't take a picture of her, thanks to the Bitch, but he could damn sure get a good close-up look with his field glasses.

So he'd hurried away to get them.

Hurried so fast that he'd ended up with three nicks from the rose bush thorns.

No more than four minutes later, he'd returned to the wall, binoculars in hand, ready and eager.

No Sheila.

She was gone. Her book was gone. Her plastic bottle of suntan oil was gone.

She had gotten up, and he would never know whether or not she'd been careless about her top. He'd missed it. Gone for the binoculars and missed it!

In a rage, he had slammed the binoculars against the wall. Pounded them, smashed them.

Now, he realized that he had missed more than a chance to see Sheila rise from the lounger, possibly revealing her breasts.

He had missed his *last* chance.

Because now she was somewhere under all that rubble.

Crushed, ruined, dead.

Stanley walked over to the lounger. Its green cushion, faded in places so it was almost white, showed yellow and brown stains in the rough shape of a body. Run-off from Sheila, he thought. Some from Barbara, too, he supposed.

Crouching, he sniffed the cushion. Its dry, sweet aroma whispered to him of long summer days and sweltering beaches, the squeal of gulls, the rush of combers washing over the sand.

It's her suntan oil, he realized.

Suntan oil and sweat.

He pressed his face into the cushion. Eyes shut, he felt the warm fabric against his lids – and against his lips as he sucked, filling himself with the air from the cushion.

*Sheila was right here.*

He licked the cloth.

And sucked.

And thought he heard a voice.

The voice didn't startle him, didn't worry him. It hadn't come from someone near enough to observe what he was doing.

He hadn't been caught.

And he didn't *intend* to get caught, so he raised his head. A dark patch of wetness on the cloth showed where his mouth had been.

Glancing all around, he saw no one.

He heard no voice.

Maybe he hadn't heard a voice at all. It might've been something different. No telling what he had *really* heard through the awful clutter of noises: the wailing, blaring, hooting alarms from cars or houses; the sirens nearby and far away; the car horns beeping over on Robertson Boulevard; the whup-whup-whup of a helicopter that was out of sight but not very far away; the bangs and pops and blasts (none alarmingly loud) that might be backfires or slams, but were probably gunshots; a scream of car brakes; the sound of a crash; various other clamors and roars.

A regular chaos of noises.

Stanley heard such noises every day, but not so many of them, not all at once.

One of the neighborhood's normal sounds was missing, though. Probably the worst of all. The leaf-blowers. This morning, they were silent.

All the little crews of lawn workers must've decided to take the day off on account of the Big One.

Just three days ago, Mother had demanded that Stanley 'do something' about the Mexican gardeners who'd shown up across the street at seven-thirty and demolished the morning peace. First, they'd slammed the tailgate of their antique pickup truck. Then they'd gone into action with the power mower and the leaf-blower. The din of the blower had destroyed the last of Mother's restraint.

'You go out there right this minute and *do* something, Stanley!'

'What am I supposed to do?'

'Have a *word* with them. They've no right, no right in the world, to be raising such a Godawful racket at an hour like this.'

'They'll be done in a while.'

'Stanley! '

'It won't do any good, anyway. They won't understand a word I say.'

Behind her glasses, her eyes narrowed. 'I suppose you're right. Damn wetbacks. They've got no business coming to this country if they can't learn to speak . . .'

'I know, I know.'

'Call the police.'

'The *police?* I'm not gonna call the police about a leaf-blower.'

'*I* will.' Scowling, she had wheeled herself toward the telephone. After passing Stanley, she'd looked back at him. 'You're totally worthless, do you know that? You've got no balls at all. Your father was a complete pervert and a moron, but at least he had balls. But not you. I've never seen such a worthless excuse for a man.'

Remembering, Stanley smiled.

*Had the balls to bust your head in, Bitch.*

As he thought that, he heard a voice again. This time, it seemed to find its way through a gap in the tumult of noise. A woman's voice. It called out, 'Hey!'

From somewhere in front of Stanley.

From somewhere in the rubble.

He felt an explosion of wild hope.

He shouted, 'Hello!'

'Help!' the voice called back. 'Helllllp!'

He stepped to the very border of the debris. Off to the left, a portion of the chimney rose out of the mess. The fireplace itself was buried, but a seascape still hung on a remnant of wall above the mantel. The painting looked only a little crooked.

No other artwork was visible. Nor could Stanley spot any piece of furniture, any book or garment, utensil or knick-knack. Except for the lone painting, the only signs that the house had been inhabited were the refrigerator and oven that still stood upright in what must have been the kitchen – near the right front corner. Every other possession of Sheila and her family was apparently entombed beneath the fallen walls and ceiling and roof. The scatter of mounds and slopes, he supposed, showed where there might be hidden sofas, beds, dressers, counters.

Under one of the piles might be Sheila herself.

'Where are you?' Stanley yelled.

'Down here!'

The sound seemed to come from an area somewhere ahead and to his right – near the oven? At the time of the quake, he had pictured her taking a bath or shower, but maybe she'd been in the kitchen.

'I'm on my way,' Stanley called. He reached out his leg, planted his foot atop of a tilted slab of stucco, wondered for a moment if it would hold him, then stepped aboard. The stucco wobbled, but he kept his footing.

From there, he surveyed the area ahead.

The tumbled remains of the house bristled with shards of window glass, with rows of nails. The thin leather soles of his moccasins might save his feet from cuts, but . . .

Just don't step on a nail, he warned himself as he risked another stride.

And for God's sake don't fall.

He spread his arms for balance.

He picked his route carefully and moved slowly, trying to avoid slabs or chunks or boards that didn't look stable. Some broke apart anyway. Many teetered. A few flipped and dropped him ankle-deep into laths or plaster.

'Are you there?" the voice called.

It *had* to be Sheila's voice. Though it sounded louder, more distinct than before, it was still battered by conflicting noises. Besides, he'd only heard her speak a few times. He couldn't be sure this was Sheila.

Must be, he thought. It's her house. Who else could it be?

'I'm coming,' he answered. 'Are you hurt?'

'I think I'm okay. But I'm trapped. I can't move.'

Her voice didn't actually seem to be coming from the kitchen area – from that general direction, but not from that distance. Sheila was not so far away. Maybe ten or fifteen feet this side of the oven.

He couldn't see her, though. Between Stanley and the place where Sheila seemed to be, there stood hills of rubble and the low remains of a few interior walls.

Heading that way, he called, 'Was anybody else in the house?'

'No. Just me.'

'What's your name?'

'Sheila. Sheila Banner.'

*Yes!*

'I'm Stanley Banks. I live in the house behind you.'

'Sure am glad you showed up, Stanley.'

'I was checking around the neighborhood and saw the condition of your house.'

'You mean they didn't *all* go down?'

'Nope. From what I've seen so far, maybe one out of three or four got leveled.'

'My God!'

'Could've been a lot worse.'

'I just hope to God the school's okay.'

*Careful*, Stanley thought. 'Do you have a child?'

'Yeah. She goes to Rancho Heights High. Have you heard anything – any news?'

'None. It must've been a hell of a quake, though.'

'They always said we'd get it.'

'Yeah.' He began to climb a slope of wreckage. Until now, he had avoided anything so high. He could've detoured around this one, but knew there would be a good view from its top.

*If I can just get there in one piece.*

He made his way upward slowly, crouching, open hands down low so that he might catch himself if he should slip.

'How about your house?' Sheila called.

'It got . . .' His left foot suddenly triggered a small avalanche. He scrambled higher and found solid footing. Hunched there, he panted for breath. He was shaking, drenched with sweat. His pajamas felt sodden. His moccasins felt gooey inside, as if they'd been lathered with lard.

'Stanley?'

'Yeah?'

34

'Are you all right?'

'Fine.'

'Are you sure? Did you fall?'

'Some stuff . . . gave out under me. I'm okay.'

'Be careful. I don't want you hurting yourself.'

'Thanks.' Slowly, he straightened up. With a damp pajama sleeve, he wiped his face.

'What about your family?' Sheila asked. 'Are you married?'

'My wife died last year.' He resumed climbing.

As he gained the summit, Sheila said, 'I'm very sorry about your wife.'

'I appreciate that. Thank you.'

'You sound a lot closer.'

'Yeah, I . . .' He had been gazing at the debris under his face while he climbed. The moment he lifted his eyes, he saw the blazing house. And the handful of people gathered to watch it burn.

They were the *only* people he saw.

The burning house had apparently drawn every available spectator, leaving none to notice Stanley.

'What is it?' Sheila asked.

'A house fire. Over on the other side of Swanson. At the corner of Livonia.'

'Is the fire department there?'

'No. Not yet.'

'Police?'

'Afraid not. Just a few neighbors.'

'My God. What if it spreads?'

'Its pretty far away.'

'Oh God.'

'Don't worry.'

'I'm *trapped*.' Though the voice came to him along with a confusion of overlapping noises, he heard Sheila's fear. 'I don't want to burn up.'

'I'll get you out,' Stanley said. 'I'll save you. I promise.'

'Hurry? Please?'

'I'm coming.' Moving as fast as he could without taking reckless chances, he descended to the bottom of the mound without trouble. From there, he could still see the thick black smoke curling into the sky. But the burning house and the spectators were out of sight, blocked from his view by remnants of Sheila's walls.

*I can't see them, they can't see me.*

He liked that.

*If they can't see me, they won't be coming over to snoop.*

'Sheila?'

35

'You sound *very* close.'

He looked toward the sound of her voice.

It seemed to come from straight ahead – no more than a few strides away. But he could see only more tumbled, broken ruins of the house.

'I can't see you.'

'There's a bunch of stuff on me.'

He took a step. Another step. Halting, he studied the debris.

'Where are you?' he asked.

'You're almost on top of me.'

*On top of you. Yes. Oh, yes!*

'Can you see me?' he asked.

'Too much in the way. But you sound like you're somewhere above my feet.'

How could that be? The rubble in front of him looked fairly level and close to the floor. Unless Sheila'd been mashed – but she claimed to be unharmed. And she sounded fine. Scared, but not in pain.

'I don't get it,' he said. 'Where *are* you?'

'I think I'm in the crawlspace.'

'What?'

'The *crawlspace*. Under the house. I felt the tub drop. All this junk came crashing down, and the tub dropped out from under me. We must've landed in the crawlspace.'

'You're in your *bathtub*?' Stanley asked.

'Yeah. The luckiest break I've ever had.'

Me, too, Stanley thought.

'The stuff would've mashed me. But it's all across the top. Too much for me to budge.'

'Well, I'll start clearing it away.' He took off his pajama shirt. It felt good to be free of the wet, clinging fabric, to feel the air against his skin. He wanted to remove his pants, as well.

*We'd both be naked.*

*Yeah, and what if somebody comes along? And what'll Sheila think? She'll be able to see me as soon as . . .*

'How's that fire doing?' she asked, interrupting his thoughts.

Stanley twisted around for a look. Nothing had changed much. Black columns of smoke still climbed the sky. 'It isn't getting any closer. Don't worry about it. We've got all the time in the world.'

# FIVE

Wellen had only avoided a head-on collision with the RTD bus by steering even farther to the left, *two* lanes away from their proper side of the road and into the path of a gray Mercedes. He swerved right. Filled in the space between the rear of the bus and the front of an oncoming Ford. Then again to the right, abandoning the westbound lane with an instant to spare.

And it had gone on like that.

Bursts of speed, lurches from side to side, skids and abrupt halts, near misses one after another. It seemed that Wellen would no sooner save them from a crash than still another car or bus or delivery truck would be rushing straight at them.

Barbara, belted into the passenger seat, sat rigid and squeezed her thighs and tried not to scream.

Heather, in the backseat, screamed plenty. And sobbed and pleaded.

Earl and Pete shouted.

Barbara barely noticed anything that wasn't a direct threat to their Nova. She was only vaguely aware of what they passed: collapsed buildings, fires, wrecked cars, sheared off fire hydrants spouting white geyers into the air, people sprawled on the sidewalk, all bloody, or hurrying somewhere or stumbling along like zombies. Such sights hardly registered on Barbara's mind. They didn't matter. They were background. They weren't real. Only the ride was real – the Nova piloted on its suicidal course by the driver's education instructor.

On and on and on he sped with his students.

Putting their lives at risk with every turn of the wheels.

Taking them farther from school and from their homes with every second.

A few times, Wellen made detours to avoid sections of Pico Boulevard that appeared to be completely blocked. He whipped around corners, sped down sidestreets, gunned his way through alleys. But always back to Pico.

Until finally, a few blocks past Western, he drove into a trap.

Ahead, all lanes were blocked, a solid row of vehicles side by side from one curb to the other.

Wellen cried out, 'No!' and mashed the brake pedal. The Nova skidded. It stopped less than a foot behind the rear bumper of a van. He shifted to reverse. Hit the gas.

The Nova jumped backward and bucked, slamming into something.

'Great move!' Earl yelled.

Barbara twisted her head around to look out the rear window. 'A bus,' she said.

Wellen glanced back.

At first, Barbara thought he was just curious to see what he'd bumped. From the way his eyes shifted, however, she realized he was looking for an escape route – a gap in the traffic that would permit him to speed backward and resume his mad rush for the school where his daughter worked.

'No way,' Barbara muttered.

She shot her arm out sideways and twisted the ignition key.

Wellen didn't seem to notice.

He flung open his door, leaped out, threw the door shut and ran. There was a nice, clear path for him between the two rows of motionless traffic. Seconds after abandoning the Nova, he sprinted past a dumptruck and vanished.

He no sooner vanished than a lean black woman in a brown uniform – the RTD bus driver? – dashed by.

'Get him, lady!' Pete yelled. He sounded delighted.

Barbara laughed. She couldn't *believe* she could possibly be laughing, but there was no doubt about it. Her laughter had a certain frantic, crazy ring to it.

She looked back at Pete. He was laughing, too.

We've flipped out, she thought.

Heather was in no danger of laughing. She looked as if she might never stop bawling.

Earl opened his door. He climbed outside and stood next to the car for a moment, apparently hoping to see the bus driver catch Wellen. Then he looked to the rear.

'Did she get him?' Pete called.

Earl ducked into the car. 'Who knows?' he said. 'They're outa here. And so am I. You guys gonna come along? 'Cause I gotta tell you, the car's going nowhere. Traffic's backed up to hell 'n gone.'

'Just leave the car here?' Barbara asked, no longer laughing.

'It's *gonna* stay here. Don't matter if we're in it or not, it's *staying*. Guys're bailing out. Nothing's gonna move for hours. Maybe not all day.'

Frowning, Pete said, 'I don't think we're more than six or seven miles from school.'

38

'Walk it?' Barbara asked. 'Yeah. A couple of hours, it shouldn't take much longer than that. Four miles an hour.' The single mile from school to home should take an extra fifteen minutes. 'Let's do it,' she said. 'Better than sitting here. How about you, Heather?'

Heather sniffled. 'Okay.'

'Just in case Wellen comes back,' Barbara muttered, and plucked the key out of the car's ignition. She dropped the key ring into her denim purse, slipped the strap onto her shoulder, and shoved open her door.

The car had been air conditioned. Its windows had been shut. Except for the hole in the windshield, it had been sealed tight until Wellen, then Earl, had opened their doors.

Barbara had thought she would be glad to get out of the car. From the start of Wellen's mad race, it had seemed like a deathtrap.

She climbed out.

And wanted to climb back in.

'My God,' she muttered.

The deathtrap had been a haven.

Sanctuary from the heat, the stench, the smoke, the noise, the chaos and destruction.

The heat felt like the breath of an oven. Exhaust fumes and smoke from nearby fires stung Barbara's eyes, scorched her nasal passages. Her ears hurt with the blare of car horns.

*Why does everybody have to honk!*

*Everybody* wasn't honking. It only sounded that way. In fact, many of the vehicles in sight had nobody in the driver's seat. Some people were standing beside their cars, studying the situation. Others were sitting on hoods or perched atop their car roofs. In a few cases, people had banded together; strangers only minutes ago, they now stood in the midst of the traffic, chatting, nodding, pointing. Barbara supposed that plenty of people hadn't stuck around at all.

*Everybody isn't honking, just every jerk still sitting in his car.*

She longed to shut herself inside the Nova and lock its doors.

*But I'll never get home if I do. This is the only way.*

Heather had the right idea, plastering her hands against her ears.

'Let's get outa here!' Earl yelled. Without waiting for any replies, he swung around and began to stride alongside the line of stopped cars.

Pete gestured for Heather and Barbara to go on ahead of him. Heather held back. She didn't want to go second. Hardly surprising. Barbara wasn't eager to be up there near Earl, either. The guy was a major creep. But she knew she was better equipped than Heather to handle him. So she hurried forward.

When she caught up to Earl, she called, 'Let's get away from Pico when we can! Take the first sidestreet! Get away from this mess!'

He frowned back at her, nodding.

At the first corner, they turned to the left.

They bypassed the sidewalk to avoid its collection of broken glass and other debris. This section of road had metered, curbside parking. All the spaces were taken.

They walked in the road, alongside the parked cars.

The vehicles to their right were moving no faster than those harbored at the curb to their left.

At least twenty were stacked up in the two northbound lanes because of the blocked intersection, but this road wasn't completely jammed. With cars plugging one side and rubble from a collapsed building piled in the other, no vehicles could escape onto it from Pico. The rubble was only at the corner, so the southbound lanes were clear. In a fairly orderly fashion, the cars at the rear were backing off, turning around and heading away. All those trapped here would soon be free.

The drivers were waiting their turns.

Without honking.

With every stride that Barbara took, the din of the car horns on Pico diminished.

So did the smoke. Several buildings had collapsed along this section of road, but none was on fire.

'This is a lot better,' Barbara said.

'Glad I thought of it,' said Earl.

She looked back. Heather, ears uncovered, was walking beside Pete, pressing herself against his side and clutching his arm as if her life depended on keeping herself attached to him.

Give the guy a break, Barbara thought. Maybe he doesn't *want* you hanging all over him.

He didn't look like he minded, though. In fact, he seemed pretty much oblivious to Heather. With a worried frown on his face, he glanced every which way as if he expected trouble and wanted to see it coming.

'Watch where . . . !'

Barbara couldn't stop in time. Head turned toward the others, she walked smack into Earl, ramming him with her right upper arm and breast.

'Geez!' he gasped, and shoved her away.

'Sorry.'

'What're you trying to do to me?'

'I *said* I'm sorry. If you hadn't *stopped* like that . . .'

'What's going on?' Pete asked.

'We had a little collision,' Barbara said. 'It wasn't anything.'

'Yeah, right,' Earl muttered. 'Ban-butt tried to flatten me with her Flying Tit Express.'

She was already so hot she could imagine steam rising off her skin. Earl's remark, however, boosted the temperature. A lot. 'Jerk,' she said.

The heel of his hand pounded her shoulder. The blow didn't hurt, but it twisted her torso and she stumbled backward.

Seething, she raised a fist.

'Oooo. I'm so scared.'

'Leave her alone,' Pete said.

'Leave *her* alone? She's the . . .'

'Let's not fight!' Heather blurted. 'It's stupid! Stupid! We're lucky to be alive, you people. Honestly! Just look around. The quake . . . Maybe thousands of people are dead, for all we know. We might get killed our*selves* before we ever make it back home through all this. We've *got* to depend on each other. We've got to be friends!'

'You're right,' Barbara said, amazed by Heather's outburst. The girl was new in school this year, but she'd been in three of Barbara's classes. In each of them, she had cowered at her desk, huddled in isolation. She had rarely spoken. Several times, she had burst into tears for no apparent reason. A basket case. But mostly a *silent* basket case. Until now.

'We don't have to be *friends*,' Pete said, 'but it is pretty stupid to fight among ourselves. We're in this together.'

Hugging his arm, Heather gazed up at his face.

Wonderful, Barbara thought.

She met Earl's eyes. 'Anyway, I should've watched where I was going. I'm sorry.'

'Yeah, sure. Okay. So the thing is, the reason why I stopped – I was thinking why don't we cross over to the other side, you know? Maybe we can hitch a ride.'

'Hitchhike?' Barbara asked. 'Are you kidding? That's a *sure* way to get ourselves killed.'

'What? There's four of us. Who's gonna pull something when there's four of us?'

'It's really asking for trouble,' Barbara said. 'Besides, these cars may be getting out of *here*, but they won't get far.'

For a while, they all watched the cars that were peeling away from the tail ends of the jammed lanes, making U-turns and heading south. The road was fairly clear for a couple of blocks. In the distance, however, Barbara could see a backup at Venice Boulevard. Cars going in that direction would be stopped again.

About half drove straight toward Venice Boulevard, but the rest turned off – taking their chances on little sidestreets.

'Maybe we oughta give it a try,' Pete said. 'If we can get any kind of ride at all, it'll save us time. As long as it's going in the right direction. Even a few blocks would be better than nothing.'

41

'I don't know,' Barbara said.

From the time she'd been a toddler, Mom and Dad had warned her against involvement with strangers. You didn't talk to strangers, you didn't believe anything a stranger might tell you, and you most certainly did not enter a stranger's car. On the subject of what might happen to her inside a stranger's car, Dad had frequently scared the wits out of her. *I can't even tell you how bad it might be. There are nuts out there who'll do things to little girls that you don't even want to think about.*

Barbara used to spend a lot of time thinking about it, wondering what Dad had meant by that.

He'd never come right out and explained. But Barbara had gradually figured out, from watching TV and listening to her friends, that the men who picked you up took you away and kept you. They made you take off your clothes, then they did things to you. They hurt you where you go to the bathroom. And then they choked you or shot you in the head or cut you into pieces and threw you away.

For years, that was how Barbara had imagined her fate if she should ever get lured or dragged into a stranger's car.

More recently, she'd read some books about serial killers. And found out, shocked, that her childhood version of the horrors had been almost charming compared to the real thing.

You were *lucky* if all they did was rape and murder you. If you weren't so lucky, they ripped at you with pliers, burnt you with matches or cigarettes, took off your fingers or toes or nipples with hedge clippers, jammed your vagina with screwdrivers or broken bottles or broom handles or God-knows-what. All that before you were dead.

Dad had been right: you don't even want to think about such things.

But there are *four* of us, Barbara reminded herself. And this is an emergency. And these are mostly just morning commuters. And . . .

'Okay,' she said. 'We can try it. But I won't get in a car unless the driver's a woman.'

'Yeah, right,' Earl muttered. 'Like women are a bunch of saints?'

'They're rarely homicidal rapists,' Barbara pointed out.

He huffed.

'Why don't we just ask somebody who's waiting?' Heather suggested as they walked alongside the line of cars. 'Wouldn't that be easier than trying to hitchhike?'

'Nobody's gonna go for it,' Earl said. 'Too many of us. Not a chance. It'll scare 'em off. What we gotta do, we gotta use our heads.'

He led them to the end of the line. They waited while a couple of cars turned around. Then they hurried to the other side and headed south. While they walked, several cars sped by. Two turned right at the first cross-street.

'That's where we'll get one,' Earl said. He raised his eyebrows. 'You wanta be the bait, Heather?'

'Me? Huh?'

'Bait. You stand out in plain sight, charm a driver into stopping. The rest of us hide. You open up the door, and we all run out and jump in.'

'Cute,' Barbara said.

'I don't see why we need to be sneaky about things,' Pete said.

'Depends. Do you want to ride or walk? If you want to ride, this is how it gets done.'

They reached the corner.

To the right, 15th Street stretched into the distance.

This didn't look like a good place to be. On both sides of the street were two-story, woodframe houses with gables and bay windows and front porches. They looked as if they'd been uprooted from a quaint, midwestern town back in the days of the Great Depression, planted here in Los Angeles, and left to rot. About half of them were down. Barbara was surprised that *any* had survived the quake.

Every yard was enclosed by a six-foot chain link fence.

Protection against marauders.

Except for a lone derelict pushing his shopping cart down the sidewalk at the far end of the block, nobody seemed to be around.

No trees. No people.

'Where *is* everybody?' she asked.

'Maybe dead,' Heather said, her voice hardly more than a whisper.

'Dead, my butt,' Earl said. 'They're probably all off on a looting spree.'

'At least the cars are getting through,' Pete pointed out.

'Yeah!' For as far as Barbara could see – perhaps three blocks – the few cars traveling this street seemed to be moving fast.

*We could make fantastic time.*

*Who knows? If we're really lucky, maybe the driver will take us all the way home.*

*But even a mile . . .*

*Dad probably won't be there, but Mom . . .*

*She might need me. Maybe just a few minutes could make all the difference.*

'I'll do it,' she said. 'I'll be the bait.'

Heather looked greatly relieved.

'Fine,' Earl said. 'Just don't be picky. You don't gotta marry the guy, just ride in his car for a while.'

'No guys, remember?'

'Just do whatever you think is best,' Pete told her.

An old green pickup truck was parked at the curb. Barbara positioned herself beside its driver's door. The others ducked out of sight by the front bumper.

Seconds later, a white Honda rounded the corner. The woman behind its wheel was middle-aged, chubby, and wore rollers in her hair.

Perfect.

Barbara stepped away from the pickup's door, turned toward the driver, and waved her hands. 'Could you help me?' she called.

The woman gave her a glance, then turned her head forward very fast. As if afraid she might be caught looking.

It's the way people act with bums, Barbara thought.

*I'm not a bum!*

She supposed her hair might be a little messed up, but otherwise . . .

She looked down at herself. Her short-sleeved white blouse was clean, neatly pressed, buttoned almost to her neck, and tucked into the waist of her pale blue shorts. She fingered the zipper of her shorts. It was shut, of course. So the driver hadn't been put off by an open fly. Her shorts were clean. They weren't skin-tight short-shorts, either, but baggy-legged things that reached almost down to her knees.

Bending forward slightly, she inspected her socks and shoes. White crew socks, white athletic shoes. And a very nice tan between the tops of socks and the hem of her shorts.

I look terrific, she thought.

*Maybe the creepo just doesn't like teenagers.*

*Maybe she's afraid I'm a serial killer. Like maybe I've got a chainsaw in my purse.*

The next car to turn onto 15th Street was a Mercedes convertible driven by a man. His hair was mussed. He wore sunglasses, a blue sport shirt and a necktie.

Barbara settled back against the door of the pickup. She folded her arms and gazed away.

The Mercedes stopped.

'Do you need a ride somewhere?' the driver asked.

'No. Thanks, anyway.'

'Are you sure? I don't normally give people a lift, but under the circumstances . . .'

'No, that's all right. I'm waiting for someone.'

'Is everything okay?'

'Yes. Fine. Thank you for stopping.'

He shrugged and drove on.

He looked like a nice guy, she thought.

Yeah, and so did Ted Bundy.

'What's the matter with you?' Earl called from the hiding place.

'I told you, no guys.'

But the next two cars that passed were driven by women, and neither stopped.

Earl yelled, 'Hey, got a great idea! Why don't you lay down in the road?'

# SIX

After trading seats with Mary and strapping himself in, Clint had reached out to turn on the radio. He'd needed news of the quake. And of traffic conditions.

Where a radio should've been, there was an empty space in the instrument panel.

'Where's your radio?' he'd asked.

'Gone.'

He had shaken his head and started driving.

He'd *really* wanted to hear some news!

The Valley had been hit hard, that was obvious. But what about the rest of Los Angeles? If the epicenter had been somewhere near here, maybe L.A. got off easy. Maybe at home there was nothing but a minor tremor, the sort of thing you might mistake for a big truck driving by the house. Maybe Sheila didn't know it was a quake until she saw the chandelier above the dining room table swinging.

The chandelier, their home earthquake meter.

*Yep, that was a four-point-two on the Chandelier Scale.*

'It's the fourth,' Mary had said.

'What? What're you . . . ?'

'I've had four stolen. And they always break a window.'

Oh. Car radios.

'I even tried not locking the car at night. But they broke a window anyway. So I just gave up. I stopped buying new ones. After the fourth. They'd just get it, anyway. Why waste my time and money? Now I don't have a radio, but my window got broken anyway.' She'd glanced at it, but looked away fast. 'I love this car,' she'd murmured. 'And people keep . . . hurting it. Why can't people be *nice*?'

'People are fine,' Clint had said. 'Nine out of ten.' Two blocks ahead, the road had appeared to be jammed with traffic. Clint could avoid the mess with a detour. But which way to go? Probably right.

'Trouble is,' he'd continued, 'nine out of ten adds up to ten in a hundred who are jerks. They foul up the works for everyone else. Which is why my car's locked away in a parking lot and why *you* don't have a radio. I'd *really* like to know what the hell is going on with this quake. I've got

46

a wife and kid over in West L.A. I'd *really* like to know if there still *is* a West L.A., damn it!'

He'd turned right.

'Where are you going?' Mary had asked.

'Laurel Canyon. I hope. You wouldn't happen to know how we might get there from here?'

'We need to get onto the Golden State, and . . .'

'Not today.'

South on the Golden State Freeway was Clint's usual route home. The Golden State south, then west on the Ventura Freeway to the Laurel Canyon Boulevard offramp – about a ten-minute drive on the freeways. Ten minutes to cover ten miles through smoothly moving traffic in the early afternoon.

But the quake had struck at eight-twenty when the commuter rush was at its peak.

Even without an earthquake, every freeway in the Los Angeles area was usually crowded at that time of the morning with bumper to bumper traffic that barely moved at all. The quake had probably turned the freeways into parking lots.

Clint knew enough to stay clear of them.

But he wasn't sure at all about which surface streets to take, so he'd picked his route at random – trying to avoid areas where the traffic appeared heavy, trying to keep a course that carried them south and west.

Some of his choices worked fine. Others didn't.

After swinging into a road that dead-ended, he turned the car around and asked, 'You aren't at all familiar with the streets around here?'

'Not really,' she admitted.

'Do you have a map?'

She shook her head.

'Are you sure?'

*What kind of person doesn't have a map!*

'It's just that . . . I don't normally go places when I don't know where they are. I'm sorry.'

'It's all right.'

'Do you have maps?' she asked.

'Sure, but they're in my car.' *Where they belong*, he thought.

'Do you think we should maybe go back and get them?'

Clint shook his head.

How long had he been driving? About ten minutes?

It would take at least that long to return for the maps – if he could even manage to find the office building.

'I don't think I could find my way back if I *wanted* to,' he said. 'Besides, it'd take too much time. Every minute . . . no.'

The minutes lost by backtracking might be the minutes that mattered, that delayed them just enough to make all the difference.

*For want of a minute . . .*

Clint *had* to get home. He had to be with Sheila, with Barbara. He had to see them with his own eyes, know they were all right, hold them in his arms.

Any delay could mean arriving at an intersection *after* it'd jammed.

They'd all be jammed soon. Most of them, anyway.

Because the traffic signals were dead.

People who believed in the rules would take turns crossing, but the few who were out for themselves would mess it up, trying to cross when they shouldn't. Every intersection that didn't have a cop directing traffic would soon be clogged, impassable.

It had to be happening already.

Five, ten more minutes, Clint thought. That's probably all we've got before the roads'll be totally screwed up. We've got to put some miles behind us while we can.

As long as we're heading in the right general direction, that's the main thing.

*If we can just make it over the hills . . . as far as Sunset . . . we could walk from there . . . maybe four miles, five at most. Easy. We could cover that in an hour or so. Mary'll still be a long way from home, but . . .*

Rounding a corner, he found the street ahead blocked by police cars and fire trucks.

He braked to a halt.

Halfway down the block, an enormous, two-story apartment complex was ablaze.

Forty or fifty people stood around, watching: few men, mostly women and small kids. Many were dressed in nightgowns or robes. One man, hair still slicked down from a bath or shower, wore nothing except a blue towel wrapped around his waist.

'Can you get around it?' Mary asked.

'Doubt it.'

Besides, a police officer was waving them off.

Clint shoved the gearshift into reverse. He started to back away, then noticed the woman. She was calling to someone as she hurried into the street.

Calling to us?

Her arms were busy hugging a baby to her chest. Her hair was wrapped with a pink towel. She wore a long, paisley robe and pink slippers.

Clint stepped on the brake.

'What does *she* want?' Mary asked.

'Guess we'll find out.'

'Let's not. Let's get moving.'

'We'd better wait and see what . . .'

'She'll want us to take her somewhere. I *know* it. We haven't got time. Every minute . . .'

'Yeah.' Lifting his foot off the pedal, he shook his head at the approaching woman and saw a look of despair crumple her face.

'Wait!' she called. 'Don't go!'

Mary squeezed his thigh. 'Do you want to get home to your wife and daughter or don't you?'

Clint backed up and swung the rear of the BMW into the cross street, retracing his course.

The woman was running, waving one arm, the baby jostling against her chest, the colorful robe open below its sash and flapping behind her. Her legs were very pale. Her pubic hair was a heavy black thicket, startling to see but not arousing. Disturbing, pathetic, and vaguely repulsive because somehow it reminded Clint of Holocaust pictures. 'No!' she yelled. 'Wait!'

He didn't wait.

He forced his eyes away from the woman and sped the car forward, leaving her behind.

Then he muttered, 'Shit.'

'Don't worry,' Mary said. 'It couldn't have been anything that urgent or she would've gone to the cops. That's what they're for, to help people.'

Good point, Clint thought. It made him feel better. Though not much.

'I just wish I knew what she wanted.'

'A ride. Either that or money. She would've given us some kind of a sob story and we'd still be sitting there listening to her.'

'You're probably right.'

'I know I'm right.'

But Clint wished he had waited, let the woman say her piece.

It would not have been the smart thing to do; speeding away had been the smart thing. He hardly needed a total stranger to be robbing time from him – time that he owed to Sheila and Barbara.

Lose a minute listening to some distraught woman, and maybe you end up on the wrong side of a crash that shuts your road.

Stupid.

But he wished he had risked it. He wished he had stayed to hear out the woman, then done whatever he could to help her.

Not the smart thing to do, but the right thing.

He felt a little bit sick inside.

Ashamed.

Not only ashamed of himself for fleeing from the stranger, but for allowing Mary to talk him out of doing what he knew was right.

Was he so used to letting Sheila and Barbara have their ways that he'd forgotten how to stand up to a woman?

*Of course, mine're usually right about stuff.*

The thought made him start to smile, but a terrible sadness suddenly swept through him.

*If they're not okay . . .*

# SEVEN

Stanley savored the job of uncovering Sheila. He took his time at it, scooping up double handfuls of debris, lifting away a chunk of this, a slab of that, a broken beam, a section of fallen wall.

Though he simply tossed the smaller obstacles aside, he lifted each large piece, carried it a few paces, and set it down carefully.

Slow work. Exciting work.

When Sheila had asked if he could go any faster, he'd explained, 'It's awfully precarious up here. I don't want to start an avalanche.'

'I know you're doing the best you can.'

He *was* doing the best he could – to remove the material silently. Let Sheila think he was taking great care to prevent her from being injured by falling rubble; his actual purpose was to maintain the secrecy of his project. There would be an awful clamor if he started hurling the big stuff aside.

Though remnants of walls protected him from being seen by anyone who might pass in front of the house, loud noises might draw attention. The last thing he wanted was an intruder – a nosy neighbor coming along to investigate or help.

*Sheila's mine.*

He had cleared away rubble all the way down to floor level before she began to appear.

Low and out of reach.

The bathtub *had* apparently dropped into the crawlspace underneath the house, just as Sheila had told him. The rim of the tub seemed to be about two feet lower than the floor. And she was lower still, at the bottom of the tub.

Most of the scrap was jumbled atop the tub like a roof.

As Stanley carried it away, she came into view a part at a time. First a foot, then a knee, next a shoulder.

She was a wondrous jigsaw puzzle being assembled by Stanley, growing piece by piece as he removed the debris that concealed her.

A thigh, a hand tucked between her legs, her chin, a breast partly covered by a forearm.

Sunlit parts, dirty, powdered with dust, strewed with flakes and crumbs of wood and plaster. Stanley wondered why she hadn't brushed some of the litter off her skin. Maybe she appreciated the coating. Maybe it gave her the feeling that she wasn't totally naked.

Only when he worked near the foot of the tub could he see her face. From every other location, it was hidden beneath a wooden four-by-eight beam that lay across the far end of the tub like a wide, thick shelf.

He wondered how much *she* could see of him.

*When I can't see her eyes, she can't see mine.*

Still, just to be on the safe side, he took only small glimpses of Sheila. He tried not to stare. And he made small talk. 'We'll have you out in a jiffy, now . . . That one was heavier than it looked . . . I'm getting a pretty good workout here.' Talking as if he hadn't particularly noticed – or didn't care – that she was sprawled out naked below him.

She talked, too, as if unconcerned by her nudity. But she kept the hand between her legs and the arm across her breasts.

Stanley needed both hands for his work, so he couldn't use one to hide the jutting front of his pajama bottoms. Most of the time, however, he was bent over or crouching. Maybe she hadn't noticed the bulge.

She *might* have noticed, though.

*Maybe it turns her on.*

Stanley had a sudden urge to pop open the snaps of his fly.

*Give her a good look.*

*No!*

She might start yelling, and maybe somebody would come along to investigate . . .

Just keep it all normal and friendly, he told himself. Wait until just the right time.

Soon, Sheila was clear.

Except for the beams.

Stanley had saved them for last, knowing they would give him the most trouble.

Four-by-eights, both of them. He guessed they must be support beams that had broken and shifted under the house's floor. One lay across the far end of the tub, above Sheila's face. The other was jammed *into* the tub, braced up by the edge to her right, slanting downward and shoved tight against the left side. From its position, it looked as if it should've chopped off Sheila's left leg at the thigh. But she must have kicked upward in the nick of time.

Flat on her back, she had the beam between her legs – on top of her right, under her left.

The knuckles of the hand covering herself down there were less than half an inch from its rough wood surface.

Stanley supposed he probably *could* lift or shove the beams out of the way. If he got down and stood on the rim of the tub and really worked at it.

Moving them, however, might not be necessary.

He got to his hands and knees above Sheila's right hip. From there, he had a pretty good view of her. He hunched down so that he could see more of her face – chin, lips, the tip of her nose.

'Do you think you can work yourself out of there now?' he asked.

'I'll try.'

She raised her left leg off the beam. Keeping it high, she placed both hands on the beam. Her arms, nearly straight, pressed her breasts together. She pushed. Her skin suddenly writhed over flexing muscles and she slid toward the rear of the tub. But only a bit. An inch. Maybe two. Then the top of her head thumped the underside of the other beam.

She winced. Her muscles unbunched and she let herself slide back down a bit.

'You okay?' Stanley asked.

'Yeah, it just . . .'

'I should've warned you.'

'I knew it was there. Just didn't think it was so *close*.' Tilting her head toward her right shoulder, she again pushed at the beam between her legs.

Stanley watched the muscles come up in her arms and shoulders. She even had pecs that bulged near the tops of her breasts.

A moan growled out of Stanley.

A slip. But Sheila didn't react. Probably hadn't heard it through all the other noises.

She twisted herself and raised her left leg even higher and swung her arm from the beam to shove at the edge of the tub.

Though her right hand still thrust at the beam, Stanley could see past its wrist. Coils of golden hair. Pink, open flesh.

'*Damn* it!' Sheila cried out.

Thinking he'd been caught, Stanley flinched and looked away fast.

At once, he knew she hadn't seen where he'd been looking.

She was too busy squirming, straining upward, twisting herself, trying to work her tilted head out from under the other beam. Her face was red, teeth gritted, lips peeled back.

Abruptly, she quit that tactic. She flung both hands overhead and clutched the forward edge of the beam and thrust against it. Even as she shoved, her body made a quick slide toward the foot of the tub. She didn't get far in that direction before she was stopped by the lower beam.

Stanley grimaced when he saw it mash her.

She squeezed it between her thighs as if using it for a brace.

Then she struggled like a trapped savage.

Whether she was trying to force the beam out of her way or shove herself in front of it, Stanley couldn't tell. Either outcome would've worked. And she tried hard. Her whole body shuddered with the effort. Sweat poured, cutting skin-colored trails through her coating of powder and dust. Her muscles trembled. Her breasts shook.

At last, she let go and sank down against the bottom of the tub, panting for air. Her arms lay limp by her sides. She shook her head. 'Can't. The beams . . . not with . . . them . . .'

'They're sure in the wrong places, all right.'

'I can't . . . believe it,' she muttered.

'Yeah,' Stanley said. If the beams had fallen differently, she might've been able to squirm free – or they might've crushed her. But the quake had rammed them into the perfect positions to trap her.

If she were a few inches shorter, or the tub a bit deeper, she would be able to curl herself forward until her head cleared the four-by-eight that loomed above her face. Then, sitting up, she could slide clear of the beam between her legs. But she was too tall for that, the tub too shallow.

It's almost like a miracle, Stanley thought.

Everything had happened *just so* to pin Sheila naked and unhurt at the bottom of her bathtub.

*Just for me.*

*She was put here for me.*

Does that mean I'm supposed to *leave* her down in the tub?

It's not a question of *supposed to*, he told himself. She's like a gift. I can do whatever I want with her.

Right now, it seemed like enough just to *be* with her – to look at her and talk to her.

'Just relax for a while,' he said. 'We'll get you out, don't worry.'

She nodded, took a very deep breath, then blew the air out through pursed lips. Her arms still rested by her sides.

No more point in covering herself, Stanley realized. I've already seen what there is to see.

Or maybe she's just too distracted to care.

*Thank you very much, my dear. Thank you oh so much.*

'It's really a miracle you weren't killed,' he said. 'If you hadn't been in the bathtub . . .'

'I wasn't. Hadn't even started the water yet. But I was in leaping distance.'

'You *leaped* into the tub?'

'More of a dive. It was very impressive. Wish Clint had been here to see it.' She smiled in the shadow cast by the beam. But the smile lasted only a moment, then trembled and vanished. 'I just wish he was here, at all.'

54

'Clint's your husband?'

'Yeah. He works in Glendale. God only knows how long it'll take him to get home. If he *can* get home.' Her chin started to tremble. She pressed her lips together in a tight, straight line.

'I'm sure he's just fine,' Stanley said. 'Your girl, too.'

'I just wish they were here.'

'Yeah.'

'That's the worst part. Not knowing if they're okay. I don't mind the rest so much. You know? The house . . . As long as *they're* okay.' Her smile came back. 'Not that I'd mind getting out of this tub.'

'We'll get you out.'

'Maybe you could go and find some help,' Sheila suggested.

'Let's see if I can't move one of these beams out of the way for you.'

'It's no use. *I* couldn't budge them. They don't seem to have any give at all. I think they're wedged in, somehow.'

'Well, I could give it a try.'

'No.' She shook her head. 'Don't. You might hurt yourself. Or fall or something. Really, there's no point.'

'We might both try one together,' Stanley suggested.

'I doubt . . . Do you know what would work? A saw. I don't think even two or three people could manage to budge either of these beams, but . . . you could saw right through one. It'd be easy.'

'That sounds like a really good idea.'

'We've got saws in the garage.'

'Your garage went down. I'm sure I can find a saw somewhere, though. Might take a few minutes, but . . .'

'Before you go, can you take a look around? I'd like to have *some*thing, you know . . . to cover myself with.'

'I'm afraid I already checked,' he lied. 'While I was clearing the stuff away. All the clothes must be buried under . . .'

She shook her head. 'What about curtains? Or a towel? A bedsheet. Maybe a pillowcase?'

'Unless you want a plank of wood . . .'

She let out a small, quiet laugh. 'No, that's all right. When you go for the saw, though, maybe you can find me something?'

'Sure,' he said.

When Hell freezes over, he thought.

He was glad he'd taken off his pajama shirt earlier. If Sheila had known about it, he would've had to toss it down to her as soon as she'd come into view. Either that, or risk making her suspicious. But nobody could be expected to give up his pajama pants. She hadn't asked for them, and she would think he was weird if he even offered to let her have them.

'Anything'll be fine,' she added. 'Just so I can . . . make myself decent. Even an old sack or a rug.'

'I'll find something.' He frowned. 'I just hate to leave you alone down there.'

'I'll be okay.'

'Yeah. It's just . . .' He stopped his voice.

'What?'

'Never mind. It's all right. The chances of someone coming along while I'm gone are pretty remote. And if anybody *does* find you, it probably won't be . . . anyone to worry about. It's just that you're so vulnerable down there. If the wrong sort of person . . .'

She smiled. A game smile, only a trifle nervous. 'Trying to cheer me up, are you?'

'Sorry. The thing is, I noticed a couple of strange characters over near where that house is on fire. They looked . . . unsavory, you know?'

'Terrific.'

'I didn't mean to worry you.'

'It's all right. How's that fire doing, anyway?'

Stanley glanced over his shoulder, but couldn't see much. In the way, near his back and about five feet high, was the remnant of an interior wall. 'Just a second,' he said. He crawled backward so Sheila couldn't watch him stand. On his feet, he turned around.

Off in the distance, beyond the low, ragged corner of Sheila's house, a column of smoke still surged into the sky.

'It doesn't look like it's spreading,' he said.

'Is the fire department there yet?'

'No,' he answered. 'No police, either.' He was guessing. The ruins of Sheila's house blocked his view of the street, and he wasn't about to climb a pile of rubble just to inspect the situation. 'There's hardly any breeze. I don't think we need to worry about the fire getting here.'

'So, as long as we don't have one of our own . . . I don't smell any gas. Can you smell gas?' she asked.

Stanley sniffed. The hot air made his nostrils sting. He smelled a faint aroma of smoke, a dry odor that might have been concrete or plaster dust, and a scent of suntan lotion that quickened his heartbeat and filled his head with images of beaches, surf, girls in bikinis, Sheila stretched out on her lounger.

Her lounger had smelled that way.

He closed his eyes, breathed deeply, and moaned with pleasure.

'Stanley?'

How wonderful to hear his name spoken by that sweet voice.

'I can't smell any gas.'

'Maybe you should turn it off at the main valve, anyway. It's what you're supposed to do after a big quake. And there almost *has* to be leaks.'

'Okay. I'll take care of that. Do you know where the shutoff is?'

'It's outside the house.'

'Okay.'

'It's near the chimney, on the outside wall. There ought to be a special wrench attached. All you've gotta do is turn the wrench.'

'I'll find it.' He stepped close to the edge of the floor, leaned forward and looked down at Sheila. 'I'll turn off the gas, then go and find a saw . . . and something for your decency.'

'That'll be great, Stan. Thank God you found me.'

'I'll second that.'

'Hurry back, okay?'

'I'll get back as fast as I can. You can bet on it.'

# EIGHT

No matter what Barbara did – motion with her thumb, call out, jump up and down waving both arms – female drivers simply wouldn't stop their cars. Some scowled at her. Others pretended not to notice her.

It had taken Barbara a while to figure out why, but now she thought she knew the answer. It had little to do with how she was dressed. Nor was it because the drivers didn't like teenagers or were afraid she might be a criminal.

They weren't stopping, she decided, for the simple reason that women take an immediate dislike for any female they consider more attractive than themselves.

As Mom had put it, 'If you make them feel plain or ugly, they hate you for it.'

Mom knew from first-hand experience. She'd been a target for spite and envy all her life. Nearly everyone really liked her once they got to know her, but she seemed to be despised from a distance. By women. Barbara had seen it happen many times. Just as men gaped at Mom with wide eyes and sagging mouths, women glared, narrow-eyed, tight-lipped.

Barbara had been the object of such attention, herself. Not nearly as much as Mom, but often.

This has to be part of the same deal, she thought as one woman after another drove past her without stopping.

Men, of course, stopped even though she gave them no encouragement. Not all of them, but several.

The sixth was in a black Pontiac. The passenger window slid down even before the car had come to a full halt. The driver leaned across the seat. He appeared to be about forty. He looked fairly prosperous and serious in his gray suit and necktie. His glasses had silver rims.

'Climb on in,' he said.

'Thanks for the offer, but I'm just waiting here for somebody.' She had used the line successfully with the other men who'd stopped.

But this one smirked. 'Hey, come on, don't give me that. It's no secret you're looking for a ride. I saw how you tried to flag down that Rabbit.' He nodded toward the white VW that had already gone some distance up 15th Street. 'Now all of a sudden you've lost interest? Come on, climb in here.' The passenger door swung open. Fast. Straight at Barbara's thighs.

She backstepped. The edge of the door made a whissing sound against the front of her shorts. It just missed her legs.

'Thanks for stopping,' she said. 'I appreciate it. But I'm waiting for . . .'

'Come on, where are you going? Do you need a ride home? I'll take you wherever you want to go. Traffic permitting. The streets are a mess, in case you haven't noticed. I'll be lucky if I can get home myself . . .'

'Don't you think that's where you *ought* to go instead of trying to pick me up?'

'Pick you *up*? You're *hitchhiking*. Christ!'

'I've got a policy not to ride with guys. Just women.'

'Just women,' he muttered. His thin upper lip lifted and stretched across his gums. 'Wonderful. Figures. Boy, how it figures. A gal looks like you, it just goes to figure she's a . . .'

The man's door flew open.

On *his* side of the car.

He'd been leaning sideways, braced up with a hand on the passenger seat, bright red face raised toward Barbara. At the sound of his door unlatching, he shoved himself upright and snapped his head to the left.

Earl sprang into the V of the open door.

'Hey!' the man yelled.

Earl grabbed him, tugged, brought the face close to his own and snarled, 'Hey yourself.'

'Earl!' Barbara yelled. 'What're you . . . ?'

Her voice stopped as if her own breath had been smashed out. But it was the driver of the Pontiac who lost his air, lost it when Earl hauled him from the car and kneed him in the belly.

'Leave him alone!' she shouted, breaking into a run.

Pete and Heather both popped up in front of the old pickup where they'd been crouching along with Earl to wait for a ride. Pete looked confused, Heather excited.

'He's pounding the guy!' Barbara yelled.

By the time she reached the other side of the Pontiac, the driver was curled on the pavement, arms hugging his head, knees up close to his stomach. In a high, squealy voice, he cried out, 'Stop!' and 'Quit it!' and 'Please!' as Earl pranced around him, kicking him.

Barbara had already shouted for Earl to leave the man alone. Earl hadn't listened then. He wasn't likely to listen now.

So Barbara didn't waste her breath.

As Earl kicked his victim in the back, she threw herself over the squirming man. She went at Earl sideways, hunched low, head down. Her right shoulder bashed him in the chest.

He let out a grunt.

And another grunt when his back hit the street.

Barbara smashed down on top of him. The instant his body stopped skidding, she rolled off.

Earl lay sprawled on his back, eyes and mouth wide open. He made sucking noises.

On hands and knees, Barbara watched him struggle to catch a breath. His face was awfully red. He seemed to be having a very hard time. She frowned.

She hadn't meant to *hurt* him, just stop him.

'You okay?' she asked.

He glanced at her, said nothing, and kept on wheezing.

At the sound of quick footsteps, Barbara looked over her shoulder. Pete and Heather were rushing around the car. The man scurried for his open door. They gave him a wide berth, glancing from him to Barbara to Earl.

He clambered into his car and slammed the door. Through the open window, he shouted, 'Bastards! Fucks! I'm getting the cops!'

His car lunged forward, squealing and laying rubber, smoke rising behind its rear tires.

Barbara returned her attention to Earl just in time to see his arm shoot out.

'Watch it!' Pete yelled.

Before she could make a move to get away, Earl clutched the front of her blouse and yanked her toward him. Her arms went out from under her. She flopped on top of Earl. Twisting and bucking, he threw her sideways. He scrambled onto her, straddled her. Pinning her arms to the pavement, he bounced his rump on her belly.

'Get off her!' Pete snapped.

'You see what she did to me?'

'You were beating the hell out of that guy!' Barbara gasped.

'Yeah! Damn straight!'

'Get off her!' Pete said again.

Earl ignored him. 'We needed that car.'

'You aren't gonna steal a *car*,' Barbara gasped. 'Just 'cause we had a quake . . . doesn't mean all the *rules* are gone.'

'Oh yeah?' He bounced on her belly again, driving her wind out.

'Okay,' Pete muttered. 'Okay.' He rushed in from the side, ducked low, grabbed Earl's right forearm and jerked it toward him.

Earl lost his grip on Barbara's wrist.

The instant her left arm was free, she punched him in the face. The blow jolted his head. Spit flew from his lips.

He yelled and released her right wrist and grabbed her throat – and his right arm was loose, somehow. Barbara had time to think, *What did*

*Pete do, let go of it?* before the fist struck her face.

The blow rocked her.

But she still had enough strength to tear Earl's hand away from her throat. As she shoved it aside, he punched her again. This time, he went for her jaw instead of her cheekbone.

Just as the punch landed, Pete kicked him in the head. The toe of the gray Reebok caught him in front of the right ear. His head snapped sideways. He tumbled off Barbara.

Propping herself up with one arm, she looked at him.

He was sprawled out, motionless.

'Geez,' she murmured.

They all stared at Earl. He lay on his back, arms and legs spread out, eyes shut, mouth open. His right cheek wore the rosy imprint of Barbara's fist. Otherwise, he looked okay. Except that he wasn't moving.

Barbara worked her jaw from side to side. It hurt on the left side, down below her ear. And a clicking sound came from there.

What did he do, break it?

Probably not, she decided. It doesn't hurt that bad.

The clicking noise made her nervous.

But it only came when she slid her jaw sideways.

So quit doing it, she told herself.

While Barbara worried about her jaw and experimented with it, she watched the front of Earl's shirt. Trying to see movement there.

Is he breathing? she wondered.

Heather suddenly let out a tiny, odd laugh. 'Lookit, lookit!' She pointed, and Barbara noticed a dark stain on the faded blue denim at the crotch of Earl's jeans.

Heather leaned forward, her face aglow with delight. 'He wet his pants! Jones! Mr Tough Guy! He peed in his pants!'

'Knock it off,' Barbara said.

Pete looked scared. 'What does it mean?'

'Wittow Err-owe need a die-dee,' Heather said.

Pete ignored her. 'Did I kill him?'

'I don't know,' Barbara said. Keeping her eyes on Earl, she slowly got to her feet. She felt dizzy for a moment, but it passed. She fingered her face. The jut of her cheekbone seemed twice its usual size, and the skin over it was tight and hot.

'God,' Pete muttered. 'I bet it means he's dead.'

'Maybe it's just 'cause he's unconscious,' Barbara said. 'I don't think he necessarily has to be dead to . . . you know . . . lose it.'

'I hope he *is* dead,' Heather said.

Barbara looked at her. 'I thought you wanted us all to be friends.'

'Yeah, but that was before.'

'Don't wish him dead, for Godsake,' Pete said. 'I'm the guy who kicked him.'

'He's such a creep.'

'Yeah,' Barbara said. 'He's a creep, all right, but that isn't a capital crime.'

Heather's lip curled up. 'Huh?'

'Nothing.'

Pete crouched over Earl. Bending low, he pressed his ear against the boy's chest.

'Is he okay?' Barbara asked.

Pete didn't respond. Barbara waited.

'He had it coming,' Heather muttered.

'Shhhh.'

Then the energy seemed to drain out of Pete. His eyes drifted shut, and he looked as if he might stretch out and fall asleep using Earl's chest for a pillow. Suddenly, he flinched. His eyes jumped open. He sprang to his feet. He pranced away from Earl and darted his glance from Heather to Barbara. 'Come on, quick. We've gotta get out of here.'

'He's really *dead*?' Barbara asked.

'All right!' Heather clapped her hands.

'Hell no, he isn't dead,' Pete blurted. 'Let's get outa here quick!'

Oh, Barbara thought. I get it.

*Jeez!*

At least he's not dead, she told herself. That's a good thing. Right? Yeah, sure.

'Come on,' Pete said.

'Wait. We can't just leave him in the street. What if a car hits him?'

'You're right,' Pete said.

Heather rolled her eyes upward, shook her head, and said, 'Boy.'

Barbara and Pete each crouched over Earl and took one of his arms. They pulled until his back came up off the pavement. Then, side by side, they towed him toward the curb. He skidded on the seat of his jeans. He left a broad, wet trail like a mop being dragged across a floor. His head, hanging limp between his stretched arms, wobbled and swayed. Barbara watched it, hoping it wouldn't suddenly jerk upright, eyes open.

They pulled Earl over the curb. He still seemed to be unconscious when they eased him down onto the sidewalk.

'Good enough?' Pete asked.

'Good enough,' Barbara said. 'Let's beat it.'

'Should we tie him up, or something?' Heather asked.

'Are you kidding?' Barbara asked.

'What if he comes after us?'

'We took care of him this time, didn't we?'

'Yeah, but . . .'

'Besides,' Pete said, 'he'll have to find us first. Let's go! Let's haul it!'

Pete in the lead, Barbara taking the rear so that she wouldn't need to worry about Heather falling behind, they raced up 15th Street.

# NINE

After making so many detours to get away from blocked streets, Clint hardly knew which way to turn. He couldn't go straight; the road dead-ended just ahead.

We're lost, he thought. Really lost.

Payback for running away from that woman back at the fire. We're getting the lousy luck we deserve.

'Which way do we go?' Mary asked.

Clint shook his head.

'We can't just sit here.'

From the angles of the shadows, he knew the sun was behind him. He'd been driving from east to west, so a turn to the left would head them south.

He turned left. 'At least we'll be going in the right general direction,' he said.

'Are you sure?'

'Yep. Left is right.'

He glanced at her. She twitched her lips to let him see that she wasn't much amused.

His choice had been good, though. It took them to Burbank Boulevard. He'd been doing all he could to avoid the major thoroughfares, figuring they'd be jammed, but on Burbank the traffic was moving along in a slow, steady flow.

A car eased back to let him in.

Clint waved a thank you to the driver and turned right onto Burbank.

Just ahead was Lankershim Boulevard. A police officer stood in the middle of the intersection, directing traffic.

'Fantastic!' Clint blurted. 'A cop!' A motorcycle cop, he realized when he saw the Harley parked at the corner. 'Wish we had one of those,' he said, nodding toward the bike. 'We could go just about anywhere.'

'Do you know where we are now?' Mary asked.

'I'm not positive,' he admitted. 'But doesn't Burbank go parallel to Ventura Boulevard?'

Mary frowned and shrugged.

'I think it does,' Clint said. 'And that'd mean it should run straight into Laurel Canyon.'

'Does Laurel Canyon go this far north?'

'Hope so.'

'Yeah, me too.'

And then Clint saw, up ahead, the Hollywood Freeway.

Below the freeway, an underpass.

'Oh, have we lucked out!' He made no attempt to control his excitement. 'I didn't know *how* we'd ever get across the freeway, you know? Only the major roads go through, and they were bound to be totally jammed – but they're not! *This* one isn't! There's still the Ventura Freeway, but . . . hell, we'll worry about that when we come to it.'

They entered the shadows of the underpass.

They came out on the other side into the sunlight.

And brake lights.

Ahead, every westbound lane appeared to be jammed with traffic.

'Great while it lasted,' Clint muttered, and cut hard to the left. Just as he made it to the center lines, a break appeared in the stream of cars going east. He swung into the gap, jamming the gas pedal to the floor.

Mary gasped and grabbed the dashboard.

They shot through, untouched.

She let her breath out, let her hands drop to her lap. 'You're something else,' she said, and almost smiled.

'Just wanta get us where we're . . .'

He saw the girl.

She was striding down the sidewalk, head forward, her short hair shiny in the sunlight. She wore a big pink T-shirt that drooped down crooked over the seat of her white shorts. One pink sock hung lower than the other.

She reminded Clint of his daughter.

She was not as tall as Barbara, but just as slim. Though her hair was cut very short, it was Barbara's pale shade of blonde. Like this girl, Barbara often wore T-shirts and shorts to school. And they both lugged huge, bulky book bags in just the same manner, slung over their right shoulder by one strap, the weight swinging against their backs.

This girl's resemblance to Barbara was enough to make Clint slow the BMW and stare at her.

He wouldn't have considered stopping because of it.

But she was also walking alone through an area that had been slammed by a devastating earthquake. And she was injured.

At least, Clint *thought* she must be injured. Behind her left shoulder, her T-shirt bore a brown-red stain that looked a lot like blood.

'She's hurt,' he said, and aimed for the curb a few yards in front of her.

'A *lot* of people are probably hurt,' Mary said. 'What're you doing?'

'I want to make sure she's okay.'

'Oh, for Godsake. No! Don't!'

'It won't . . .'

'Keep going! You don't even know her.'

'She's a kid.' He stopped at the curb and twisted around to look out the rear window. The girl, walking just as briskly as before, looked in at him and frowned a little.

'Damn it, Clint! This is *my* car.'

He said, 'Yup,' and plucked its key from the ignition.

'Clint!'

'Take it easy. I'll be right back.' Taking the key with him, he climbed out of the car.

The girl looked wary, but not frightened.

Instead of trying to intercept her, Clint stopped in front of the BMW.

The girl stopped on the sidewalk adjacent to the passenger door. She cocked her head a bit to the left, narrowed her left eye, and gnawed the left side of her lower lip.

At least she didn't have Barbara's face. For one thing, she was younger. Maybe thirteen or fourteen. Though she had sharp blue eyes like Barbara, her face was longer, more boyish, cute but not with Barbara's obvious beauty. She had the looks of a real tomboy – short hair mussed and hanging across her forehead, a sprinkle of freckles across her nose and cheeks, no lipstick or any other makeup.

She might have been mistaken for a boy except for the small, pointed breasts pushing out the front of her T-shirt.

A girl, all right.

Girls like this used to break Clint's heart when he was their age. Even now, something about her made his throat go tight.

'What's up?' she asked.

'I know you've probably been warned about strangers,' Clint said, 'but you look like you might be able to use some help. I'd be glad to give you a ride somewhere.'

'Clint!' Mary snapped from the car.

'Hi,' the girl said to her – the way she might speak to a growling dog, trying to soothe it. 'How are you?'

The treatment didn't warm up Mary. 'I've been better,' she muttered, and turned her eyes to Clint. 'We're wasting time, you know.'

'You're welcome to climb in,' Clint told the girl. 'We'll take you where you're going.'

With a nod, she hurried to the back door. She opened it and swung in her book bag while Clint returned to the driver's side. Their doors bumped shut at almost the same moment.

Plugging in the ignition key, Clint said, 'I'm Clint Banner. This is Mary Davis.'

Mary looked around at her. 'Where *are* you going?'

'Home?' she asked. 'That's where I was heading.'

'And where is that?'

Before she could answer, Clint said, 'Just point me in the right direction,' and started the car moving.

'Go straight for a while. My name's Em, by the way, in case you're wondering.'

'M?' Clint asked. 'Like 007's boss?'

'Cute,' Mary said.

'It's E-m. Short for Emerald. Emerald O'Hara. Could you just call me Em, though?'

'How old are you?' Clint asked.

'Thirteen.'

'I've got a daughter who'll be sixteen next month.'

'Do you live around here?'

'Nope. West L.A.'

'Guess I wouldn't know her, then. What about you, Mary? Do you have any kids?'

'I'm not married.'

'Do you have any kids, though?'

'Is that supposed to be a crack?'

'A crack? No. My mom isn't married. Never was. I've got a father, of course, but only in the strictly biological sense if you know what I mean. I don't have the vaguest notion who he might be. Mom won't tell me, either. He doesn't even *know* he's my father, can you beat that? All *I* know is that he was in her Chaucer seminar at UCLA umpteen years ago, and that isn't a whole lot to know about your own father. Mom doesn't believe in men, see. She only went with this one guy until he got her pregnant, and then she dumped him.'

'Your mother sounds like an interesting woman,' Clint said.

'Most people think she's a pain in the keister. I'd have to agree with them. Not that I don't love her, and everything, I do. But she's pretty hard to take most of the time.'

'Nice way to talk about your mother,' Mary said.

'I always try to be strictly honest about stuff. I mean, if you're going to tell lies, why talk at all?'

'Is your mother at home?' Clint asked.

'I hope so.'

'She doesn't work?'

67

'No. But that doesn't mean we're poor or anything like that, 'cause we're not. Mom calls it her sabbatical. But what it is, she won this huge lawsuit over sexual harassment at her previous workplace. I mean, it was a bundle. So she's staying home and writing a book. Like a handbook for women who are getting pestered at work?'

'Anyway, you're pretty sure she'll be at home?'

'Oh, yeah. I just hope the house hasn't fallen down or anything. Not that I'm terribly worried. It made it through the Sylmar quake okay. Not that we were living there at the time. Not that *I* was living anywhere, if you know what I mean. But I bet the house made it through this one. Not all that many went down, have you noticed? Just a few here and there. They're saying the Valley got off pretty easy. The epicenter's supposed to be over near downtown.'

'You've heard *news*?' Clint blurted.

'Oh, yeah. Mostly from this guy I walked for a while with. He had a Walkman that was picking up the Emergency Broadcasting Network. Think that's what he called it. They're saying it was an eight point one, but it wasn't on the San Andreas.'

Mary looked shocked. 'You mean this *wasn't* the Big One?'

'Big enough to suit me,' Clint said. 'What else did the radio say, Em?'

'Well, I only know what the guy told me. He said the power's out all over the place, and there're a lot of fires, a lot of buildings down, and whole bunches of people have gotten killed and hurt. They don't know how many yet. It's really supposed to be a mess. There're even some reports of riots and looting. The cops and firemen are having a real hard time getting anyplace because the streets are so bad. But it's not supposed to be nearly as serious over here on this side.'

'My family's on the other side,' Clint said.

'Yeah. Well, I sure hope they're okay. It doesn't sound too swift. I'm not even sure you can *get* there.'

'I'll get there.'

Em leaned forward. Her head appeared between the seatbacks. 'You ought to make a right when you get a chance. We'll need to go under the Ventura Freeway pretty soon. Maybe at Laurel Canyon would be the best place.'

'How far are we from there?' Clint asked.

'Just a few blocks. Once we get past the freeway, we're almost to my house.'

'We're almost to the freeway and Laurel Canyon?'

'Sure.'

He grinned at Em. 'This is great. I've got to tell you, we've been kind of lost for a while.'

'I can show you anyplace you want to go,' Em said. 'I do a lot of walking.'

'By yourself?'

'Sure. We get along fine, me and I.'

'It's awfully dangerous for a girl to be out on the streets alone.'

'You're telling me? I just got clipped by a *brick*. Not even during the quake, if you can believe that. I just happened to be walking by when half a stupid wall decided to fall. If *I* hadn't been so quick on my feet, it would've killed me. Only one brick got me, though. See?' She twisted her body to show Clint the back of her shoulder. Straining her head around in an attempt to see the damage for herself, she said, 'Is the cloth ripped? Can you tell?'

'Maybe snagged a little. It's not really torn.'

'I wonder if the blood'll come out.'

'What about *you*?'

'Oh, I'm okay.'

'You can't be *that* okay if that's your blood on the T-shirt.'

'It isn't bleeding now, is it?'

'I don't think so.'

'I just hope the shirt'll come clean. It's one of my favorites.'

'Were you on your way home from school when you got hit?'

'Yeah. We were supposed to stay and wait in the yard, but I'm not all that big on waiting around, so I made myself scarce.'

'You ditched?'

'Well, it's not like I'll be missing any lessons. I figured Mom might worry about me, and it's not *all* that long a walk to get home. Why should I stick around school, you know?'

Clint wondered if Barbara had seen things that way, too. The high school wasn't much more than a mile from their home. She could walk it easily.

No, Barbara wouldn't.

Not right away, anyhow.

She would know enough to wait at school.

*You just stay put*, Clint had told her when discussing what to do in case of a major quake. *One of us will come and pick you up. You're not to walk home under any circumstances.*

*What if you can't pick me up?* she had asked.

*Stay at school.*

They had never allowed Barbara to walk anywhere by herself. Too many perverts cruising around. Every day, the news brought stories of kids who disappeared a block or two from their homes, of frantic parents, of futile searches, of bodies being located. The bodies were almost always found naked, with evidence of torture and sexual abuse.

Boys and girls both. Girls more often than boys, though.

Clint and Sheila had no intention of ever letting such a thing happen to their daughter.

So they walked with her, or drove her, anywhere she needed to go.

Over-protective. That's what some people called them.

Right.

No such thing as being over-protective in L.A.

*Whatever it takes to keep your kid alive.*

A cute kid like Em was lucky she had lasted this long. Breaks the most basic rules: walks alone, gets in a car with strangers.

I ought to have a talk with her mother, Clint thought.

Yeah, and she'll probably tell me to mind my own business. She's obviously some sort of radical feminist. She'll really appreciate a *man* telling her how to raise her daughter.

Forget the mother.

'All this walking around, Em, aren't you afraid you might run into the wrong sort of person?'

'You mean like a mugger?'

'Or worse.'

'He means like a psycho,' Mary explained. 'One of those guys who grabs girls like you and rapes them and cuts them into pieces.'

'Hey,' Clint said. 'That isn't necessary.'

'Isn't that what you were getting at?' Mary asked. 'I mean, if you've got an urge to warn her, *warn* her, don't pussyfoot. Just lay it out straight, tell her about all those guys out there who'd like nothing better than to get their hands on such a cute young thing – and how lucky she is that she was picked up by *you*, who's a gentleman and a father, not to mention a Knight of the Fucking Roundtable.'

Clint gazed at Mary, astonished. 'What's the matter?' he asked.

'Nothing. Not a thing.'

Em, very calmly, said, 'This is Laurel Canyon coming up. You'll want to turn left.' Then she patted Mary's shoulder. 'A couple more minutes and I'll be outta here. Then you'll have Clint all to yourself, and everything will be splendid again.'

# CHAPTER TEN

While shutting off Sheila's gas, Stanley had wondered about the gas at Mother's house.

His house, now.

If only he'd taken care of the gas before coming over to look for Sheila! He hadn't *thought* of it, though. That was the problem.

Stupid.

He could lose everything.

Even though much of the house had collapsed, Stanley figured that he would be able to salvage plenty from the mess. If it didn't all go up in smoke first.

From the top of the cinderblock wall, he could see that his house was fine.

He grinned and shook his head. Hardly *fine*.

More like half a house, at this point. And no garage at all.

But at least there was no trace of fire.

Instead of leaping, he lowered himself down from the wall. At the bottom, he turned sideways to slip through the rose bushes. A thorn scratched his bare chest while another nicked his rump through the thin cloth of his pajama pants.

Gotta cut the bastards down, he thought as he jogged toward the house.

The earlier wounds felt itchy, like mosquito bites. The new ones stung. Cold water would sure feel good on them.

He saw the water spigot at the rear of the house, nothing covering it or blocking it, nothing to climb over. The back wall looked as if it had been battered away just below the roof, but the area beneath it was clear; the rubble must've all tumbled inward.

Better take care of the gas first, he thought.

*What for? No fire, yet. Maybe there isn't even a leak.*

He hurried over to the spigot. The garden hose was still attached. He unscrewed the hose and let it fall, then twisted the handle. Instead of the normal gush, only a few drops of water fell from the spout.

The disappointment clogged his throat.

'Stan?'

He almost cried out. The sound of his name felt like an icy spike being

71

shoved into his belly. Cringing, he straightened up and turned toward the voice.

Judy Wellman stood only a few yards away, at the edge of the patio. Nothing to worry about. Stanley hoped.

Judy lived next door. She and her husband, Herb. They seemed like nice people. Though they usually kept to themselves, they always had cheerful, friendly things to say whenever Stanley happened to run into them.

Last night, Stanley had seen Herb carry a suitcase out to the car. Judy had driven him away and returned an hour later without him.

Which meant, to Stanley, that she had delivered him to LAX.

He had flown somewhere, likely on a business trip.

So Herb was out of the picture.

*This could be interesting.*

Stanley liked the looks of Judy.

She was no Sheila Banner, of course. Nobody was in Sheila's league.

Still, she looked pretty good. Very good, in fact. Hard to believe she was old enough to have twins in college. Her tanned face had plenty of crinkles when she squinted or smiled, and a few threads of silver gleamed in her thick brown hair, but her body was trim. Though Stanley had never gone out of his way to spy on her, he'd seen her many times simply because she lived next door. He frequently saw her when she went out for the morning newspaper, when she went to her car, when she did yard work. He'd seen her last week wearing shorts and a bikini top while she hosed off her car in the driveway.

This morning, she wore a faded blue shirt so large that Stanley figured it must belong to her husband. Its sleeves were rolled up her tawny forearms. The top couple of buttons were unfastened. The shirt wasn't tucked in. It hung so low that it nearly covered her cut-off jeans. Her brown leather boots, ankle-high, looked very big and clumsy at the ends of such slender legs.

Had she been dressed this way when the quake hit?

Maybe not. Maybe she'd been in her nightgown.

If she'd changed clothes after the quake . . .

Stanley gazed past Judy. All he could see of her house was a rear portion of the side wall. The bedroom window was broken, but the wall appeared to be intact.

'Your house came through okay?' he asked.

She nodded. She looked very solemn. 'I'm awfully sorry about your mother, Stan.'

*She knows!*

He tried to hide his shock and fear behind a mask of sorrow.

72

She can't know I did it, he told himself. If she knew, she would hardly be giving me condolences.

'You saw her?' he asked.

'I came over to make sure everyone was all right. After I saw how badly your house . . .' She shook her head. 'Anyway, your front door wasn't locked. I knocked a few times, but . . . I hope you don't mind. I don't normally go barging into people's homes.'

'No. It was very thoughtful of you.'

'I guess you'd already left. Actually, I figured you were buried under the mess. You didn't answer when I called out. I looked around for a while. There wasn't any sign of you, so . . .'

'I went through the backyard to check on the Banners,' he explained .

Even as he heard himself speak the words, he wondered why he was giving such information to Judy.

*Should've lied, damn it.*

Why? he asked himself. Why bother?

From the vague expression on Judy's face, he guessed that she didn't know the Banners. 'They live directly behind us.' He nodded toward the wall behind the rose bushes.

'Oh. I saw you jump over.'

'The bushes got me pretty good.' He looked down at his sweaty chest, at the stripe of bright red blood above his left nipple. And he saw his pajama pants hanging so low that they looked ready to fall. Trying to appear embarrassed, he pulled the pants up above his hips. Then he folded his hands in front of his groin. 'Sorry,' he muttered.

'Don't worry about it. Why don't you come on over to my place? We'll patch you up a bit, and I'll find you something to wear.'

The offer made his heart pound quicker.

'Is Herb there?' he asked.

'Lucky dog, he flew to New York last night.'

*She's asking me into her house. And she made it clear that Herb won't be showing up.*

*Oh, man.*

Then he thought, Who do you think you're kidding? The last thing on Judy's mind is seducing a guy like me. She's just being friendly, trying to help. Probably feels sorry for me.

So what? The minute we step into her house, she's mine.

But Sheila's waiting, he reminded himself. Sheila's better than Judy – no comparison – and she's naked, and she can't get away.

Then he thought, *Judy'll keep.*

Her husband was in New York, some three thousand miles away. Sheila's was only about thirty or forty miles away in Glendale. No telling how long it might take either husband to return home, but the one coming from Glendale was bound to arrive first.

*Gotta get Sheila out and away to someplace safe, or I'll miss my chance.*

'I don't think I should go into your house,' he said, 'if Herb's not there.'

Judy looked perpiexed. 'What?'

'It wouldn't look good.'

'To whom? Are you kidding? Who would notice *or* care?'

'I don't know. It just . . . anyway, I've gotta get back. I only came around to find a saw and turn off the gas supply at Mother's.'

'I took care of the gas for you,' Judy said. 'I smelled a leak while I was inside looking for you.' The gloom returned to darken her face. 'It's . . . so awful about your mother. I'm so sorry.'

'It happened very fast. I don't think she suffered.'

'You saw it?'

'Yeah. A big chunk of ceiling dropped straight down on her head. She never had a chance.'

'But you're all right?' Judy asked.

'The quake never touched me.' He felt a corner of his mouth turn up. 'Just the damn rose bushes.'

Judy smiled slightly, herself. 'Well, why don't you come over? Under the circumstances, I really doubt that any of the neighbors are likely to tell on us. We'll wash you off and put some disinfectant . . .'

'That really isn't necessary. And I've got to get going.' Stanley frowned at the spigot. 'The water main must be broken, or something.'

'My faucets don't work, either.'

'I bet it's the whole neighborhood,' he said, realizing that Sheila's bathroom pipes probably would've sprayed all over the place if she'd had any water pressure. 'Maybe the whole city,' he added.

'I've got some water in the refrigerator,' Judy said. 'We can use that to clean your wounds. You're probably thirsty, too.'

'Maybe later, okay? But have you got a saw I can borrow?'

'What sort of saw do you need?'

'The best thing would be a chainsaw, I guess. It's a *thick* beam.' He held up his hands to show her the size.

'I don't know. We haven't got one of those. Honestly, I don't know of anybody around here who *does* have a chainsaw. Would a regular handsaw do you any good at all? We've got a couple of those in the garage.'

'Worth a try,' Stanley said.

'Come on.'

He followed Judy down his driveway and through the gate. As they started across her own front yard, she said, 'That beam you need to cut, did it fall on something?'

The question didn't surprise him much. After all, he had asked for a saw. It was only natural for a person to wonder why he needed it.

Very quickly, he tried to think of a lie.

But he had already told her about going to the Banner house.

*Doesn't matter, anyhow.*

'It's got Mrs Banner pinned down.'

Judy looked over her shoulder, frowning. 'You mean she's trapped?'

'I'll have her out in a few minutes once I get back with a saw.'

'Is she hurt?'

'No, I think she's in pretty good shape. But I left her alone. I really need to get back to her as fast as I can.'

They headed up Judy's driveway toward her garage at the far end. Stanley walked slightly behind her, enjoying the view of her slim, dark legs. Threads dangled from her frayed cut-offs and brushed against the backs of her thighs.

He liked the look of the cut-off jeans, though he couldn't see much of them below Judy's hanging shirt tail.

Hardly anyone seemed to wear cut-offs anymore. Apparently, they'd gone out of style.

Too bad, Stanley thought.

'I haven't been into the garage yet,' she said. 'God only knows what kind of mess it'll be.'

'At least it didn't fall down.'

'Everything *inside* it probably did.' With that, Judy grabbed the handle and hauled the garage door sideways. It slid with a low rumble, rolling almost four feet before it thumped to a sudden stop. She looked around at Stanley, shrugged, and said, 'At least we can get in.'

She took one step into the garage before groaning, 'Oh, man. Maybe you'd better wait there.'

Remaining outside, Stanley watched Judy make her way deeper into the gloom. She kept near the wall and moved toward the back, nudging boxes aside, shoving a power lawn mower out of her way, stepping over long handles that Stanley supposed must belong to shovels, rakes, hoes, and brooms that had been propped up until the quake knocked them over.

Soon, she stopped and studied the wall. 'Ah. We're in luck. Right where it's supposed to be.' She stretched out an arm and lifted a saw down off the wall, where it had apparently been suspended by a nail.

She returned with it.

The saw in her hand looked shiny and new. It almost looked unused, but Stanley noticed some crumbs of yellow sawdust clinging to its teeth.

'Think this'll do the trick?' Judy asked.

'It should.'

She handed the saw to him. 'Maybe we should take her some water. It's awfully hot out.'

*We?*

'Right back,' she said, and hurried toward the rear door of her house. Now what? Stanley wondered.

*Judy's planning to come along, that's what.*

The door bumped shut.

*Why didn't I keep my big mouth shut?*

Picturing Sheila sprawled out in the tub, he moaned.

Judy would ruin it all.

*Oh, no, she won't!*

The door flew open and slammed shut. Stanley watched Judy bound down the couple of stairs and stride toward him, swinging a plastic jug by her side. The jug was almost full. He could see the water through the frosted plastic, hear it sloshing. 'Have some?' she asked.

He wanted to be rid of her.

*No, I don't want any of your fucking water. Get out of here and leave me alone!*

But in his imagination, the water was as cold as a high Sierra stream spilling down from melting glaciers.

He clamped the saw handle between his knees, took the offered bottle, uncapped it, and raised it to his mouth. The water burbled out, flooding over his parched tongue, filling his mouth. Its sharp chill made his teeth ache. Cheeks bulging, he held the water in his mouth and capped the jug. He swallowed a small bit at a time until his mouth was empty.

'Thanks,' he said. 'That sure hit the spot. Want some?'

'Not just now.'

He took a deep breath. 'I've been thinking, Judy. Maybe you oughta stay here while I go over and take care of Mrs Banner. Her whole house is caved in. There's broken glass, all kinds of nails and stuff. I wouldn't want you to get hurt.'

'I'll be careful. Anyway, look at you. You're wearing moccasins. If it's that bad . . .'

'I made it okay last time.'

'I'd find you something for your feet, but you're so much bigger than Herb.'

'Doesn't matter. I'm fine. But look, I'd better get going.' He shifted the water jug to his left hand, then bent over and took the saw from between his legs. 'I'll bring these back to you as soon as I've got her free.'

Frowning as if she didn't understand, Judy shook her head. 'It's all right, I'll come with you. You don't need to worry about me. If I get hurt, I get hurt. The thing is, there's no point in you trying to rescue this woman by yourself. I'm not totally useless, you know. I might be able to help. If nothing else, I can keep the two of you company – give you some moral support.'

'I don't . . . just stay here. You must have a lot that needs to be done. Picking up, and . . .'

The look in her eyes stopped him. 'What's going on, Stan?'

His heart thudded. In spite of the drink he'd just taken, his mouth suddenly felt dry. 'Nothing,' he said.

'*Some*thing's going on.' She sounded more curious than suspicious. 'Why don't you want me to go with you?'

Think *think THINK!*

'Because . . . you make me nervous. The way you keep looking at me.'

'Looking at you? What are you talking about?'

'You know.'

'I don't know.'

'Let's just drop it, okay? The thing is, you're a very attractive woman. Very. But you're married. That might not mean much to you, but . . .'

'What?' She gasped out a single, strange laugh.

'I'm sorry. I just have a rule that I don't fool around with married women.'

'Hey, now.' Blinking, she shook her head. She looked astonished. 'Let's not get the wrong idea, here. You seem like a nice guy and everything, Stan, but if you think for one minute that I'm interested in . . .'

'You keep *looking* at me. You keep trying to get me into your *house*, and your husband isn't even there. What else am I supposed to think?'

'You're *supposed* to think we've just gone through a major earthquake, that we're neighbors and I want to help you. Because that's the truth. That's it.'

'Is it?'

She jerked her head up and down once, fiercely. 'Yes, that's it. My God, Stan, I realize we barely know each other, but how you could ever get it into your head that . . .' Her eyes, watching him with a narrow glare, widened a bit.

'What?' he asked.

'You didn't,' she said, her voice little more than a whisper.

'Didn't what?'

'Get it into your head. You knew good and well.'

'Knew what?'

Now, he saw fear in her eyes.

She shrugged her shoulders. She tried to smile, but her lips trembled. 'If you didn't want my help, you should've just said so. It's all right. Hell, I've got plenty of stuff to do around the house without butting in on your little rescue effort. So just go on ahead.' Still trying to smile, she began to step backward. 'You can bring her over later on if you want . . . or not. Makes no difference to me. If you need anything, you know where to . . .'

Stanley dropped the saw and water jug. Before they had time to hit the driveway's pavement, he sprang and grabbed the front of Judy's shirt. She started to yell as he jerked her toward him. He pumped his knee into her belly.

The blow picked her up.

She landed on her knees. Hugging her belly, she pressed her forehead against the pavement.

Stanley went to her side.

He bent over and swept her shirt up, baring the lower portion of her back. She wore no belt. The waistband of her cut-offs bulged upward slightly. He peeked into the gap and glimpsed shadowy skin, the cleft of her buttocks, the white of her panties.

He shoved his hand in.

Clutched the denim.

Hefted Judy off the pavement and swung her around and hauled her to the back door of her house.

# ELEVEN

'I can't . . .' Heather gasped. 'Can't . . . gotta stop.' She'd done fine for a while, but her running had finally deteriorated to a stagger. Panting and hunched over, she held her stomach and grimaced.

Barbara, at her side, wondered if the girl was faking it.

They hadn't run all that far since leaving Earl unconscious on the sidewalk. Though they'd taken off at a very quick pace, they'd slowed down after turning the first corner. From then on, they'd merely jogged.

Only a few moments before Heather's first 'I can't,' they'd entered an alley that stretched westward behind house fences, garages, carports and garbage bins. Nearly every flat surface had been spray painted with gang signs. The alley ahead looked clear, though. No traffic, no major piles of rubble, no lurking strangers.

'Keep going,' Barbara urged the girl.

'Can't.'

'Just to the next street.'

'I . . . I'll try.'

Heather's agony almost had to be an act.

Barbara might've been able to understand the huffing, moaning and stumbling if it came from a fat slob. But Heather was thin, almost skinny except for her chest. For such a small person, she had awfully big breasts. Maybe being so top-heavy made it hard to run. Maybe that's what wiped her out.

Could be, Barbara thought. But also her legs aren't as long as ours. And she just isn't in very good shape.

Heather's strides shortened, slowed.

'Keep it up. Come on. Just a little farther.'

Shaking her head, Heather halted. She bent over, clutched her knees and panted for air.

'Pete!' Barbara shouted. 'Hold up!'

Pete jogged in a tight circle and came toward them. He didn't seem to be out of breath, but he was red and sweaty from the heat. He stopped in front of them.

'How you doing?' he asked Heather.

She shook her head and kept on panting.

'We did pretty good,' Barbara said. 'We might as well take it easy now.'

'I don't know.' Pete lifted the front of his shirt and wiped sweat off his face. He was smooth and tanned above his belt. His gray trousers looked heavy, hot. 'Think we managed to ditch him?'

'I've been keeping an eye out. He isn't on our tail. Not that I could see, anyhow. That doesn't mean he won't find us, but we'd better quit running. Heather's pooped. And it's too hot.'

'Hot, all right.'

'You must be dying in those pants.'

'Yeah.' He'smiled. 'Want to trade?'

Surprised, Barbara laughed. 'No, that's all right. I'll keep my shorts.'

'They wouldn't look as good on me, anyhow.'

When he said that, Heather let go of her knees and straightened up. She glanced from Barbara to Pete. 'We just gonna stand around, or what?'

'Are you ready to go?' Barbara asked her.

'I've *been* ready. I'm not a weakling, you know.' She switched her purse strap to her other shoulder. 'Just because *you* happen to be some sort of Amazon . . .'

'You've got the wrong Banner. The Amazon's my mom.'

Pete started walking. Heather hurried and caught up to him.

Barbara hung back.

*Let Heather fall all over him . . .*

Pete looked over his shoulder, then stopped and waited. 'Are you coming?'

'Yeah. Sure.'

'Your mom's not really an Amazon, is she?' Pete asked when Barbara came up next to him. He studied her eyes.

And she studied his. They were pale blue, their whites like fields of sunlit snow. They seemed intelligent, earnest.

'She isn't *from* the Amazon, if that's what you mean. She doesn't throw spears.'

Pete smiled. 'Does she file her teeth into points?'

'Nope. And she hasn't cut off . . .' In mid-sentence, Barbara found herself reluctant to finish. 'She's just large, that's all. Large and strong. A bodybuilder.'

Pete looked impressed. 'You mother *pumps iron?*'

'So do I. Not like her, though. Compared to her, I'm sort of a pipsqueak.'

'You're not any pipsqueak,' Pete said. 'How tall are you?'

Can't you tell? she wondered, looking straight forward into his eyes. She decided not to answer his question. So she shrugged.

'I'm five-eleven,' he said, 'and you're almost as tall as me.'

She grinned. *Almost, huh?* 'Mom's six-one,' she said.

'Man, that is big.'

'If you ask me,' Heather said, 'it sounds pretty freakish.'

Barbara leaned forward and scowled at her. 'Watch it, okay? You don't even know my mom. How would you like it if I called *your* mom a freak?'

'My mom's dead.'

The remark worked.

It hurt. A lot.

It felt like the time last year when an elbow had rammed Barbara in the solar plexus during a basketball game. Not only had the jab knocked her wind out, but it had sent a cold ache radiating through her whole body. The pain had numbed her, driven her to her knees. Later, the coach had explained that the solar plexus was a nerve center, so sensitive that a blow to it would drop just about anyone. Later still, in the locker room, her friend Lynn had informed her that it was exactly like getting kicked in the balls.

Stunned now with pain from Heather's words, Barbara thought, *It's just like catching that elbow.* And then she thought, *What the hell did Lynn know about getting kicked in the balls?*

She muttered, 'I'm sorry.'

'I hope you're happy.'

'I'm not happy. I told you, I'm sorry.'

'Yeah, sure.' Heather returned to Pete's side and took hold of his hand.

He glanced at Barbara. He looked uncomfortable, downright squirmy. After the glance, he faced forward.

She stayed next to him, but kept her hands to herself.

Nobody said anything.

Beyond the end of the alley, the street appeared to be blocked solid with traffic. Barbara saw no people inside the cars. Some were milling about, others relaxing on their hoods or trunks.

'How did you lose your mother?' Pete asked.

*I don't want to hear this!*

'I didn't lose her. She killed herself.'

Barbara winced.

'She committed suicide?' Pete asked. He sounded appalled, impressed. As if he'd never heard of anything quite so astonishing.

*Don't ask how she did it, Pete. Please.*

'How . . . ? I mean, maybe you don't want to talk about it.'

*Maybe we don't want to* hear *about it.*

'No, it's all right.' Heather leaned forward to see past Pete. 'I bet *you* want to hear all about it.'

81

'Not really,' Barbara said.

'She jumped out a window, that's how. She checked into a motel, but there was only just one vacancy for that night and it was on the third floor. The third floor, right?' Heather laughed. The laugh was harsh, off-key. Barbara saw tears in her eyes.

*Why is she telling us this?*

'Mom went on ahead and jumped anyway, though. The thing was, three stories up wasn't really high enough. She landed flat on her back on the sidewalk, and it like split her open all over, but it didn't kill her. She was still conscious. And screaming. Her brains were oozing out, and blood was coming out her ears and eyes and *everywhere.*'

They had all stopped walking.

Pete and Barbara both gaped at the girl.

She was grinning and weeping as she talked. A long string of snot dangled from her nose.

*Why is she telling us this? How does she even know all this yucky stuff? What the hell is going on?*

'So you know what Mom did? She couldn't get up because she was too busted apart, so she wiggled across the sidewalk like a worm and dragged herself down into the street and a car ran over her head and popped it like a grape.'

With a look of frantic glee on her face, Heather sniffed and wiped her nose.

Whacko, Barbara thought. The girl's gone completely whacko.

Pete didn't seem to share that opinion. He looked stunned. 'That's . . . that's horrible,' he said. 'That's the worst thing I ever heard.'

Heather suddenly flung herself against him. She pressed her face to his chest, hugged him, and wept. With one hand, Pete patted her back. With the other, he stroked her hair.

*Method in her madness.*

*She probably made up the whole thing.*

At least Pete didn't seem to be enjoying the attention. As soon as Heather quit weeping, he eased her away. 'Are you okay?'

She blinked up at him and sniffed.

'Can we go now?' Barbara asked. She didn't wait for an answer. She walked to the end of the alley, then turned around. The other two were following, but farther away than she expected. 'Maybe we oughta make another turn,' she called. 'Just to make things tougher for Earl.'

'I don't know,' Pete said. 'Do you think we need to bother?'

'If he finds us, it won't be pretty.'

'Well, which way do . . . Watch out!'

Barbara glimpsed a quick motion to her left. Jerked her head toward it. Saw a bicycle speeding toward her, a kid hunched over its handlebars.

He looked no older than twelve. He had a big grin. 'Beep beep, babe!' he called.

She leaped backward, yelling, 'Hey!'

The bike missed her.

As it shot by, out darted the kid's arm. He caught a handful of her blouse just below her right shoulder. Her blouse and the denim strap of her purse. She felt a quick tug. Buttons popped open. The right side of her blouse was tugged sideways and down off her shoulder before she could grab the kid's wrist. She kept the grip for just an instant, then lost it.

The kid raced away, Barbara's purse swinging at his side.

'You bastard!' she shouted. She swept her blouse shut and dashed after him.

The kid was moving off fast, butt up, head low, the bike wagging from side to side as he pumped its pedals.

Barbara sprinted after him.

A guy sitting on the hood of a car off to the side clapped and shouted, 'All right!' After him, a small group of people standing beside a long white car watched her run by. They made comments among themselves, a woman pointing at her, a man staring, another man letting out a hoot. Then two landscape workers drinking beer in the bed of a pickup truck whistled as she rushed by. 'Yo, baby!' one called. 'Marry me!' called the other. 'I make you smile all over!'

Creeps, she thought. So they can see my bra. Big deal.

Big men. Don't see any of *them* trying to stop Bike Boy.

Though Barbara ran at full speed, she didn't seem to be gaining on the kid. The sidewalk made a perfect getaway route for him: level and straight, unlittered by any debris from the quake.

*Never catch him.*

She kept on chasing him, anyway.

She tried to remember what she had in her purse – what she would lose: six or seven dollars; her house key and, oh yeah, the keys to the school car they'd left a long time ago somewhere in the middle of Pico Boulevard; her learner's permit; her library card, brush and comb, compact and mirror, lipstick, tissues, some bubble gum, and a few photos in her wallet.

Nothing really major.

Except maybe the pictures. Mom and Dad, and what if they've both been . . . ?

*Those snapshots might be all I ever have of them again.*

'Damn it, you bastard! Stop!'

He glanced over his shoulder and showed Barbara a big, white-toothed grin.

'Give me my purse!'

He swung an arm out behind him and hoisted his middle finger.

*I'll never get him. It's useless.*

She staggered to a halt. Gasping for breath, she started to fasten a button. The skin showing between the edges of her blouse was so sweaty it looked oiled. Her bra felt soaked.

She glanced back. Pete was coming toward her. He had Heather by the hand. He appeared to be towing her, trying to hurry but being held back. Obviously, Heather was in no rush.

Barbara took another look at the thief.

He was almost to the end of the block, still pedaling like mad, the purse swinging from his shoulder. And suddenly a man dressed like a banker leaped at him from behind a tree. The kid tried to swerve away. The man clubbed him in the face with a slim dark rod – a crowbar, maybe a tire tool.

The kid's head jerked back. He flung his arms out wide. Then he tumbled backward off his seat and fell. He smacked the sidewalk behind his bike. Barbara saw his head snap down against the concrete. His bike kept going. Riderless, it veered toward a lawn.

The man in the gray suit chased the bike. The moment it fell, he ducked and grabbed the handlebars. He dragged the bike to the sidewalk, tilted it upright, ran with it for a few strides, then mounted and pedaled away.

Nobody yelled. Nobody rushed from a house or from the street or from any of the waiting cars to stop him.

*Maybe I'm the only one who saw it,*

*Hardly. They just don't care. Or they're scared.*

The kid still lay sprawled on the sidewalk.

At his side was Barbara's purse.

The man sped around the corner at the end of the block and vanished.

Barbara looked back at Pete and Heather. They weren't much closer than before. She couldn't wait for them.

She ran to the kid and her purse.

The kid had a puddle of blood under his head. The blow had crushed a deep, leaky ditch above his left eyebrow. His eyes were open. One stared straight up and the other cast its gaze off low to the side as if nervous about something crawling toward his knee.

He wore tan trousers. They were wet in front.

Just like Earl's jeans.

He was sprawled out on the pavement like Earl. He was a creep like Earl, a thief like Earl, and he'd been bashed in the head and he'd peed his pants like Earl. But he was much younger than Earl and he was dead.

Barbara felt cold and numb and trembly inside.

Crouching, she lifted the strap of her purse. She was careful not to touch the kid as she slid the strap off his shoulder and out from under his arm. She stood up. She looped the strap over her head so that it crossed her chest like a bandolier, the blue denim purse at her hip.

She stepped aside for Pete. He stopped and looked at the body. 'Jeez,' he said.

Heather, holding Pete's arm, said, 'Wow.'

'Did you see it?' Barbara asked. 'Did you see how that guy got him?'

'I wasn't looking,' Pete said.

'You were in the way, anyhow,' Heather explained.

'A guy just jumped out and smacked him in the face. It was so weird. The guy was really well-dressed. He didn't look like someone who'd . . . kill a little kid.'

'Maybe he saw the kid snatch your purse,' Pete said.

'No. That wasn't it. He wanted the bike.' Her voice sounded far away as she spoke. 'That's all. He just wanted the bike. His car . . . it's probably stuck in the traffic somewhere.'

'You could really make time if you had a bike,' Pete said.

'Killed for a bike.'

Heather sighed. 'Let's not go feeling *too* sorry for the jerk. He was nothing but a purse snatcher.'

'He . . .' Barbara started.

'I know, I know. He didn't deserve to die for it. Well, he didn't – he died because some *other* jerk wanted his bike. Big loss.'

'Don't talk like that,' Pete told her.

Heather's face went red. She turned her head away.

'Let's get moving,' Barbara said, 'or we'll never get home.'

They stepped around the small body. Once past it, Barbara moved ahead of the other two.

'Can you imagine killing someone for a bike?' Pete asked.

Barbara turned sideways to watch him. 'It's crazy. This whole thing is crazy. You know? You always hear about how people pull together when there's a disaster.'

'You hear about looters, too,' Pete pointed out.

'Yeah, I guess so. But mostly it's acts of sacrifice and heroism, that sort of thing. They don't tell you about the people who go nuts. It seems like *everybody's* going nuts. Mr Wellen goes nuts with the car, Earl tries to *swipe* a car, that poor kid snatches my purse, some kind of executive breaks the kid's skull open for a bicycle. It's all like some kind of a huge, awful joke.'

'Maybe the quake released some kind of a nerve gas into the air,' Pete said, his mouth tilted by a crooked smile. 'It makes everybody go insane.'

Barbara found herself smiling. 'Right,' she said.

'I've read books about stuff like that.'

'Horror novels.' It wasn't a question.

'Well, yeah. It almost makes sense, though.'

Heather studied Pete. 'Could there really be a gas or something that makes people crazy?'

'I doubt it,' he said.

'Are you sure?'

'How could there be a gas like that?' Barbara asked her.

'Look at me and Pete. We haven't gone bonkers yet.'

'It's the quake,' Pete said. 'That's all. It shook everyone up too much.'

'Is that supposd to be a pun?'

'Everyone's scared.'

Barbara nodded. 'Everyone's scared and wants to get home and be safe.'

'Not me,' Heather said.

'Sure you do,' Pete told her.

'Oh yeah? How would you like going home if you didn't have any mother?'

'You've got a father, don't you?'

'Oh, sure.'

'He's probably at work,' Barbara said. 'Mine is. Though I bet he's trying awfully hard to get home right now.'

*If he's okay.*

'I don't know where my father is,' Heather said. 'And I don't care.' They walked a little farther before she added, 'Hope a roof fell on him.'

Pete frowned. 'You can't mean that.'

She didn't answer.

But Barbara saw the look in her eyes. 'I think she means it.'

# TWELVE

'Uh-oh.'

'What?' Clint asked.

'That's our house,' Em said. She stretched out her arm through the gap between the seatbacks, pointing. 'The one with that pickup in the driveway.'

'It looks all right,' Clint said. In fact, none of the homes along this quiet, dead-end street appeared to have been demolished by the quake. The only damage he'd noticed since turning the corner were a few broken windows and minor cracks in some of the stucco walls. 'Looks like your whole neighborhood got off pretty easy.'

'Yeah,' Em said.

Clint swung to the curb in front of her house.

'Bye-bye, Emerald,' Mary said. 'It's been a treat.'

'Yeah,' Em said again, still staring through the windshield.

'What's wrong?' Clint asked.

'It's that pickup. It shouldn't be there.'

Mary sighed. 'I thought we were supposed to be in a hurry, Clint.'

'That's where our Cherokee goes,' Em said. 'When Mom's home, she leaves it right there in the driveway. We use the garage for storing stuff, you know? So Mom isn't home. And that pickup's got no business sitting in our driveway.'

'Have you seen it before?' Clint asked.

'I don't think so.'

The front door of her house opened. Out stepped a burly man carrying a large cardboard box. His hair stuck out in all directions. His eyebrows were black thickets. His jaw was shaped like a brick. Though much of his upper body was hidden behind the box, Clint saw that he wore a grimy white T-shirt. His arms were thick and hairy. The trousers that sagged around his hips showed, in a few places, where they used to be green. Just looking at them, Clint thought he could smell garbage.

'One of your mother's boyfriends?' Mary asked.

Em didn't answer.

A woman followed the man out of the house.

She, too, carried a box.

87

Her gray-streaked hair, parted in the middle, drooped straight down the sides of her face. With each step, her cheeks wobbled. Though Clint guessed he must be forty feet from the woman, he could see her bristly mustache. A cigarette hung from a corner of her mouth, its smoke crawling up her cheek and into her eye so she had to squint. The sleeves were missing from her old, plaid shirt. Her arms were thick and white and floppy. So were her legs. Her short skirt left them bare from mid-thigh all the way down to the tops of her red cowgirl boots.

'And I guess that's Mom herself,' Mary said.

'Oh boy,' Em muttered.

The man carried his box down from the stoop and lumbered along the walkway toward the pickup truck.

'Do you know them?' Clint asked.

'I sure don't.' Em threw open the back door and leaped out. 'Hey! Put that stuff down!' She ran onto her lawn. She ran *at* the pair.

'Jesus,' Clint muttered.

'Is she nuts?'

Not totally, Clint thought. Because she'd stopped on the lawn at least ten feet away from them.

They turned and stared at her. The man looked confused, the woman annoyed. So far, neither of them had glanced toward the car.

'What've you got in those boxes?' Em demanded.

'Buzz off,' the woman said.

'Put them down!' Em snapped. 'Right this instant!' She planted her fists on her hips.

A grin slowly stretched the man's heavy lips. He turned his head to the woman. 'Let's take *her*, Lou.'

She guffawed.

They both twitched at the noise of the car horn.

Once he had their attention, Clint climbed out. The man's eyes grew wide. The woman's narrowed.

'You don't scare me none,' she said.

He stepped around the front of the car. 'I'm not here to scare you, ma'am.'

'Let's get outa here, Lou.'

The man hurried toward his pickup. Lou didn't budge.

'Put down the box, mister,' Clint said.

The man set it down on the grass, then waved his open hands at Clint and sidestepped away. 'I don't want no trouble. We're goin'. Come on, Lou.'

She ignored him.

Clint walked toward her.

She spat out her cigarette. Em did a quick prance to dodge it.

'Put down the box, ma'am, and leave.'

She put down the box. Then she stepped out from behind it. Leaning forward, she grinned at Clint. Her crooked teeth were brown. 'Come 'n' get it.'

Off to the side, a door clanked shut. An engine rattled and wheezed. 'Less go, Lou!'

'Hold yer water!' she called.

'Why don't you just go away?' Em said to her.

Lou wiggled her fingers at Clint. 'Less tangle. You 'n' me.'

'I don't want to fight with . . .'

Lou lurched at Em. Her flabby arm swung out. Her fist struck Em like a hammer just beneath the throat.

Em flew backward off her feet.

Lou grinned at Clint. 'How y'like that?'

He'd only known Em for a little while. But he liked her a lot.

He took a step toward Lou. When she threw the punch at his jaw, he blocked it. His other hand chopped. He heard her collar bone break. Then all he heard was her squealing.

She was down on her knees, walking on her knees, waddling and squealing as Clint towed her by her greasy hair to the driveway.

He opened the passenger door for her.

Squealing and whimpering, she climbed up and fell into the passenger seat.

'Whad y'do to-uhr?'

'Get out of here. Both of you.'

The red cowgirl boot on Lou's right foot was still hanging outside when Clint started to swing the door shut. He stopped. 'Pull in your foot, Lou.'

When the boot was in, he slammed the door.

He glanced into the bed of the pickup. A dozen or so boxes were scattered about. They looked as if they'd been thrown in. Some lay on their sides. Clint didn't see any that weren't empty.

*Must've been their first trip out with stuff.*

The pickup sped backward to the end of the driveway, swerved out into the street, and sped off.

Em was already on her feet. 'Boy, you really *destroyed* her!'

'Are you okay?' Clint asked.

'Sure.' She rubbed her chest through the T-shirt. 'Not that it didn't hurt, but I'm okay.'

He looked into the box that the man had carried from the house. 'Looks like he cleaned out your mother's bar.'

Em bent down over the other box. 'Food here. Mostly stuff from the freezer.' She lifted it. 'Will you bring in that one?'

'You bet.' Clint picked it up. 'Watch when you go in,' he warned. 'I'm assuming there were just the two of them, but you never know.'

As he followed Em toward the stoop, Mary called from the car, 'Where are you going?'

'I'll be right back.'

'You're not going in, are you?'

'Just for a minute or two. I've got to make sure it's safe.'

'Oh, fine. Just fine. Wait for me.'

He didn't wait, but he left the front door open after stepping into the house.

Em stood in the middle of the living room, the box in her arms. She turned around slowly, surveying the mess, making a face. 'I guess it could be worse, huh?'

'A lot. If it doesn't get any worse than this, you're in great shape.'

'I don't know about *that*.' She wrinkled her nose. 'Those two were *in* here. Yuck.'

'I doubt they were responsible for . . .'

Mary hurried in. 'Everything all right?'

'Too soon to know,' Clint said.

'Who were those awful people?'

'Looters. They seemed to be after food and booze.'

'They sure looked like they needed it,' Mary said, and tried to smile. 'You really handled them well, Clint.'

She's trying to make amends, he thought. He told her, 'Thanks.'

Em started toward the dining room.

'Hold it,' he said. 'Let me go first.' As he walked past her, he asked, 'Are you pretty sure your mother's gone?'

'Oh, yeah. The Jeep isn't in the driveway. She's probably out shopping. She only goes shopping just about every day.' Em followed Clint into the dining room. 'Personally, I don't think Mom much cares for staying home. She's *always* looking for an excuse to go out for an excursion.' They entered the kitchen. 'She's probably at a mall. I suppose those malls are pretty sturdy, don't you imagine so?'

'Probably,' Clint said. 'She's just lucky she wasn't here.'

'Yeah. That's for sure.'

They set the boxes onto the kitchen table.

Mary, entering after them, stepped over some debris of broken dishes and swung the refrigerator door shut. 'We really *should* get going,' she said.

'You don't need to rush off,' Em said. 'Maybe you'd like a drink?' She lifted a bottle of Jim Beam out of the box. 'Name your poison.'

'We really don't have time,' Mary said. Though she was speaking to

90

Em, her eyes were fixed on Clint. 'The longer we stay here, the more trouble we'll . . .'

'I'll give the place a quick once-over,' Clint said. 'Then we'll go.' He left them in the kitchen and began to explore the rest of the house.

The walls and ceilings appeared to be intact. He saw no significant damage.

In the bathroom, the medicine cabinet door stood open. Toothbrushes, tubes of paste and creams, plastic bottles of pills and fluids were heaped in the sink, scattered about the floor. Maybe the looters had done it. More likely, however, it was the work of the quake.

In the mother's bedroom, a full length mirror on the closet door was cracked. Bureau drawers stood open, and one had dropped to the floor. The floor was an obstacle course of things that had been cast down from walls, shelves, the tops of the bureau and nightstands.

After checking under the mother's bed and inside the closet to make sure Em didn't have any hiding visitors, he went down the hall to the other bedroom.

Obviously, Em's room.

A poster on the wall showed Bart Simpson riding a skateboard.

Em's swivel chair had rolled away from her desk and stopped near the head of her bed. Two desk drawers were on the floor. All of her bureau drawers were open, but none had dropped.

Clint saw the jumble of books and dolls piled along the base of her built-in shelves. Like his own daughter, Em had a collection of Barbie dolls, a couple of Kens, and even Barbie's '57 Chevy. The big, plastic car must've been hurled off its shelf and hit the carpet bumper-first, throwing out Barbie. Its rear end was propped up high against an upright. Barbie lay in front of the Chevy, stiff, gazing at the ceiling.

As Clint crouched over Barbie, he heard footsteps. He picked up the doll. As he stood, Em came into the room.

She looked around, moaning and shaking her head. 'What a dump.'

'There's not much that didn't end up on the floor,' he said. He set Barbie on a shelf. 'I haven't spotted any particular damage to the house, though. And I haven't found any stowaways so far.'

'Are you sure you've looked everywhere?'

'Not quite done yet.' He opened the closet door. 'Nobody here. '

Em, herself, checked under the bed. Standing, she brushed off her hands. 'Actually, I just came in to grab a clean shirt.' She stepped over to her bureau, pushed the top drawer shut, then searched through a stack of T-shirts in the second drawer. She took a faded blue one from the bottom. 'No point wearing a good one on a day like this,' she said. 'I'll be with Mary in the kitchen,' she said, and hurried away.

Clint spent a few more minutes checking through the house for intruders, then returned to the kitchen.

Em was facing the sink, bare to the waist, while Mary stroked her below the left shoulder with a wet cloth. In front of Em, water hissed from the faucet.

'Glad to know there's water pressure,' Clint said.

Mary scowled at him. 'Hey. Get out of here. Can't you see she isn't dressed?'

'That's all right,' Em said. 'Just stay, all right? It's no big deal.'

'You shouldn't be . . .'

'Nothing *shows*, for heaven's sake. See?' She turned slightly, and Clint saw that she was pressing the blue T-shirt against her chest. The pink one was draped over the front edge of the sink. 'We're cleaning my wound,' she explained. 'You want to see it?'

Nodding, Clint stepped closer. Mary moved aside. The girl's back was white except for a few freckles and a very raw, red scrape where the brick had struck her. Most of the skin on her shoulder blade was ruddy and striped with fine, bright rows of scratches.

'Looks like it hurts,' Clint said.

'It stings, is all. It's not so bad.'

'Did you land on it when that gal knocked you down?'

She let out a soft laugh. 'Yeah. Now *that* didn't feel terribly swift, I must say.'

'You can put on your shirt now,' Mary said.

'Does it need a bandage?' Em asked.

'The air'll do it good.'

'Won't it stick to my shirt?'

'Here.' Clint sidestepped, pulled a square of paper towel off a roll suspended under the cupboard, and pressed it gently against Em's scrape to blot up the moisture. When he took his hand away, the paper adhered to her. It showed lines of pinpoint red dots. He took it away, tore off another square and folded it into a pad. 'Just leave this one against it loose under your shirt for a while,' he said.

He smoothed it against her, then turned away while she pulled the blue T-shirt over her head.

'Okay.'

He faced her. The T-shirt was printed with a dead cat, legs up, and the legend, I ONLY EAT ROADKILL AT J.R.'s, MOAB, UTAH.

'I guess it's time for us to get going,' Clint said.

'And then some,' Mary added.

'Will you be all right here by yourself?'

Shrugging, Em made a face that almost brought a smile to Clint. Her expression – lips curling, eyebrows writhing – showed a fine mix of deep thought, worry, revulsion and hope. 'What if somebody *else* comes along?'

'Your mother will probably be home soon,' Mary said.

'Yeah, but what if she isn't? *I* don't know where she went. Maybe she *can't* get back.'

'Is there a gun in the house?' Clint asked.

'Mom allow a gun in the house? I don't *think* so. The world's biggest pacifist?'

'Is there a neighbor you can stay with?' Clint asked.

Em shook her head. 'I don't know. I don't know much of anybody around here.'

'You don't know your neighbors?' Mary asked her. It sounded like an accusation.

'I don't know mine either,' Clint admitted. 'Just a few of them here and there. It was worth a shot.'

'I know everyone in my building,' Mary said.

'So do I,' Em said. 'Me and Mom.'

'What do you *want* to do?' Clint asked.

Her eyebrows climbed her forehead. 'Could I go *with* you?'

'With us?'

'I really don't want to stay here. Those people might come back. *Anybody* might come. I mean, I'd be all alone here. Maybe for hours. Or maybe even all day. Mom might not show up till tomorrow or something.'

She might never show up, Clint thought.

*She's probably fine.*

'And I especially wouldn't like to be here alone after it gets dark,' Em said. 'With no lights? And with no gun? And with no way to get any help?'

'The phone's dead,' Mary added. 'We checked.'

'Anyway,' Em went on, 'the point is that I'd much rather stick with you two, if you know what I mean.'

'No way,' Mary said. To Clint, she said, 'We're really losing a *lot* of time here.'

'I know, I know.'

'I'll leave a note for Mom so she won't worry about me.'

'Em, we're going all the way to West L.A.'

'And Santa Monica,' Mary said.

Em kept her eyes on Clint. 'That's okay. I'd sure rather go there than stay by myself.'

'We might not be able to get you back here tonight.'

'I don't *want* to be here. Not unless Mom gets home.'

'The whole idea's ridiculous,' Mary said. 'Her mother might walk through the door two minutes after we're gone.'

Clint nodded. 'She might.'

'You could wait here till she comes,' Em suggested.

'I've gotta get home to *my* family. And I have to leave now.'

'Is it okay?' Em asked him.

'No,' Mary said.

Em didn't even glance at her. 'What would you do if I was *your* daughter?' she asked.

He didn't need to think about it. 'Come on along. But you have to leave that note.'

Mary sighed and shook her head.

Em found a pad and pen beside the telephone.

Clint watched over her shoulder as she wrote, 'Mom, I'm fine but some sleezoids broke into the house. I can't stay. I've gone with Clint Banner. He lives at . . .'

Clint gave his address and telephone number.

'What else should I say?' Em asked.

'Tell her you'll stay with my family. I'll bring you back home as soon as conditions permit.'

When the note was finished, she stepped into the dining room. She folded the note in half and stood it upright on the table there.

'Are we ready?' Mary asked.

'Do we have a minute for me to use the john?' Em asked.

'We should probably all go,' Clint said. 'It might be a long and johnless day.'

Em laughed, then headed for the toilet.

When she was gone, Mary said, 'What is it with you and her?'

'We can't leave her alone here. She's just a kid.'

'You're not her father.'

'I'm aware of that.'

'You like her, don't you!'

'Sure I like her. She's a good kid.'

'A swell kid,' Mary muttered.

'We don't know where her mother is. We don't know if she's coming back at all. I hate to think what might've happened to Em if she'd been in the house when Lou and her pal broke in. They *might* come back. And there's absolutely no way for us to know how bad things are, how bad they might get. It's pretty obvious the cops won't be doing people a lot of good, not till the phone system is operating again and the roads clear. With a deal like that, you could end up with big-time chaos. A girl Em's age shouldn't have to face that sort of stuff alone.'

'I wonder if you'd be saying that if she was fat and ugly,' Mary said. Then came the sound of the flushing toilet. She left the dining room. She and Em crossed paths near the doorway.

Em looked at Clint, one eye narrowed. 'Don't you think maybe we should take some stuff with us? Water, for instance? And some food, at least something to snack on? Because we might very well need to walk part of the way. Have you considered that? I mean, I wouldn't be one bit surprised to find Laurel Canyon closed. Or totally jammed with traffic so we wouldn't be able to go an inch all day.'

'It's very possible,' Clint said.

'Maybe we'll be able to zip right over the top in the car, but we ought to be prepared for the opposite.'

'You're right. Let's take some food and water.'

'And maybe we should arm ourselves.'

'I thought you said . . .'

'Oh, we don't have any guns. But we could take along some knives.'

'Your mother allows knives in the house?'

Em smiled. 'She hasn't figured out how to get by without them. Not yet, anyhow.' As they walked into the kitchen, Em said, 'If we didn't eat meat, of course, I think we could manage without sharp knives. I'm certainly not about to tell her that, though – she'd turn us into vegetarians. Life is bizarre enough without that. I don't know what I'd *do* if I couldn't eat meat.'

The carving knives were on the floor, three still jutting from the slotted block of oak that served as their holder. The other five were scattered nearby. Em picked up the holder while Clint gathered the knives that had fallen out.

After setting the block onto the counter, she pulled its knives and arranged them beside those that Clint had spread out. 'Which should we take?'

'If we need any of them, we're in a whole lot of trouble.'

Mary came into the kitchen. 'Now what?' she asked.

'We're choosing weapons,' Em answered.

Mary stepped up to the counter. 'Terrific. You can count me out.'

'That's all right,' Em told her, 'I'll take two.'

'Take your pick,' Clint said.

'You go first.'

'Ladies first.'

'But you're in charge. You ought to . . . '

'Jesus H. Christ!' Mary snapped. 'Stop playing games!'

Clint quickly grabbed a paring knife with a four-inch blade.

'Is that *it*?' Em asked.

'Suits me. Shorter the blade, the less likely I am to cut myself. You go ahead and pick. I'll be right back.' He hurried to the bathroom. He urinated. Then he found the cardboard core of a toilet paper roll in the wastebasket. He took it out, mashed it flat, and slipped the blade of his knife inside. In the sink, he found a roll of adhesive tape that had apparently fallen from the medicine cabinet. He taped the end of the tube shut, then ran a strip down the knife handle and onto the cardboard to secure the knife within its makeshift sheath.

Keeping the roll of tape, he returned to the kitchen. Em, at the refrigerator, was stuffing food into a paper bag. Mary, at the sink, was filling a two-litre plastic Pepsi bottle with tap water.

Two knives lay side by side on the counter. The remaining knives had been put back into the holder.

'These the ones you want?' Clint asked.

Em smiled over her shoulder. 'I picked the biggest.'

'So I see. What I'm going to do is run a length of tape along their sharp edges. That way, you won't have to worry about slicing yourself open. If you need to cut something, you just strip off the tape.'

'Nifty.' She swung the refrigerator door shut. Crumpling the top of the bag, she came over to Clint.

Mary shut off the faucet. 'Okay, we've got three bottles. One each.'

Clint got to work taping the knife blades. 'You'll be a regular Jim Bowie,' he said.

'Didn't he bite it at the Alamo?'

'Well, yeah.'

'Real swift comparison, Mr Banner.'

'That's all right,' he said. 'We're nowhere *near* the Alamo.'

Em laughed. She laughed hard. She cracked up. She had never fallen apart like this in front of Clint, and he enjoyed seeing her so delighted.

After she regained control, Clint handed the knives to her. 'The trick with these is to keep them out of sight. They make an excellent secret weapon. Once the enemy becomes aware of them, though, they loose a lot of their effectiveness.'

Mary frowned. 'What is this? How do you know about that stuff? And I saw the chop you gave that woman. Who are you?'

'Bond. James Bond. And this is M.'

'Very funny.'

He glanced from Mary to Em. 'Are we all set? Are we forgetting anything?' They shook their heads. 'Then let's move out.'

He carried two of the water bottles for Mary. Em carried the bag of food and her two butcher knives. On the front stoop, he scanned the neighborhood. He saw no one. He saw no signs of trouble.

When Em finished locking the front door of her house, they walked across the yard toward Mary's BMW.

Clint was almost to the curb when he noticed that the right front tire was flat.

*Shit!*

Another delay. But as long as Mary's spare was okay . . .

He saw that the right rear tire was also flat.

His stomach dropped.

He rushed out into the street. Both tires on the left side of the car were flat.

Mary stood motionless and stiff, her mouth hanging open. 'Whuh . . . ? What happened to . . . *to my car?*'

'That pair we chased off,' Clint said. 'I'd bet on it.'

'Lou and the guy,' Em explained.

'Did us a little payback.'

'My God! My Beamer! They . . . they *ruined* it!'

'All they did was slash the tires,' Clint said. 'Probably.'

'Why didn't you just let them take the goddamn boxes?' she blurted. 'Why did you have to *bother* them? Look what they did! Look what they did to my Beamer!'

Ignoring her outburst, Em asked Clint, 'What'll we do now?'

'Do you still want to come with us?'

'You must be kidding. They snuck back while we were inside. I'm not sticking around here.'

'If you people think for one minute that I'm going to leave my car on this street in the middle of God-knows-where . . .'

'Studio City,' Em broke in. 'And it's right in front of my house. It's not like it's *lost*. You can pick it up when Clint brings me back.'

'It might not even *be* here by then.'

'It'll be fine,' Clint said.

'It's not fine *now*!'

'Well, look, there's nothing we can do. Not with that many flats. If you try to drive it in that condition, you'll ruin the rims. In a day or two, after things have settled down, I'll bring you out and help you take care of it. Okay? But right now, we've gotta get moving or we'll never get home.'

'What're you planning to do, walk?'

'Yup.'

'Oh, fine and dandy. Have you forgotten about the *mountain range*?'

'It's just a ridge of hills. I've driven over it every day for the past three years. From Ventura Boulevard to the top, it's only two miles.'

'Two miles?' Mary grimaced.

'Two miles up, two miles down the other side to Sunset, and it'll be a level hike of about four miles from there to my house.'

'Right here,' Em said, 'we're about a mile from the bottom. So that'll make a grand total of nine miles.'

'I'm not going,' Mary said.

'You don't want to stay here,' Em told her. 'Besides, it'll be a cinch once we get to the top. The first part'll be tough. After Mulholland, though, no sweat.'

'And we'll take it easy on the way up,' Clint added.

'I'm not going. I'm staying right here.' She walked around to the other side of her BMW, opened the driver's door, and climbed in. She slammed the door shut.

Clint muttered, 'Women.'

Em gaped at him. 'Say again?'

'Just kidding. Women are terrific.'

'That's better.'

'Let's go, Em. *You're* still coming, aren't you?'

'Are you going to leave her?'

'It's her choice.'

He followed Em to the driver's window. The girl bent her knees and looked in at Mary. 'Are you sure you want to stay?'

'Buzz off.'

'It's not that far. Less than ten miles.'

'This isn't about walking.'

'What *is* it about?'

'What do you care? Just go. You've got Clint to take care of you now. Have a good time.'

'If you're really planning to stay, I'll give you my house key.'

'Don't bother.'

'You can at least go inside and . . .'

'*Fuck off!*'

Em lurched backward as if struck. Turning away, she glanced at Clint with startled eyes. 'Let's go.'

Mary was still sitting in her car when they reached the end of the block.

'What do you think's wrong with her?' Em asked.

'Plenty.'

'She certainly got upset about her tires.'

'I guess the car means a lot to her.'

'That's for sure. Not to mention she hates me.'

'Aah, she doesn't hate you.'

'Sure she does. That's okay, though. I'm used to it. People either love me or hate me – has something to do with my winning personality.' She grinned. 'Anyway, I didn't mean to come between you two, or anything.'

'Don't worry about it. We're probably better off without her.'

'I just hope nobody jumps her while she's . . .'

'Hey! Wait for me!'

Looking back, they saw Mary jog around the corner, waving. Her purse swung at her side oy its shoulder strap. It was open, the top of her water bottle jutting out.

'Oh, joy,' Em said. 'Let's see if we can ditch her.'

Clint laughed. 'You have a cruel streak.'

Now that they had halted to wait for her, Mary slowed to a walk.

'Hurry up,' Clint called.

'Sorry.' She quickened her pace.

She looked different to Clint. Less formal and sour, somehow. And her suit jacket was gone.

'Change your mind?' Em asked when Mary stopped in front of them.

The woman nodded, shrugged, looked sheepishly from Em to Clint. 'I don't know what I was thinking,' she said. 'Honestly. I mean, how stupid can a person be? Guess I'll have to plead temporary insanity.'

'It's been a rough morning,' Clint said.

'You're telling me.' She fluttered the front of her blouse. 'Hotter than the dickens, too. Do you believe this heat?' She pursed her lips, blew, and fanned the air in front of her face.

'We'll take it slow,' Clint told her. 'We'll be all right.'

# THIRTEEN

Stanley never meant to do any of this. He'd only wanted to borrow Judy's saw and hurry back to Sheila.

But Judy couldn't let it go at that.

Oh, no. Huh-uh. She had to stick her nose in. She had to push. She had to insist on going *with* him.

Stanley'd had enough of interfering women, women who butted into his business, women who wanted to control him and stop him from doing the good stuff.

Judy would've ruined his plans for Sheila.

So she had to be put out of action.

That was all Stanley had meant to do – take her out of the game. That's why he had driven his knee up into her belly. He'd meant to incapacitate her, haul her into her house, maybe tie her up and gag her, then hurry on back to Sheila.

But the moment Stanley felt his knee sink into her belly and heard her breath gush out, she'd stopped being an obstacle in his way. She'd suddenly become an unexpected gift.

An earthquake prize.

We'll just make it quick, he'd told himself as he lugged her into the house by the back of her cut-off jeans.

*What if this ruins Sheila for me?*

It won't, it won't. And anyway, who knows? The Sheila thing might fall through.

Shit, it probably will.

Something was bound to mess it up. Nothing ever turned out right for Stanley, and getting Sheila for himself wasn't likely to be the exception.

Anyway, a bird in the hand . . .

Even though Judy couldn't compare to Sheila, she was in his hands, in his power.

He'd never had a woman that way before.

They'd always held the power: he'd always been the beggar.

And he'd never even come close to having a woman who wasn't fat or ugly.

Sure, Judy was no Sheila. But compared to the few women who had

100

allowed Stanley to touch them during his thirty-two years of life, Judy Wellman was incredibly gorgeous, breathtaking, stunning.

He *couldn't* just tie her up and go away.

So he'd carried her into the master bedroom, climbed onto the king-sized bed with her, swung her feet toward the ceiling while holding onto her cut-off jeans, and shaken her until she dropped headfirst onto the mattress, leaving the jeans in his hands. Panties halfway down her thighs, she'd flopped and rolled. Before she could get to her hands and knees, Stanley had pounced.

It seemed like ages ago.

I've gotta get back to Sheila, he told himself.

*She'll keep.*

Maybe not. Someone might come along. I've been here way too long.

He hated to give it up, though.

Judy had struggled in the beginning, but her resistance had caved in almost right away once he'd shoved into her for the first time. It was as if her only reason for fighting had been to keep him out of her body. After that, she'd cried a lot. Then, the crying had stopped. She'd let Stanley do whatever he wanted, and she'd followed orders.

Which had seemed great for a while.

He'd studied her all over, explored her, delved into her, caressed and squeezed her, kissed and licked and sucked her everywhere, commanded her to suck on him.

Absolutely great.

For a while.

After a while, however, Stanley began to feel cheated. Betrayed. Judy was letting him do whatever he wanted and she was doing everything he asked of her, but without *feeling*. As if her mind and spirit had taken a hike.

*So long, Stan. Have a merry old time with the bod. We'll come back when you're done.*

Thelma used to do that. Flop on the bed and gaze at the ceiling. As if he wasn't there at all. After a year of that, he'd quit bothering.

It made him feel a little sick inside to remember how it had been with Thelma.

And now Judy was pulling the same stunt.

*Denying my existence.*

'Fucking bitch!'

He rammed his cock up Judy, slamming his pelvis against her so hard that he jolted her whole body. Her breasts jerked and wobbled. Her teeth clashed together. But she stayed limp and kept her empty gaze on the ceiling.

'I'm here,' Stanley said. 'Hey!'

101

No response.

'Hey! Judy! Damn it!'

Nothing.

So then he pulled out of her. He slid down her body. She was slick and sticky. He scooted backward until his knees reached the edge of the bed. Then he slipped his arms underneath Judy's wide open legs and clutched the tops of her thighs.

He pressed his mouth against her.

He licked and probed.

His tongue got no reaction.

But his teeth did.

Judy shrieked and bucked.

*Yes!*

Stanley raised his face. He looked up from between her legs. She was all shiny and flushed, her belly pulsing as she gasped, her breasts shaking, her arms up, hands clenching the sides of the pillow under her head, her face crimson, her lips peeled back in agony, tears rolling down from the corners of her tightly shut eyes.

*What a sight!*

*What a beautiful sight!*

'Did you like that?' Stanley asked.

'No!' she cried out.

'Do you want more?'

'No! Please!'

'Who am I?'

'Please! Don't . . . !'

'Who am I?'

'Stan! Stanley!'

'Stanley who?'

'Banks! Stanley Banks!'

'Very good.' He kissed her. Not a bite, a kiss, but she flinched anyway as if scalded. 'Where am I, Judy?'

'Huh?'

'*Where?*'

'I don't . . . What do you want me to say?'

'Am I in outer space?'

'No!'

'Where *am* I?'

'In . . . in Los Angeles?'

'Yesss. But *where?*'

'On Marlene Street?'

'More.'

'What?'

'*Where?*'

'In my house!' she blurted. 'In my bedroom! In my bed!'

'*Where?*'

'Here! Right here!'

'Right! And you made a really big mistake when you decided to pretend like I wasn't.'

'I'm sorry.'

'Why?'

'Why what?'

'Why sorry?'

'Because . . .'

'Because you hurt my feelings?' Stanley asked.

'Yes! I didn't mean to. Honest.'

'Bull-fucking-shit.'

'I'm *sorry*.'

'Do you wanta know why? There's only one reason you're sorry, and that's because I'm in charge now. You can't make me go away. You can't make me stop. And you can't ignore me. You bitches think you own the fucking world. But you don't own me. Not today. Not here. It's *my* turn to be the boss.'

In a quiet and trembling voice, Judy said, 'I never did anything to you. I've always been nice to you.'

'Yeah. And I'm sure you're always nice to dogs, too.'

He made her scream again.

# FOURTEEN

'You're not quitting?' Mrs Klein asked, alarm in her voice.

'Just taking a breather,' Barbara said as she climbed backward down the slope of rubble.

'A brief rest,' Mrs Klein said.

'Yeah.' Feet on the flat, safe surface of the alley, Barbara stood up straight. She stretched, arching her spine, twisting, thrusting her shoulders back. Then she bent over and held on to her knees and panted for air. Sweat dripped off her face. Her blouse was so wet that it hugged her back. A couple of the top buttons had come undone, so the front drooped open to her belly and let air in. Her bra felt sodden. Her panties were glued to her rump.

'Such wonderful young people you are,' Mrs Klein said.

'Glad to help,' Barbara muttered.

They'd hardly gotten away from the body of the kid who'd snatched Barbara's purse before they'd been waylaid by Mrs Klein. Actually, Barbara supposed they'd gone two blocks. Maybe three.

The woman had come stumbling out of the alley just in front of them, weeping, frantically flinging her head from side to side, then spotting them and calling out, 'Help me! Please! Help me!'

'Quick!' Heather had whispered. 'Let's get out of here!'

'Not me,' Pete had said. 'Sorry. I mean, look at her.'

About fifty years old, fashionably dressed, she looked like a woman who might've just been mugged on her way to a luncheon in Beverly Hills. Her brown hair was mussed, her face streaked with mascara as if she'd wept blue tears, her ivory silk blouse filthy and untucked, her stockings snagged and split with runs, her knees bloody beneath the hem of her skirt, her shoes missing.

'Are you okay, ma'am?' Pete had asked as she hobbled toward them.

'Am I okay? Is my outfit a ruin? Is my heart broken? Help me! Help me save my baby!' Without waiting for an answer, she'd dragged Pete into the alley. As Barbara and Heather had hurried after them, she'd gasped out, 'How could this *happen* to me? My poor Susie! I only left her for two minutes. Two minutes, not a second longer. I'd forgot my checkbook in the house. My checkbook! A checkbook I don't need. Do I have credit cards? Who doesn't? But off I go for a checkbook I don't need, and all God's hell breaks loose, do you know what I mean? The house? A shambles, but up it stays. The garage, down it goes like a bad stock. On top of my baby! My poor baby! You'll save her?'

'We'll do whatever we can,' Pete had assured her.

'Is she in the car?' Barbara had asked.

'Yes, yes. Such a fool I was to leave her alone. But only for two minutes? What can happen in only two minutes? An earthquake, for instance! The end of the world? Who knows! For two minutes I leave her alone. If I'd *known*! But we don't know these things! These things are rocks thrown at us – we're not paid to duck, if you know what I mean.'

Barbara had no idea what she meant. That didn't matter, though. It only mattered that her daughter was trapped. More likely her granddaughter, considering the gal's age – though Barbara supposed Mrs Klein might be the child's actual mother.

When they came to the ruin, Heather realized that more than a simple garage had fallen. 'Was it two stories?' she asked.

'An apartment up above. But it was vacant, thank God.'

'Your car's buried under all of *that*?' Heather asked.

'It's not so much. You should've seen it before. A mountain, that's what it was. Me, I've whittled it down. But I . . .' Shaking her head, she raised her hands. They were shredded and bloody.

'It's okay,' Barbara had said. 'We'll get her out.'

With Mrs Klein watching from the alley, Barbara and Pete and Heather had climbed the rubble and gotten to work. They'd made good progress for a while. Then Pete had gashed his forearm on the point of a nail. The wound not only took him out of commission while Mrs Klein hustled him into her house for first aid, but put a stop to Heather's half-hearted labors.

Crouching on the slope, Heather had watched the woman lead Pete away. Just when they were about to enter the back door of the house, she'd called, 'Wait! I'm coming, too!' and started to hurry down.

'You don't have to go with them.'

'I do, too. Anyway, I'm thirsty.'

'How do you think her *kid* feels?'

'She's probably dead.'

'Maybe not. The car could've protected her.'

'Yeah, sure. This is a big waste of time. I'm only helping 'cause Pete wants to. Anyway, I'm taking a break.' Then she'd hurried on to the house.

A while later, Mrs Klein had come back alone. Not only had she returned to the alley without Pete and Heather, but without a soda or even so much as a glass of water for Barbara.

That's when Barbara had decided it was time for a breather.

'Such wonderful young people you are.'

'Glad to help.'

Barbara raised her arms, one at a time, to wipe her face on the short sleeves of her blouse. 'What happened to Pete and Heather?'

'They'll be along. The poor girl overheated herself.'

'I'm pretty hot, myself.'

She suddenly seemed to *see* Barbara. 'Why, you're soaking wet.'

'I could sure use a drink.'

'A *drink*? You look ready to collapse, you poor thing.'

'No, I'm not that . . .'

'You shouldn't be standing out here, you'll drop dead from heat prostration. Into the house with you, right this minute. Find yourself a drink in the fridge.' She patted Barbara's arm. 'Sit, rest, cool off. I won't have you dropping dead from the heat. Come out when you're ready. You and your friends. But don't take too long. My Susie . . .'

With that, Mrs Klein staggered to the pile of debris, leaned forward, and picked up a chunk of stucco.

'I'll just get a drink and come right back,' Barbara told her.

'Cool off,' Mrs Klein said without stopping her work. 'A few minutes you should take to cool off.'

'Sure,' Barbara said, though she had no intention of relaxing inside the house. Maybe after they'd found Susie.

A narrow walkway led from the side of the demolished garage, through a neatly trimmed back yard to the patio of Mrs Klein's single-level, stucco house. The outside of the house looked undamaged.

A faded awning shaded the patio. Barbara let out a sigh as she stepped beneath it.

So great to get out of the sun.

On her way to the back door, she lifted the front of her blouse and wiped the sweat off her face. Then she fastened the buttons.

She pulled open the door and entered the kitchen.

Most of the cupboards were open, their contents thrown out and scattered on the counters and floor.

No sign of Pete or Heather.

'Hey, you guys,' Barbara called.

'In here,' Pete called to her. He sounded as if he were a room or two away.

'Be right there. What're you drinking?'

'She's got Pepsis in the fridge.'

The refrigerator was still standing, but looked as if it had been dragged toward the middle of the kitchen. Barbara headed for it. She stepped over a small pile of broken plates, kicked a can of Campbell's tomato soup out of the way, and tugged open the refrigerator door.

No light came on. But the kitchen was bright, so she had no trouble finding several cans of soft drinks lined up inside a rack on the inner side of the door.

She lifted one of them out. It felt fairly cold. But cool slime suddenly slipped onto her hand. She gasped, 'Uck!' and kneed the door shut.

'You okay?' Pete called.

'I think so.' Barbara looked at the top of the can. It was coated with a clear, mucous substance. Floating on the ooze, and embedded in it, were bits of broken eggshell.

'You oughta get in here,' Pete said. 'We wanta show you something.'

'Just wait'll you see *this*,' Heather added.

'I'll be right there.'

Barbara spotted a roll of paper towels beside the sink.

She made her way toward it.

She wondered if her kitchen at home looked this way: everything shaken off shelves, hurled out of cupboards – broken jars and bottles and cans and boxes and plates and glasses and mugs all over the floor – a strange jumbled mixture of containers, spilled ingredients, and utensils: as if a mindless dolt had hurled everything onto the kitchen floor in the hope of creating a surprise feast.

What a mess!

Maybe Mom'll have it cleaned up by the time . . .

*Please, Mom, be okay . . . And Dad.*

At the counter, she tore off a handful of paper towel and cleaned the top of her Pepsi can. Then she sidestepped to the sink, held the can underneath the spout, and twisted the cold water faucet handle.

No water came out.

*Of course not.*

No water, she thought, and here we are drinking up this woman's sodas.

Barbara raised the can to her face. She sniffed.

A lingering odor of raw egg.

She took the unopened can back to the refrigerator, opened the door, and set it into the rack.

She noticed there were five or six other cans.

It won't kill her if I drink one, she thought.

*Ah, the can stinks anyway.*

The egg couldn't have gotten them all.

But she left them all there, anyway, and shut the door.

At the end of a short, dim hallway, she found the living room. Pete and Heather were sitting on a sofa beneath a crooked watercolor of a Paris street in the rain. They looked dirty and sweaty. They each held a can of Pepsi.

'You didn't get yourself a drink?' Pete asked.

'Nah. I don't feel like one. Too sweet.'

'You need to get some liquid in you. You don't want to get dehydrated.'

'I don't know.' Barbara shrugged with one shoulder, and felt her top button slip out of its hole. Ever since the kid had grabbed her purse and tugged her blouse open, her buttons hadn't worked the way they should. Pete and Heather didn't seem to notice the problem, so she left the button alone.

On her way to the sofa, she looked around. Mrs Klein's living room had fared better than her kitchen. Except for a table lamp that lay on the floor with one side of its shade mashed in, there didn't seem to be any real damage.

'I bet you didn't find Susie,' Heather said.

'Not yet.' Barbara sat down beside Pete. 'How's the arm?'

He held it up, showing off the neatly taped patch of gauze on the underside of his forearm. 'Not bad. Doesn't even hurt. Mrs Klein, though, she said how I'd better check with my parents and make sure my tetanus shots and things are up to date.'

'Will you need any stitches?'

'Nah, it's mostly just a scratch.'

'Good thing.' She leaned back, and sighed at the wonderful feel of the soft cushion. She hadn't realized how sore she was: how much her neck and back and rump and legs ached.

I'll just stay here forever, she thought.

But suddenly realized that her sweaty hair and back might stain the upholstery.

So she sat up straight, and groaned.

'Why don't you take a drink of mine?' Pete asked. He held his can toward her.

'Well . . .'

'Go ahead. I'm done, anyway.'

'Well . . . Okay. Thanks.' She accepted the can. It felt half full.

'You'll never guess what we found out,' Heather said.

Barbara took a few swallows. The soda *did* taste too sweet.

It's not too sweet, she thought. It's just not cold enough. Medium cool just doesn't do it when you're drinking colas.

Better than nothing, though.

She stopped herself from drinking more, and held the can out to Pete. 'Here, you finish it.'

'No, you go ahead.'

'I have to get back outside and help Mrs Klein.'

'I don't think there's a big hurry about that,' he said.

'What do you mean?'

'Get a load of this,' Heather said. Leaning forward, she stretched her arm past Pete. Her hand stopped above Barbara's left knee. It was holding a small tin of Whiskas cat food.

'What?' Barbara asked.

'Three guesses,' Heather said.

'We looked around,' Pete said. 'There's only one bedroom, and . . . no sign that Mrs Klein has any children.'

Heather, still leaning forward, gave Barbara a smug grin.

'Get it? Her Susie eats Whiskas.'

'Susie is her cat,' Pete explained, and shook his head.

'You're kidding,' Barbara muttered. 'Are you sure?'

'There's a plastic bowl on the kitchen floor,' Pete said. 'It has Susie's name on it.'

'Really?'

'And milk *in* it,' Heather added. 'Most of the milk's on the floor, but there's still *some* in the bowl. Susie's bowl.'

Barbara shook her head slowly from side to side. 'I don't believe this,' she muttered. 'Susie is her cat? We've been busting our butts out there, *cooking* in that sun, wasting God only knows how much time when we could've been on our way home to rescue that woman's *pussycat*?'

'It sort of looks that way,' Pete said.

'Terrific.'

Heather grinned. 'Cute, huh? I knew we shouldn't stop and help her.'

'We didn't know it was just a cat,' Pete said.

'She didn't exactly say it *wasn't*,' Barbara pointed out. 'She called it her baby, but a lot of people do that sort of thing.'

'She *wanted* us to think it's a person,' Heather said. 'She just figured we wouldn't help if we knew it was only a cat.'

'She would've been right,' Pete said.

Barbara shook her head. 'I mean, there are probably people trapped under buildings. If I'm gonna bust my butt trying to dig somebody out, I'm gonna do it for a human being.'

'I'd do it for my own dog,' Pete said. 'If I had one.'

'I'd do it for my cat, Mickey,' Heather said. 'Except that my father pounded his brains out with a claw hammer one time.'

'You're kidding,' Pete said.

'Huh-uh.'

'Why'd he wanta do that?'

Here we go again, Barbara thought. Another story of sickness and blight from Lady Cheerful.

'Mickey got into the Thanksgiving turkey.'

'Oh, man,' Pete muttered.

'It was right out of the oven and we were waiting for it to cool, and watching a rerun of the *Rose Parade* on the TV. Mom went in the kitchen to mash the potatoes, and she yelled – this was before she killed herself.'

Never would've guessed, Barbara thought.

'So then Dad went in, and he went totally ape. First off, he punched out Mom for leaving the turkey out where the cat could get to it.'

'Where'd she leave it?'

'On the kitchen counter.'

'Where was she supposed to . . . ?'

'Nowhere. That wasn't the thing. Hell, *Dad's* the one who put it on the counter, anyhow. But that didn't matter. Mom was the one who got smacked for it.'

No wonder she killed herself, Barbara thought. Married to a guy like that . . . and with a daughter like Heather.

'Then he grabbed up Mickey by the tail and hauled him outside. I went running out after him, 'cause I knew he meant to kill him. But then he slugged me.'

A mad, gleeful look appeared on Heather's face.

No tears, this time.

Maybe because this one isn't about her mother, Barbara thought. And maybe she hadn't liked Mickey all that much in the first place.

'He slugged me in the stomach. He never hits me in the face, 'cause it'd show. But anyhow, he knocked my wind out and I was down on my back in the driveway, laying there and trying to catch my breath, when he came back from the garage. He'd gone there to get his claw hammer. So then he dangled Mickey right over my face and starting swinging at him with the hammer. It took him . . . oh, a long time. He kept missing. That's because of how Mickey was squirming around and everything. He didn't miss all the time, though. He'd wham Mickey in the back, and in the jaw . . . blood was flying, pouring down on me, getting in my face . . . but then finally he caught him a good one right on top of the head, and . . .'

'Could you knock it off?' Barbara said. 'You're making me sick.'

'Can't take it, huh? I bet *you* never had to take anything like that, did you?'

'My parents aren't a couple of lunatics,' she said.

Pete seemed to cringe.

Barbara stood up. Heather's grin looked crooked and frozen. 'I'm sorry your mother's dead,' Barbara told her. 'I'm sorry your father's a crazy vicious madman. I'm sorry he killed your cat. I just don't wanta hear about it, okay?' To Pete, she said, 'I'm going back outside.'

'Me, too.' Pete crushed his Pepsi can. Leaning forward to set it on the table, he turned to Heather. 'You ready?'

'I guess so.'

They both stood up at the same time.

Heather took hold of Pete's hand. Her other hand, Barbara noticed, was out of sight behind her back.

'What've you got?'

'None of your business.'

'You're right,' Barbara said. And up yours, she thought.

On her way to the rear of the house, she looked back once. Heather's left hand was still behind her, and her right was still holding Pete's hand.

*How can he stand her?*

*He can't. He's just being kind to her because she's such a loser.*

After the cool shade inside the house, the sunlight was blinding, the air heavy with heat. Barbara squinted and lowered her head as she made her way across the back yard.

She wished she could've stayed inside.

Things seemed worse, now, out here.

She supposed that nothing had actually changed very much. Spending time in the house – though probably no more than ten minutes – she'd simply forgotten how bad all this was: the heat, the glare of the sun, the sour odor of smoke in the air, the sounds of sirens, amplified voices, shouts, screams, car alarms, and occasional bangs that were obviously gunshots.

'What I wouldn't give,' Pete said, 'for some air conditioning.'

Barbara glanced back at him. 'An air-conditioned movie theater.'

'Yeah. With a big old Pepsi full of chopped ice.'

'And an Eastwood movie on the screen.'

'You said it!'

'How about an ice-cold shower?' Heather asked. She bumped softly against Pete's side. 'With you and me in it.'

A grin spread across Pete's dirty face. 'Well, now.'

'Charming,' Barbara said, and turned away. She was already sweaty again. And her eyes burned. Lifting the front of her blouse, she wiped her face.

'Maybe somebody around here has a swimming pool,' Pete said.

'I wouldn't count on it,' Barbara said, not looking back.

She stopped and gazed at the piled jumble of the demolished garage.

'Mrs Klein?' she called.

No answer.

'Where is she?' Pete asked.

'Maybe around the other side,' Barbara said. Then she shouted, 'Hello! Mrs Klein! We're back!'

Still no answer.

'Well,' Barbara said, 'it's kind of noisy around here.'

'She should've heard that.'

'Oh,' Heather said, 'I sure hope nothing happened to her. Wouldn't that be such a shame?'

'Hey, cut it out,' Pete said.

'Don't give me that. You *like* the idea that she had us digging through this crap for her *cat*?'

'Not exactly.'

Barbara began to make her away around the fallen garage, eyes down, carefully watching each footstep to avoid stumbling or gouging herself on debris. She planned to keep going, and not check the pile again until she had reached its opposite side.

But Pete said, 'Oh, Jeez.'

Barbara stopped fast and snapped her head sideways.

And saw a pair of legs.

Like the legs of a clothes store mannequin that had been jammed headfirst into the side of the pile of rubble, jammed in so deep that only the legs stuck out.

It is a mannequin! Barbara thought.

*Oh, Jesus, no it's not.*

A mannequin wouldn't have bloody feet. Or torn stockings. Or varicose veins or cuts or scratches on its calves and thighs.

'Mrs Klein?'

*Somebody'd stuffed her into the . . .*

*No, maybe not. Maybe she'd worked her way to the car and tried to squeeze her way in through one of the windows to reach Susie.*

*And gotten trapped.*

*And suffocated?*

Suddenly feeling breathless and sick, Barbara rushed toward the protruding legs.

'Careful!' Pete shouted.

She didn't need to go far. She didn't need to climb at all. After staggering over a few scattered roof tiles and splintered boards, she grabbed the ankles.

'Mrs Klein!' she yelled. 'Can you hear me? Are you all right?'

Nothing.

'Dead?' Heather asked.

Barbara glanced back. Heather had forgotten to keep her left hand out of sight. It hung by her side. It was clinging to the can of Whiskas.

Apparently, she'd intended to confront Mrs Klein with the evidence of her treachery.

Pete was on his way.

'Here,' he said. He rubbed against Barbara's side, forced his way through more debris, and wrapped his arms around Mrs Klein's thighs. 'Okay,' he said. 'Let's try and ease her out. Gently.'

'Yeah.'

They both began to pull.

Mrs Klein came out slowly. When her rump was clear, Pete said, 'Wait.' He reached out and grabbed the hem of her skirt and pulled until the backs of her thighs were covered. 'Okay,' he said.

They resumed pulling, inching her out of her burrow in the side of the mound.

'Is she dead?' Heather asked.

'I don't know,' Pete called.

'Let's not worry about it till we've got her out,' Barbara said.

Above the waist of her skirt, the woman's back was bare. Barbara saw fresh, raw scratches on her skin. From crawling into the rubble? Or from being dragged out feet-first?

'Almost got her,' Pete said.

They pulled some more, and met resistence.

'Hold it. Let's not force her.'

They stopped pulling. She was bare halfway up her back.

'Something's stuck.'

'Her boobs are in the way,' Heather said.

'Try lifting,' Barbara suggested. 'Raise her as much as you can, and I'll pull.'

Hugging her around the belly, he pulled her upward. Barbara tugged her ankles and she suddenly came out so fast they both staggered, gasping with alarm and fighting to keep their feet.

As Barbara tried to stay up in a moment that seemed to stretch on and on forever, she glimpsed the broad, black cross-strap of Mrs Klein's bra . . .

. . . vertical straps that disappear under the ivory fabric of her rucked-up blouse . . .

. . . blouse rumpled high across her back, still clothing her shoulders and arms, shrouding the back of her head . . .

. . . speckled and splashed with shiny blood . . .

. . . arms still stretched out like a diver . . .

. . . blouse-hidden head coming out now . . .

. . . coming out of a dark gap in the mound . . .

. . . a squawling '*rrrroowwww!*' that races a shiver through Barbara . . .

. . . a cat leaping out of the darkness, pouncing on the shrouded back of the head – a cat so drenched in blood that a glimpse of it reminds Barbara of Carrie on prom-night – and then it springs away, blood flying from its fur.

The endless moment ended when Barbara heard herself cry out. Her own '*Yahhh!*' drowned out whatever noises might've come from Pete or Heather, but she saw Pete lurch aside and stumble and drop Mrs Klein.

Feet elevated by Barbara, the woman was about to smash her face into the alley pavement. Too late to help by letting go. So she flung the ankles at each other, made them miss, crossed them and thrust, twisting the body as it fell.

The shoulder, not the face, struck the pavement. Barbara was glad.

But not for long.

Mrs Klein flopped onto her back.

Barbara glimpsed her shredded, eyeless face, her ripped throat. Whirling away, she dropped to a crouch and squeezed her eyes shut and clutched her own face with both hands.

*No no no no no!*

Then she felt hands on her shoulders.

'You okay?' Pete asked.

She shook her head.

'I guess that was Susie.'

'Yeah.'

'What a way to go,' Heather said. She sounded far away, and impressed. 'Good thing it wasn't one of *us* tried to crawl in and save her cat. God! Look what it did to her. Just look at that, will you?'

# FIFTEEN

Time to get back to Sheila.

Way past time, Stanley thought.

But he had to deal with Judy first.

She was slippery underneath him. Slippery and sticky, and motionless except for her breathing.

He got to his knees, and stared down at her.

Her skin was shiny with wetness. Smeared with a little blood here and there. Rosy where Stanley had used her roughly – places where there would soon be bruises.

'What a beaut,' he muttered.

Saying that, he felt a small rush of guilt.

'But not in Sheila's league,' he added. 'Not even close.'

He pictured Sheila in the bathtub.

*Gotta get back to her, get her out of there. Clean her off . . .*

But something had to be done about Judy, first.

Don't wanta kill her, he thought. That wouldn't be any good. Ruin her for later, in case something goes wrong with the Sheila thing.

*Nothing better go wrong!*

'Gotta get,' he reminded himself.

Not without taking care of Judy, though.

'First things first.'

He climbed off the end of the bed.

Bending over, he grabbed Judy by the ankles. He backed away, dragging her until her rump slid off the mattress. She bent at the waist and sat down hard on the carpeted floor. The abrupt landing made her breasts do a quick bounce.

Stanley pulled her away from the bed. When she was flat on her back, he lowered her legs to the floor.

She was unconscious now, or appeared to be. But she was sure to come out of it, sooner or later. He needed a way to secure her so that she wouldn't be able to run off and get help.

*How about pinning her down in her bathtub?*

The idea made him laugh.

But right away, he realized that it was a very good idea. Sheila had

115

sure gotten trapped in her tub. The thing was almost as good as a cage.

Crouching, he shoved his arms under Judy's body. Her head dipped toward the floor and wobbled when he lifted her. He walked quickly across the bedroom toward a door that was open no more than a crack.

He hadn't looked behind the door, so far, but he suspected that it belonged to a connecting bathroom.

As he hurried along, Judy's limp body kept slipping through his arms, her hip sliding down his belly. Twice, on the verge of dropping her, he had to pause and give her a knee in the rump and readjust his hold.

He bumped the door with her head to make it swing open. Then he turned her sideways and carried her into the bathroom and was amazed by the aroma that engulfed him.

A rich perfume.

Vanilla? Marshmallow? Cotton candy? Sweet and mouth-watering, it teased him with old memories.

He squinted his eyes.

He sucked the wonderful scent in through his nose, filling himself with it.

Something from when he was a boy . . .

Carnival midways?

That's it!

Midways he'd walked a few times with his parents. Always with his parents, and always in daylight.

But oh, how he'd longed to explore them in the night, alone, with nobody to tell him no or stop him. Midways brilliant as Christmas with colored lights, dark and secret and mysterious in the shadows. Midways where forbidden rides could kill you with their thrills, where strange men promised to show you terrible wonders hidden in tents, where all the women seemed to be gypsies full of wild magic.

He had longed to sneak in all by himself at midnight and become part of it.

But, of course, he hadn't.

Hadn't dared.

*What if Mother catches me!*

Stanley inhaled deeply again. He felt a smile float on his face.

*I've got my own carnival now.*

'Step right this way, folks. See the Amazing *Limp* Woman. She jiggles, she shimmies, she shakes.'

He shook her, and smiled.

But suddenly she reminded him of Sheila.

'Sheila the Woman of Steel, who . . .'

*Gotta get back to her.*

Stanley glanced around the bathroom. Except for a crack in one large mirror, it looked unharmed by the quake.

It couldn't have gotten off this easily.

Judy had obviously spent time picking up whatever had been hurled out of its medicine cabinet and cupboards – including a bottle of wonderful perfume that must've broken or spilled.

I oughta check and see what's in the wastebasket, he thought.

Later, he told himself. For now, I've gotta take care of Judy.

He scanned the bathroom.

A very *nice* bathroom.

Twin sinks, counters that looked like marble, mirrors everywhere, a shower stall with a clear glass door (exactly like the one in his fantasy of Sheila when she showered after her morning runs), and a step-down tub.

The tub looked like a miniature swimming pool.

Only not all *that* miniature.

Stanley stood above it, gazing down past the body cradled in his arms.

Gleaming, royal blue tiles.

What a great tub. So much nicer than the one at Mother's house. So much nicer than Sheila's. He wished he could fill it high, right now, with cool clear water.

*Damn quake.*

It's not a damn quake, he told himself. It's my *friend* the quake. Yes yes yes. I wouldn't be here except for the quake. None of this great stuff would be happening. Just too bad it had to screw up the water system.

*Oh, how I'd love to take a bath in this. Judy on one side of me, Sheila on the other. We'd be all cool and soapy and slippery . . .*

Judy suddenly slipped down through his arms again. He planted his knee against the moist crevice of her rump, thrust her upward, and struggled to hold on while he hurried down the tile steps.

The bottom of the tub was as flat as a floor. He crouched and laid her down on her back, feet toward the faucets. Then he climbed out.

He looked down at her.

A tub this big wouldn't be much help in confining her. He wondered if there might be a guest bathroom with a normal tub somewhere in the house.

I'm not gonna lug her around looking for one, he thought. This'll do. Long as she's tied up good and tight.

*With what?*

He doubted he would find anything useful in the bathroom, so he hurried into the bedroom. He glanced from the bed to the dresser to the closet, considering what they might have to offer: bedsheets, pantyhose, scarves, neckties . . . ?

117

*I don't wanta be tying her with rags – nothing that's gonna stretch and rip.*

Belts?

In the closet, he found a good collection of leather belts hanging by their buckles from a rack on the inside of the door. They were men's belts – her husband's, he supposed. He grabbed several and hurried back to Judy.

She didn't look as if she had moved.

Stanley dragged her closer to the faucets. The two chrome handles were slightly higher than his own knees, and about twenty inches apart.

He twisted both handles. As he'd expected, no water came out.

Would've been nice, though. Could've had a nice, cold bath.

Just as well, he told himself. I've gotta get back to Sheila.

He lifted Judy's right leg up between his own legs. He pressed its ankle against the side of the cold water handle, then squeezed his legs together to hold it in place. With both hands free, he wound a belt three times around her ankle and the faucet. He pulled it tight, then buckled it.

He did the same with her other foot, binding it to the hot water faucet with a second belt.

Legs elevated and separated as they were, she was probably secure. It would require a major effort to reach the belts, and Stanley doubted that Judy had the strength.

Bet she can't, he thought.

And he imagined how much fun it would be to watch her try.

He could just see it! Fabulous struggles and contortions! Grunting and sweating and weeping, she would fight to sit up, strain to stretch her arms to the faucets and, failing, flop back down and resort to twisting and bucking and kicking.

It'd be great!

But Stanley knew he couldn't stay and watch. He'd already stayed too long.

*Can't leave her this way, though. Not for real.*

To leave her arms free would be tempting fate.

When you tempt fate, you get screwed.

He remembered seeing a straight-backed chair someplace.

Returning to the bedroom, he spotted it in a corner. His pajama pants were wadded on its seat cushion, where he must've tossed them at some point – though he couldn't remember when.

He flung the pants to the floor and carried the chair into the bathroom. At the bottom of the tub, he set it down on Judy. Its back legs fit nicely above her shoulders. The rungs pressed against the fronts of her shoulders like the straps of a peculiar wooden bra, and the chair's front legs touched her sides just above her hips.

Squatting above her head, Stanley picked up another belt. He held it in his teeth, lifted both her arms over the padded seat, and forced her hands toward each other. Her arms weren't long enough. He couldn't get her hands to meet. Which meant he wouldn't be able to strap her wrists together with the belt.

*If I just had some handcuffs . . .*

He could change his plan, he supposed. But he really liked the idea of fastening her hands together above the seat as if she were clutching the chair against her chest. She wouldn't have a *chance* of sitting up and going for the ankle restraints – not while she was hugging the chair.

But a leather belt wouldn't work.

There must be some sort of belt or tie or strap that'll do, he told himself. Something handy. Don't wanta go rooting through the whole house.

Back in the bedroom, he returned to the closet.

*Maybe two or three neckties . . .*

*Maybe Judy has a belt made out of rope, or . . .*

Nothing useful near the front, so he worked his way deeper into the closet. He couldn't see much, and felt his way along. He liked the way some of the clothes rubbed against him.

Maybe I can find a robe, he thought. A terri-cloth robe like mine at home might have a belt that'll work.

As he felt among the blouses in search of one, however, his hand collided with several empty wire hangers.

*Hangers!*

He snatched a few out of the darkness.

Moments later, he was again squatting at the bottom of the tub. He swung Judy's arms up, pulled them toward each other above the seat of the chair, and slipped a hanger over both her hands. Then he forced them toward the sides until their wrists were wedged between the narrowing wires.

'Beautiful,' he muttered.

He collapsed the middle of the hanger, trapping Judy's wrists at each end, then bent and twisted the wires to make his trap secure.

Got her now, he thought. She'll never get out of this.

He tossed the unused belts and hangers out of the tub. On his knees, he smiled down at Judy. Her face was upside-down. It looked strange that way; her mouth was where her forehead ought to be, her eyebrows *under* her eyes. For the first time, Stanley noticed that she had a few freckles on her eyelids.

'Yoo-whooo,' he said. 'You still out?'

She didn't react.

'I'm going away for a little while. You gonna miss me? Huh? Anyway, I'll be back, so don't worry. Just stay here and relax.'

119

With his left arm for a brace, he eased down and kissed Judy's mouth. Her lips felt dry and scratchy, so he licked them. That seemed to soften them up some. He went on kissing her. While he did that, he reached his right arm around and under the chair and fondled her right breast. It was slippery and sticky, but he enjoyed squeezing it. He tried for the left breast. He couldn't get to it, though, so he stayed with the right.

He had his tongue deep in her mouth.

He was hard again.

He wondered what it might be like to fuck her the way she was tied like this to the faucets and chair.

'It'd be fuckin' impossible,' he muttered, and laughed.

He gave her nipple a final pinch, pulled his tongue out of her mouth, and struggled to his feet. He climbed out of the tub.

By the side of the wastebasket, he crouched. He sniffed.

*Cotton candy.*

But a perfume, really.

At the bottom of the plastic recepticle were wads of pink facial tissue, loose pills, pieces of broken bottles, a tooth brush.

Stanley scooped out a handful of the tissues. They were still moist. He lifted them to his nose. He gave them a small, careful sniff.

Yes!

He inhaled deeply, then rubbed his face with the tissues, smearing himself with the wonderful aroma.

When he was finished, he put the tissues back inside the wastebasket for safe keeping and headed for the bathroom door.

He stopped and glanced one more time at Judy.

She looked like the victim of an exotic, failed contraption.

'I shall return,' Stanley said, and left the bathroom.

He pulled the door shut, crossed the room and stepped into his moccasins. They felt mushy and slick under his feet, as if they'd been lathered inside with lard. Barefoot was better, but he had to wear *something* on his feet when he went outdoors.

He found his pajama pants, stepped into them and pulled them up. They stuck to him. They seemed to trap the heat against his skin.

He supposed he could probably find a pair of shorts to wear, instead. Something of Herb's.

*But then Sheila's gonna know I found clothes.*

'Can't have that,' he said.

He liked the idea of shorts, though.

So he went into Judy's kitchen to hunt for something sharp. He'd been through the kitchen when he carried Judy into the house, but he hadn't noticed much about it. Now, he realized that it seemed untouched by the quake.

Maybe Judy had already picked up all the things that had fallen. Sure, she had. Must've started scurrying around and cleaning house the second the quake stopped – even before rushing out to check on the neighbors.

Busy girl, Stanley thought.

Or maybe the kitchen had simply gotten off easy, the way some places do for mysterious earthquake reasons.

He started looking in the drawers for a sharp knife. But he found a pair of scissors, first. He took off his pajama pants, snipped off both the frail legs, and put the pants back on.

*Much, much better!*

He started to set down the scissors, then changed his mind. They might come in handy, later on.

What else? he wondered. There's a whole house full of stuff here, and it's all mine.

Food? Probably plenty of good stuff in the fridge.

He wasn't hungry yet. Besides, he could come back whenever the urge might strike him. Sheila shouldn't be needing food yet, either.

*We'll have a little party after I get her out. Maybe even come over here. Yeah, bring her here.*

Judy and Herb were drinkers, he knew that. He'd seen their empty bottles in the recycling bin that they put out to the curb once a week for trash day.

*I'll offer Sheila a nice, tall vodka and tonic. We'll sip cocktails together on the sofa.*

He pictured Sheila sprawled on the sofa, naked, smiling, sipping her drink, beads of icy condensation falling off the bottom of the glass and splashing her breasts, sliding down them, dripping off her nipples.

He groaned.

He wandered through the kitchen, checking cupboards. The cupboard doors had either stayed shut during the quake – which hardly seemed likely – or Judy had gone around and closed them afterward. She *must've* done some tidying of the kitchen: it couldn't have gotten off this lightly.

After tugging open the doors of several cupboards, he found the liquor supply.

'This'll be great,' he said. He shut the cupboard. 'Great.'

He hurried to the refrigerator. Planning to check for ice, he reached toward the handle of the freezer compartment.

*No no no no no! Don't open it, you'll let out all the cold.*

The voice inside his head sounded a lot like his mother, the Bitch. He grinned.

'Just can't get rid of you, can I?'

*No no no no no.*

In this case, however, he appreciated the warning. Judy and Herb were certain to have plenty of ice in their freezer, so there was no reason to look. The only question was how long the ice might last with the power down. It would last a lot longer if the door stayed shut.

Stanley turned away from the refrigerator.

'Okay,' he said. 'Anything else?'

*Bet Sheila could use some sun block.*

He laughed.

Then, with the scissors in his hand, he stepped outside. The sunlight made him squint, but he liked how it felt on his body. He took a deep breath. He smelled smoke, but he also detected a fresh scent of the ocean air, and the sweet candy aroma of Judy's perfume.

In the driveway, he bent down and picked up the saw and the plastic jug of water. The jug was dripping. It left a wet place that looked brown on the gray concrete.

With the saw and scissors in one hand, the jug in the other, he made his way down Judy's driveway. As he walked, he rubbed the jug against his chest. Its wet plastic was slightly cool. Too bad it wasn't ice cold, the way it had been when Judy brought it out.

That was a long time ago, Stanley told himself. I'm lucky the water isn't hot enough to boil eggs by now.

He crossed Judy's front yard. On his own driveway, he stopped and looked at the door of his mother's house.

*My house.*

He wondered if anything needed to be done inside.

*Go in and give the Bitch a kick for good measure. One to grow on.*

Laughing and shaking his head, he walked up his driveway. The garage in front of him was a collapsed ruin.

At least I've still got half a house, he told himself.

Too bad I can't change houses with Judy, he thought. Hardly fair, hers getting off with nothing more than a few broken mirrors and windows while mine is half destroyed.

I *can* change houses with her, he realized. At least for the time being. Who's gonna stop me?

When he came to the cinderblock wall at the back of his yard, he turned sideways and raised his arms and started to ease himself in between two of the rose bushes. A nettle snagged his shorts. He stopped.

He glanced at the saw in his hand.

'Ho! No time like the present!'

Backing clear, he set down his scissors and jug of water in the grass. Then he knelt in front of a rose bush. Bracing himself up with his left arm, just as he'd done in the bathtub to kiss and fondle Judy, he reached low with his right hand and pressed the teeth of his saw against the base of the stalk, no more than two inches above the garden's soil. The bush shook as he worked the saw back and forth. The teeth bit a deep slot into the stalk.

Sweat got into Stanley's eyes, making them burn. It dripped off his chin and the tip of his nose. It tickled him as it spilled down his body.

But soon, the bush keeled over sideways against its neighbor.

Stanley cut down that bush, too.

Then another.

He used the blade of his saw to drag and shove the three rose bushes out of his way. Then, breathless from the labor, he sat on the grass. He unscrewed the lid of the jug and took a swallow of water.

The grass felt prickly through the seat of his shorts.

He stood up, and rubbed his rump. With a slick bare forearm, he tried to wipe the sweat off his face. He wished he'd gotten himself a rag before leaving Judy's house: just something he could use for his sweat. His pajama legs would've been fine, but he'd left them in Judy's kitchen.

So he pulled down his shorts and stepped out of them. He wadded them and mopped his face and hair. The cloth felt sodden after that. He twisted his shorts into a tight stub and managed to wring out some of the wetness. Then he shook them open. He wiped his face once more.

He wished he didn't have to put the shorts back on. But Sheila might start screaming, or something, if he reappeared naked. Then he would need to hurt her, and he didn't want to do that until he had her someplace private – in Judy's house, maybe.

Gotta keep her thinking I only wanta rescue her, he told himself.

So he stepped into the shorts and pulled them up. They clung to him, but the elastic waistband seemed limper than before. He popped open the front, drew the slack out of the band, and resnapped so they didn't feel quite so loose.

Then he picked up his jug, scissors and saw. He carried them across the newly cleared strip of ground, and set them on top of the cinderblock wall. After that, he stepped to the side so they wouldn't be in his way when he climbed over.

He placed his hands on top of the wall and jumped. Braced high on stiff arms, the edge of the wall pressing against his waist, he got ready to swing a leg up.

But straight ahead, beyond the lawn and patio, a man was standing in the ruin of Sheila's house.

Stanley felt as if an octopus had suddenly wrapped its tentacles around his bowels and started to squeeze.

He groaned.

This is exactly what he'd been afraid of – someone else discovering her.

'I knew it,' he muttered. 'I knew it, I knew it.'

Shouldn't have stayed so long with Judy, he thought.

And then he swung himself over the top. He dropped to the other side, stumbled, fell to his knees, then got to his feet and returned to the wall. Reaching up, he took down his jug of water, his scissors and his saw.

He headed for Sheila's place.

# SIXTEEN

'Hey, all right, a *saw*, cool. Thata way to go.' The stranger hopped down from a pile of rubble and landed on a clear area of the patio.

He didn't look much older than twenty. His blond hair was almost white. Parted in the middle, it hung straight down past his bony shoulders. He didn't have a shirt on. His tan was so deep that Stanley suspected his pale hair might be a dye job. He was very skinny. Stanley could see his ribs. He wore faded old blue jeans. There was no belt, and the jeans hung low on his hips. He wore cowboy boots with pointed toes.

'You're Stan,' he said, head bobbing.

'That's me,' Stanley said, and smiled.

'Cool. We been waiting for you, me and Sheila.'

'Who are you?' He tried to sound friendly. It was easy; he'd been making himself sound friendly to people all his life, especially to those he feared or despised.

'I'm Ben.'

'Good to meet you, Ben. How's she doing?'

The young man bobbed his head some more. 'Good, good. Just scared, you know? Being stuck that way. She thought maybe you'd got hurt, or something, the way you didn't come back.'

'I had a delay. How long have you been here?'

'Aah. Five or ten minutes. I been going house to house, you know, looking to see if anyone's needing help. She's my first trapped one. Now we got that saw, we'll have her outa there real fast.'

'Yep,' Stanley said. 'Let's go.'

Ben led the way. As he trudged into the debris of the collapsed house, he looked back at Stanley. 'Watch your feet. Stuff'll poke right up through them moccasins. What you need is a good pair of sturdy boots, like me.'

'Nice boots,' Stanley told him.

'Yeah, thanks.' Ben smirked. 'Where the hell's the rest of your clothes, anyhow?'

It wasn't much fun being almost naked with a *guy* around.

Embarrassed, Stanley managed a small laugh. 'What am I supposed to be wearing? The quake caught me in my p.j. pants.' As he said that, he wondered if Ben had stumbled across the shirt of his pajamas. He'd taken it off and thrown it down in the mess before starting to clear the debris covering Sheila. The shirt would make a liar out of him.

*So what if he found it. What's he gonna do, report me?*

'Then my house fell down around my ears,' Stanley added. 'I'm just glad I don't sleep in the buff.'

'Whatever,' Ben said. 'You can run around buck naked, for all I care.'

Asshole, Stanley thought.

Ben resumed picking his way through the rubble. Stanley followed. He kept his gaze down and stepped carefully.

They circled around the high mound that Stanley had climbed that morning when searching for Sheila. As they passed in front of it, she called out.

'Ben? Is that you?'

Her voice saying Ben's name gave Stanley a sick feeling.

Jealousy?

No need to be jealous, he told himself. No need at all. Ben doesn't count. She's mine. I found her first, and I'm the guy with the saw.

The saw and the scissors.

'Guess who's here,' Ben called. Before she had a chance to answer, he said, 'Your old friend Stan.'

'Hey, Stan!' The greeting sounded almost cheerful. It soothed his sick feeling.

'Hi, Sheila. I'm back, and I've got a saw.'

'Great! Terrific!'

'Sorry it took so long. Had some trouble.'

Ben was first to reach the edge of the opening. Stanley moved in close to his side. Bending over, he gazed down at Sheila.

She was still sprawled inside her tub, pinned down by the four-by-eight support beams: one across the head of the tub and the other jammed down between her legs.

She looked exactly the same as Stanley remembered her.

Except for one detail.

From her breasts to her groin, she was draped with a faded green T-shirt.

Ben's shirt, no doubt.

*The bastard!*

'You okay, Stan?' she asked, frowning up at him.

'I'm fine,' he said. 'I guess.'

'You're sure a sight for sore eyes,' she told him.

You, too, he thought. What a wonderful sight. The most incredibly gorgeous, sexy woman in the world. But why did this bastard have to cover you up?

'I'd about given up on you,' she told him.

'Like I said, I had some trouble. I tried to get back sooner, but . . . How've you been doing?'

'Could be worse. It's not too comfortable down here. But mostly I was just scared. Not knowing, you know . . . And I'm not exactly used to being helpless.'

'You won't be down there much longer,' he said. He placed the scissors on a slat of broken board near the edge, then held out the saw so she could see it.

A smile spread over her face. 'My hero.'

'Brought you this, too.' With his other hand, he lifted the jug of water.

'Yes!'

'Do you think you'll be able to drink, lying down like that?'

'I'll sure give it a try.' She raised her arms toward Stan. Her hands waited, spread apart, fingers open. Below them, her chest was hidden beneath green fabric.

Stanley stretched his arm out above her and lowered the jug.

It remained well above Sheila's reach.

'I'll climb down,' he told her.

'I can catch it. Just let it go.'

'Drop it?'

'Sure.'

'Okay. Ready?'

'Bombs away,' she said.

Stanley let go of the jug, but gave it a slight push with his fingertips as he released it. The jug started to tumble. He gasped, 'Damn!'

Sheila almost caught it.

But she bobbled it, knocking it farther off course, and it fell between her hands. It landed on her belly with an impact that sloshed the water inside the jug and disrupted her carefully spread T-shirt.

As the jug slid, she grabbed it.

'Are you okay?' Stanley asked, trying to sound concerned. He realized, now, that she had tucked the T-shirt between her legs. That part of it remained in place. The rest of the shirt was now a rumpled heap beneath her breasts.

*Oh yes, oh yes!*

'I should've had it,' she said.

She picked up the jug with one hand. With the other, she pulled gently at the T-shirt and rearranged it to cover herself.

'I sort of lost my hold,' Stanley explained.

'No problem. It didn't hurt.' Holding the jug above her chest, she twisted off its cap. Then she sat up as much as possible, stopping when her forehead met the underside of the heavy beam. She tilted the round opening to her mouth. Some water slopped out and ran down her chin and neck. But then she had the opening tight to her lips, and she drank.

After a few swallows, she eased the jug away. 'Great stuff, water.'

'Why don't you hang on to that,' Stanley said. 'Ben and I have to leave you for a while.'

'What?' Ben blurted.

Stanley nodded, turned his head, and grimaced at the young man. 'I'm gonna need your help.'

'I'm not going anywhere. Not till we've got Sheila outa there.'

'I'm with Ben,' Sheila said. 'You're kidding about leaving, aren't you?'

'I wish I was. There's this girl I found. She can't be more than about four years old. I ran into her when I was looking for the saw, and I tried to get her out. That's what took me so long. She's trapped under part of a fireplace chimney that fell. I could just barely lift the thing. But I needed both hands for that, so there wasn't any way to drag her out from under. I need somebody else, someone to pull her out while I hold it off her.'

'You should've said something,' Sheila told him.

'Figured you needed a drink. Anyway, I wanted to make sure you're all right.'

'Thanks, but . . .'

'Give me the saw,' Ben said. 'I'll have her out of there in five minutes.'

'Is that what you want, Sheila?'

'No. For God's sake, get going. Both of you. Ben, go with him. Take care of that kid.'

Ben looked pained. 'Are you sure?'

'I'm fine down here. In fact, why don't you hand the saw down? Maybe I can cut myself out of this while you're gone.'

'That wouldn't be such a good idea,' Stanley said, rising. 'Just can't tell, those beams might be holding something up. You don't wanta start a slide . . . better just wait till we get back.' Before she could object, he turned away. 'Come on, Ben.'

'How long's this gonna take?'

Stanley shrugged. 'I don't know, twenty minutes. The house is a couple of blocks from here. It's a question of getting there and back – rescuing the kid shouldn't take any time at all. So I'd say we oughta be back in half an hour, at the most.'

Looking down at Sheila, Ben asked, 'Is that okay? Half an hour?'

'It's fine,' she said. 'Get going.'

'We'll hurry,' Stanley assured her, and headed through the rubble toward the rear of the house.

Ben followed him. He was silent for a while. He waited until Stanley had hopped down onto the patio, then said, 'I don't like this.'

'What don't you like?'

Ben jumped down. 'Leaving her.'

'Do you want the kid to die?'

'No, but I don't see how five minutes is gonna make a big difference.'

'Five minutes can make all the difference.'

'Yeah?'

'Yeah. Try holding your breath that long.'

'If this kid ain't breathing, she's dead already.'

'I didn't say she isn't breathing. I'm just saying five minutes can be the difference between life and death, sometimes. In this case, the kid *might* be bleeding. Down under the chimney where I couldn't see her? Do you want her bleeding to death while we saw on wood to untrap Sheila – who isn't in any danger at all and isn't even hurt?'

'Who says she's not in danger?'

Stanley turned around and walked backward, studying the distant sky. Smoke from the burning house across the street still drifted up, but it didn't seem as heavy as before. There were no other fires near enough to worry about.

'Long as a big wind doesn't come up and blow the fire this way . . .'

'It's not the fire,' Ben said.

'Then what?'

'You know. People. What if somebody finds her down there? I mean, she's buck naked.'

Not quite, Stanley thought, thanks to you.

'A lot of guys, you know, might get ideas. They might *do* stuff to her, you know?'

'You worry too much, Ben.'

'There's a lot of sick people in this world. Rapists and perverts . . .'

'I don't think Sheila is in much danger from a guy like that.'

Ben smirked. 'You don't, huh?'

'Nope. First, he'd have to *find* her. Then he'd have to *get* to her. A pervert's gonna be shit-outa-luck unless he's got a saw with him.' Stanley raised his own saw and waved it. 'Another good reason for taking this with us.'

'Yeah, right.'

'Can't rape her if you can't get to her. Can't get to her without a saw.'

'I guess you're right,' Ben said.

'Sure I'm right. Nobody's gonna touch Sheila till we get back.'

# SEVENTEEN

Though they walked slowly so that Mary wouldn't be left too far behind, they still made better progress than the traffic beside them on Laurel Canyon Boulevard. The cars and trucks in the northbound lanes moved very slowly. The vehicles in the southbound lanes, heading in the same direction as Clint and his companions, remained motionless for minutes at a time before creeping forward a few feet and stopping again.

'There must be some real trouble up ahead,' Clint said.

'I'll say,' Em agreed. 'Bet it's Ventura Boulevard. That street's a zoo, no matter what. It must be *crammed*.'

'Hey,' Mary called, 'wait up, will you?'

Turning around, they watched Mary saunter toward them. She was even farther behind than usual. As she walked slowly closer, she stuffed her plastic Pepsi bottle down the top of her purse.

'Guess she stopped for a sip,' Clint said.

'Good thing we're not in a hurry,' Em muttered, and flicked a sly grin at him.

'Be nice,' he said.

'She's lost some of her *freshness*, hasn't she?'

Clint laughed softly. 'I'll say.'

Mary's hair hung in limp, damp strands. Her face was flushed and dripping. Her white blouse was twisted crooked from the pull of her purse strap. It looked drenched. It stuck to her skin and even to her bra, which showed through as if the fabric of her blouse had been melted thin by the heat. The blouse had come partly untucked from her skirt, and hung down sloppily. Even her skirt appeared to be crooked.

'Who won the wrestling match?' Em called out to her.

'Very funny. You're a million laughs, you little brat.'

'Part of my charm.'

'Em,' Clint said. 'Hey.'

'I know, "be nice." '

As Mary ambled nearer, she gave them an injured look. 'I sure wish you wouldn't walk so fast, you two.'

Em shrugged one shoulder. 'I don't know about Mr Banner, but I'm walking as slow as I can.'

'It's not my fault if I'm not a fast walker,' Mary said. 'And we wouldn't have to be doing this, at all, if we hadn't gone over to your house and gotten my car destroyed by that pair of throw-backs. It was being nice to you that got us into this mess.'

'Hey,' Clint said. 'That isn't necessary.'

'Yeah,' Em added. 'You oughta try being cheerful and polite for a change – or would that be too much of a strain on you?'

'Screw you.'

'That's sure a big improvement,' Em said.

'Up yours.'

'Do you know any *two* syllable words?'

'Fuck you.'

'No good. That's two words, one syllable each. Give it another try?'

Clint blurted out, 'Stop all this! Both of you cut it out, okay? Women! Bicker bicker bicker. Sometimes I think God created woman just to watch the bickering.'

'Whew,' Em said. 'That was certainly a sexist remark.'

'I'm allowed. I have a wife and daughter.'

'I'll forgive you,' Em said. Grinning, she bumped herself against him.

'Very cute,' Mary muttered. 'Anyway, it *is* her fault we lost my car.'

'It's just as well,' Clint said. 'I think they did us a favor, slashing the tires.'

'Oh, sure.'

'Saved us from getting stuck in all this traffic.'

'At least we wouldn't have to be walking.'

'I *would* be walking,' Clint said.

'We don' need no steenking car,' Em said, sounding very much like a Mexican bandito. 'Or badges.'

Mary glowered at her. 'Yeah? Well what about air conditioning?'

Em's head bobbed up and down a bit. 'That's another story,' she said. 'That'd be nice, air conditioning. I could sure use that. Or a swim. How would you like to jump into a swimming pool right now?'

'I'd rather jump in my car.'

'You don't like swimming pools?' Em asked.

'Not much.'

'I love 'em. You got a swimming pool, Mr Banner?'

'Nope.'

'We don't, either. We've gotta have about the only house in the valley without one.'

'Do you have friends with pools?' he asked.

'Sure. I'm in 'em a lot, too, but it's not the same. You've gotta be invited over, for one thing. You can't just hop on in any old time you feel like it. And your friend has to be there, so it's not like you can go in by yourself. And there're usually parents around. And maybe siblings. Thank the Lord *I* have never been blessed with a sibling. I've *seen* them. They'll drop whatever they're doing if they spot an opportunity to pester you. Frankly, I would go buh-zonkers. Thank the Lord my mom hates men.'

'But you don't,' Clint said.

Em grinned up at him. 'I don't hate *you*.'

'Thank you very much.'

'Very cute,' Mary said.

Still grinning at Clint, Em said, 'I think Mary believes I'd like to seduce you. That's ridiculous, of course. I mean, I'm thirteen. I'm way too young to even *think* about seducing someone.'

'Glad to hear it,' Clint said.

'Also, I have some fairly strong reservations about the entire sexual process.'

'You have *what?*'

'I mean – if what I've heard is true and I have every reason to believe that it is – it doesn't sound like something I would want to rush out and get done to me. I mean, really. I can't imagine anything grosser, if you want to know the truth.'

'Well . . .' Clint said.

'And talk about unsanitary.'

'I think it's about time to change the subject.'

'Bravo,' Mary said. 'I thought you'd never notice.'

'What should we talk about?' Em asked. 'Mary! Have you got a boyfriend?'

'A *boy*friend?'

'You know, a guy. A sweetie? A lover?'

'None of your business.'

'That's a no,' Em explained to Clint.

'Not necessarily.'

'It doesn't mean no,' Mary said. 'It means none of your business.'

'Maybe if you had a slightly more cheerful temperament, you'd have more luck with the fellas.'

Clint struggled not to laugh.

Mary's open hand smacked the back of Em's head.

Em yelped, 'Ah!' and flinched and staggered forward, ducking.

'Hey!' Clint shouted, whirling to face Mary. 'What the hell is the matter with you?'

'The little shit's got a big mouth!'

'That's no call to hit her, for Godsake! She's just a kid!'

'She's a little shit and I'm sick of her!'

'Then take a hike!'

'What?'

132

'You heard me, take a hike.' Clint turned to Em. The girl stood nearby, bent over, a hand clasped to the back of her head. She had dropped her paper bag to the sidewalk, where the two water-filled Pepsi containers inside had made it tumble over.

Clint curled a hand gently against the back of her neck. It felt moist, and very hot. 'Are you okay?'

'I seem to be getting knocked around an awful lot today,' she said, her voice quiet but steady.

Clint felt a thickness in his throat.

'Somebody oughta tell her it's not nice to hit people.'

He felt heat and wetness in his eyes, and Em's bowed blond head went blurry.

'I hardly touched her,' Mary muttered.

'Do you want *me* to hardly touch *you* that way?'

'Don't,' Em told him. 'I don't want you hitting her.'

'I wasn't planning on it, but I'm tempted.'

'I'm sorry, okay?' Mary said.

'You sound sorry.'

'I won't do it again.'

'Just leave. Just get the hell out of here.'

Mary shook her head. She looked shocked, angry. 'I told you, I won't do it again.'

'You shouldn't have done it in the first place.'

'I'm sorry! Okay? I'm *sorry*!'

'So what?'

She raised her chin and stiffened her back. 'You've gotta give me another chance, that's what.'

'No, I don't.'

'Yes, you do. You can't just . . . send me away. You *have* to give me another chance.'

'In what rule book does it say that?' Clint asked.

'Everybody knows that.'

'Not me. I don't believe in second chances, apologies, or any of that crap – not when you pull a stunt like whacking my kid or . . .'

'She's not your kid!'

'She's *someone's* kid, and she's *my* friend, and if you *had* done that to my kid Barbara you wouldn't be talking back to me right now about second chances, you'd be on your ass on the sidewalk *bleeding*!' He took a quick step toward Mary and shouted in her face, '*DO YOU UNDERSTAND?*'

The color drained from her face. She staggered backward as if bludgeoned. Her lips twitched. Her chin quivered. Tears filled her eyes.

Em turned around and watched her.

'I'm *sorry*!' Mary blurted. This time, she looked and sounded as if she meant it.

'Who cares,' Clint said.

'You can't just leave me here!'

'Maybe we oughta tie her up,' Em suggested.

'See what a bitch she is! See!'

'She's *kidding*. Just stay away from us, that's all. Stay out of reach and keep your mouth shut, or else I *might* tie you up.'

Mary sniffed, rubbed her nose, and glared at both of them.

Bending down, Clint picked up the sack that Em had dropped. 'I'll take this for a while.'

'No, that's okay. I don't mind carrying it.'

'It's awfully heavy. I'll carry it. What about the food?'

'What about it?' Em asked.

'Do you still want to share any of it with Mary, after what she did?'

Mary shifted her gaze from Clint to Em. 'Don't do me any favors,' she said.

Em pulled her head back and made a face as if Mary were threatening her with a fingertip loaded with snot. Then she turned to Clint. She made a crooked smile. 'She can have stuff. I don't care.'

'I don't want any of your damn food.'

'It'll be a long day,' Clint told her. 'You'll probably be getting hungry, so you'd better take something now. I'm not letting you anywhere near us once we start moving.'

'Big deal. I'm not gonna eat any of your precious food. If you're gonna leave me, go. Get outa here. Hope you croak.'

Clint nodded to Em. 'Let's go,' he said.

They started walking again. After taking eight or ten steps, Clint glanced over his shoulder. Mary was already following. She abruptly halted.

Sneering, she said, 'Do you want me to count to a hundred first?'

He shook his head. To Em, he said, 'Let's just pick up our pace a bit, and we'll leave her in the dust.'

They both began to quicken their strides. They walked side by side, Clint clutching the bag by its crumpled top. It was heavy. He felt bad about letting Em carry it for such a long time.

'You should've told me it was so heavy,' he said.

'It's not so heavy.'

'It weighs a ton.'

'I'll take it,' Em said, reaching out.

'No, you won't.'

'I don't mind. My book bag is a lot heavier, and I lug it around all the time.'

'That's okay. I'll carry this.' He kept hold of the bag, kept swinging it as they hurried along.

When he glanced back, Mary was chugging along at a fair clip. 'I can't believe it,' he said. '*Now* she's walking fast.'

Em looked over her shoulder. 'She's scared of being left behind.'

'Guess so. Knows we won't stop to wait for her any more.'

But they did have to stop. At Ventura Boulevard, the lanes they needed to cross were jammed with traffic. The signal lights were dead, just as Clint had expected. And nobody was out in the road, trying to direct traffic. Horns blared. People yelled. Cars and trucks, packed bumper to bumper, crept through the intersection while some inched off onto the crowded lanes of northbound Laurel Canyon and others struggled to turn right from Laurel and squeeze onto Ventura.

On the far side of Ventura, Laurel Canyon Boulevard was deserted. Its pavement stretched southward toward the hills, broad and sunlit and empty.

'What a mess,' Em said.

'It looks like they've got Laurel Canyon closed,' Clint told her.

'Yeah?' She stood on tiptoes, but shook her head. 'I can't see it.'

'There's no traffic at all over there.'

'Figures,' Em said. 'Laurel is always getting shut down. If it isn't a mud slide, it's a car crash . . . or a fire . . . or an earthquake. Always something.'

'*We'd* better be able to get through,' Clint said. He felt his lips pull back, baring his teeth.

'We could go over to Coldwater Canyon.'

'It'd be miles out of the way.' He shook his head. 'It has to be Laurel.'

'I'm waiting!' Mary called, her voice only slightly audible over the noises of engines and sighing brakes and car horns and radio music and shouts.

She stood about fifteen feet back, hands on hips, head tilted toward her left shoulder.

'Stay where you are,' Clint ordered.

'Are you gonna cross the street,' she called, 'or what?'

'Let's go,' Clint said to Em. 'Stay close to me, and keep your eyes open.'

For now, the lead cars on Laurel were motionless, waiting for small gaps between bumpers so that they might risk nosing out onto Ventura for their right-hand turns. It looked like it might be a long wait; the traffic on Ventura seemed to be at a dead halt.

With nobody likely to make a right turn and hit them, they only needed to worry about being crushed between cars that were waiting, going nowhere on Ventura.

Clint stepped off the curb. There was room for one leg at a time between the front of a Dodge pickup and the rear of a Mazda. He stopped beside the right front tire of the Dodge. The driver behind the windshield wore a cowboy hat. A cigarette dangled from a corner of his lips. He gave Clint a wave. Clint smiled, called, 'Thanks,' and moved in front of the truck.

As he started to sidestep through the gap, he beckoned for Em. She gave the driver a big smile, and came in.

Mary failed to stay back.

Don't worry about it, Clint told himself. The thing is to get across the street in one piece. Forget about her.

*She'd better just behave, that's all.*

The Escort and Cherokee in the next lane were bumper to bumper. Clint walked through a narrow space toward the rear of the Escort, and found a Cadillac that hadn't pulled up all the way. The Cadillac's driver was a young woman who reminded him strongly of Mary. A career woman, severe in her business suit. Though she faced forward, she wore sunglasses. Clint couldn't see her eyes.

He patted the hood with his open hand, and saw her head jerk. Smiling, he gestured his intention to walk in front of her car .

She didn't respond.

'We're coming through!' he yelled.

Her lips seemed to tighten slightly.

She looks like a real bitch, he thought. But she might be a perfectly nice person. Anyway, it'd take more than a bitch to run into you on purpose. It'd take a complete lunatic.

It's probably safe, he told himself.

*If you're wrong, you get your legs crushed at the knees.*

He gestured for Em to wait. Then he stepped in front of the Cadillac. He took another step.

It'll be all right, he thought.

VROOOOOMMM!

At the roar of the engine, he sucked a shocked breath and jammed his left hand against the hood and thought, *This is it.*

Should've jumped!

A moment later, as the roar faded to a quiet idle, he realized that the car had not suddenly lurched forward and demolished his legs.

The gal had gunned it, all right. But she must've taken it out of gear, first. Gunned it in neutral, just to give him a thrill, and kept her foot on the brake.

He looked at her.

The pointed corners of her mouth turned upward.

Clint hurried through. Safe on the other side of the Cadillac, he glared in at the driver.

136

She continued to smile toward him.

Em still waited.

'Don't go in front of this idiot,' Clint called to her.

Em nodded. Then climbed up onto the hood and crawled across on her hands and knees, grinning toward the windshield.

The driver's smile quit.

Crawling by, Em smacked the glass hard with her open hand. The driver flinched. Then Em stood up and jumped to the pavement.

Clint shook his head as she came toward him.

She grinned.

'You're a little wild,' he said.

'I was gonna spit on her windshield, but I held back. Sometimes I've gotta hold back on these tendencies I've got. I could be a pretty unsavory person, if I let myself go.'

Laughing, Clint gave the top of her head a quick rub. Her hair felt soft and dry and very hot from the sun. It made him think about Barbara, the many times he had rubbed her hair – usually to her annoyance. *Cut it out, Dad!* It hurt him to think about Barbara.

*What if she's dead?*

*She could be dead right now, mashed underneath the school or . . .*

*And Sheila might be dead, too. Buried under the house.*

*No!*

*Not both of them. I couldn't stand it if I had to lose both of them . . . Couldn't stand it to lose* either *of them.*

They're both fine, he told himself. They've got to be. We'll all get through this just fine, and . . .

'Are you okay, Mr Banner?'

He realized that his hand was motionless on top of Em's head. They were standing in the narrow space between two lines of stopped cars, and she was gazing up at him with a worried look on her face.

'I'm fine,' he said. 'I was just thinking about my wife and kid.'

'I bet they're all right.'

'Yeah. I sure hope so.'

He turned his head and saw Mary. She still stood at the far side of the Cadillac. She was watching them.

'Are you coming?' Em called to her.

'After what *you* did?'

'Cheerio, then.'

Mary seemed to sag. She looked like a traveller who had arrived at a rushing stream only to find that the bridge had been washed away.

Clint could almost feel sorry for her. 'Let's go,' he said to Em.

Passing through a gap between two more cars, they reached the middle of Ventura Boulevard. As they headed toward the front of an

137

eastbound RTD bus, Clint looked around for Mary. He couldn't spot her.

Em looked, too. 'Gone,' she pronounced.

'I'm sure it's a temporary reprieve. She's probably just *behind* something at the moment. Like that van way over there.'

'Maybe she got into a car.'

'That's possible.'

Em gave her eyebrows a playful wiggle. 'She sounded *very* fond of air conditioning.'

They made their way carefully through another lane of halted traffic, then scanned the area again for Mary.

'Maybe she *did* get in a car,' Clint said.

'You don't suppose something happened to her . . . ?'

'Like what?'

Em bounced one of her slim shoulders. 'She might've gotten grabbed, I suppose.'

'Can't imagine who would want to *grab* her.'

'Someone who doesn't know her?'

Clint laughed.

'But really,' Em said, 'I'd hate for anything to happen to her. I mean, even though she is a major pain in the rumpazoid. It'd be my fault, you know?'

'Wouldn't be your fault,' Clint said. 'I'm sure she's fine, though. She's probably just taking a long way around. We can wait for her when we get to the other side.'

He led the way. A couple of minutes later, they hurried across the last lane and stepped up onto the curb. 'Made it,' Clint said.

Em pursed her lips and blew out a breath. 'Glad that's over with.'

'And no more major intersections to worry about until we get to Sunset Boulevard.'

'Which isn't till the other side of the hills, right?'

'Right.'

'By then, maybe they'll have the traffic lights working.'

'You never know.'

'What about Mary?' Em asked.

They both scanned the lanes of stopped traffic. No sign of her.

'I don't know,' Clint said.

'Do you think we should go back and look for her?'

'*No.*'

'Are you sure?'

'I'm sure.'

'What if something happened to her?'

'Nothing did. If she'd gotten nailed between a couple of cars, we would've heard the commotion. And I really doubt that she was grabbed in the middle of Ventura Boulevard on a day like this by a psychopath or serial killer or anything like that. Too many witnesses. Nowhere to go. My guess is, she made a big detour looking for better openings in the traffic, and she'll be showing up in a minute or two.'

'You think so?'

'Sure.'

'Maybe we oughta wait around for her,' Em said.

Clint smiled. 'This is our big chance to lose her.'

'I know, but then I'd have to go around feeling guilty about it.'

'Okay. We can wait for a while. Let's see what's going on over here.'

The entrance to Laurel Canyon Boulevard on this side of Ventura was blocked by two police cars and a cordon of bright yellow plastic that stretched across the entire road. The streamer was printed with black lettering that read, 'POLICE LINE – DO NOT CROSS.'

Clint stepped off the curb and walked behind it toward the patrol cars.

Two uniformed officers leaned against the side of one of the cars. A man and a woman, both with very young faces and short dark hair, both with their arms folded across their chests, both keeping their eyes on Ventura as they talked and smiled and nodded.

When Clint and Em approached them, they turned their heads.

'Can we help you?' asked the female. According to the silver tag on her chest, her name was Baker. She had a friendly, calm smile.

'How come you aren't out there directing traffic?' Em asked.

Clint gave her a dirty look.

'Not much point, is there?' Officer Baker said. 'Where would we direct it *to?*'

'We're just keeping an eye on the situation,' the man explained. Murphy was engraved on his nameplate. 'Making sure nothing gets out of hand. And keeping traffic off Laurel.'

'What's the problem with Laurel?' Clint asked.

'You can't get through,' Murphy said. 'This side of Mulholland, the pavement's buckled in several places. Down on the other side, they've got slides.'

'A real mess,' Baker said. 'We spent half the morning trying to clear out the vehicles that got stuck between here and the top. Were you hoping to get through?'

'I live in West L.A.,' Clint explained. 'I've got to get home. My wife and kid . . .'

'Who's this?' Murphy asked, nodding at Em.

'I'm his other kid.'

'Would there be a problem with *walking* over the top?' Clint asked.

'It'd be a tough hike,' Murphy said.

139

'We wouldn't stop you, though,' Baker explained. 'We just don't want cars trying to go up.'

'How is it on the other side?'

'A couple of slides,' Baker said.

'Probably nothing you wouldn't be able to climb over or walk around,' Murphy added.

'I guess we'll give it a try. Is it true that West L.A. got hit pretty hard?'

Baker shook her head. 'Not that much worse than over here.'

Murphy nodded. 'Moderately worse.'

'It's pretty bad everywhere,' Baker said.

'Pretty bad,' her partner agreed. 'But not catastrophic. I mean, this isn't India.'

'Or Afghanistan.'

'Or Mexico City.'

'This is L.A.,' Baker said.

'We're ready for this sort of emergency.'

'That's right.'

'I'd be surprised,' Murphy said, 'if we have more than a few hundred dead.'

'Four or five hundred.'

'If that.'

'It'd probably be a hundred thousand, any place but L.A.'

'Well, California in general.'

'Right,' Baker said. 'I was speaking in terms of a quake of this magnitude happening in an undeveloped place.'

'India, for instance.'

'Afghanistan . . .'

'Major loss of life.'

Baker frowned as she nodded. 'Not that four or five hundred is anything to sneeze at.'

Em nudged Clint. She glanced past him. Turning his head to the left, he saw Mary step onto the curb half a block to the east.

'. . . makes you appreciate the building codes.'

'I'd sure rather be here than . . .'

'We'd better be on our way,' Clint interrupted the officers. 'Thanks for the help.'

Baker met his eyes. 'Hope everything turns out well for you, sir.'

'Thank you.'

'You, too,' she told Em.

'Thanks.'

'It'll be a tough hike,' Murphy pointed out, 'so take a break now and then. Don't over-exert yourselves.'

Mary, on the sidewalk now, noticed them and quickened her pace.

'Thanks again,' Clint said. 'So long, now.'

They turned away from the police officers, walked around the rear of the patrol car, and began to stride quickly up the empty middle of Laurel Canyon Boulevard.

'This is slick,' Em said.

'What?'

'No traffic. We've got the whole road to ourselves.' They both looked back in time to see Mary arrive at the corner. Murphy glanced at her. She ignored him, and started to walk up Laurel.

She looked angry. She didn't wave.

'Do you want to wait for her to catch up?' Clint asked.

'Not particularly.'

'Good,' Clint said.

Grinning, Em waved at her.

Mary scowled.

'She must be too tired,' Clint said, 'to give us the finger.'

# EIGHTEEN

'This is it, here,' Stanley said, leading Ben toward a house across the street and partway down the block from his own home. It was half-collapsed, as if one side of it had been stomped down by a monster.

He hoped nobody was inside.

He had thought about taking Ben into his own place. It was deserted except for Mother, so they would have plenty of privacy. But why litter up the place with another body? If he killed Ben there, he would have to dispose of the corpse; it would be idiotic to put himself to so much effort when the neighborhood had plenty of other houses to choose from.

He had also considered taking Ben into Judy's, but he planned to keep on using her house. Why mess it up and have Ben's remains lying around? If all went well, he might be staying there for several days. Ben would start to stink the place up.

No, he would have to take his chances with the house of a stranger.

'You sure this is the place?' Ben asked as they crossed the front lawn.

'Yeah, this is it.'

'But you said the kid's stuck under the chimney.'

'Huh?'

Ben pointed.

Stanley saw the chimney jutting above the section of the house that still stood. 'Oh,' he said. 'That's the part that didn't fall.'

'Huh?'

'You'll see. Come on.'

The front door was shut – probably locked. But most of the house at the other end of the porch had collapsed. 'This way,' Stanley said, heading for the wrecked area. 'Here's where I got in, last time.'

With Ben close behind him, he waded through the rubble. He made his way toward the section of the house that still stood. One of the interior walls had a doorway through which Stanley could see a shadowy carpet, a chair and a corner of a table.

'This is it,' he said. He leaned into the doorway. A dining room. Off to one side, he could see through an archway to the living room.

Both rooms looked as if they'd been kicked apart by a tribe of lunatics.

But the ceilings and walls appeared to be intact, and curtains hid whatever damage had been done to the windows.

From where he stood, Stanley couldn't see the living room fireplace.

'Hello!' he called into the gloom.

No answer came.

'Hello! Little girl? I'm back! I went and got some help, just like I said I would.'

Still, no answer.

Either the house was deserted, or its occupant was in no condition to speak.

Stanley looked over his shoulder. 'Hope she's still okay.'

'Let's get this over with,' Ben said, and tossed his head to fling some stray hair away from his face. 'I wanta get back to Sheila.'

'Here we go.' Stanley stepped through the doorway. The floor creaked under his weight, but it felt firm. Holding the saw by the side of his right leg, he walked slowly around the end of the dining room table. As he approached the archway, the fireplace came into view.

It looked as if it hadn't been damaged at all.

*When Ben sees this . . .*

Stanley stepped through the archway.

Nobody else in the room. No way to see in from outside.

*Perfecto!*

'Oh, my God!' he blurted. 'Ben! Ben!'

'What . . . ?'

Quick footfalls behind him.

He whirled around, bringing the saw up from his side, flipping it over to put the teeth forward and chopping it at Ben's neck in a clumsy, underhand swing. Ben yelped and flung up his arm to block the blow. He cried out as the teeth bit into him, then squealed as Stanley tugged the weapon, dragging its tiny steel teeth across the skin of his forearm.

'You nuts?' Ben yelled. He stumbled into the living room, clutching his wound and backing away.

'Nuts? Me?' Stanley raised the saw overhead. He walked toward Ben.

'Don't. Hey. Come on. Look. You don't gotta hurt me. Okay? What do you want? Just tell me. Okay? Whatever you want.' He kept backing away.

'If you go for the door,' Stanley said, 'I'll have to kill you.'

Ben stopped moving. 'Okay. I won't. I won't do anything, okay? What do you want me to do? There isn't any kid, right? Nobody's trapped. It was just to get me here, right?'

'Right.'

'Okay. Fine.' Letting go of his bloody arm, he reached back with his left hand and pulled a billfold out of the rear pocket of his jeans. 'This what you want? You can have it. I got almost fifty bucks in here.' He held it toward Stanley.

'Don't want it.'

'What *do* you want?'

'Make me an offer.' As he said that, he saw Ben's gaze slide down past his waist.

'Oh,' Ben said. 'I get it.'

'Get what?'

Ben smirked. 'Had me fooled. I figured it was Sheila you had the hots for.' He tucked the wallet back into his pocket. 'This is okay, Stan. This is cool. Shoulda just asked, though, if you know what I mean. You didn't have to go nuts and cut me.'

'What're you talking about?'

'Can we bandage my arm first?'

Stanley shook his head.

'I'm bleeding all over the place.'

'So what?'

'*Okay.* Okay. First things first, huh?' With an odd, slanted smile, Ben walked slowly closer.

Stanley stood motionless, the saw still raised. His heart was pounding and he had a hard time filling his lungs. 'What do you . . . ?'

His voice died as Ben knelt in front of him.

Ben popped open a snap. The loose remains of Stanley's pajama pants clung to him with sweat, but only for a moment. Ben plucked them down.

'Oooo, look at you. You're a big boy, aren't you?'

Even without looking, he could feel that Ben was right. He lowered his gaze.

Can't be, he thought. No way. Must be some other reason. Not because of *him*.

But he squirmed with the feel of Ben's sliding fingers.

'Hey,' he said. 'Stop it.'

'You don't want me to stop.'

'Yeah. I do. I don't go for this kind of stuff.'

'Who're you trying to kid? Look at you. You're aching for it.' Head back, eyes tilted upward and staring directly into his eyes, Ben reached up behind Stanley and squeezed his buttocks. Kneaded them with slick, bloody hands and leaned forward.

His lips felt like a soft, moist O.

The pliant ring slipped forward and Stanley felt himself being sucked deep into Ben's mouth.

This is sick, he thought. This is perverted. The little rat's a fag and . . .

Gotta stop him . . .

Gotta . . .

But it feels so . . .

Judy's mouth had been a dry, unwilling hole doing what it had to do. Nothing like this.

*But he's a guy! Can't let a guy do it to me! I'm not a fucking fairy!*

'Stop it!' Stanley gasped.

Ben didn't stop.

*I don't want him to stop.*

*Not yet.*

*Not till . . .*

'No!' Stanley blurted.

He raced the toothed edge of the saw across the top of Ben's skull. Ben's mouth flew open. Stanley pulled out of it and kneed him under the chin. Ben fell backward and slammed against the floor, clutching his head with both hands. His face was twisted with pain. He cried out, 'Are you *insane*? Why'd you *do* that? My God! My God!'

'Shut up.'

'You wanted it! You *loved* it! Look what you've *done* to me!'

'Yeah. And just look what I'm doing to you now.' He scurried around to Ben's side and slashed down with the saw.

'No!'

Ben blocked it, but the blade ripped his hands. Squealing, he flung himself over. He tried to scurry away on hands and knees, but Stanley drove a foot down on his back, stomping him flat. As he pushed himself up, Stanley sat on him.

'No!' Ben shrieked. 'Get off me!'

Stanley grabbed the long, bloody hair with one hand and swatted Ben's rump with the flat of the saw. 'Giddy-up!'

Ben crawled. Stanley rode him, liking the slippery feel of the back underneath him.

Shouldn't be liking it, he told himself. Shouldn't be liking any of this.

*But he looks like a woman. From up here. He's almost like one.*

Yeah, but he isn't one. He's a guy.

*You wouldn't know it from up here. The hair. The skin. You can't see she hasn't got any tits under there.*

Not *she*!

He!

Trying to make a fag out of me!

Stanley jerked Ben's head back by the hair and sawed into the side of his neck. Blood flew.

The scream made his ears hurt.

Ben tried to buck him off.

Stanley planted his feet on the floor and clamped Ben tight between his thighs and hung on to the long hair and sawed and sawed.

Soon, Ben stopped struggling.
Stanley kept on sawing.

# NINETEEN

They walked slowly down the alley. Barbara knew that, if she turned around, she would still be able to see the fallen mess of Mrs Klein's garage.

She didn't look.

She wished they had never stopped to help the woman.

If they hadn't stopped, they would be a lot closer to home by now. And maybe Mrs Klein would still be alive.

*Maybe we killed her by helping her.*

It seemed like a crazy idea, but it made sense to Barbara. After all, they were the ones who had cleared away the really heavy debris. If Mrs Klein hadn't been able to make it through to her car window . . .

We can't exactly call it our fault, she told herself. We didn't rip her up, the cat did.

Barbara was a few strides ahead of Pete and Heather, so she turned around.

She couldn't stop herself from gazing past them.

The tumbled garage wasn't in sight, after all. Thank goodness for that, she thought.

Walking backward, she said, 'My dad claims an earthquake never killed anyone – it's the stuff that falls on your head.'

Pete smiled. 'Cool.'

'Stupid,' Heather said.

'I'll have to tell him quakes can also kill you with cats.'

'Man,' Pete said. 'Do you believe that? I've never heard of anything that crazy.'

'I have,' Heather said. 'I've heard of worse stuff.'

Of course you have, Barbara thought.

'I've heard about people getting *eaten* by their pet cats,' Heather explained. 'At least Susie didn't *eat* her.'

'I'm not so sure of that,' Barbara said.

'You didn't really look at her.'

'I looked at her plenty. I saw her better than you did. You didn't have to carry her around like me and Pete.'

'You didn't *have* to,' Heather said.

'Not if you'd helped, maybe.'

'It was your idea.'

'You still could've helped,' Barbara said.

'We should've just left her in the alley.'

'That would have been a lousy thing to do.'

'Yeah,' Pete said. 'I mean, I wasn't overjoyed about touching her, exactly, but Jeez . . . How can you just leave her there? If I got myself killed in some lousy alley, I think it'd be pretty nice if somebody'd take me back into my house.'

'Not me,' Heather said.

Pete looked as if he didn't believe her. 'Don't tell me you wouldn't rather have someone carry you inside and put you on a nice sofa in your own house so you don't have to lay out there in the sun and . . .'

'You think she *knows* she's on a nice sofa in her own house? Or that you two busted your humps hauling her in? You just wasted your energy, that's all. Dead's dead. Doesn't matter where you end up.'

'You'd like to get left in an alley?' Barbara asked.

'Sure, why not?'

'A car might come along and run over you,' Pete pointed out.

Heather shrugged.

'A cat might eat your face,' Barbara said.

'So?'

'A wino might come stumbling along,' Barbara added, 'and throw up on you.'

'Big deal.'

'Or rape you.'

'Sick,' Pete said. He wrinkled his nose at Barbara. 'That's really sick, Barbara.'

'It could happen,' she said. 'I've read about people who do stuff like that. Serial killers do it all the time.'

'Yeah, but . . .'

'So what if some wino came along and raped me?' Heather said. 'That'd be his problem, know what I mean? I'd be dead, so how's it supposed to matter to me? I'd sure rather get raped when I'm dead than when I'm alive. It's no picnic, getting raped. I'd rather be dead if it's gonna happen again.'

*Oh, Jeez. She's been raped.*

Big surprise, Barbara thought. Is there anything horrible that *hasn't* happened to Heather?

Pete looked shocked and embarrassed. 'You mean . . . somebody raped you?'

'Oh, do tell us all about it,' Barbara said.

Heather gaped at her. 'You think it's funny?'

'I didn't say that.'

'You oughta try getting raped and see how you like it.'

'Thanks, anyway.' As she said that, she saw how Pete was looking at her. 'Oh, give me a break. She's *dying* to tell us in great gory detail all about it, and I'm a little tired of hearing about Heather's endless stream of weird tragedies. My God, she makes Anne Frank sound like a lucky kid.'

'Who?' Heather asked.

'Look!' Pete blurted, pointing behind Barbara.

Barbara whirled around.

Out from behind a garbage bin strolled a husky cat. It stopped and stared at them. Its up-curled tail was golden brown with a white tip. Its eyes were amber. Its nose and muzzle must've been licked clean; the rest of the cat looked as if it had been dipped in a vat of blood. The fur was matted flat, clumpy, dripping.

'It's Susie,' Heather whispered.

Barbara stomped her foot down hard against the alley pavement.

The cat didn't so much as flinch.

'Don't scare it away,' Heather said.

Barbara looked back at her. 'What do you want to do, adopt the thing?'

'I don't wanta have it around *me*,' Pete said.

'Let's just keep going,' Barbara suggested. 'Maybe it'll mind its own business and go off on its own. Just don't do anything to entice it, Heather.'

As she walked forward, the cat turned away and began sauntering up the middle of the alley. It glanced back. Its jaw worked and it made a noise that sounded like '*Raw.*'

Barbara stomped her foot again.

The cat continued to stroll up the alley, staying a small distance in front of her.

'Great,' Pete muttered.

'The cat's meow,' Barbara said, and slowed her pace until Pete and Heather caught up to her. 'Think I'll just stick with you guys,' she said.

'She's probably just lonely,' Heather said.

'Me or the cat?' Barbara asked.

'Susie.'

The cat looked back again.

'Great,' Barbara said. 'Try not to say her name, okay? The thing's a psycho.'

They walked in silence, their eyes on the cat. It stopped looking back. Once in a while, its tail twitched. It crossed a deserted street and entered an alley on the other side.

'Maybe it'll keep going,' Pete said. He nodded to his left. 'Let's try *that* way.'

149

They turned and started up the sidewalk, but only took a few strides before Pete suddenly stopped.

Near the end of the block, four young men were coming out of a house, yelling and laughing, their arms loaded. One seemed to be carrying a television. Another had an electric guitar.

Before Barbara saw what the others were taking, Pete said, 'Uh-oh.'

'Let's get out of here,' Barbara whispered. Whirling around, she found the cat staring up at her. She feigned a kick at it, then broke into a run.

Susie scampered ahead of them as they raced into the alley.

They sprinted past a hedge, past garbage bins and car ports and backyard fences. Pete kept looking over his shoulder as he ran. Soon, he slowed to a jog. 'I don't think they're coming,' he gasped.

Heather staggered to a halt. She bent over and clutched her knees and panted for air.

Barbara walked in slow circles, hands on hips, head back as she tried to catch her breath. She was dripping wet. 'We'd better . . . stick to the alleys.'

'Yeah,' Pete said. 'Yeah. Jeez.' He picked up the front of his shirt and wiped his face with it. 'Those guys . . . they had to be looting . . . don't you think?'

'Sure looked like it.'

'Man.'

Heather, still bent over and huffing, raised her sweaty red face. 'What if they . . . come?'

'They won't,' Pete said.

'But if . . .'

'They'd be here by now,' Barbara said. 'Probably. Anyway, they . . . had their hands full.'

'We oughta hide.'

Barbara shook her head. Sprinkles of sweat flew off her hair. 'We'll never get home if we . . . hide. Gotta keep . . .'

'We won't get home . . . if we get jumped by . . . guys like them.'

'Over here,' Pete said. He pointed, and walked toward a recessed parking area at the rear of an apartment building. Except for a few minor cracks in the stucco walls, the overhanging structure looked as if it hadn't been touched by the earthquake.

There were stalls for six vehicles.

Four were empty.

A pickup and a station wagon were parked side by side. Pete entered the narrow space between them. Barbara hurried after him, and Heather followed her. 'We'll just rest here for a minute or two,' Pete said.

They sat down. The concrete floor felt slightly cool. Barbara started to lean back, but the pickup's front tire was behind her. She was filthy enough already. Besides, how comfortable could a tire be? She crossed her legs, leaned forward, and propped her elbows on her knees.

The top of her blouse was wide open, thanks to the ruined buttonholes. Her chest looked dark and shiny. Her white bra had gotten smudged with dirt. The moisture from her sweat made the cups a little transparent. She could see the color of her skin through them, but her blouse wasn't open quite far enough to let her nipples show.

Pete had probably seen plenty.

Nothing I can do about it, she told herself. Not unless I wear my blouse backwards, and that'd look pretty stupid.

Pete hadn't exactly seemed to be overwhelmed by the view, anyway. Why should he be? Next to Heather, I've got nothing to look at. A couple of humps. I've got mounds and she's got mountains. And maybe Pete's got a few things on his mind that don't include what's on my chest *or* Heather's. We'll be lucky if we make it home, and maybe home won't even *be* there anymore. If his mind is on boobs, he must be nuts.

Though *my* mind is on boobs.

She laughed softly.

'What?' Pete asked.

'Nothing.' There was no point in trying to fasten the buttons; they would only pop open again. Besides, she rather liked how she looked and felt with the blouse open this way. 'The shade's nice,' she whispered.

'If somebody comes,' Pete said, 'we'll sneak around in front of the pickup.'

'I just don't want to stay here long. We'll never get home if we keep stopping.'

'Should've thought of that,' Heather said, 'before you wasted all that time with what's-her-face.'

'Mrs Klein,' Pete said.

'Yeah. Her.'

'Let's not start in on her again,' Barbara said. 'Anyway, I was all set to leave as soon as we got her into the house. *You're* the one who made us sit around and drink her Pepsis.'

'Like the both of you weren't dying.'

'She was sure heavy,' Pete said. 'Jeez, that was awful.'

'I'm glad we did it, though,' Barbara said.

'Yeah. Me, too. I guess. Gross, though.'

'Well,' Heather said, 'I figure you wasted maybe an hour, and all because you wouldn't let her stay in the alley.'

'I don't think it was that long,' Barbara said. Then she wondered if Heather was wearing a watch. She didn't think so, but she wasn't sure.

She twisted around for a look.

But forgot all about wristwatches when she saw Heather leaning back against the pickup truck, legs stretched out straight, smiling at the cat by her right side as she stroked it with a gory hand.

'Aw! Jesus H. Christ!'

'What?' Pete asked.

'Look at her!' Barbara dropped back against the tire as Pete leaned forward. He gazed past her.

'Heather!'

The girl raised her eyebrows and continued to pet the cat. 'She's a nice kitty.'

'Have you lost your mind?' Pete blurted.

Barbara scrambled to her feet. 'I'm getting out of here.'

'Yeah,' Pete said. 'God almighty, Heather.'

Barbara leaped over the girl's legs and hurried toward the alley.

'You two sure freak out easy,' Heather said. She sounded amused.

Clear of the car port, Barbara felt the sun pound down on her. She squinted, and looked both ways. Nobody seemed to be coming. Except for Pete. He hurried forward, hunching down slightly when he left the shade.

In the car port, Heather was already standing. 'If you think I'm gonna *stay* here . . .'

'We just don't want that cat around us,' Pete said.

'It's a psycho,' Barbara repeated. 'It *killed* Mrs Klein.'

'That doesn't mean she's a bad kitty.' Heather came out of the shadowy car port, the cat swaggering along beside her. 'She felt trapped, that's all. She was only trying to survive. You can't go blaming her for that.'

'Just keep it away from us,' Pete said.

He and Barbara started walking, but they continued to look back. Heather and Susie were gaining on them.

'Just stay back there,' Barbara said.

'I don't wanta.'

'What *do* you want?'

'The front.'

'Okay, take the front.'

As Heather and the cat approached, Barbara took Pete by the arm and guided him toward the other side of the alley.

'It'd be funny if it weren't so sad,' Heather commented. 'Scared of a nice little kitty.'

Barbara wrinkled her nose when she saw all the blood on Heather. Not only was the girl's hand a mess, but the cat must've put a lot of effort into rubbing itself against her. She had blood on the side of her white sock and on her calf. The tan fabric of her baggy dress was smeared with blood on the right side from her thigh almost to her armpit.

'Look what it did to you,' Barbara said.

152

Heather looked, and shrugged. 'I'm not any dirtier than you.'

'Yes, you are. And I don't have *blood* all over me.'

'You oughta wash that off,' Pete said as Heather walked by.

'Doesn't matter. My dress is ruined, anyhow.'

'Maybe, but you don't want it on your hands all day.' He looked at Barbara. 'We need to find someplace where she can wash up.'

'Won't be easy,' Barbara said.

They'd both gotten blood on their hands carrying Mrs Klein into her house. Barbara had been frantic to get it off. It made her feel contaminated by the woman's death. She hated the rusty brown color and the tacky feel of the stuff.

She had hurried to the kitchen sink and twisted a faucet handle, forgetting that the quake had knocked out the water pressure – her memory returning when the faucet was silent and nothing came out. 'What're we gonna do?' she'd gasped. 'I've gotta get this off me!'

Pete had remained calm. 'Don't worry. We'll think of something.'

After a discussion that included searching for pre-moistened towelettes (good luck finding any), using Pepsi (sticky) or water from the toilet tank (gross), they'd pounced on Pete's idea of dipping paper towels into water from melting ice in the freezer compartment of the refrigerator. It had worked great.

Now, Pete came up with a fresh idea. 'Maybe we can find a garden hose that still has some water in it.'

'Can't get much out of a hose,' Barbara said. 'Besides, she'll just get bloody again messing with the cat.'

Heather suddenly looked pleased. 'Let's wash Susie. I bet we can find a swimming pool or something around here.'

Pete frowned, apparently thinking about it. 'Yeah,' he said after a few moments. 'You never know. This is sort of a lousy neighborhood, but if we start looking in back yards . . .'

'Courtyards of apartment houses have swimming pools,' Barbara pointed out. 'A lot of them do. Maybe even some around here. Couldn't hurt to keep our eyes open. One thing though.' She looked from Pete to Heather. 'If we do find a pool, I wanta have a crack at it before it gets screwed up with blood and cats. Okay?'

Pete smiled. 'Yeah. Me, too.'

'Let's find us a pool,' Barbara said.

# TWENTY

Stanley opened a curtain to let in more sunlight. Seeing nobody on the other side of the window, he gazed down at himself.

He looked as if he'd been wallowing in blood.

'Beautiful,' he murmured.

He rubbed his hands over his body. He liked where the blood felt slippery, but didn't care much for the sticky places where it was drying. He wished he could mix it with oil, so it would stay slippery everywhere.

A large mirror above the fireplace had survived the quake. He stepped close to it. His reflection was large, but the bottom of the mirror cut him off halfway down his chest. So he went to the far side of the room. From there, the mirror showed him only to the waist. So he stood on the sofa.

Able to see himself all the way down to his knees, he was stunned by how large and powerful and *savage* he looked. Like some sort of jungle warrior naked and wild, washed in the blood of his enemies. The blood on his face was mostly around his lips and down his chin.

'Anyone might think I'd *eaten* him,' he said.

He laughed, but the grin made him look stupid, so he made a fierce face. Much better. He growled. He sucked in his belly and flexed his muscles.

'Oh, yeah,' he murmured.

It's me, he thought. This is how I oughta look *all* the time. Except work out better and build up some muscles. And let my hair grow. I can do that. Nobody to tell me no, anymore. Nobody to make fun of me. This *is* me. Naked and wild and covered with blood.

The blood made him a little itchy, but he could live with that. A minor nuisance. Like putting up with the itch of a wool shirt because the shirt makes you look like a lumberjack.

He stood on the sofa for a while longer, posing and watching himself in the mirror.

He wished he could go outside like this.

That'd be stupid, though. Hugely stupid.

Even if he was lucky enough to avoid meeting any strangers, he didn't want Sheila to see him drenched with blood. She might guess that it wasn't his.

He jumped down from the sofa.

Wandering through the rooms that hadn't been destroyed, he looked for water. He found no water, and no other liquid except for the blood on the carpet around Ben.

He had an urge to lie down there and squirm around.

'Gotta get back to Sheila,' he told himself. 'Had enough fun here.'

Instead of squirming in the blood, he sprawled on the sofa. He rolled and writhed, rubbing himself against the nubby upholstery. He left a great amount of blood on the sofa. After climbing off, he wiped himself with both of the sofa's pillows. The pillows worked especially well on his neck and armpits, his groin and the crease of his rump.

By the time he finished with the pillows, he was no longer wet. But he looked as if his skin had been stained with reddish-brown shoe polish. He felt sticky and itchy all over.

He looked at himself in the mirror and shook his head.

'Gotta do better than this,' he said.

He *had* to find water.

A swimming pool!

He knew just where to find one.

He'd seen it from the roof of Mother's house – *his* house.

Amazing what you could see from up there. Though the house was only a single story high, it seemed to tower above the neighborhood when he stood on it.

It's the standing that does it, he had figured out. Puts my eyes about six feet higher up than everything else.

He'd gone up there often. Not often enough, though. And he'd never dared to stay for very long. The problem was, his perch atop the roof not only gave him a great view of the neighborhood, but it gave the neighbors a great view of him. The nearly flat plain of the roof, surrounded by knee-high walls, provided nowhere to hide unless he lay down. Not only that, but there were often helicopters in the sky. He didn't dare take binoculars up with him. Nor did he dare to spend much time looking down at the surrounding houses.

No privacy at all, up there.

He'd gone up, anyway, for a few minutes at a time – usually taking a bucket of asphalt 'roof patch' with him so he would appear to have a legitimate excuse. On those occasions, he'd relished the view: his mother's back yard; beyond the cinder-block wall to Sheila's yard and patio and back door and windows; the rear grounds of the houses to the right and left of Sheila's place; the back yard of the Taylor house, his first neighbor to the north; the Donaldsons' on the far side of the Taylors; Judy and Herb's house directly to the south, and the Benson place on the other side of Judy's.

It was the Benson place that had the pool.

Behind their small stucco house, with a redwood gate across the driveway and fencing around the borders of the back yard, the pool was like a guarded secret. Stanley supposed he would never have known of its existence at all, if he hadn't spotted it from his roof.

He had never seen anyone in the pool, or even sunbathing on the padded loungers beside it.

Not that he'd spent much time looking. Whenever he was on the roof, he occupied most of his time keeping an eye on Sheila's house. Hoping for a glimpse of her. Or a glimpse of Barbara. Though the girl was no match for her mother, she was still a great-looking piece, well worth watching. The best on the block, after Sheila. With Judy running in third place.

The Bensons had never interested him until now. He did know that they were a middle-aged couple and they rarely seemed to be home. Judy had once mentioned that they were school teachers. Stanley doubted if he could recognize either one of them, though he knew that he'd seen Mrs Benson and had judged she was nothing worth looking at.

He also knew that they had a fine-looking swimming pool in their back yard.

They're bound to be gone, he thought. Barbara's at school. That's what Sheila'd said. So if these Bensons are teachers, they'll be at school, too.

Probably.

'Doesn't matter,' he said.

He put on his cut-off pajama pants again. As he snapped the waistband shut, he saw that the front was spotted with blood. Not a lot of blood, though. He had enough scratches and minor cuts on his body to explain it away.

He thought about leaving his fly open.

That'd be stupid, he decided. You don't wanta look *too* conspicuous.

So he tucked himself inside the fly and fastened a snap in the middle. Then he stepped into his moccasins. He took his saw to a window and used a curtain to wipe the blood off its handle and blade.

That it? he wondered.

Think so.

Lifting the saw to his brow, he offered a salute to the dismembered corpse on the floor.

'So long, Ben – it's been good to know you. Been a treat. Been a hoot.' He laughed and went to the front door of the house. Opening it a crack, he peered out.

He saw no one, so he stepped outside. On his way across the yard, he looked all around. He saw a few people here and there, milling about in the distance. They were too far away to matter – so far away that they hardly seemed to exist, at all.

He heard distant noises, too: sirens and alarms, bangs, engine noises of cars and trucks and airplanes and helicopters, even a tinny voice amplified by a loudspeaker. But all these noises were far away, and the neighborhood itself seemed oddly quiet.

A ghost town, he thought. *My* ghost town. All mine.

From the curb, he looked across the street and down the block. Past the Taylor house, past his own house, past Judy's . . .

He wondered how Judy was doing.

Should he pay her a visit?

No no no. A waste of time. She's right in the tub where I left her. It'd take Houdini to get loose, the way I had her tied to that chair and the faucets.

As he started to cross the street, he gazed at Judy's house. He remembered the look and feel of her.

It'd only take a minute to drop in and check on her, he thought. Make sure she isn't getting loose.

He laughed softly.

It'd take a *lot* more than a minute.

First, he would have to untwist the hanger and free her hands and take the chair off her. Then for the fun. But he wouldn't want to kill her, so he'd have to make her secure again after he got finished. Re-do the bit with the chair and hanger. Only *then* would he be able to go next door to the Benson's pool.

He wanted to do it.

He couldn't stop thinking about it.

He got stiff, thinking about it. He was stiff when he walked past his own house. He looked at the broken picture window and imagined Mother sprawled on the floor of the living room.

*If she could see me now!*

*'Just what do you think you're doing, young man? Have you lost your senses? Get inside this minute and put on some clothes! What's got into you? You look like some sort of a pervert, galavanting around that way. You're positively indecent!'*

By the time he had left his house behind, he was laughing regularly, and no longer aroused. He decided not to bother with a visit to Judy.

'She'll keep,' he said as he walked past her house.

Anyway, he'd already had her. She'd been terrific, but it would be a shame to use himself up on a third-rate gal like Judy when he had a Sheila waiting for him.

What'll I tell Sheila about Ben? he wondered. Better come up with a good one. Maybe tell her they rescued the kid just fine, but she couldn't be moved, so Ben volunteered to stay with her.

157

Hell, he thought, I can tell her *anything*. Doesn't really matter. She's in no position to cause trouble. The worst she can do, stuck down there, is start yelling. If she tries that, I'll shut her up quick.

He pictured himself leaping down onto her.

*What'll I do to her?*

What a question.

*What won't I do to her?*

The real question is, where to start?

Start by making her shut up.

Stanley had to stop thinking about it, however, when he found himself in front of the Benson place.

It reminded him of house facades he'd seen during tram rides through the back lot of Universal Studios. The house's front still stood. It looked just fine except for the shattered picture window. He could see sky through the window.

Behind the front wall, the house was down.

'Perfect,' he said.

If the Bensons weren't away from home, they were no doubt underneath it.

Their driveway was empty, though. More than likely, the couple had driven off to work this morning and were marooned at a distant school or two.

Stanley crossed the front lawn to the driveway. The redwood gate at the far side of the house was padlocked shut, but the stucco wall to its right had been knocked down. Stanley detoured around the gate, climbing over broken stucco and lathe and plaster, then jumping to the pavement and continuing up the driveway.

As he walked toward the back, he scanned the ruin of the house. The roof had caved in completely, taking down most of the interior walls and crushing whatever else might have been inside the house. The front wall, of course, still stood. So did most of the northern exterior wall.

It had gotten off better than Sheila's place, but not by much.

He saw nobody.

He thought about calling out, but decided against it.

*If there are dead Bensons in the vicinity, they aren't likely to hear me.*

*If a Benson is trapped, who cares? Not me.*

Besides, someone might hear a shout and come to investigate.

I sure don't need that, he thought. All I want is a couple of minutes to wash off in the pool. Get myself all spiffy clean for my sweet Sheila.

Behind the wreck of the house, he spotted the pool. He halted, shocked. Empty! No! Can't be!

He could *feel* the cold water. He *longed* to plunge in and glide through

158

the chill. He *had* to wash the blood off his body. He needed to get clean for Sheila. And the itch was driving him mad!

'No fair,' he muttered, feeling his throat tighten. 'No fair!'

He had counted on the pool. He felt cheated, betrayed.

Everything had been going so well, until now.

Shaking his head, he shambled closer to the pool.

Do people drain the things in June? he wondered. For a spring cleaning, or something? No, that's crazy. This is the time of year when you'd want to be *using* them.

Maybe the Bensons are idiots.

He wished they *were* here, so he could kill them.

There must be other pools somewhere, he told himself.

He didn't know where, though. And he sure couldn't afford the time to go searching for one. Sheila was waiting. He needed to get back to her and cut her free and . . .

Stanley suddenly smiled.

At the shallow end, which was all he'd been able to see at first, the bottom of the pool was dry. But walking closer, he noticed that the blue tile floor sloped downward toward this end, the deep end. Partway down the slope, water glimmered.

He hurried forward and stopped at the edge of the pool.

Below him, the water looked blue and cold.

The Bensons *didn't* drain it, he realized.

And the pool looked undamaged, so the water hadn't leaked out through breaks.

The earthquake, he realized, must've done this – sloshed out tons of water, tidal waves of it – leaving nothing but a few feet of water at the very bottom of the deep end.

He wondered where all the lost water had gone. There was no trace of it, now. During the hours since the quake, the run-off must've spread out, spilled down drains and onto neighboring property, been absorbed by the ground. The concrete apron surrounding the pool had obviously been baked dry by the sun.

Amazing, he thought.

He'd heard of earthquakes throwing water out of swimming pools, but he'd never heard of a pool being *emptied* by one.

It isn't quite empty, he reminded himself. It left enough water for me.

'Saved some for the fishies,' he said.

*My luck hasn't gone bad, after all.*

He couldn't get into the water from here. At this height, jumping into such shallow water would probably break his legs. Even the chrome ladder, over at the corner, didn't reach down far enough to let him enter the water without a risky drop.

So he hurried to the other end of the pool and stepped out of his moccasins. The concrete seared the bottoms of his feet. Quickly, he slipped back into the moccasins. He kept them on as he trotted down three tile stairs and walked on the bottom of the pool toward its deep end.

As the bottom slanted downward, the walls surrounding him seemed to grow. They were higher than his head by the time he stopped at the edge of the water.

He looked around at them.

This is great, he thought. Nobody can see me down here.

Nobody's *here* to see me, but even if people were around, I'd be out of sight. Unless they're right on top of me, looking down, they'd never know I'm here.

'Fantastic,' he muttered.

My own, secret place.

This, he realized, was even better than if the pool had been full to the brim with water.

A lot better!

I could even bring somebody here, he thought. Like Sheila, after I get her loose. We'd be outside, but still have all the privacy we need.

And we'd have water. I could wet her up. I could do stuff to her *in* the water, and that way she'd be all clean and cool and slick.

Holding images of Sheila in his mind, he stepped out of his moccasins and walked into the water.

# TWENTY-ONE

Heather stayed well ahead of Barbara and Pete. The cat pranced along beside her as she hurried through the alley with energy that Barbara had never seen in her. She rushed from side to side, peering over rear fences and gates, running up walkways to search for a swimming pool.

After ten or eleven tries, she bounded back into the alley from the shadows of an apartment complex's parking area and shouted, 'Found one!' Susie darted past her feet. 'Come on! Looks great!' She whirled around and rushed out of sight. The cat swiveled its head to watch her, then looked at Barbara. It blinked a couple of times, twitched its tail, then slowly turned and followed Heather.

'If she goes in that pool before us,' Barbara said, 'I'm not going in.'

'She'd better not,' Pete said.

'She found it.'

Pete made a face. 'If she goes in and gets it bloody, we'll just have to find our own.'

'I'm with you.'

From the rear, the two-story apartment building looked as if it hadn't been damaged by the quake. Barbara didn't even see any cracks in the stucco wall or balconies above the parking area.

There were parking spaces for twelve vehicles. Three were occupied. If this was like most apartment houses, additional spaces could probably be found at the front.

Barbara wondered how many cars might be parked there.

Too bad we can't have the place to ourselves, she thought.

She followed Pete across the parking area and through a narrow passageway to a wrought iron gate. The gate was shut. Pete pulled it open, stepping backward, watching Barbara and nodding for her to go ahead of him.

'Thanks.' She stepped past him and entered the pool area.

Heather was waiting, just off to the side.

With Susie cradled in her arms.

She smiled at Barbara. 'How about *this*?' she asked. Her voice sounded too loud.

'Not bad,' Barbara said, unable to look at anything except Heather

161

and the cat. The bodice of Heather's tan dress was smeared with rust-colored blood. So was the skin of her throat, as if the cat had been nuzzling her with its gory head.

The gate clanked shut, and Pete came to her side. He met her eyes, then looked at Heather. His lips peeled back. 'You're getting it all over you,' he said.

'No big deal. It's only a little blood.'

Mrs Klein's blood, Barbara thought. Blood from a dead woman. A woman killed by the very cat that Heather was hugging to her chest and caressing.

'You'd better hope Susie doesn't decide to rip *your* throat open,' Barbara said.

'Aw, she's a nice kitty.'

'My butt,' Barbara said.

'You'd *better* be careful with that thing,' Pete warned. 'Maybe it just went temporarily insane, or something, but it *did* kill her, and maybe it – you know – wouldn't mind doing something like that again.'

Heather gently kissed the top of Susie's head.

'Oh!' Pete blurted in disgust. 'Man!'

She grinned at him. Her lips now had more color than before.

Barbara grimaced. 'I'm going in the pool.'

'Same here,' Pete said.

She waited by his side.

He faced Heather. 'You'll stay out till we're done, won't you?' he asked.

'Maybe I will, and maybe I won't.'

'Hey. Please?'

'I found it, you know.'

'We know, but . . .'

'What'll you give me?'

'Let's not play stupid games,' Barbara said. 'Come on. Before somebody shows up and kicks us out of here and none of us gets to go in the water.'

'Susie and I *both* need a swim,' Heather explained.

'Just wait till we're out,' Pete told her.

'All right.'

'Thanks. It's not you. It's just that we don't want to be in the blood.'

'But I will require a small favor.'

Barbara considered punching her in the face.

*If I slug her, I'll probably get some of that blood on my fist.*

*And that damn cat'll probably rip my face off.*

'Okay,' Pete said. 'What do you want?'

'One favor.'

'What?'

Heather tilted her head. 'Anything I ask.'

'Let's just get in the pool,' Barbara muttered, turning her scowl toward Pete.

He ignored her. '*What* favor?'

'I haven't decided yet.'

'Oh, I'm supposed to . . .'

'The hell with all this,' Barbara said. She left them where they stood, and walked toward the pool. The surface of the water glimmered with sunlight.

At the edge, she stopped.

She turned slowly, scanning the windows and doors of the apartments surrounding the courtyard. All the doors were shut. The draperies appeared to be drawn behind most of the windows. Through a few windows, however, she could see the dim interiors of rooms.

Everybody can't be gone, she thought. Somebody almost *has* to be home.

Home, and watching us.

Why do they have to be sneaky about it? she wondered.

*Maybe afraid of us. Scared we might be dangerous, or something.*

*What if they're the dangerous ones?*

'Just stay out,' Pete said to Heather.

'I will. But you owe me.'

'Yeah, sure.'

Hearing Pete's footsteps behind her, Barbara slipped her purse strap off her shoulder. She set the purse down by her feet, then started to take off her shoes and socks. The concrete was very hot. After taking off her socks, she stood on them and twisted sideways to watch Pete get ready.

As he unfastened the buttons of his shirt, Barbara said, 'Did you bring your suit?'

He threw her a nervous smile and shook his head. 'Guess I'll just empty my pockets and go in the way I am.'

'Same here.' She nodded at the bandage on his forearm. 'You'd better try to keep that dry.'

'It's not really much of a cut.' He let his shirt fall, then started to take off his shoes.

'Oh!' Heather called, looking over her shoulder as she walked toward the far end of the pool. 'I forgot to tell you about the jacuzzi!'

Barbara saw it now – a low circle of tiles at the pool's corner.

'I wasn't even *gonna* get in *your* pool. Not till I was clean. So, ha! But you still owe me a favor, anyhow, Pete. A deal's a deal.'

'Fine,' Pete muttered. 'We'll see.'

'Watch this!' Heather called.

Still a few strides from the spa, she hurled Susie through the air. The cat cried, '*Rowwwwww!*' as it tumbled. In mid-air, it flipped over. It dropped paws-first into the spa. Water splashed high. Heather clapped her hands and hopped with delight.

An instant later, the cat sprang out of the spa. In a blur of speed, it scampered across the concrete away from Heather, away from the pool, and under the gate at the front entrance to the courtyard.

'Susie!' Heather shouted.

'Quiet down!' Barbara snapped. 'Do you wanta get us kicked out of here?'

'She's running away!'

'What did you expect? You don't throw cats into water like that.'

'Oh.' Heather looked agonized. 'I just wanted to wash the blood off her.' She glanced toward the gate, then turned to Barbara. 'Will she come back?'

'I doubt it.'

'Maybe you'd better go and find her,' Pete suggested. 'If you don't, that's probably the last you'll ever see of Susie.'

'Will you come and help?'

'We'd better not,' Barbara said. 'Cats get spooked awfully easily. If Pete and I come, we'd probably scare it off. You'd have more luck by yourself.'

'You'd better hurry,' Pete added.

Heather started jogging toward the front gate. She looked back. 'You guys won't leave . . .'

'We'll wait right here,' Pete said.

'Promise?'

'Cross my heart.'

'Okay, then.' She reached the gate, opened it, and walked quickly out of sight.

Barbara and Pete looked at each other. They both smiled. Barbara shrugged.

Pete said, 'Well . . .'

'Did you *see* her throw that cat?'

Pete laughed. 'I couldn't believe it.'

'I could. The girl's odd.'

Pete's smile vanished. 'Well . . . yeah. She's had a tough life, though. You know?'

'I know, I know. All she does is talk about it. Like she's *bragging* about it.'

'Yeah. Sort of. I guess she does get annoying but . . . I feel kind of sorry for her.'

'That's what she wants.'

'You think so?'

Barbara shrugged. She wished she hadn't started in on the girl. Now, Pete probably figured that she was heartless. 'I don't know,' she said. 'I've got nothing much against her, I guess. I'm going in.'

With that, she dived into the pool. It didn't look quite as full as it should be, so she didn't dive deep.

The water seemed to hit her everywhere at once, shocking her with its cold. She felt as if every inch of her body had suddenly been clamped by icy pliers. Almost immediately, however, the pain faded. She glided through the water, just beneath the surface, relishing the coldness.

It caressed her. It licked away her heat.

Surfacing, she rolled onto her back. She floated and watched Pete. He still stood above the other end of the pool. He was barefoot and shirtless. His pants looked big and hot. She wondered if he would change his mind and take them off.

No, not Pete.

Even if he was wearing perfectly decent underwear, he didn't seem like the kind of guy who would take his pants off in public, in broad daylight.

Not that I'd *want* him to, Barbara thought.

Not that I'd *mind*, as long as he keeps his underwear on. Might be kind of neat.

Maybe he doesn't even *wear* any underwear.

Of course he does, she told herself. Don't be ridiculous.

'What are you waiting for?' she asked.

He shrugged. 'I don't know.'

Lowering her legs, she found the bottom of the pool. She stood up. The water covered her to the waist.

Pete stood motionless and stared at her.

'Are you gonna take off your pants?' Barbara asked.

He didn't answer. He acted as if he hadn't even heard the question. He simply stood there, mouth hanging open, and continued to stare at Barbara.

She glanced down at herself. Her blouse had come unbuttoned all the way. It was open, showing a lot of tanned, wet skin. And showing too much of her bra. This time, the cup on the right side was exposed. It held her breast like a white, flimsy pouch. It was almost transparent. Her nipple pushed at the clinging fabric like a stiff, dark cone.

*Oh my God!*

Her heart slammed and heat flooded through her. She felt as if her breath had been stolen.

Her hand trembled as she raised it out of the water and fumbled with the right side of her blouse and covered her breast.

It's no big deal, she told herself. It's nothing. So what if he saw . . . ?

'How's the water?' Pete asked. He sounded awfully nervous.

*Sure he's nervous. He's been staring at my boob. And he knows I saw him.*

'The water's fine. Are you coming in?'

'Should I?'

'Yeah. Come on.'

'Okay. Okay, sure.' Bobbing his head, he rubbed his hands together. 'Here I come, ready or not.' He dived off the edge.

Obviously, he was used to easier methods of entering pools. Barbara found herself grinning, but trembling, as he came down flat and smacked the water hard.

'Ouch!' she gasped.

Water from his huge splash rained down.

She stayed where she was, and watched him swim closer. He stopped just out of reach, and stood. The water was halfway up his chest. He blinked and wiped his eyes. 'It's *cold*!' he gasped.

'Yeah. Are you okay? You sure did a belly-whomper.'

He smiled. 'I'm not the greatest diver in the world.'

'You're okay, though?'

'Sure.' He nodded. His gaze darted down from her face, but he looked away fast.

Suddenly very aware that she was standing higher than Pete and in water just to her waist, she squatted down until the water lapped over her shoulders. Letting go of her blouse, she raised her arms away from her sides and moved them slowly to keep herself steady.

Pete went lower, too.

Only his head was above the water, but Barbara could see his neck and shoulders and arms and chest and belly below the surface. The way the water bent the light, his bare skin seemed to wiggle and shimmy.

Barbara supposed that she must look the same, to him.

*Except I'm wearing stuff on top.*

With her arms out, her blouse had probably drifted open. She didn't check to find out.

*What I don't know won't hurt me.*

Pete seemed to be sneaking glances and looking away fast, meeting her eyes for a second, trying to smile, looking all around, finding her eyes again.

'This is pretty neat,' he said after a while.

'It's probably the best place to be. Under the circumstances.'

'A hot day like this,' Pete added.

'Yeah. And safe. There's nothing much that can fall on us here.'

'And if nothing falls on you, you're okay.'

'Unless a cat gets you,' Barbara said.

He laughed softly, glanced down through the water at her, then turned his head away and appeared to study the upper level of the apartment building. 'I wonder where everyone is,' he said.

'It's kind of spooky.'

'Yeah,' Pete said. 'I'm glad, though. That nobody's around. I mean, we're sort of trespassing. We could get kicked out if anybody cared.'

'I know.'

'But where are they all?'

'Who knows?' Barbara said. 'Mostly at work, maybe. But there were cars back by the alley.'

'Yeah. Somebody must be here.'

'Probably spying on us.'

Pete wrinkled his nose. He slowly turned all the way around. His nose was still wrinkled when he faced Barbara again. 'Maybe we oughta get out of here.'

'We have to wait for Heather.'

'Yeah. But . . .'

'We might as well stay in the water till she shows up.'

'I guess so.'

She smiled. 'Scared?'

'Nah.'

'Let 'em spy all they want. As long as they stay in their apartments and don't come out to get us.'

'Oh, real nice.'

She started to scan the apartments, herself. As her gaze moved slowly past doors and windows, she noticed that Pete seemed to be looking straight ahead – at her.

*Now that I'm not watching him . . .*

Let him, she thought. It's fine.

It's nice.

Let him look all he wants.

'I really do wonder where everyone is,' she said, keeping her eyes away from Pete. 'It isn't just here, either. It's all over the place, ever since we got away from the main streets. I mean, it's not that *nobody* is around. But there just don't seem to be as many people as there *should* be. We're in the middle of Los Angeles. There oughta be people everywhere. They can't *all* be at work. Have they gone into hiding, or something? They can't be *dead*. I guess some are. Maybe a couple of hundred? But that's not so many. Even *thousands* wouldn't be enough to account for everyone being *gone* like this. It's sort of like they *vanished*.'

She glanced at Pete.

He was watching her, all right. Staring at her.

At her face, not at the areas below the water line.

She wasn't sure whether she ought to feel pleased or disappointed. And she found that she felt a little bit of both. 'What do you think?' she asked.

'It's sure funny,' he said.

'Maybe the monsters got them.'

His face broke into a smile. 'That's probably it.'

'I wonder where Heather is.'

'Maybe the cat ate her,' Pete said.

And Barbara laughed. 'Oh, that's real nice. A minute ago, you were sticking up for her.'

'Actually, I like it better when she isn't around.'

'Me, too.'

Pete's eyes seemed to be searching her eyes, almost as if trying to get *into* them. 'I really . . .' His voice quit.

'What?'

He shook his head and looked away. 'I don't know. It's . . . I just wanta . . . I mean, it's really awful, all this stuff that's happened. And how we're kind of stuck out here and things are sort of dangerous. And we don't know if our families are okay or anything. But . . . it's just that . . . I'm not glad any of it happened, nothing like that, but . . . I'm sort of glad we got a chance to . . . I've had a chance to, you know, *be* with you like this.'

'Me, too,' Barbara said.

Pete looked stunned. 'Really?'

'Really.'

'Oh, man.'

'Yeah,' Barbara said.

''Cause, what I mean to say . . . I really sort of *like* you, you know?'

'I really sort of like you, too.'

'You do?'

Barbara reached out through the water. Pete's arm swept forward and he took her hand. She gave his hand a gentle pull that brought him toward her, walking up the slope of the pool's floor but staying low and keeping his head level with Barbara's.

A single stride away from her, he stopped.

He had a very strange look on his face. Barbara couldn't tell whether he was terrified or ecstatic.

'Oh, man,' he said, his voice shaky.

Barbara's lips felt dry. She licked them.

'I can't believe this is happening,' Pete said.

'What?'

'This. You. Would it be . . . is it okay if I . . . Do you want to kiss?'

'Yeah.'

Still holding her hand, he put his other hand against the back of her head. His face came closer. It was sprinkled with tiny bright sparkles of water. His eyelashes came together in tiny, dark points. His eyes jumped a little bit from side to side as if he couldn't make up his mind which of her eyes to look at. He licked his lips. And Barbara shut her eyes.

And waited.

And wondered why he wasn't kissing her yet.

This'll be my first, she realized. My first *real* kiss – not Mom or Dad or a relative or a friend of the family or whatever but a *boy*.

*A real boy kissing me.*

And now she felt his mouth against her lips. Moist and cool, then warm, pressing gently as he held the back of her head.

This is it, she thought. This is really it. My first kiss, and I'm almost sixteen and it's Pete in a swimming pool on the day of the big quake. And here I am *thinking* about it instead of just *enjoying* it – but it *is* nice.

Nice because of how it feels, she wondered, or nice because it's Pete?

*Stop thinking!*

He's being very much a gentleman, she thought. Just a nice kiss, no funny stuff.

She wondered if anyone was watching.

From one of the apartments, maybe.

*It's not like we're doing something wrong.*

Our bodies aren't even touching, she realized. Just our mouths and hands, and his other hand back there in my hair.

*It'd be nice to be up against him.*

Just as she thought about moving in closer and maybe hugging him, he took his mouth away.

'Maybe we'd better stop,' he whispered. He lowered his hand from the back of her head. It went silently down toward his side.

'Okay,' Barbara said.

'Man.'

'What?'

'Nothing.'

'Come on, tell.'

'I never . . . that was sure a kiss.'

'In what way?' she asked.

He rolled his eyes. 'I don't know!'

'Was it a good kiss?'

'Are you kidding?'

'Felt pretty good to me,' she said.

'It was incredible,' he whispered. '*You're* incredible. I mean, *God!*'

'We'd better pretend nothing happened.'

'What do you mean?'

'Heather. She'd go nuts if she found out we kissed.'

Pete looked surprised. 'Do you think so?'

'Oh, sure. She's got a thing for you.'

'She does?'

'Of course she does. And you know it.'

'Yeah, I guess so.' Then he added, 'I'm very hard to resist,' and laughed as if he thought it a good joke.

'You are.'

'Right.' He laughed again, and shook his head.

'So anyway, if we don't want to see what Heather's like in a jealous rage, we'd better cool it.'

'I guess that means no more kissing.'

'She'd probably pop up right when we're in the middle of one.'

'Yeah. Like on TV.'

'We'll have to just save it for some other time,' Barbara said.

'Any time is fine with me.'

'I'll bet.'

'So . . . what should we do now?'

'Swim around?'

Pete looked toward the front gate. His smile slipped away. 'I wonder what's taking her so long.'

'She must be having trouble with the cat.'

'It's probably not extremely eager to get caught,' Pete said.

'No kidding. Cats hate water. One sinking was probably enough for it.'

After a moment, Pete said, 'I hope nothing's happened to her. She *has* been gone an awfully long time. I mean, if she couldn't catch the cat, don't you think she'd come back?'

'I don't know. She seems like the stubborn type.'

'Something really might have happened to her, though.'

'Do you think we should go and look for her?' Barbara asked.

'I don't much want to.'

'Me, neither. Besides, we said we'd wait here. What if she shows up while we're gone?'

'Can't let that happen.'

Barbara raised her eyebrows. 'Of course, one of us could go looking for her while the other stays here.'

'I'm not sure that's such a good idea,' Pete said.

'It's a *rotten* idea.'

He suddenly smiled again. 'It was *your* idea.'

'Figured somebody oughta bring it up. Doesn't mean I'm in favor of it. I'm totally against splitting up.'

'It'd be stupid to split up.'

'Exactly. Asking for trouble. Besides, she'll probably get back any minute.'

'If we're lucky, without the cat.'

Barbara laughed. 'Exactly.'

# TWENTY-TWO

Pete boosted himself up and sat on the edge of the pool.

Barbara, floating on her back near the other end, flipped over and swam to him. She stood up in the waist-high water and checked her blouse. It was unbuttoned and clinging and open a few inches. Just wide enough. Not so wide that it showed enough to be embarrassing.

She put her hands on Pete's knees. 'What do you think?' she asked.

'I don't like it.'

'I don't, either.'

'Where could she be?'

'We can't just stay here *all* day,' Barbara said.

'It hasn't been all that long.'

'Long enough. Between this and all the time we spent . . . you know, at Mrs Klein's . . . we could've been home by now.'

'I've sort of liked it *here*,' Pete said.

'Me, too. I feel about a million times better than I did.'

'That's what kissing me will do for you.'

She let out a laugh. 'Yeah, right. That wasn't bad, either.' She squeezed his knees, gave them a playful shake that jostled the water between his legs, then let go and moved sideways. She stepped forward to the wall of the pool.

Aware of Pete watching, she planted her hands on the concrete near his hip, and jumped. She braced herself up beside him, arms stiff, the edge of the pool hard against her thighs. Then she stayed that way – because of how Pete was trying not to stare at her. She didn't look down at herself. Didn't need to. Just by the feel, she knew that her arms, in tight against her sides, were pushing her breasts together and thrusting them forward. She took a deep breath. The smoky air made her lungs hurt, but she filled them anyway, expanding her chest to improve the view even more.

Pete turned his head away.

'I think we'd better go and find Heather,' Barbara said – just to make him look at her.

It worked. Pete faced her again. He met her eyes and nodded. 'Yeah. Guess we'd better.' He glanced down, began to turn away, then looked again and stared for a few moments before forcing his gaze away and studying the other end of the pool.

Barbara smiled. She swung a leg up, slapped a bare foot onto the ledge, and climbed out of the pool. She stood up straight, her legs apart. Water raced down her body and spilled off her clothes, splashing the concrete between her feet.

Must look like I'm peeing, she thought. So she took a few steps away from the pool. After turning around, she pressed her legs together.

Pete was already walking toward her. His soaked trousers dripped water. They were glued to his legs. Their front bulged, shoved outward by the knobs of Pete's fists which were jammed into the front pockets.

Why the fists? Barbara wondered. She felt a quick stir of worry.

'You okay?' she asked.

'What do you mean?'

'Planning to punch me out?'

'Huh?' He looked confused. Then he blushed and glanced down at the front of his pants. 'Oh, that. Nah. I wouldn't hit you. Are you kidding?' He smiled nervously and shook his head. But his fists remained in his pockets.

'Planning to punch out somebody else?'

'I'm not gonna slug anyone. I just . . . it's nothing, okay? You want me to bring over your shoes and stuff?'

'We can both go,' Barbara said.

Pete turned away. Taking his hands out of his pockets, he walked toward the corner of the pool. Barbara followed him past the corner, and along the side. His back was tanned and shiny. He left trails of water drops.

Halfway to the other end of the pool, Barbara looked into the water. She could see where the bottom began to slope downward.

*That's where we were standing. That's where we kissed.*

She wondered if she would be able to find this apartment complex again – this pool.

It'd be nice to come back with him some time, she thought.

*What if we got married some day and came back to live right here in this building? And we could sneak into the pool late at night when everyone else was asleep, and go to our special place right there . . . ?*

Wild, she thought. It'll probably never happen. But it might. It might, if I want it to badly enough. Dad says you can make almost anything happen if you're willing to go for it.

This is a stupid time to even be *thinking* about stuff like that, she told herself.

*No, it's not. As good a time as any . . .*

Pete sat down on the concrete to put on his socks and shoes. Barbara sat nearby, but facing him. The concrete felt warm and rather nice through the wet seat of her shorts. She used one of her socks to wipe her feet.

'Maybe we can go somewhere,' Pete said, tying one of his Reeboks.

'Like where?'

'I don't know. Anywhere. How about the beach?'

'Are you crazy?'

'What do you mean?' Pete asked.

'The *beach*? I've gotta get home. And anyway, the beach is miles . . .'

'Not *today*,' Pete said. 'Jeez! That *would* be crazy. I meant like, you know, after all this is over.'

'Oh! '

'What do you think?'

*He's asking me out!*

'Yeah!' she blurted, and saw his face light up.

'Great! That's great!'

'I'm not sure about the beach, though. We'd have to figure out something that'll be okay with my Mom and Dad.'

*If I'll still have a Mom and Dad.*

*Of course I will. Sure I will. They're fine. They have to be.*

'They might have to go along, or something,' she said. 'Depending on what we wanta do. They're awfully protective.'

'That's okay. I don't mind.'

'Maybe you could come over to *my* place,' she suggested. 'You know, for starters. They'd go along with that. As long as one of them is home.'

'That'd be great,' Pete said. 'I don't care *where* we . . .'

A clamor of iron stopped his words.

They snapped their heads sideways. The front gate, flung open by Heather, squawled on its hinges and rang out as it crashed against the fence bars.

Barbara cringed at the noise.

She heard Pete mutter, 'Oh, man.'

Something was wrong.

Huffing and red-faced and streaming sweat, Heather ran toward them with her head thrown back, her mouth sagging, her arms swinging about wildly, her breasts jumping up and down as if trying to rip free of her clothes, her feet pounding down flat so that the soles of her shoes made heavy whapping sounds with each stride.

She was still bloody from the cat.

The cat didn't seem to be with her, though.

Maybe it's chasing her, Barbara thought.

*Something* must be chasing her.

But nothing followed Heather through the gate. It clanged shut as she chugged alongside the pool, hurrying toward Barbara and Pete.

They finished with their shoes. Pete grabbed his shirt and started to get up. Barbara reached for the denim strap of her purse.

She looked again at Heather.

No purse.

It had been hanging from Heather's shoulder when she left to go chasing after Susie, but now it was gone.

*Does she know she lost it?*

*Maybe it got snatched, and that's why she's acting so weird and scared.*

*The kid who snatched mine is dead.*

*Maybe his ghost . . . yeah, right.*

Pete and Barbara were on their feet by the time Heather staggered to a halt by the corner of the pool. Wheezing, she bent over and clutched her knees. She shook her head. 'Gotta get . . . outa here,' she gasped. 'They're coming.'

Barbara felt a sudden, sinking coldness inside.

'Who's coming?' Pete asked. 'What do you mean?'

'Guys. Whole bunch of 'em. Like a gang. I saw 'em . . . pulled people outa cars . . . Killed 'em . . . Can't let 'em get us . . . Can't . . . If they get us . . . Gotta hide.'

'Where are they?' Pete asked.

Still bent over, she let go of one knee and raised her arm. She flopped her hand in the direction of the front gate, then clutched her knee again.

'How far away?'

'Don't know. Couple blocks?'

'Are they coming this way?'

'Yeah.'

'Did they see you?' Barbara asked.

'Chased me.'

'Oh, my God,' Barbara said.

'Just two . . . came after me. Think I lost 'em.' Heather stood up straight. Still gasping for air, she wiped her face on a sleeve. Then she looked toward the gate. 'Lost 'em a few minutes ago. Over on . . . a different street. Hid. Circled around. But the main bunch is coming. Just saw 'em.'

'From right out in front?' Pete asked.

'Yeah.'

'Did they see you come in here?' Barbara asked.

'Don't know. Don't think so, but . . . Maybe. We gotta hide. Gotta hide quick.'

Barbara met Pete's eyes. He looked scared. 'Go for the alley?' she asked.

'No!' Heather blurted. 'They'll get us. I can't run. Can't. But I . . . I figured it out. We can hide here. All we gotta do is . . . get in a door . . . they'll never find us.'

'Break into an apartment?' Pete asked.

'Yeah! Yeah, it's perfect. They won't . . . know where to look for us.'

They'll know if they spot a busted door, Barbara thought.

'Upstairs,' Pete said. 'We'll try upstairs.'

Pete in the lead, they ran to the nearest stairway. He rushed up the stairs, taking three at a time. Barbara took two at a time. Heather grunted and wheezed behind her.

At the top, Pete raced along the balcony and stopped at the first door. He grabbed its knob, twisted it and shoved it.

'Nobody's gonna leave their doors unlocked,' Barbara said.

'Should I bust it in?'

'No. Not this one. Keep going.'

We don't want to hide in the very first room at the top of the stairs, she thought. Besides, maybe there *would* be a door that somebody hadn't bothered to lock.

They hurried on to the door of the next apartment. Pete tried that one, shook his head, and kept going.

Barbara followed him almost as far as the third door, then veered to the side and gazed over the railing. Nobody had entered the pool area yet. But she winced at the sight of the trails they had left on the concrete.

Huge, dark splotches of wetness showed where they had climbed out of the pool. A lot of water must've spilled off them there. Not so much where they had hurried along the side of the pool; only a few traces of dampness remained to show that trail. But plenty of water remained, undried, at the end where they had sat down to put on their shoes and socks.

From there, a weak trail of dribbles, barely noticeable from Barbara's position at the railing, led to the stairway they had used.

'They're gonna know we were here,' she said.

Pete lurched to the railing. He peered down. 'It's drying fast,' he said. 'In a couple of minutes, we oughta be okay.'

As if they'd both been struck by the same idea, Barbara and Pete suddenly turned their heads to see if they'd left a trail of water along the balcony.

Just a few drops.

'We'll be okay if we can get inside,' Pete said.

'In here!'

Barbara's heart jumped. She saw Pete flinch, heard Heather gasp.

She turned in time to see the door of the next apartment swing open wide.

A man stepped out.

He had a pistol, but it was pointed upward, not at them.

He was young – probably not much older than twenty – stocky and muscular. His hair was so short that the pale skin of his scalp showed through. His face looked handsome, but grim, with bright blue eyes and a broad jaw. He wore a white T-shirt, tight blue jeans and combat boots of gleaming black leather.

'Get in here,' he said. He gestured them forward with his pistol.

Pete looked back at Barbara and Heather. He shrugged, then turned again to the man in the doorway. 'Uh . . . Do we *have* to? I mean, what's going on? Are we supposed to be, like, your prisoners, or . . . ?' He shrugged again.

The man stared at Pete, eyes narrow.

After a moment, he said, 'You don't wanta see your day ruined, you'd better get in here fast.'

# TWENTY-THREE

On their way to the top of Laurel Canyon Boulevard, Clint and Em walked side by side up the middle of the road. Mary followed them at a distance. Sometimes, she gained on them when they stopped for a rest. But soon afterward, she would need to stop, herself, and they would leave her farther behind.

They stepped right over a few minor cracks that ran across the pavement.

When they came to the first of those, Clint had said, 'Watch out. Step on a crack, break your mother's back.'

Em had stepped over it, then given Clint a puzzled look. 'What was that about my mother's back?'

'An expression. "Step on a crack, break your mother's back." You've never heard it before?'

'Not that way. It was "step on a crack, snap a fella's back." '

'Bet your mom taught you that one.'

'You mean it doesn't go that way?'

'It's "break your *mother's* back." '

'I've been misled.' Grinning, Em had shaken her head. 'We used to chant it – Mom's version – and jump up and down on every crack we found.'

'I can't *wait* to meet your mother. I think I'll have to send you home in a taxi.'

'Oh, don't worry about her. She'll like you. How can she not, you know what I mean? You may be a man, but . . .'

'Hey, there's no "may be" about that. Please!'

'Anyway, you're not a jerk like most guys.'

'Why, thank you. I'm honored.'

They'd crossed several more cracks during the next few minutes. Though nothing more was said about the expression, Clint noticed that Em avoided stepping on any of them.

Higher up the hillside, they came upon a much larger break in the pavement. The jagged fissure crossed every lane of the road, but was never more than about two feet wide. Over to the right, several smaller cracks led away from it.

Em, striding along by Clint's side, suddenly halted and said, 'Wait wait wait. Whoa.'

'What?'

'Look at that thing.'

'The crack? It's no big deal. We can step right over it.'

'I'm not so sure about *that*. How deep is it?'

Clint walked closer to it.

'Be careful! Don't fall in.'

One more stride carried him near enough to see the bottom. 'It's not even three feet deep.'

'Are you sure it doesn't drop down into some sort of chasm or abyss?'

'Positive.'

'Okay. I didn't think so. Not really. But, you know, they *do* in the movies. I've seen movies where the ground opens up and swallows people whole – and like the crack goes all the way down to the center of the Earth, or something. Which is ludicrous. But one can't be too careful, if you know what I mean. I've never been in a quake of *this* magnitude, so who knows what might happen? Have you heard about "liquefaction"? Now *that's* pretty scary. And it's real, too. It's like the ground right under you can turn into quicksand? I've never seen that in the movies, though, have you?'

'I've seen quicksand in the movies,' Clint said, and crossed over the crack with one long stride.

'I mean liquefaction.'

Safe on the other side, he turned around and watched Em staring at the split. 'I haven't seen that in movies,' he said.

'Me, neither. I guess it's not as dramatic as falling into a bottomless chasm.'

'I don't know if liquefaction would swallow a person the way quicksand does,' Clint said. 'For that matter, I have my doubts that quicksand swallows people for real the way it does in movies.'

'You're probably right.' Em began to step toward the crack carefully, like someone walking on the frozen surface of a pond. 'The movies basically never get anything right, do they?'

'Mostly not.'

'I love 'em anyway, though.'

Clutching the grocery sack against his chest, Clint reached out his other arm. Em took hold of his hand. She clutched it tightly as she stepped across the gap.

'A cinch, right?'

'Right,' Em said. 'Thanks.' She let go, then turned around. She frowned down the road toward Mary, who was slogging her way slowly toward them. 'Maybe we oughta wait for her.'

'I don't see why,' Clint said.

'She might need a hand.'

'Tough tacos. She should've thought of that before she whacked you.'

'You aren't exactly brimming over with forgiveness, are you?'

'Nope. Come on, let's go.' They resumed walking. 'I am fairly forgiving of mistakes,' he explained. 'Screw-ups, accidents, errors in judgment . . . People should pay attention to what they do and consider what the consequences might be, but everybody makes mistakes. Meanness is something else. There's no excuse for it. There's no excuse for the way she hit you.'

'Does that mean you're *never* going to forgive her?'

'Not in the foreseeable future.'

'Whew. Hope *I* never tick you off.' As she said that, she looked back.

Clint looked, too. Mary was trudging up the road, the fissure behind her. 'See,' he said. 'She didn't need help, anyway.'

'Guess not.' They continued uphill. 'But you'll help her in case of *real* trouble.' It didn't sound like a question, more like a statement of fact.

'That remains to be seen,' Clint said.

Soon, they came upon a tree that had dropped across the road.

'The cops didn't say anything about this,' Em said.

'Nope, they sure didn't.'

The tree roots had left a dark pit in the hillside just above the road. The clump hadn't gone far; it rested at the edge of the hole like a ball joint popped from its socket. It was eight to ten feet high, and clotted with dirt. It elevated that end of the trunk.

'Your choice,' Clint said as they walked toward the fallen tree. 'Over, under, or around?'

Em turned her head, studying the tree from one end to the other. 'Looks like there's some room to crawl under it,' she said.

Still in the middle of the road, they angled to the left so they would reach the tree near its roots. Em took the lead. Stopping short of the trunk, she squatted down. She looked from side to side. Clint stopped behind her.

'Problem?' he asked.

'Maybe we'd better climb over, instead. It might not be the safest thing in the world, crawling under there.'

He walked past Em, placed a hand against the trunk, and shoved. The tree didn't budge. 'I don't think it's going anywhere.'

Em stood up. She made a face at Clint, and shook her head. 'I wouldn't want to be crawling under it if there's an aftershock. That would not be at all swift, if you know what I mean. A person could get squashed like a bug. And I think we're past due for an aftershock.'

'We're probably having them all along,' Clint said.

'Oh, I know. I'm sure we've had dozens, so far. Even hundreds.'

'I haven't felt any yet, have you?'

'I don't think so. But you don't have to feel them. They're there, all right. And we'll have a really big one sooner or later. Maybe even one as big as the first quake. Or bigger, though that isn't very likely.'

'You know your quakes,' Clint told her.

'Sure. How can you *not*?'

'I guess we all do,' Clint said.

'But I also did a paper on them in sixth grade, so I learned a lot then. It's only a matter of time . . .'

'That's close enough,' Clint called.

Mary, a few yards downslope from Em, stopped and uncapped her plastic bottle. She held the bottle of water by her side and panted for air, apparently too winded to take a drink.

Em turned around. 'The tree's in our way,' she said.

Mary found enough breath to gasp, 'No fooling.'

'We're gonna climb over it.'

'Be my guest.'

'In case of an aftershock.'

Mary smirked. 'What's an . . . aftershock . . . got to do with it?'

'Make it fall and smash you.'

'While you're crawling . . . underneath?'

'Yeah.'

'Right. You'd only be under the thing . . . couple of seconds. Wouldn't fall, anyway.'

Clint agreed with her, but he kept it to himself.

'You go ahead and crawl under if you want,' Em told the woman. 'But I'm going *over* it. Better safe than mashed like a bug.'

Mary raised the plastic bottle to her mouth and tipped back her head. She only took one swallow, then had to stop for a breath. After another swallow, she lowered the bottle. 'Do I have to wait?' she asked Clint.

He shook his head. As Mary stepped closer, he watched her.

'Don't worry,' she said, 'I'm not gonna *beat up* on anybody.'

'I'm not worried.'

'Just looking for an excuse to smack me, aren't you?'

'No.'

'Yeah, right.' She sidestepped past Em and Clint, then turned away and sank to her knees. She crawled under the trunk, the plastic bottle dragging against the pavement, her rump swaying from side to side. Clint noticed that she didn't have stockings on. Had she been wearing them earlier? He thought so. The lack of stockings made her legs seem strangely vulnerable.

Maybe I shouldn't be so tough on her, he thought.

But his moment of regret was pushed aside by the memory of Mary striking Em.

Don't go soft, he told himself, just because she looks a little bedraggled and pathetic.

'She'll make it,' Em said.

Mary must've heard her. 'The aftershock's waiting for *you*, sweetie.' A moment later, she cried out, '*OW! Shit shit shit!*'

Clint and Em crouched and looked.

Mary was only visible from the rump down. She seemed to be standing, hobbling away from the tree.

'Are you okay?' Em called.

'No!'

'What happened?'

'I wracked myself.'

'What happened?' Em asked again.

'As if anybody cares,' Mary said, and kept going.

'Wait!' Em rushed forward, dropped to her hands and knees, and started to scurry under the tree.

So much for climbing over it, Clint thought.

And realized that he wasn't concerned about the possibility of an aftershock – such a slim possibility that a huge one would hit at exactly the wrong time and drop the tree onto Em.

He found himself more interested in the look of her. She was crawling on her hands and knees, the same as Mary had done. Her white shorts were tight across her rump. Dirt smudges and grass stains on their seat reminded Clint of the fall she'd taken in front of her house – after being punched in the chest by that horrible, ugly woman named Lou. Lou the looter.

Even before that, before he had met Em, she'd gotten her back scraped by a brick. And finally, Mary had given her head a swat.

She'd been through plenty. A lot more than Mary. But there was nothing at all vulnerable or pathetic about how she looked as she crawled under the tree.

A kid on an adventure, eagerly crawling into the mouth of a cave.

*Barbara.*

This could've been Barbara, a couple of years ago. They're so much alike.

Em's a lot wilder, feistier, but . . .

'Watch it when you stand up,' Mary said. 'That's how I wracked myself. Stood up too soon and it got me in the back.'

*She's warning Em. Good for her. Trying to get back in our good graces?*

Doesn't matter why she warned Em, Clint told himself. Not much, anyway. She did it, and that's what counts.

Em stayed down. As she crawled a little farther, Clint got to his hands and knees. They were scraped raw. He winced and gritted his teeth. He thought about his dive to avoid the speeding Toyota pickup truck. The quake had still been going on when he'd thrown himself out of the way and skidded on the pavement. It seemed like a very long time ago. Days ago, not a few hours. So long ago that the abrasions on his palms and knees should've healed by now. But they hurt like hell.

Bracing himself up on his knuckles and thumbs, he scuttled underneath the tree on the balls of his feet.

No aftershock.

In probably no more than three seconds, he was on the other side. He started to rise, then remembered Mary's warning to Em and stayed down a few moments longer. To make sure that he was clear of the tree, he looked over his shoulder. And saw a broken limb jutting straight down from the trunk. A miniature stalactite, no larger than a thumb but sharp at its splintered end.

Em was lifting the back of Mary's blouse. Clint sidestepped for a better angle. He glimpsed blood on the fabric. Then Mary's skin was there. The gouge started just below the cross-strap of her bra. It was about three inches long, and looked as if someone had tried to plow a furrow down her back with a stick.

'Bet that hurts,' Em told her.

'God, what if it leaves a scar?'

'It won't,' Clint said.

'How would *you* know?' Mary snapped. 'This is all your fault!'

Of course, he thought. Should've known. As much as he loved Sheila and Barbara, they were usually quick to put the blame on him – no matter how remote his involvement might be in whatever mishap had befallen them. He had come to figure out that this was normal behavior for women.

'My fault?' he asked.

'You had me so upset,' Mary said, 'that I couldn't pay attention to what I was doing!'

'I had you upset?'

'Treating me like I'm some kind of a criminal.'

'Oh. I see.'

Em, still frowning at Mary's wound, said, 'We oughta put some water on it, maybe.'

Clint set down the bag. Em took out a water bottle and a paper napkin. She moistened the napkin. While Clint held up the back of Mary's blouse, Em gently dabbed at the wound.

'How does that feel?' Em asked her.

'Better.'

'Weird, huh? It wasn't all that long ago, you were doing this to me.'

'I liked it better that way,' Mary said.

Em laughed, and so did Mary. Even Clint found himself smiling.

'Now,' Em said, 'Clint's the only one who hasn't gotten screwed in the back.'

Looking over her shoulder, Mary gave him a tight smile. 'The day isn't over yet.'

'Real nice,' he said.

Em smoothed the wet napkin against Mary's wound. 'We'll leave it there,' she said. Guiding Clint's hand, she lowered the blouse. He let go of it. Em tucked it under the waistband at the back of Mary's skirt. 'That might hold it for a while.'

Clint looked at Em's back. Her T-shirt was clinging with sweat, spotted a little with blood near her shoulderblade. 'What happened to your paper towel?' he asked her.

'Oh, it fell out a long time ago.' She suddenly grimaced. 'Is there blood on my shirt?'

'Some.'

'Poop!'

'That's all right,' Clint assured her. 'Your blood goes nicely with the shirt's "road-kill" motif.'

She grinned. 'Hadn't thought of that. Speaking of road-kill, who's hungry?'

Mary turned around and faced them. She glanced from Em to Clint. 'I'll leave, now. Thanks for nothing.'

'You don't have to go,' Em said. 'Does she, Clint? Come on, tell her she can stay. I mean, I'm the one she whacked. And anyway, I might've gotten porked by the tree if it hadn't been for Mary.'

'If it hadn't been for Mary, you would've climbed over it.'

She grinned. 'Might've fallen and broken my neck. So see? That makes *twice* she's saved me.'

'Oh, sure,' he said.

'Anyway, don't you think she's been banished for long enough?'

Not really, he thought. It's asking for trouble.

But Mary *had* warned Em. That had to count for something. And she hadn't done any serious damage to Em by giving her the smack on the head. And Em herself wanted Mary to be given a second chance.

'Okay,' he finally said. He met Mary's eyes. 'Are you going to behave from now on?'

She glared at him. 'I guess so.'

'You guess?'

'I don't wanta be left behind any more.'

'This is sort of going against my rules, so don't blow it. Don't make me regret being nice to you.'

Mary's upper lip twitched.

'Why don't we all settle down and take a break and have something to eat?' Em said. 'This is as good a place as any.'

Gazing up the slope, Clint could see the unlighted traffic signals at Mulholland. They marked the crest of the ridge. Just beyond them, Laurel Canyon Boulevard began its long, curving way downward to Hollywood.

To Sunset Boulevard.

On the other side of Sunset, there would be no more hills to climb. The road would stop being Laurel Canyon and become Crescent Heights, and following it would lead him most of the way home.

Clint had wanted to reach the top before taking a break for lunch. But his bouts with Mary made him feel like a dictator. He didn't enjoy the feeling.

'Fine with me,' he told Em. 'Let's have lunch here. This looks like a great place for it.'

'Good, 'cause I happen to be starving.'

# TWENTY-FOUR

The curtains behind the sofa were shut across the picture window, filtering out the sunlight, giving the room a murky yellow glow.

Barbara and Pete sat beside each other on the floor across from the sofa. Barbara figured that Pete had picked this spot because it was low and away from the big window. But maybe he'd avoided the furniture out of simple courtesy, because his trousers were wet. Either way, she liked where she was. She felt fairly safe down here. She had a wall at her back and she had a full view of the curtained window, the door, Heather and Lee.

Heather had taken a seat on the sofa as if she'd forgotten all about the blood on her legs and arms and hands. She sat sideways, one leg tucked under her, her hands resting on her thighs, her face toward Lee.

Lee was kneeling in the middle of the sofa, elbows on top of the back rest, peering outside through a bright sliver of space between the curtains.

His pistol was stuck down the waistband at the back of his jeans. Beside him on the sofa was a mean-looking, stubby rifle with a leather sling. It looked to Barbara like a military weapon. Just in front of its trigger guard, a big chrome magazine jutted downward.

A similar magazine was on the table in front of the sofa. At the open top of this one, Barbara could see a couple of slim pointed cartridges that were almost golden in the mellow light. A much smaller magazine was also on the table. Barbara figured that this one must belong to the pistol. The cartridge showing at the top was fat – its slug, a dull gray dome.

On top of the same table were several boxes of ammunition. And a pair of binoculars.

The first words out of Barbara's mouth, after being ushered into the apartment and glimpsing the collection, had been, 'Charles Whitman, I presume?'

'Lee Nolan,' he'd corrected her, grim-faced. Barbara's reference to the Texas Tower sniper had apparently gone over his head. 'I'm the manager here,' he'd said. 'Your two friends are Pete and Heather. Didn't catch your name.'

'Barbara. How do you know . . . ?'

'Their names? You wouldn't believe the way sound carries in this place. From up here, I can hear the *ripples* in the swimming pool.'

'You were listening to us.'

'And watching.'

A heat of embarrassment had spread through Barbara as she pictured Lee at the windows, spying on her and Pete in the pool, treating himself to close-up views with the help of his binoculars. At such close range, it must've been like watching them from about two feet away.

'Terrific,' she had muttered, and glanced down to make sure that the top of her blouse hadn't somehow come open in spite of her left hand clutching it shut. The tight fist in the middle of her chest could only draw attention to the problem – and to her breasts. Especially how her left one stuck out and pretty much hid her wrist.

Still, she'd been determined to keep her hand there and hold her blouse shut.

'It's my job,' Lee had explained, 'to know what's happening in and around my facility. And to protect it.'

'We weren't doing anything,' Pete had told him.

'Sure you were. But you weren't doing any harm to my tenants or property. That's why I didn't interfere until you started trying to get through doors.'

'We don't normally do stuff like that,' Pete had explained.

'It's all right. This isn't a normal day. Sit down. Everyone sit down. Heather, start talking. I want every detail of what you saw out there.'

Heather then started in on an expanded version of the story she'd blurted to Pete and Barbara down by the pool. Lee didn't seem to pay much attention. He kept gazing out through the tiny gap between the curtains.

Barbara figured that he must've overheard the original . . . he'd heard everything else said down there.

*Seen everything, too.*

She'd been aware, all along, that people might be watching from the apartments. Peeking out from time to time, maybe. It hadn't occurred to her, though, that anyone would study them with binoculars – and listen to every word.

From where she sat, she could hear enough to know that the windows were open. She listened for the sound of ripples in the pool.

Not quite. There was a vague, hollow murmur that she thought of as 'pool noise' – a sound as faint as the whisper of a seashell held close to the ear.

But she couldn't hear ripples.

Though maybe if Heather weren't talking . . . Maybe if there wasn't that undercurrent of noises from outside the courtyard: faraway shouts and barks and sirens and bangs and horn blasts and engines . . . tires squealing . . . a scream now and then so muffled that she couldn't tell whether it belonged to a cat or a person.

Such background noises were barely noticeable unless you listened hard for them. Some of them must've gotten in the way a *little*, though.

Lee couldn't possibly have heard everything.

A lot, though.

She hated the idea that he might've heard Pete's shy, stumbling speech about liking her. Somehow, that seemed even worse than knowing he'd probably focused those damn binoculars in on her breasts.

*He saw our kiss, too.*

It really hurt that he'd watched that.

*The creep.*

'How many were there?' Lee asked, and Barbara realized that she'd been paying no attention to Heather's story.

'I don't know,' Heather said.

'Yes, you do. Think.'

'Well, maybe ten or twelve.'

He carefully shut the crack between the curtains, then turned sideways on his knees and frowned down at Heather. 'How were they armed?'

'Some had guns.'

'How many guns did you see?'

Heather shrugged, then quickly said, 'Four? Maybe five. That I saw. Maybe they *all* had guns, but just weren't using them. I saw knives, too. And one guy had an axe.'

Pete grimaced at Lee. 'What'll we do?' he asked.

'There're too many to take on,' Lee said.

'Glad to hear it,' Barbara said.

Lee twisted his head around and gave her a sharp look. 'You find humor in this situation?'

'Not really.'

'I can do without your wise-ass comments.'

She tried not to cringe. 'I'm sorry, okay? I didn't mean anything.'

'Didn't mean anything by that Whitman crack, either, did you?'

She felt herself suddenly blush. 'Oh, that. Whoops.'

'Yeah, whoops.'

This guy had no sense of humor at all.

'It's just that . . . you've got these guns and you sort of look like you're itching for a shootout. So I was sort of surprised when you said that about not wanting to take on that mob, or whatever it is out there. That's all. Okay? I didn't mean to . . . you know, insult you.'

'Is that supposed to be an apology?' he asked.

Barbara shrugged. 'I guess so.'

'Never apologize. It's a sign of weakness.'

'Oh, for . . .' *What does he want?* 'Right,' she said. 'Whatever you say, sir.'

'Cut the attitude,' Lee said.

Heather grinned.

'*You* shut up,' Barbara told her.

'Me?' Heather asked, all innocence. 'What did *I* say?'

'It's your fault we're here in the first place, you and that damn cat.'

'Leave her alone,' Lee said.

And Heather glowed as if she'd been blessed.

Lee turned toward the window and parted the curtains.

Barbara bared her teeth at Heather.

Heather smirked at her.

'What *is* the plan?' Pete asked.

'We wait and see,' Lee said, peering out the window. 'If we're lucky, the marauders bypass us. There's a whole city out there. They can't hit everyplace.'

'What if they do show up here?'

'My first responsibility is to my tenants.'

'Tenants?'

'I have people in four of the units.'

'Right now?' Pete asked.

'You've got it. I made the rounds after the quake hit. Minimal damage, and no casualties. Most of my tenants had already left for work. A few are away on trips. But I've got people in those four units, like I said, and I have to protect them.'

'I thought you weren't going to take anybody on,' Barbara reminded him.

He didn't bother to look around at her. 'That only means I'm not planning an offensive operation. It doesn't rule out a defensive action.'

'Oh.'

'Maybe you think we should hunker down and hide in here while they slaughter my tenants.'

'I don't think that,' Barbara protested.

'I don't see why *we* should stick around, though,' Pete said. 'We aren't gonna be of much help if we don't have guns. I mean our idea was to lay low. But if you're planning to fight, maybe we oughta try and get away while we've still got a chance.'

'Fine with me,' Lee said.

Pete leaned closer to Barbara and said in a soft voice, 'What do you think? We could take off out the back and make a run down the alley.'

'Not me,' Heather said.

Pete's gaze stayed on Barbara. 'Whatever. We don't have to let that stop us.'

189

'Leave without her?'

'Go ahead,' Heather told them. 'I'm not going out there, not unless Lee *makes* me.'

'You're free to stay here,' Lee told her. 'It's your call.'

'Are you sure? That's so sweet of you. But are you sure you wouldn't mind? I don't want to get in your way, or anything.'

Barbara looked at her.

*Obsequious, is that the right word?*

*Or fawning?*

*Or does she suddenly adore this guy?*

*Nah. She's gotta be faking it. Laying it on thick, so he won't toss her out.*

Sickening, Barbara thought. The girl's pathetic.

'Stay,' Lee said. 'Or leave. Either way is fine with me. I'd think you might want to go with your friends, though.'

'Are you kidding? That mob's out there! I don't wanta get gang-raped and torn apart. Anyhow, I'm just in the same driver's ed class with those two – it's not like they're my friends.' When she said that, she cast a hurt look at Pete.

As if he'd betrayed her.

What does she know? Barbara suddenly wondered.

*Maybe Lee isn't the only one who was spying on us.*

No, she thought. Heather didn't see us, she's just mad because we didn't go with her to chase the cat.

'Even if we aren't friends,' Barbara said, 'we probably oughta stick together.'

'I don't see why.'

'How will you get home?' Pete asked.

Heather's shoulders bobbed up and down. 'I don't care. It doesn't matter.'

'Getting home,' Lee said, 'shouldn't be anybody's top priority at this point. Number one priority is survival.'

'Yeah,' Pete said. 'I agree.' He turned again to Barbara. 'That's why I think we should get out of here. With or without Heather. I think we'll stand a better chance if we're on the run. I mean, if anything goes down, Lee's planning on a shootout. It'll be like the OK Corral around here.'

Barbara nodded. 'I'm with you.' She glanced at the others. Lee was peering out the window again. Heather met her eyes, and had a strange, sly smile. 'You're sure you want to stay here?' Barbara asked her.

'Why would I wanta go anywhere with you two?'

'Can't imagine,' Barbara said.

'I'll take my chances here, thanks anyway.'

'Okay.' Still holding her blouse shut with her left hand, Barbara shoved at the floor with her right as she drew in her legs and started to stand up. Her rump felt a little itchy. On her feet, she rubbed the damp seat of her shorts while Pete got up. 'So,' she said, 'I guess we'll be going.'

'You sure you don't want to change your mind?' Pete asked Heather. 'Once we're gone, it'll be a little too late.'

'Too late for you, you mean.'

They were almost to the door when the sound of a soft *clank* hit Barbara like a blow to the heart. She gasped and halted. Pete froze. Heather snapped her head toward Lee.

Lee's back stiffened.

'One of the gates?' Heather whispered.

*Of course it's one of the gates, you idiot! They're here. They're down by the pool.*

One eye at the gap between the curtains, Lee raised an open hand.

Nobody moved.

Nobody spoke.

My God, Barbara thought, what if we'd gotten to the door a few seconds sooner? We'd be out on the balcony in plain sight, and . . .

After a few moments, Lee reached behind his back and tugged the pistol out of his jeans.

'Oh, man,' Pete murmured.

'Who's out there?' Barbara asked.

'Visitor,' Lee whispered.

'Just one?' Barbara asked.

'So far.'

'What's he doing?'

'Shhh.'

Like Lee's little assistant, Heather frowned at Barbara and pressed a finger to her lips.

Barbara listened hard for sounds from the intruder.

*He's sure being quiet down there.*

*She?*

No, Barbara thought. Can't be a woman – Lee wouldn't have pulled his gun.

'Heather?'

Not a shout, but a soft call as if the person below knew how well his voice would carry to the surrounding apartments – knew, and wanted to make no more noise than necessary.

'Heather?' he called again.

The voice sounded familiar.

Barbara met Pete's eyes.

'It's Earl,' Pete whispered.

'My God. Where'd *he* come from?'

'*Earl?*' Heather asked. She looked stricken. 'What's *he* doing here?'

'He's calling your name,' Barbara said in a hushed voice.

'I didn't see him.'

'He saw you,' Pete said. 'Must've.'

'Great,' Barbara muttered. 'Just great.'

'Who is he?' Lee asked, not looking away from the window.

'He's a jerk,' Barbara said.

'He was in the driver's ed class with us,' Pete explained. 'He's kind of a trouble-maker.'

'Heather?' Earl called again. 'Are you here? Pete? Barbara? Where are you?'

'Right after the quake,' Pete said, 'he tried to steal some guy's car. We had a big fight about it, and we . . . sort of knocked him out cold and left him behind.'

'No kidding,' Lee said, still gazing out.

'Are you here?' Earl called. 'Come on, guys! I'm not gonna hurt anybody, I promise. I just . . . I don't like it out here by myself. There's scary shit going on. Okay? Can you hear me? Hey, I'm sorry I screwed up back there, okay? I wanta get back together with you. Please!'

Lee looked over his shoulder at Pete and Barbara. 'I don't like this. He'll give us away. Let's bring him in.'

'You sure you want to do that?' Barbara asked.

'I don't want him down there yelling, that's for sure. Pete, tell him to come up.'

'If you say so.'

'Do it.'

Pete slipped past Barbara, unfastened the deadbolt, and pulled the door open. He stepped over the threshold. Raising an arm, he called out quietly, 'Up here, Earl. Make it quick.'

'Hey hey, Pizzaria! My bud!'

'Quiet! Jeez!'

'Hey, hey, don't have a cow. Anybody else around here?'

'Don't ask so many questions. Just hurry up.'

'I'm coming, I'm coming. Hey, don't rush me. I've been in better shape, you know. It's not every day I get the crap beat out of me.'

Barbara heard Earl start pounding his way up the stairs.

'You got Banner with you?'

'She's here.'

'Good, good. Didn't see her. Or you either. Thought maybe something might've happened. Which'd be a real shame. Wouldn't want nothing happening to my old pals. You miss me?'

'Sure.'

'How'd you get yourselves a place?' Earl asked. From the sound of his voice, he had reached the balcony. 'Rent it? 'Cause knowing how fucking *moral* you and Banner are, you sure as hell didn't *bust* in.'

Not bothering to answer, Pete stepped backward out of the doorway.

A moment later, Earl strolled in. He grinned at Barbara.

She felt her mouth drop open.

'Greetings and salutations, Banner-babes.'

'What happened to *you*?' she blurted.

'You oughta know.'

'We didn't do all *that*.'

The right side of Earl's face was puffy and smudged with dark bruises – damage, she supposed, that had been inflicted by herself and Pete. But the hair above his left ear was pasted down flat with dry blood. They hadn't done that to him. Nor were they responsible for his change of clothes. Barbara wasn't sure what he'd been wearing before, but not this: a white shirt so large that it hung down almost to his knees, pin-striped blue slacks that looked as if they might go with the business suit of an obese executive, and brightly polished black leather dress shoes.

Someone, probably Earl, had torn off the sleeves of the shirt so that his arms were bare to the shoulders. The shirt was unbuttoned, too, showing sweaty skin with bruises and scratches. Earl's huge, bulky slacks were cinched in around his waist with a striped necktie. The cuffs were rolled up. He had bare ankles above the fancy shoes.

'Greetings, Heather,' he said. 'And who's this?'

'Lee Nolan,' Lee said. 'I'm the manager of this facility.'

'No kidding. Figured maybe you was Rambo.'

'He's not amused,' Barbara said.

Ignoring them, Lee looked at Pete. 'Anybody else out there?'

'I don't think so.'

'Check again, then shut the door.'

When the door was shut, Lee got to his feet and faced Earl. He held the pistol low by his side. 'Tell us what's going on out there,' he said.

'What do you want to know?'

Heather spoke up first. 'How did you find us?'

'Just lucky, I guess. Heading for home, trying to stay out of trouble. And then I spotted you . . . You were like two blocks away. Knew it was you, though. You got yourself an unmistakable figure.'

Heather blushed. 'Thanks,' she murmured.

'Think that was a compliment?'

The red of her face darkened.

Looking pleased with himself, Earl turned his attention to the others. 'Anyhow, I yelled. I thought she heard me, but she kept on going like she didn't. So then I chased after her, and saw her go through the gate down there.'

193

'What about the mob?' Lee asked.

'Huh?'

'Was that you yelling "Porky"?' Heather asked.

'Me, all right,' Earl said.

'You dirty . . .'

'Let's not get sidetracked, here,' Lee said. 'Heather reported that there's a group of marauders heading our way.'

'A what?'

'A wild mob,' Pete explained.

'Rampaging,' Barbara added. 'Killing people.'

'No kidding?' Earl asked.

'It wasn't exactly a *mob*,' Heather said. 'I mean, there weren't that many.'

'A dozen,' Lee reminded her. 'That's what you told us.'

'Well, it seemed like a dozen. Maybe it wasn't that many.'

Earl shrugged and made a face like someone faking perplexity. 'A wild mob of killers, huh? Only maybe just a few, but on a rampage?'

'Pulling people out of cars,' Pete said.

'Heather saw them raping and killing women,' Barbara added.

Earl's face lit up. 'Raping, huh? And to think I missed it.'

'What *did* you see out there?' Lee asked.

'I didn't see nothing like that.'

'I did,' Heather insisted. 'And some of them chased me, but I ditched 'em.'

'No kidding?' Earl asked. 'You sure about that? Looked to me like you was taking your sweet time, checking around under cars and stuff. What were you looking for?'

'A cat. But that was after those guys . . .'

'Hold it,' Lee broke in. 'I want to hear from Earl.'

Earl shrugged. 'I didn't spot any mob, that's for sure. Not around here. There was a whole bunch of looting over on Pico. A few fights and stuff, too. I saw some people who'd gotten themselves pounded pretty good – hey, you're looking at one.'

'We didn't do that to you,' Barbara said.

'Like hell.'

'I punched you in the face a couple of time, same as you punched me.' She realized that she had pretty much forgotten about her injuries. Reminded now, she noticed that she had a slight earache, probably from the punch in the jaw. She pressed her hand to her jaw. Not much swelling there. But the bulging skin over her cheekbone felt warm and tight.

'Be grateful, Banner,' Earl said. 'I improved on your looks.'

'Shut up,' Pete said.

'Screw you.'

'We didn't do that to your head,' Barbara told him. 'Not where your hair's all bloody there. That wasn't us. Maybe we should've, but we didn't.'

'I suppose you didn't steal my stuff, either.'

'We didn't steal anything. All we did was drag you out of the street so you wouldn't get run over.'

'Yeah, sure. What you did is strip me.'

'Did not.'

'We didn't do anything like that,' Pete said.

'Yeah, right.'

Heather looked as if she had made an amazing recovery from her embarrassment. She was beaming. 'Somebody took your clothes?'

'Yeah, and I know who.'

'Not us,' Heather said. 'You've gotta be kidding. You pissed your jeans.'

'Yeah, right.'

'You did,' Barbara confirmed, and found herself smiling.

'Bull.'

'It's true,' Pete said.

'That's three against one,' Heather pointed out. 'And you were out cold, so how can you say you *didn't*. Your little piggie went, "Wee wee wee wee." '

'Up yours.'

'Let's everyone knock it off,' Lee said.

'The thing of it is,' Barbara persisted, 'it wasn't us who did that to your head or stole your clothes. Somebody else must've come along and done it after we were gone.'

'What did they take?' Pete asked.

'What do you think?'

'Everything?'

'Yeah.'

'Jeez.'

'They take your *undies*?' Heather asked.

'My what?'

'Your underpants.'

'Who wears 'em?'

'And he calls *me* a pig. At least I wear underpants.'

'They left you naked?' Barbara asked Earl.

'Yeah, so what?'

'What did you do?'

'What do you mean, what'd I do? I wandered around in my birthday suit till I got this stuff.' He fluttered his fingers against the front of his shirt. 'Wasn't any picnic finding some new duds, I tell you that. It's not like people are real eager to part with what they're wearing, and I couldn't find me a clothes store that hadn't already gotten picked clean.'

'Let me guess,' Barbara said, 'you mugged a fat bank manager.'

'I don't know what he was. And I didn't mug him. He was already dead when I found him.'

'Dead?' Barbara asked, wrinkling her nose.

'Yeah, but I didn't do it.'

'I'm sure,' Heather said.

'Hey, I don't go around killing people for their pants.'

'This man you took the clothes from,' Lee said, 'did he look like he'd been assaulted?'

'Your mob didn't get him, if that's what you're getting at.'

'It's not *my* mob.'

'It's Heather's mob,' Barbara put in.

'My man was all in one piece. I mean, I don't think he was even cut. He probably died from a heart attack, or something. I'm surprised he still had his clothes, though. Every stiff in town has gotten itself stripped, from what I've seen. And this bozo's billfold was gone, but they hadn't taken his clothes. I can see why, too – the guy was an elephant. I had an awful time trying to . . .'

'Wait wait wait,' Lee said. 'What's this about stiffs? You mean corpses?'

'What do you think?'

'How many did you see?'

'I don't know. Hell, who counted?'

'How many?' Lee repeated.

'What do you think, I kept a scorecard? Aah. Let me think. Twenty? Maybe thirty?' He wrinkled his nose. 'It was pretty gross. Even the babes. Fact is, the babes were the worst, you know?' Something went out of his voice. He frowned down at the floor. 'You'd think it'd be sort of cool, seeing 'em all . . . with their clothes off like that. The way it turned out, though, it was . . . I don't know. It made me feel a little sick. The way they were dead. It didn't make me feel horny or anything, just sort of sick and depressed.' He suddenly seemed to cheer up. 'But hey, guess the good news is I'm not one of them necromaniacs.'

Lee didn't seem amused. 'These women you saw, did they look as if they'd been attacked?'

'Yeah. Attacked, all right. By falling buildings. Who knows, though? I don't know how they got killed. The men, either. I didn't go up and check 'em all, up close and personal. There were a couple I happened to notice with bullet holes, and one guy had a knife in him. But they were more like the exception. Mostly, they were sprawled around near places that'd gotten nailed by the quake. They were pretty messed up. Saw a lot of bashed heads. A lot of nasty cuts. One guy'd caught a big thing of glass right across his face. There was a gal, she didn't have any head at all. I sort of looked for it, too.' He turned to Barbara and raised a corner of his mouth. 'Fact is, thought she might be you. You know, she sort of had the same general shape and stuff. Could've been you.'

'Sorry to disappoint you.'

'Hey, I'm glad she wasn't.'

'Sure.'

'Really.'

'So,' Lee said, 'you think most of these dead people were killed by the quake?'

'Most of 'em, yeah.'

'And nearly all of them had been stripped?'

'Yeah, that's how come I had such a tough time finding myself something to wear. Fuckin' Los Angeles. The whole damn city's nothing but scavengers. Just look around on garbage day. I didn't catch any of 'em in the act, but you can bet there's gotta be all these creeps sneaking around taking what they can get off the dead people. Like the looters, only they're looting stiffs instead of stores. Maybe that's who got me,' he said. 'Took me for a goner.'

'From the look of your head,' Barbara said, 'they tried to help make you one.'

'You guys shouldn't't've left me there like that.'

'You're the one who started it.'

'I was only just trying to grab us a car. If you hadn't messed it up, we'd all be home by now.'

'You can't go around and steal . . .'

'Let's not start quarreling again,' Lee said. 'It sounds as if the situation outside hasn't deteriorated quite as much as we thought.'

'I saw what I saw,' Heather said. 'I'm not a liar.'

'Nobody's calling you a liar,' Lee said.

'If Earl didn't see your mob,' Barbara said, 'then where is it?'

'He *had* to see it,' Heather insisted. 'He's lying.'

'Get real,' Earl said.

She leveled her eyes at him. 'Maybe you're *with* them!'

He smirked. 'Bull.'

'They sent you on ahead to find us, didn't they?'

'You're outa your tree.'

'Lee! He's one of them! He has to be. The rest of them are probably sneaking up . . .'

'I doubt it,' Lee said. Pistol in hand, he walked to the door, opened it and stepped out onto the balcony. He came back in, shaking his head.

After shutting the door, he said, 'It's clear out there. Earl's not with that bunch you told us about, Heather. The rest of them would've been in here long before now.'

Heather shook her head. 'Maybe they're waiting for a signal from him, or something.'

'Give it up,' Earl said. 'You probably made up the whole damn thing.'

'Did not.'

'Then how come *I* didn't see 'em?'

'I don't know.'

'Why would she make up something like that?' Pete asked.

'Who knows? Maybe she likes the attention.'

'I didn't make it up!'

'Take it easy,' Lee told her.

'Maybe they all went inside someplace,' Heather said. 'You know? And took the bodies in with them.'

'That's a charming thought,' Barbara said.

'Sounds to me,' Earl said, 'like a crock of shit.'

Pete faced him. 'The thing is, we were just about to get out of here when you showed up.'

'Not me,' Heather said.

'Barbara and I. What about you? Do you want to come with us?'

'Yeah, sure, what do you think? I been out there on my own all morning, and it gives me the creeps. Yeah, I'll go with you. Damn straight.'

'Could you use a change of clothes before you take off?' Lee asked him.

'Yeah! Are you kidding? That'd be great. You know what else I could sure use? Something to eat. And a drink. You got some beer or something?'

Lee frowned. 'Beer? How old are you?'

'Know what?' Earl said. 'A guy's legal drinking age, it's supposed to be twenty-one around here, right? But the thing is, there's the *unwritten* law. The Quake Factor. Ever hear of it?'

'Afraid not.'

'Sort of like that wind-chill factor they talk about in places where they've got real winters? What you gotta do, you take a guy's real age and add on the Richter scale reading of the quake he made it through that morning. That's how you arrive at the Quake Factor. I'm sixteen, right? So you add about eight from the Richter scale to that. Total it up, and it makes me about twenty-three, twenty-four years old. Way past the drinking age.'

For the first time, Lee smiled. 'You convinced me. Beer it is. How about the rest of you? Could you use some lunch and a drink before you take off?'

'That'd be great,' Pete said.

'Yeah,' Barbara said. 'I'm all for that. Thanks.'

'Okay,' Heather muttered. 'I'm still not gonna leave, but if everybody's gonna eat . . .'

'How many beers?' Lee asked. 'Going by Earl's Quake Factor, you're all old enough. It might not be very cold, though.'

# TWENTY-FIVE

When Stanley woke up, he knew right away where he was. Behind the Benson house, stretched out on one of the pool-side loungers.

He'd flopped on it after climbing out of the pool.

He hadn't meant to fall asleep. He'd meant only to lie there for a couple of minutes and rest while the sun dried him. Obviously, though, he'd drifted off. Drifted off and sunk into a deep slumber.

Now, he couldn't move. He felt as if a huge, hot weight lay across his back, holding him down, pressing him into the cushion. It felt good, though, that weight. He knew it was only hot sunlight.

And the heaviness wasn't in the light, it was in him.

In his skin and muscles and bones. In his mind.

Gotta get up, he told himself.

But he didn't move.

He felt so heavy, so peaceful.

Vaguely, he wondered if anybody had found Sheila yet.

Doesn't matter, he thought. She won't get away. She'll still be there. Or somewhere. I'd better get up, though.

He couldn't bring himself to move.

*Whatever you do, don't fall asleep again.*

*I won't.*

The cushion under his face had a fresh, clean chlorine smell. He supposed it must've gotten doused by pool water during the quake. He wished it smelled like Sheila's lounger pad – of sunlight and tanning lotion, sweat and beaches and cotton candy.

Cotton candy?

This *is* Sheila's pad, he told himself. Let's just say it is.

Yes. I'm on Sheila's pad.

And he sees himself, as if from a distance, stretched out on the lounger behind the ruin of Sheila's house. His hands are crossed beneath his face. His back shines with sweat. The flimsy remains of his pajama pants cling to his buttocks.

Now he feels the soft, moist pad underneath him.

Sheila's pad. Soaked with her lotions and juices.

*I've gotta get up. Gotta get back to Sheila before . . .*

'What's the big hurry?' she asks, her voice low and teasing.

Stanley knew that it was only in his mind. And so were her hands. But in his mind, her hands are big and warm on his back. They press him down, massage his shoulders.

'You aren't going anywhere,' she tells him. 'Not just yet.'

Then she is pulling at his shorts, sliding them down and off.

She climbs onto him. She lies on him, all hot, heavier than the sunlight. He feels her thighs against the backs of his legs. His rump is tickled by her soft nest of hair. Her breasts, just below his shoulderblades, feel big and slippery and springy. As she licks and sucks the side of his neck, he squirms.

Stanley squirmed, imagining it.

He needed to roll over.

Then he imagined a hole in the pad. A hole in the pad and in the lounger directly below his groin. As big as a softball, maybe. Big enough to fit down into. With the hole there, he wouldn't be mashed and achy anymore. He wouldn't need to roll over. The hole would let him feel all loose and free down there.

And then he thought how it would be to have Sheila under the lounger. She squirms in on her back until her face is below the hole. Then she pushes herself up with her elbows. She takes him in her mouth.

But Stanley didn't have a hole in the lounger.

He flipped over, sweat sliding and spilling off him. Though his eyes were shut, he squinted as sunlight glared yellow through the thin sheaths of his eyelids. He flung a forearm across his eyes and tried to catch his breath. His heart was racing. He felt shaky all over – buzzing – as if his blood had gone fizzy in his veins and arteries.

Rolled over too fast, he told himself. Should've done it sooner, before things got so urgent.

I'll be fine in a minute, he thought. Just gotta settle down. Lie here and relax. It would help to stop thinking about Sheila, too. I can have her for real when I want, so it doesn't make any sense to get all hot and bothered daydreaming about her. That's for losers who can't get the real thing.

If I don't watch out, he thought, I'm gonna screw up and miss the real thing. Ben found her, didn't her? What if somebody else came along?

*Then it'll be just too bad for somebody else.*

*Easy come, easy go.*

But maybe the next person to find Sheila wouldn't be as easy as Ben. If he kept on wasting time, he ran a real risk of losing his chance at her.

He knew that he had to get up.

He was already feeling better – the tremors and pounding and tightness had subsided, along with the sizzling sensation in his bloodstream. But he waited a while longer. Then he sat up slowly.

201

Sweat poured off his face, streamed down his chest and sides and belly. He felt dizzy for a moment or two, but then his head cleared.

He swung his legs over the side of the lounger. His moccasins were waiting. He slipped his feet into them, leaned forward and pushed at his knees and stood up straight. Feeling a bit unsteady, he breathed deeply and didn't try to go anywhere.

Never should've laid down like that, he thought. Lucky I didn't get heat prostration, or something.

*Who says I didn't?*

No, he told himself. I'm fine. Maybe a little dehydrated, that's all. That's probably why I'm feeling weird. Too much sun. Sweated too much.

He wondered where he could get a drink.

Depends, he thought, on whether I mind a little chlorine and blood in my water.

He decided that he didn't mind.

The water at the bottom of the pool's deep end still felt chilly. He waded in until it wrapped around his thighs. Then he bent over and cupped some into his mouth. It didn't taste bad. He couldn't detect any hint of blood flavor. He drank some more. And some more.

Then he squatted until the water covered him to the shoulders. He dunked his head. He glided forward, leaving his feet, floating through the cool silence.

He felt wonderful as he climbed out of the pool. He felt *cold.* Which didn't make any sense at all. Never had. It was part of the magic of a swimming pool. The hot air cooks you before you get in. But when you climb out, it wants to freeze your butt off. The thing is, temperature of the air hasn't changed much at all. If anything, it's hotter than before.

Crazy, he thought.

He stood by the edge of the pool, shivering and smiling.

He wished he had a pool of his own.

I'll have one put in when I rebuild, he thought. Who's gonna tell me I can't? Mother?

'Oh Stanley, Stanley, Stanley,' he said in a whiny voice, mimicking her. 'We are not going to have a swimming pool. What a ridiculous idea. I don't know what gets into you sometimes. Do you think we're *made* of money?'

'No, Mother darling,' he said in his own voice. 'I think *you're* made outa dead meat, you piece of shit.'

Laughing, he stepped into his moccasins again. He walked toward the lounger. He wanted to lie down on it. On his back, this time. Just for a while. Just long enough to let the sun dry him off and take away the chill.

'No no no no no,' he said. 'And zonk out again? Huh-uh, no way, no way.'

He went to where he had left his saw.

He bent down and picked it up, squinting as its shiny blade flashed sunlight.

'Excalibur,' he said, and waved it high.

He started walking toward the Bensons' driveway.

Why take the long way around? he wondered. So he changed direction and headed for the fence that separated their back yard from Judy's.

As he hurried along, he waved the saw and proclaimed, 'This is my sword, Excalibur. Not twenty-two caliber, not thirty-eight caliber, but *Ex*-caliber!'

He laughed.

He wished Sheila could've heard that one.

I'll have to tell it to her, he thought.

When he came to the redwood fence, he reached over the top and dropped his saw. Hitting the ground on the other side, it made a whangy sound.

Stanley gave the fence a shake. It creaked and wobbled.

Not climbing over *that*, he thought.

With both hands, he grabbed one of the upright slats. He jerked it toward him, throwing his weight backward. The board came with him. The nails near its top squawled as they were yanked out of the upper crossbeam. The lower set of nails only came out part of the way. They bent silently as he stomped the plank flat against the ground.

He ripped and smashed two more slats off the fence.

Then he crouched and tore all of them free at the bottom. He might be coming back this way later on. Maybe even after dark. It wouldn't be any good to leave the boards where he might step on them when he returned.

Not with those nails sticking up.

He made a small stack of the boards, off to one side and close to the fence. Then he returned to the opening, ducked and stepped through.

His saw had landed on a narrow, grassy strip that ran between Judy's side of the fence and the edge of her driveway. He picked it up.

He was only paces away from the spot where he'd been standing when Judy had brought the water to him.

He looked at the door to her kitchen.

It would only take a couple of minutes, he thought, to run in and check on her. Make sure she isn't getting loose.

We've already gone over that, he reminded himself. I go in just to check on her, and next thing I know I've gotta be feeling her, messing around with her, and then it's an hour or something before I get out.

Forget it. What am I, nuts? *Hunting* for ways to screw myself outa Sheila?

Judy isn't worth it. No way, no how. She's not anywhere close to being in the same league as Sheila.

But he wondered if he should make a quick trip into the kitchen. Sheila was probably awfully hungry, by now. She would be grateful for some food.

I could use a bite, myself, Stanley thought. Not to mention a drink.

'No,' he said.

We'll wait, he decided. We'll wait till Sheila's free, and then we'll come back here together and go in and have a nice party in Judy's kitchen. Vodka and tonic, maybe. And sandwiches made out of salami and cheese.

He hurried on, crossing Judy's back yard. At the far side, he placed his saw on top of the cinderblock wall. Then he boosted himself up. Crouching on the ledge, he took hold of the saw handle. Then he slowly stood, arms out for balance.

From this height, he could see down his own driveway, over the top of the gate, all the way into the street in front of his house.

Where no cars passed.

Where no people roamed.

He gave no more than a glance to his half-collapsed house, his patio and back yard, his completely collapsed garage.

Nothing was on fire.

Nobody was snooping.

Everything looked fine.

He gazed out into the distance toward Sheila's house. If his garage were still standing, it would block his view. But it had gone down to rubble like a polite bystander crouching to let him see what he wanted.

At the sight of Sheila's house, he felt a quick thrill.

The ruins weren't aswarm with rescue workers.

He saw nobody.

Excellent, he thought. This is excellent.

Somebody *might* be there, of course, hidden from view, maybe hunched down behind a heap of debris or a broken wall. But the situation sure looked good from where Stanley stood.

*What if Sheila's not there?*

She has to be.

*Somebody might've gotten her out. I've been gone for an awfully long time.*

She's there, he told himself. She has to be.

The cinderblock wall, cracked in a few places by the quake but still intact, led like a narrow walk away from Stanley, along the side of his driveway, past his fallen garage to the corner where it joined the back wall.

I can do it, Stanley told himself.

It would be a lot easier than jumping down and cutting through his yard to the back wall, climbing over that . . . Quicker, too. And if he stayed up here, he wouldn't have to lose sight of Sheila's house.

His mind made up, Stanley turned and started walking along the top of the wall. He gripped the saw in his left hand. He held both arms out away from his sides to keep himself steady, and watched the block ledge just ahead of his feet.

I shouldn't be doing this, he thought. I must be nuts.

*No. This is the best way to get to Sheila's. Long as I don't fall off.*

I won't fall, he told himself. This is a cinch.

*But what if someone's watching?*

The thought sent a shiver through his stomach.

*Here I am, up here in plain sight.*

I shouldn't be up here, he realized.

But it was a bit late to change his mind. He couldn't jump down now. A drop to the right would land him in the rough debris of his garage where he was sure to get hurt. To the left, he would fall among Judy's rosebushes.

He quickened his pace.

*They'll think I'm the Wild Man from Borneo.*

Yeah, he thought. But what are they gonna do about it? Nothing, that's what. They spot me running around like this, they'll figure I'm demented. Won't come near me. I've got nothing to worry about.

'They're the ones better worry,' he muttered.

But he felt a great surge of relief when he came to the end of the wall. He was tempted to step out into space and drop.

Don't, he warned himself. It'll hurt too much. And what if I sprain my ankle?

So he sat at the corner where the walls joined, and lowered his feet over the side. The blocks felt rough and hot against his buttocks. He tossed his saw to the ground. Then he used both hands to shove himself away from the wall.

He didn't have far to drop. The landing was fairly gentle, and he managed to stay on his feet.

It was sure good to be down.

Here below the level of the wall, he felt hidden and safe.

He picked up his saw and jogged across the grass to the patio. There, he stopped to catch his breath. He gazed at Sheila's lounger.

Its green pad was faded and stained. He could almost feel the heat of its fabric against his face. He knew its aromas. He knew its taste.

205

If I need to take another nap, he thought, I'll do it right there.

*Maybe I can fuck her on it!*

He thought about that, pictured Sheila on the lounger underneath him, imagined the feel of her, all hot and slippery, and how the lounger would wobble as he thrust.

Wobble, then smash down.

It isn't strong enough to hold us, he decided. We'd probably bust the thing. Besides, we'd be out in the open. That wouldn't be any good. Somebody'd come along and try to save her.

*I have to take her where we won't be bothered. Judy's place for a party. Then maybe over to the pool.*

Stanley walked around the lounger. As he approached the remains of the house, he thought about calling out. If he called her name, Sheila might answer. Then he would know she was still here, still all right.

But what if somebody other than Sheila heard him?

Better to sneak in.

Go in silently and keep the element of surprise.

So he stepped over the broken back wall of the house and began making his way through the debris. He moved cautiously. He watched out for nails and broken glass. With each step, he lowered his feet gently, trying to make no noise. Every so often, he stopped and listened. He heard the usual background sounds, but nothing nearby.

The carcass of Sheila's house sounded dead.

What if *she's* dead? he wondered.

Why would she be dead? She wasn't hurt, and I left her with plenty of water.

*If somebody came along and killed her . . .*

Impossible, he told himself. Absolutely.

He found himself smiling as he remembered an old joke about an idiot who was caught carrying a bomb onto an airliner. The guy had carried it aboard as an act of self-preservation. 'What are the odds,' he'd asked, 'of there being *two* bombs on the same plane?'

Pretty much the same odds, Stanley thought, as two fellas like me happening to find Sheila.

*No way has she been murdered. Impossible.*

If anything, she got herself rescued while I was gone.

If that's what happened, he told himself, I'll find her. I'll thank her rescuer for saving me the work, and then I'll kill him with my little saw.

When he spotted the hole in the debris, he whispered, 'Please, please, please.'

It *looked* the same as when he'd been here before.

But he couldn't see Sheila yet.

He stepped closer.

The four-by-eight beam that had slanted down over the side of the tub and trapped Sheila's legs was still in place.

*That's a good sign.*

But he still couldn't see Sheila.

And then he did.

*Yes!*

Only the knee of her left leg that was hooked over the top of the beam, but enough.

*If her leg's here, she's here. Unless she did like a trapped coyote and chewed her leg off, which she couldn't do anyhow, the way she was pinned down. Maybe she could've cut it off with a knife, but . . .*

The rest of Sheila was there.

She lay motionless at the bottom of the tub, apparently unaware of Stanley's arrival.

Wanting the best view possible, he made his way to the section of floor above the foot of the tub. He squatted down.

When he'd last seen Sheila, her body had been draped from chest to groin by Ben's green T-shirt. Since then, somebody had pulled it higher. Now she was naked below the navel. The T-shirt still hid her breasts, but now it also covered her face.

*They cover your face when you're dead.*

That's why she isn't moving, he thought. She's dead.

Stanley saw no blood on her bare skin. No blood had soaked through the T-shirt, either. She didn't look hurt, just dead. He wondered if the sun had gotten to her. Or maybe she'd had internal injuries. A heart attack? An aneurism? Being muscular and full of energy didn't mean something couldn't go wrong inside and kill you.

Maybe someone had come along and strangled her.

He supposed that anything was possible. There were plenty of ways to die. And one of them had found Sheila.

Found her and killed her.

*No fair! She was supposed to be mine!*

She still is, he realized. She's here, isn't she? Dead, but here. Maybe it isn't such a bad thing, either. She was awfully strong. She might've given me some real trouble. This way, I won't have to fight her.

*But I wanted to fight her!*

Oh, well, he thought. That's the way the cookie crumbles. At least she didn't get away.

He wondered if he would still need to saw through one of the beams. Probably not. With her dead like this, he supposed he could simply pull her free. That'd be a lot easier and quicker than sawing through one of the beams. Use a little force and drag her out. Maybe have to break her neck or pop a leg out of its socket to help her clear the beams.

For that matter, it would be easy enough to saw off her head. With that gone, Sheila wouldn't have any problem at all clearing the overhead beam.

*I don't wanta cut off her head. Not right straight off the bat, just to get her out. It'd ruin her looks.*

Doesn't have to ruin anything, he told himself. I can take it with me. I can even set it up right in front of us so I can watch her face . . . all sorts of things I can do with it.

He got hard as he sat there and thought about uses for her severed head.

Plenty of time for that stuff later, he finally told himself. I oughta try to get her out in one piece, so at least I can start out with her whole.

Stanley set the saw aside, then lowered his legs toward the tub. He spread them wide enough to let him put his feet on the porcelain ledges.

As he started to stand, the tub wobbled slightly.

Sheila moaned.

Stanley flinched, then held still. He stood motionless on the sides of the tub and gazed down at her.

Gazed hard.

And detected the slight rise and fall of her bare belly, of the green T-shirt covering her ribcage and her breasts.

She was breathing.

Had she been breathing all along? How could Stanley not have noticed? *Unless maybe she'd been holding her breath?*

*Playing possum?*

She wouldn't do something like that, he told himself. Not Sheila. That isn't her style. She's asleep, that's all, and I just jumped to conclusions about her being dead because she had the shirt on her face.

She had probably pulled it up there, herself.

Earlier, her face had been in shadow. But the sun had changed position during Stanley's absence, taking away the shade. She must've drawn the shirt up to shield her eyes from the direct sunlight.

Of course.

Now that he realized she was alive, he wondered how he could've possibly mistaken her for dead. The breathing was really pretty obvious. And her skin was shiny with sweat, ruddy from the heat or sunburn. Dead people might be red, he supposed. But they don't sweat, do they?

Sheila looked alive, all right. And very hot.

The water bottle that he'd left with her was empty. She or someone – had set it upright on top of the beam above her face.

Might need to go and get more, Stanley thought.

*No. I'm not leaving again, no way. We'll just have to get by. We can drink all we want when we get to Judy's.*

He wished he had thought to bring more water with him, though. He didn't want thirst to ruin his good time. Or rush him. He wanted to enjoy every moment of this, and make it last and last.

Still poised on the ledges of the tub, he squatted down. He placed his left hand on the beam that angled down across the top of Sheila's right thigh. Then he leaned forward.

This was the closest he had ever been to her.

He wanted to see her breasts. But she would wake up, for sure, if he reached out and snatched away the T-shirt.

There'll be plenty of time later for them, he told himself. For right now, enjoy what shows.

So he studied her.

And longed to feel her.

If he dared, he could reach down with his right hand and actually touch the smooth, sunlit curves of her left hip – stroke the skin of her belly – slip his fingers through her shiny curls and caress the fleshy lips that he could see down lower – even get a finger or two inside her.

But any sort of touch was likely to disturb her sleep.

She wakes up and finds me messing with her, Stanley thought, and she won't trust me anymore. The longer I keep her faked out, the better.

Even if she catches me hovering over her like this . . .

Very carefully, he uncrouched and made his way backward to the foot of the tub. Instead of climbing all the way out, he sat on the edge of the floor.

*Not yet, not yet!*

He was sticking up high out of the left leg hole of his pajama pants.

She sees that, he thought, and she'll know something's up.

He laughed softly.

He tried to cover it, but the flimsy fabric just fell away.

So he waited. Finally, he settled down. He adjusted his pajama pants.

There. He still showed. Sheila would be able to get a good look up through the leg hole, but he wasn't sticking out like some sort of exhibitionist.

Don't want her thinking I'm a pervert, he thought.

Then he laughed again.

Then he quietly called, 'Sheila? Sheila, I'm back. It's me, Stanley.'

# TWENTY-SIX

Sheila took a long time waking up. She groaned. She shifted her body slightly as if searching for a more comfortable position. The way she acted, she might've thought she was coming out of sleep on a fine morning in her own bed. But abruptly, she went rigid, snatched the T-shirt down from her face, and raised her head off the bottom of the tub. She squinted up at Stanley.

He gazed down at her, stunned. She was even better than he remembered. Her beauty wasn't diminished at all by her sweaty, flushed face and the tangles of hair glued down wet against her forehead. She looked as if she had just stepped out from under a shower.

In the brightness of the sun, her blue eyes looked like the summer sky on a clear day.

The specks of sweat above her lip looked like diamonds.

She licked her lips. Then she said, 'Oh.' After a pause, she said, 'Stan.'

'Are you all right?' he asked.

'I feel . . . wasted. Guess I'm okay. My butt keeps falling asleep.' One side of her mouth twitched as if she wanted to smile.

'I'll get you out of there, now.'

'You went off with . . . Ben?'

'Yeah. He might be back later.'

'There was a girl.'

'Right. We managed to pull her out. Ben and I. I couldn't have done it without him. Anyway, she was pretty banged up. One of her arms was broken, and she had some head injuries. But she could walk, so we decided I'd come back here to help you, and Ben'd take her over to the hospital. That one over on Pico?'

'Yeah.'

'So, here I am.' Smiling, he picked up his saw. 'Me and my trusty saw, Excalibur.'

'Excalibur?'

'Not twenty-two, thirty-eight or forty-five caliber. *Ex*calibur.'

Again, she tried to smile. 'I'm sure glad you're back,' she said. 'I was afraid you'd forgotten about me.'

210

'I could never forget about you, Sheila.' Even as he spoke the words, he regretted them.

'Guess not,' she said. 'The naked babe in the tub.'

The way she said that, Stanley knew he was all right; she hadn't picked up anything strange about his remark.

'Things might've happened to you, though,' she explained. 'That's what had me scared, really. I figured you'd come back if you could.'

'You figured right.'

'It just seemed like such a long time. Felt like hours.'

'We had a hard time getting the girl out. Did anyone come by while I was gone?'

Sheila shook her head. 'Don't think so. I dropped out of the picture, though. Fell asleep, I guess. Or passed out. I don't think anyone showed up, but . . . is anybody around?'

'Not much of anyone,' Stanley said. 'I spotted a few oddballs roaming the neighborhood. Like the ones I told you about before? Creepy types. But they didn't see me. I think we'll be all right as long as we don't make a lot of noise.'

'They're close enough to hear us?'

'Probably not. Just don't shout or something.'

'Okay. God. Thank God *they* didn't find me.'

'We'd better get you out of there,' Stanley said.

'Yeah. Please.'

With the saw in his right hand, he stood up. He made his way slowly forward, sliding the soles of his moccasins along the smooth ledges of the tub. The beam across the other end blocked his view of Sheila's face, and she probably couldn't see much higher than his chest. He wondered where she was looking.

At least I'm not sticking out, he told himself. It isn't my fault if she sees something she shouldn't. Isn't my fault if I'm turned on, either. She's the one who's naked around here, not me.

'What about the fire?' Sheila asked.

What fire? Stanley wondered. Then he remembered the burning house across the street.

'Didn't see it,' he said. 'Must've burnt itself out.'

He tried to remember what he had seen over there during his return. Nothing.

At the very least, there must've been smoke rising from the ruins.

He couldn't recall.

Too focused on Sheila, he supposed. But nothing of much importance could've been going on, or he would've noticed.

'Nothing left but smoking rubble,' he told Sheila – and wished he could remember.

*What else did I miss?*

Bending his knees, he leaned forward the same as before and placed his left hand on top of the beam that angled downward between her legs. Now, he could see Sheila's face again.

*Gorgeous.*

Was there a wariness in her eyes that hadn't been there before?

*That ain't wariness – that's horniness.*

It's probably nothing at all, he told himself. Don't go reading things in.

'What are you going to do?' Sheila asked.

'Cut right through it,' he said. He tapped the edge of his saw against the beam's front corner. It bit in, digging a tiny wedge into the wood. He began to pump it back and forth.

Pale sawdust torn from the gash spilled over the front of the beam and drifted down between Sheila's legs. She gasped. Her right hand darted down and she clapped it to her body.

A flurry of sawdust fell on the back of her hand.

'Wait, Stan. Wait.'

He stopped.

'It'll still be on top of my leg,' she said. 'Maybe you should try over there.' She nodded to her right. 'Do it over by the side of the tub, and we can take off the whole section.'

'I guess I could do that,' he admitted. He moved the saw seven or eight inches up the slanted beam. 'Here?'

'Perfect.'

He drew the blade back and forth a few times. Now, the sawdust drifted down between the wall of the tub and and side of her right thigh.

He met Sheila's eyes. 'If I cut it off here, you know, your leg's likely to get mashed pretty good when it drops.'

'Oh, don't worry about that. My leg's pretty strong.'

'You'd still be able to get out if I cut through the center where I was doing it before. Nothing would end up dropping on you, either, and we'd only have half as big a piece to deal with.'

'But I'd have to squeeze my way out,' Sheila said. 'I don't like it. God knows what'll happen when this thing isn't propped up anymore. You really should cut it off there. Please.'

'Your wish is my command.'

'Don't be angry.'

'I'm not angry. I'll cut it off anywhere you want.'

'Okay. Thanks.'

He resumed sawing. It was hard work: not so much the pumping of his right arm, but how he had to stand so precariously on the edges of the tub, knees bent, waist bent, torso twisted awkwardly so that he could

212

reach the place where Sheila insisted that he make the cut. The sun felt very hot on his back. But he liked how his pajama pants were clinging halfway down his buttocks and how he felt so loose and free in front and how the sawing motion made him swing in there.

His body ran with sweat. The dribbles tickled. They felt odd when they got inside his ears. They stung when they got in his eyes. But he liked the way they dropped off his head and face and fell like small, shiny bombs onto Sheila. She still kept the hand between her legs. The sweat bombs hit the back of her hand, her wrist and forearm, and the nearby areas that the hand didn't cover. The tops of her thighs. Her curves and slanting hollows. The tender skin below her navel. Clear, gleaming bombs that hit and exploded with tiny splashes and mingled with Sheila's own sweat.

Her belly-button was full and shimmering.

Stanley's sweat fell all around it, but none wanted to land dead center. He changed his position slightly, but still couldn't find the target.

Then he thought about how he would like to put his mouth down there, seal his lips around her brimming navel and suck it empty, and afterwards thrust the tip of his tongue down into the hole.

The tongue part would probably hurt her and make her squirm.

She would try to make him stop.

I oughta do it right now, he thought. What's she gonna do about it, pinned down like that?

What's she gonna do about anything?

*A whole new ballgame, once she's loose.*

He stopped sawing. As he forced his fingers to release the handle, he noticed how badly his left arm trembled from the strain of bracing himself above the beam. The muscles of his legs and rump also fluttered. His back ached. So did his neck.

'Are you okay?' Sheila asked.

'Yeah,' he huffed. 'Just . . .' He shook his head.

Leaving the saw embedded in the deep groove, he wiped his face with his upper arm. The arm felt as slick and wet as his face. It didn't seem to do any good at all. Blinking, he glimpsed the green of Ben's T-shirt.

'Can't see . . . what I'm doing,' he gasped. 'Need a rag.'

'Maybe you'd better rest a while,' Sheila said.

'You mind?' Leaning forward, muscles juddering, he stretched his right arm down over the beam toward the T-shirt.

'No!' While Sheila kept her right hand tight between her legs, her left forearm clamped the shirt against her chest. 'Don't,' she said, and shook her head. 'I need it, Stan. Please.'

'Okay. Okay. But I . . . I've gotta be able to see. But that's okay. I'll just . . . take a rest.'

He groaned as he straightened his back. When he was standing upright, he slid his moccasins along the ledges of the tub and slowly began to make his way backward.

He sat on the edge of the broken floor. With both hands, he wiped his dripping face. Then he interlaced his fingers behind his head, pressed his hands against his drenched hair, and arched his back.

'I'm sorry,' Sheila said.

'Sorry?'

'I shouldn't have . . . You can have it.'

'What?'

'The shirt.'

'No,' he said. 'That's okay. You need it.' He pulled his legs up, scooted backward and began to stand.

'What're you doing?' Sheila asked. Her voice sounded calm but worried.

He stood up. He couldn't see her face, though, so he squatted before answering. 'I'll go and . . . find a towel. It won't take long.'

'No! Don't leave! Please!' Her eyes shifted to the saw. 'You've almost got it done, Stan. Just a couple more minutes, and . . .'

'It'll take a lot longer than that. I'm only about halfway. And I'm all worn out. So damn sweaty, too – it hurts in your eyes. I'll find a towel somewhere, and maybe lay down for a while.'

'Don't! Here!' With both hands, she snatched up the T-shirt. She crumpled it and hurled the bundle at Stanley.

He watched how the sudden movement of her right arm made her breasts jump and shake. Then the unfurling T-shirt blocked his view. He grabbed it out of the air in time to see Sheila tuck her right hand down between her legs and fling her left arm across her breasts.

Bitch, he thought.

He wadded the shirt and mopped his face with it. When he rubbed his hair, he saw that Sheila was squinting up at him.

'This helps a lot,' he said. 'Thanks.'

She didn't say anything.

Stanley winced when he rubbed his shoulders and the back of his neck.

'We're both gonna have nasty sunburns,' he said.

'Yeah.'

'We'll put something on 'em when I get you out of here.'

He rubbed his arms with the T-shirt. Then his armpits. Then his chest and sides and belly. Then his face again. Done, he held up the sodden ball of fabric. 'You can have it back, now.'

'Keep it,' Sheila said.

'Are you sure?'

214

'I'm sure.'

She didn't sound very friendly, anymore.

Stanley stood up, his knees crackling as he straightened his legs. He couldn't see her face from this height, but that was just fine; she couldn't see his, either. He allowed himself to grin.

'I'll go and find us some water,' he said.

'No!' she blurted, shock and alarm in her voice. 'Don't! Please, Stan! You're almost done with the sawing. Don't go anyplace now. Just cut through the rest of the way. Please.'

'Why should I?' he asked.

Sheila didn't answer.

There seemed to be a great stillness.

Stanley stood motionless, staring down at her. She didn't seem to be moving at all, not even breathing. She looked rigid. Her right breast was tightly clutched by her hand, while her left breast was pushed down by her forearm. Because of the middle beam, he couldn't see much of her right hand. From the position of the wrist, however, he supposed that it was welded between her legs.

'Why should I do *anything* for you?' he asked.

After another long silence, Sheila spoke. Her voice sounded low and tightly controlled. 'What's going on?'

'What've you done for *me* lately? Huh? I'm out here in the hot sun working like a slave, and what're you doing for me? Nothing. Giving me orders, that's what you're doing. Telling me what to do, like I don't know where I'm supposed to cut a fucking board. Giving me all kinds of stink when all I do is ask for your shirt so I can wipe my face. I've gotta *pry* the fuckin' shirt off you. And then you go and cover up like you're scared I'll catch a peek at your precious titties. Who do you think you are, huh? Who do you think's doing *who* a favor around here?'

'You're doing *me* the favor, Stan,' she said. She sounded as if she were trying very hard to sound calm and reasonable and sympathetic. 'I really and truly appreciate it, too.'

'Yeah? Well, you don't act like it.'

'I'm sorry. This is all very . . . difficult. My family . . . I don't know where my little girl is.' She suddenly started to cry. 'Or my husband. They might be dead, for all I know. I'm . . . I'm trying to hang on . . . don't mean to . . . to be bad to you.'

Except for her legs, her whole body seemed to be shaking and twitching as she sobbed there in the bottom of the tub. Stan watched, amazed and delighted. She was so sleek and shiny, all curves and hollows that rippled and throbbed and writhed, and the arm across her breasts couldn't hold them still.

The sight made him stiff and achy.

215

He glanced down. The front of his pajama pants jutted out so much that Sheila couldn't possibly miss it.

He thought about squatting down to conceal the bulge.

*Why should I? She sees what she sees. She better get used to it.*

Soon, Sheila's crying subsided. She sniffled a few times. She sighed. After a while, she said, 'Are you going to finish sawing the beam for me?'

'Maybe. Maybe not. What'll you do for *me*?'

Slowly, both her hands slid away from where they covered her. 'Is this what you want?' she asked.

Stanley grinned. 'I didn't say that.'

'You didn't have to.'

Her hands settled lightly on the smooth plain of skin below her ribcage. 'Okay?' she asked.

'Lovely.'

'Now get back to the saw,' she said.

'When I'm good and ready.'

Her hands slid, the right gliding downward while the left moved toward her breast.

'Don't push your luck,' Stanley said.

She didn't let the warning stop her.

'Okay, okay!' Stanley snapped.

'When you start sawing, I'll take my hands away.'

'Okay!' Once again, he lowered his legs toward the tub. He stood on its ledges and shuffled along until he came to the four-by-eight. Bending over, he braced his left hand against it. His right hand gripped the saw.

'Start,' Sheila said.

'Yeah,' he said. 'Sure.'

Tugging at the saw's wooden handle, he drew the blade out of its deep slot in the beam.

Sheila frowned. 'What're you doing?'

'You want me to start sawing. I always do what I'm told.' Her cry of pain split the quiet as Stanley ran the saw across the top of her left thigh.

# TWENTY-SEVEN

'You'd better keep down,' Em warned, 'or else you'll pork your back.'

The man crawling underneath the tree grunted and stayed low until he was well clear of the trunk. His silver jewelry jangled as he rolled onto his back. Red-faced and huffing, he raised his knees into the air. 'You hear that, Loreen?' he called.

'I heard, Caspar,' a woman answered. She sounded irritated. 'I'm not deaf, you know.'

'Never said you were, baby.' He rolled his head sideways and blinked toward Em. 'Hello, miss.'

'Just Em,' the girl said. 'That's short for Emerald. These are my pals, Clint and Mary.'

'Pleased to meet you all,' Caspar said. He pushed at the pavement, struggling to sit up. 'Whew! That's a mighty steep old road back there. And I, for one, am not as young as I used to be.'

'How old were you then?' Em asked.

Caspar, done sitting up, scowled at her. He was as fat as Santa, but beardless. He had no mustache, either, but his black eyebrows were enormous, bushy, upswept to points, and more Satanic than Santa-like.

Though his scowl looked ferocious, Em smiled.

'Just my luck,' he said. 'A scamp. Beware of geeks bearing wit.'

Em's jaw dropped. She glanced from Clint to Mary. 'I think he just called me a geek. Did you hear that? He doesn't even know me.'

'He's psychic,' Mary said.

'Hardy har.'

'Psychic indeed,' Caspar said. He turned to the woman who was poking her head out from under the tree. 'Didn't see this one coming, did we, my dear?'

'Speak for yourself.'

'Watch your back, darling,' he warned her.

She kept crawling forward. Like Caspar, she was rotund, red-faced, and out of breath. She appeared to be twenty-five or thirty years old – about half his age. Her jet black hair was shorter than his, and shaped like a football helmet while his was a shaggy mane.

Clear of the trunk, she sat on the pavement next to Caspar.

What a pair, Clint thought.

They wore matching red blouses – loose, airy affairs that gleamed like silk, had billowing sleeves, and were gathered in around their waists with broad, golden sashes. Loreen wore a peasant skirt; Caspar, a pair of crisp blue jeans. They sported sandals instead of shoes. They each wore more jewelry than Clint had seen on one person in a long time: enormous hoops that dangled from their ears, necklaces, pendants, bracelets, rings on most of their fingers.

Patting the woman's leg, Caspar looked from Clint to the others and said, 'My Loreen. What would I do without her? Smile more often, perhaps?'

She slapped the back of his hand. 'He finds himself amusing,' she explained.

'We just finished eating,' Clint said. 'We have some salami and cheese left over. Would you like some?'

'That would be splendid, I'm sure,' Caspar said.

'Help yourselves,' Em said, leaning forward and handing the bag to him. As he took it, she asked, 'What are your costumes for? Do you work in a Greek restaurant?'

'Scamp,' Caspar said.

'We're gypsies, my dear,' Loreen explained.

'Oh, delightful,' Mary muttered.

Clint gave her an annoyed glance. She smirked at him.

Em and the newcomers paid no attention. Em, sitting up straight, grabbed her knees and said, '*Real* gypsies?'

'What's real?' asked Caspar, peering into the bag.

'We're gypsy fortune-tellers,' Loreen explained.

'The Blotskis,' Caspar added. 'We're world famous in Studio City.' He took out a handful of cheese slices and the remains of the salami, and one of the knives.

'I don't think I've heard of you,' Em said.

'We won't hold that against you,' Caspar said.

'You're one among legions,' Loreen told her.

'Our parlor's in Studio City,' Caspar explained 'but our *lair* is in West Hollywood. The hike appears to be more than we bargained for.'

'Couldn't get through the traffic?' Clint asked.

'Ah. I took one peek at Ventura Boulevard and decided to leave our car in the parking lot.'

'My feet will never be the same,' Loreen said.

'The hike will do us good.'

'If it doesn't kill us.'

'You're almost to the top,' Clint said.

'Speaking of which,' Mary said, 'shouldn't we be going?'

218

'What's the hurry?' Em asked.

Though Clint hated to agree with Mary about anything, he told Em, 'We've been resting here too long already. I want to get home.'

'But these are gypsies.'

'Yeah,' Mary said. 'Sure thing.'

'I don't know about you, but I'd sort of like to have my fortune told.'

'What do you want to know, sweetie?' Loreen asked.

Em frowned. 'Don't you have to use a crystal ball or look at my palm or something?'

'Not Loreen,' Caspar said, cutting off a thick disk of salami. 'She's a face-reader.'

'I never heard of something like that.'

'A mug-inspector,' Caspar added.

'A fraud,' Mary muttered.

Clint had no doubt that everyone heard her, but nobody reacted.

Loreen said, 'Tell me what you want to know, Emerald.'

Em gnawed her lower lip. Then she said, 'To begin with, what's my last name?'

Caspar, chuckling, placed a slice of cheese on top of the salami piece. 'Such a scamp,' he said as he handed it to Loreen. 'A test! She wants to test you. How do you like that one?'

'I'm afraid I don't do parlor tricks,' Loreen told Em. 'Your last name is no mystery to you. I deal only in mysteries, in the dark secrets lurking in the mists of the future.'

'What a load,' Mary said.

Loreen didn't ignore that one. She turned her head toward Mary, smiled pleasantly, and said, 'The parting mists do show you, smart lady, coming to a very bad end in the very near future.'

Em cackled.

Smiling beatifically, Loreen chomped her salami and cheese.

'That's *real* funny,' Mary said. 'Ha ha ha. What am I supposed to do now, tremble? I'm *so* scared. Weirdos.'

Words muffled by her soggy mouthful, Loreen said, 'I just call 'em like I see 'em. So sorry. Rest in peace, honey.'

'Bitch.'

'Hey!' Clint snapped.

'She said I'm gonna die!'

'And soon,' Em added, laughing.

'That's really for shit!'

Clint tried not to smile.

'Oh, yeah, you think it's funny, too. You wouldn't think it was so funny if she said it about Em, though, would you? You'd be laughing out of the other side of your face, then.'

'I'm not laughing,' Clint explained.

'Maybe not, but you *want* to.'

'*I* am not laughing,' Caspar said. The grim tone of his voice shocked Clint. Em's laughter stopped as if crushed by a boot. 'You called my Loreen a bitch,' Caspar said, staring at Mary, his eyelids half shut. The salami was in his left hand, the knife in his right. He raised the blade of the knife. 'Perhaps I should remove your tongue?'

Oh, Jesus, Clint thought. 'She didn't mean anything,' he said.

'She called my Loreen a bitch.'

Clint turned on Mary. 'Tell them you're sorry. You didn't mean it.'

'The hell I will.'

'Do it!'

Her eyes suddenly shimmered with tears. 'You're just gonna let this asshole threaten me?'

Em rolled her eyes upward. 'Oh, wonderful, now she's called *him* an asshole. The fun never ends. Jeezle-peezle, Mary!' Leaning forward, she patted Caspar's knee. 'Don't let her get to you, okay? Sometimes, she's a *putz*. You know what I mean? You've just gotta basically ignore her.'

Caspar slowly nodded. 'For you, my little scamp, I'll let the woman keep her tongue.'

'Only because you're so nice,' Loreen added.

Mary wiped her eyes, then glared at Clint. 'Thanks a heap, He-man.'

'I'm not here to save your butt when you go running off at the mouth. I don't know what your problem is, but . . .'

'I'm a *putz*.'

Frowning, Em tilted her head and asked nobody in particular, 'Can a female person *be* a *putz*? Or is that a term that only applies in a strict sense to men?'

'It applies in Mary's case,' Loreen said, smiling.

Mary's face darkened and her mouth opened. But she shut her mouth fast.

'We're all friends again,' Caspar said. 'Aren't we, Mary?'

'Yeah, sure.'

He bared his teeth at her. 'Of course, I was kidding about cutting out your tongue. Just kidding. A little joke. I would never cut out the tongue of a pretty woman like you.'

Clint fully expected the next words out of Caspar's mouth to be, 'Of course, I would cheerfully *slit your throat* from ear to ear,' and mean it.

From the looks on the faces of Mary and Em, they seemed to be thinking pretty much the same thing.

Whoever this guy is, Clint thought, he's dangerous. Friendly and cheerful, but definitely dangerous. And probably no more of a gypsy than I am – just some sort of showman or con artist, or God knows what. Same with Loreen.

What's she, anyway? His wife? His daughter?

Ask?

Yeah, right, and risk the Wrath of Caspar? No, thanks. Leave that sort of thing to Em.

'Can we get going, now?' Mary asked.

'Let's wait till they're done eating,' Em said, 'and we can all walk together.'

'And why would we want to do that?'

'Well, for starters, it wouldn't be very polite to walk away and leave them. Also, I happen to find them very fascinating people.'

'Thank you, dear,' Loreen said.

'You're welcome.' She returned her attention to Mary. 'And also, it's a well-known fact that there is safety in numbers.'

'Excellent observation,' Caspar said, and stuffed his mouth with salami and cheese.

'Thank you,' Em told him. 'I'll just bet you'd be handy to have around if we should happen to run into a hooligan or two.'

Busy chewing, he nodded and twirled the blade of the knife.

'You can have some of that water, by the way,' Em added. 'You two are probably parched. I should've mentioned it. Those bottles in the bag there . . .'

'Ah.' He reached into the bag and pulled out one of the plastic bottles. Only about a cup of water remained in it. 'Thank you, my dear. You are a life saver.' He took a single swallow, then passed the bottle to Loreen.

Like Caspar, she restricted herself to one swallow. Then she licked her lips and said, 'Delicious.'

'Drink some more,' Em said. 'Both of you. That was hardly enough to wet your whistles.'

'Maybe later,' Loreen told her. She handed the bottle back to Caspar, who capped it and returned it to the sack.

'I think we could use a couple more people,' Clint said. 'Especially in case of trouble.' Eyeing Mary, he added, 'As long as we can all get along together. Are you going to behave?'

'I'll behave,' she said. Lowering her eyes, she muttered, 'Like I have a choice.'

'If you act up,' Em warned, 'we'll let Caspar cut your tongue out.'

'Oh, you're real funny.'

Clint sighed. 'That's no help, Em.'

'But fun.'

'Such a scamp,' Caspar said.

'She doesn't need any encouragement,' Clint told him.

'You're right. Emerald, be a sweetheart and stop pestering Mary.'

'Thanks,' Clint said. 'Anyway, what do you think about joining up with us?'

'Which way are you heading?' Loreen asked.

'Some psychic,' Mary muttered. And quickly added, 'Sorry.'

'They're heading the same as us,' Caspar told her. 'You didn't see them on the way up?'

'I wasn't looking up.'

'I saw them. I saw *someone*. It was you?'

'Probably,' Clint said. 'Nobody else seems to be up here.'

'I didn't see anyone,' Loreen said.

'We know that,' Caspar told her. 'Tell us something we don't know.'

'We're in for big trouble,' she said in a very casual voice, as if commenting on bland weather.

Clint felt his stomach sink.

'Wonderful,' Mary muttered.

Em curled her upper lip. 'Is that a prediction?' she asked Loreen.

The woman didn't answer, but Caspar said, 'I'm afraid so.' Then he asked Loreen, 'What sort of trouble?'

'Big trouble.'

'Is she getting this from someone's face?' Em asked Caspar. 'You said she's a face-reader.'

'From the face of the day,' Loreen said. 'I see blood on the face of the day.'

Mary let out a huff of air. She said, 'This is such . . .' But she didn't let herself finish.

Everyone stared at Loreen.

'Tell us more,' Caspar said.

'I see death at sunset.'

Something down low inside Clint seemed to shrivel.

'One of us?' Caspar asked.

'All right,' Clint said. 'That's enough. Just cut it out. I don't know who you people are, but I don't want to hear any more of this. Nobody can predict the future . . . and you're giving me the creeps. So knock it off, okay? I don't want to hear this kind of stuff. Just keep it to yourselves, or . . .'

'I don't want to be *around* them,' Mary protested, standing up. 'Okay? Let's just go.'

'If you leave now,' Em said, 'you won't find out who's going to die at sunset.'

'As if I didn't know. Who do you *suppose* the fat lady's gonna finger? She's got it in for me. You've *all* got it in for me.'

'No, we don't,' Em said. 'That's silly.'

222

Mary frowned down at Clint. 'Are you coming?'

'Is everybody ready?' he asked, glancing at the others.

'Those two don't have to come with us, do they? Come on, Clint, they're . . . they scare me.'

'I'm done with banishing people.'

'You oughta be happy about that,' Em told her.

'As far as I'm concerned,' Clint said, 'the Blotskis are welcome to come along.'

'You're a fine and decent man,' Loreen said.

'True,' Caspar added. 'And that's not a prediction, it's a fact. Mind if we eat while we walk?'

'Go ahead. Just lay off this fortune-telling stuff. Nobody wants to hear it.'

'Or maybe,' Em suggested, 'you could tell us just the nifty stuff, and leave out anything that's ooky.'

'No,' Clint said. 'Any more predictions, nifty, ooky or otherwise, and *I'm* going to take off and leave everybody behind.'

'Same here,' Mary said.

'Those are the ground rules.'

'Fine by me,' Caspar said. 'Loreen?'

She pressed a forefinger to her greasy lips. 'Mum's the word,' she said.

Clint got to his feet. 'Let's get moving,' he said. 'We're almost to the top, so the worst is behind us.'

# TWENTY-EIGHT

They had eaten a lunch of barbeque-flavored potato chips and peanut butter and jelly sandwiches. Barbara had tried a beer, but she'd given up on it after one taste, and switched to Dr Pepper. The others had seemed to enjoy their beers.

Leaving Heather to keep watch out the window, Lee had taken Earl into the bedroom for a change of clothes. Barbara and Pete had sat beside each other on the floor while they were gone. Barbara could hear quiet talking from the other room, but she couldn't make out the words.

'Cool, huh?' Earl said as he swaggered into the living room. He'd kept the dead man's huge, white shirt. But the pin-striped slacks had been replaced by a pair of camouflage trousers and he now wore white socks and faded blue running shoes. He fluttered a baggy leg of the pants. 'Gets all his stuff at Supply Sergeant.'

Heather looked over her shoulder and smirked. She said nothing, though.

'All I need's like an M-16, or something, and I'd be all set to rock 'n' roll.' He grinned at Lee. 'Anyway, thanks for the duds. I'll get 'em back to you, promise.'

'No hurry,' Lee said.

'Thanks for feeding us,' Barbara said, getting to her feet.

'Yeah,' Pete said. 'It sure hit the spot.'

'Glad I could help,' Lee told them.

'Now, if you *really* wanta help,' Earl said, 'how about letting us borrow one of your guns?' He said it smiling, as if it were a big joke, but Barbara knew he meant it.

'No can do.'

Earl made a mock-pouting face. 'Hey, I thought we were pals.'

'I don't loan out my weapons.'

'You don't need both of 'em, do you?'

'Yes.'

'Hey, come on. How am I gonna protect Banner if I don't have a gun? Look at her. She's a beauty, isn't she?'

Lee glanced at Barbara. His eyes darted from her face to the hand that held her blouse shut, then back to Earl. He said nothing.

'Don't you care what happens to her?'

'I care.'

'All we gotta do, you know, is run into the wrong sort of guys out there on our way home, and . . .'

'Stay here,' Lee said. 'Nobody's pushing you out the door.'

'I have to get home,' Barbara told him. 'My parents . . .'

'Same here,' Pete said.

'But we don't need one of your guns,' she added.

'Speak for yourself,' Earl said.

'I just did. I don't want one.'

'I do.' Earl frowned at Lee. 'Come on, you've got that *assault* rifle.' He nodded at the carbine that was leaning against the sofa near Heather. 'What do you need the pistol for? It might save our lives. Might save Banner from getting herself reamed by a gang of drooling maniacs.'

Barbara scowled. 'Shut up.'

Heather smirked over her shoulder at Earl. 'You said there *isn't* any gang of maniacs out there.'

'Yeah, well, who knows? Just 'cause I didn't see it . . . I sure saw plenty of poor jerks who'd gotten themselves trashed real good. It ain't exactly a picnic out there.'

'Then don't leave,' Lee said. He looked at Barbara. 'I know you want to get home. I know you're worried about your parents . . .'

'And it has to be killing them, not knowing if I'm okay.'

'Same here,' Pete said.

Lee nodded. 'I understand. But you'd be better off playing it safe. Do you think that your parents would want you to risk your lives, just in order to get home a little bit sooner? Not a chance. The National Guard'll be on the streets tomorrow.'

'The Guard?' Pete asked. 'Really?'

'How do you know?' Barbara asked.

'Heard it on my radio,' Lee said.

'You've got a radio that works?'

'Down in my car.'

'Sure!' Pete said. 'Car radios. They'll still work.'

'What else did you hear?' Barbara asked.

'Not much. I had to get back into the building. The car was no good as a defensive position, so . . .'

'But they said for sure the National Guard will be here tomorrow?' Pete asked. He seemed very excited.

'That's right.'

'Jeez, Barbara. Maybe we *should* stay here. You know?'

'Not me. I can't wait till tomorrow. Besides, how do we know the Guard will really show up when it's supposed to? It'd be crazy to wait

225

that long on the chance that things'll be safer. I mean, we're only a few miles from home. An hour or so, that's all it'll take.'

'On the other hand,' Lee said, 'you might not make it at all.'

'I'll take my chances,' Barbara told him.

'See that?' Earl said. 'She's going, with or without a gun.'

'I don't want a gun,' Barbara repeated.

'I do,' Earl said. 'Come on, Lee. You afraid I won't bring it back?'

'That's not . . .'

'I'll *buy* one of 'em off you? Okay? I'll give you five hundred bucks for the forty-five.'

Lee shook his head.

'Six hundred.'

'We both know you don't have any money, Earl.'

'Maybe not on me . . .'

'I'm going,' Barbara said. 'Thanks again for the lunch, Lee.'

'Welcome.'

'Pete, are you coming?'

'Just hang on a minute,' Earl said. 'Nobody's going anywhere. We're in the middle of some negotiations here.'

Barbara smirked. 'Negotiations, my butt. You haven't got any money.'

'How much have you got?'

'Not nearly enough. Maybe five bucks.'

'Pete?'

'Six or seven, I guess.'

'Heather?'

'I'm not paying nothing,' Heather told him. 'I'm staying right here.'

'Okay,' Earl said. 'Okay. So, we don't buy it with money. What'll you take for the forty-five, Lee?'

Lee was beginning to look annoyed. 'I won't take anything for it. I'm not selling.'

'What'll you take to let us *borrow* it just for . . . say, three or four days? I mean, we only need it for an hour or two, but I'm not sure when I'll be able to get it back to you.'

'Forget it,' Lee said.

'How about an hour with Banner?' Grinning at Barbara, Earl patted her shoulder.

She swatted his hand away.

'Hey! Watch the merchandise!'

'Keep your hands off her!' Pete snapped.

'Yeah, yeah, sure, don't wet your pants. How about it, Lee? Look at her. A fair trade – you get an hour in the sack with Banner, and we get the loan of your forty-five.'

Lee met her eyes.

226

*My God, he's thinking it over!*

'No,' she said. Her voice sounded hollow and seemed to ring in her ears.

'How about it, Lee? A deal?'

'She said no.'

'What if she changes her mind?'

'Cut it out,' Pete warned.

'Shut up.'

'She isn't gonna do something like that.'

'Maybe she is and maybe she isn't. Lee's gonna let us have the gun if she comes across.'

'No.' Lee shook his head. He seemed less sure of himself than before. After a moment, he added, 'Not unless she wants to.'

'Look at him, Barbara. He's a handsome guy, isn't he? A real hunk. Wouldn't you like to have him put it to you?'

'Stop it,' she said.

'I'm pretty sure she must be a virgin, Lee. Everything in mint condition, if you know what I mean.' He faced Barbara. 'Is that the problem? You wanta save it for . . . ?'

'She asked you to stop,' Lee said. 'So stop. I'm not going for this. I'm not about to have you brow-beat her into doing something against her will.'

'Ah, don't be such a Boy Scout.'

'Knock it off, Earl!' Pete yelled.

'*I'll* do it,' Heather said.

The room suddenly went silent.

Everyone turned to Heather, who was kneeling on the sofa, looking at them over her shoulder. 'I'll do it,' she said again. Then she climbed off the sofa and turned around and faced Lee. A corner of her mouth trembled. 'How about it?'

Lee looked flustered. 'I'm sorry. This is all . . . don't know how this got started, exactly, but I don't want any part of it. Earl's crazy if he thinks I'm going to trade one of my guns for . . . for sex . . . with you or anybody else.'

Heather gaped at him. She blinked. She looked as if she couldn't believe her ears. Then she muttered, 'What's so wrong with *me*?'

'Nothing. Nothing's wrong with you. This is all a mistake.'

'Wasn't a mistake when it was *Barbara*.'

He shook his head. 'I wasn't going to . . .'

'She didn't *want* you, or you would've.'

'That's not true,' he said.

The hell it's not, Barbara thought. If I'd said yes . . .

'So why not me?' Heather blurted. 'Am I so ugly and disgusting . . . ?'

227

'You're not. You're very attractive.'

'Screw it,' Earl said. 'He's just trying to spare your feelings. It's Banner or nothing. Right, Lee?'

'It's nothing,' he said.

Barbara gripped Pete's arm. 'Let's get out of here. Right now.'

Whirling around, Earl blurted in her face, 'We need that gun, Banner! You wanta get us killed out there? Fuck the guy and we walk out with a gun! What's your pussy worth, for . . . !'

Pete grabbed Earl by the front of his shirt.

'Stop it!' Lee shouted and reached for Earl.

The blast of a gunshot slammed through the room.

Lee's head jerked as if it had been struck in the side by a baseball bat. His lips flopped. Spit flew from his mouth. The bullet came out the left side of his head an inch above his ear, throwing out a heavy red splash. He went sideways as if chasing it, tripped on his own feet, and crashed to the floor.

Heather took aim with the rifle and put another shot into him.

'No!' Barbara yelled.

'Good job!' shouted Earl. 'Way to go, Heather! Now we get *both* his guns.'

'The dirty rotten son of a bitch,' Heather muttered, scowling at Lee's sprawled body.

Still holding Pete's arm, Barbara staggered backward on flimsy legs. She stopped when her buttocks bumped softly against the wall.

Oh God, she thought. Oh, my God. Oh, my God.

*She gonna shoot me next?*

'Got just what he deserved,' Earl said. 'You're terrific, Heather. Not only beautiful, but damn smart!' He knelt beside the body. 'Don't know what we would've done without you,' he said. Nodding and smiling at her, he pulled the forty-five out of the back of Lee's jeans. 'Thanks to you, Heather, we'll have a real fighting chance out in the streets.'

'Is he dead?' Heather asked. Her voice sounded strangely flat, as if she was speaking from a trance.

'You killed him deader than hell,' Earl said. 'I couldn't have done better myself.'

'He was a rotten son of a bitch,' Heather said.

'Yeah. Sure was. Who else do you think we oughta shoot?'

'Her.' Heather swung the muzzle toward Barbara.

'No!' Barbara yelled.

She heard Pete yell, too, and felt him shove her out of the way.

As she stumbled, she watched Earl jab the forty-five at Heather and fire. The noise was low and heavy and didn't stop. He was pulling the trigger very fast. The black pistol jumped in his hands, spitting brass out its side, smoke and fire out its front. Slug after slug punched Heather. They hit her in the chest and breasts, poking holes through her blouse, flinging out gouts of blood, shoving her backward. She dropped the rifle and sat down hard on the sofa.

Barbara's ears rang.

Shreds of white smoke drifted silently through the air.

'God!' Earl cried out. 'I had to do it! Did you see her? Did you see what she did? I had to do it!' Earl's voice sounded very far away. Barbara could barely hear it through the ringing. He was standing in front of her, looking from her to Pete. 'You're my witnesses, right? You saw what happened. I had to shoot her. She flipped out. No telling who she was gonna shoot next. Right?'

Pete muttered, 'Guess.'

Barbara nodded her head.

'Damn right,' Earl said. Pointing the pistol toward the floor, he pushed a button to release its magazine. His hands started to shake. Badly. Then more than his hands. He stood there with his shoulders hunched, arms tight against his sides, chin jumping up and down – shuddering all over like a wet, naked man standing in a blizzard. Finally, the magazine came sliding down out of the pistol's handle. He fumbled it and it fell to the floor.

He stared down at it.

'Why'd she do it?' he asked. He looked at Barbara. 'She *shot* him. He was a good guy. He helped us. What the hell did she want to go and shoot him for? Does that make any sense? Was she nuts?'

'You . . . said he deserved it,' Barbara muttered.

'Yeah. That was *after*. Anyway, I didn't mean it. Had to say something.' He held the pistol toward her. 'You want this?'

'No. Huh-uh.'

'I'll take it,' Pete said. Earl handed the pistol to him.

'Better reload,' Earl said, and turned away. Turned toward the sofa. 'Jesus,' he muttered. 'Jesus, look at her.'

Heather sat slumped against the back cushion, her mouth hanging open, her arms limp by her sides, the rifle across her lap, her legs apart and stretched out underneath the coffee table. Her face was spattered with blood. From the shoulders down, her dress was sodden. She looked like she'd caught a bucket full to the brim with red paint square in the chest.

There's that woman's blood under all that somewhere, Barbara thought. The woman the cat killed.

She couldn't think of the woman's name.

She couldn't think of the cat's name, either.

That's Heather, though, she told herself. I know that's Heather. But what's her last name?

Doesn't matter, she decided. I don't have to know.

'I did that to her,' Earl said. 'Can you believe it? Jesus. I did that to her.'

Pete bent over the table and picked up the full magazine. He shoved it up the handle of the Colt, then jacked a fresh round into the chamber. 'She flipped out,' he said. 'Maybe we all had something to do with it, I don't know.'

'We did,' Barbara said.

'Yeah, I guess so.'

'One way or another.'

'Yeah,' Pete said.

Earl shook his head. 'I'm the one that blew her out of her socks.'

'We helped,' Barbara said. 'She was . . . so jealous. Of me.'

'It's almost like we led her right up to the brink,' Pete said.

'I think she saw us in the pool.'

'What'd you do in the pool?' Earl asked.

'Kissed,' Barbara said, looking him in the eyes.

'That's all?'

'It was plenty,' Pete said. 'We wouldn't have done it with her watching. Not if we'd known.'

'She had a thing for Pete,' Barbara explained.

'Maybe she didn't see us.'

'But what if she did? And then, on top of that, Lee won't . . . sleep with her.'

'She just lost her marbles and I had to shoot her,' Earl said. 'That's all there is to it. She went nuts. Doesn't make any sense to blame anybody but her.'

'Maybe not,' Barbara muttered. 'God, I don't know.'

'What should we do about . . . all this?' Pete asked.

'Nothing,' Earl said. 'Let's just get out of here. Get the rifle, Barbara.'

'I don't want it.'

'Shit. I'll get it.' He stepped toward the end of the coffee table. 'Just don't shoot me, Pete. You aren't gonna shoot me if I go for it, are you?'

'You aren't gonna try and shoot *us*, are you?' Pete asked.

'Gimme a break.'

'So we can't testify.'

'Are you kidding? I'm gonna *want* you to testify. You can tell 'em how it was self-defense.'

'Yeah,' Pete said.

'It *was* self-defense,' Earl said, and picked up the rifle. 'No telling who she was gonna shoot next. I had to put her down. It was her or us. Isn't that so, Banner?'

'I guess so. Yeah.'

'Okay. Okay. Now let's take whatever we need and get the hell out of here.'

'Take what?' Barbara asked, frowning.

'The ammo, for starters. And anything else we want.'

'We can't steal from him.'

'If you think we're walking outa here without the guns and ammo, you're crazier than Heather.'

'I'm not a thief,' she said.

'You don't have to be. Leave it to me and Pete. Anyhow, it isn't really stealing – he's dead.'

'It's still stealing.'

'Right, sure. Screw that. You and your morals, Banner. If you weren't such a damn prude, Lee'd be balling you right now in the other room instead of lying here with his brains on the floor. And Heather'd still be alive.'

'Oh, suddenly now it *is* my fault?'

'Not saying it's your fault. Just saying none of it would've hit the fan if you'd done what I said and let him fuck you.'

'Go to hell.'

'Leave her alone,' Pete said. 'You had no business trying to push her into something like that in the first place.'

'He was gonna go for it.'

'We didn't need a gun that badly.'

'Oh, no? You might just be singing a different tune, Pizza face, if we get out there and run into trouble. Anyway, we've got 'em now. No thanks to Banner. Now, let's get what we need and hit the road. Startin' to stink in here.'

# TWENTY-NINE

He'd made Sheila call out that they should go away, that she was fine and didn't need help and wanted to be left alone. But they had come, anyway.

Two men and a woman.

Earlier, Stanley had warned Sheila about 'oddballs' and 'creepy types' he'd seen roaming the neighborhood. It had been a lie to keep her from shouting for help. But these three fit the bill perfectly.

Too perfectly.

They *are* real, aren't they? he wondered.

*I might be nuts, but I don't hallucinate.*

They've gotta be real, he told himself as he watched their approach from his hiding place in the rubble.

Not only could he see them, but he could hear them: their voices, the crunch of their footsteps, the heavy breathing of the big guy. He could smell the woman's cigarette.

If that wasn't enough to prove they weren't some sort of phantoms concocted by his imagination, he'd heard Sheila calling to them, answering them, telling them to go away. So she was aware of them, too; they had to be real.

Unless I'm imagining *all* of this, Stanley thought – including Sheila.

The notion made him smile. Then it sent a chill through him.

What was that story?

*An Occurrence at Owl Creek Bridge.*

*Shit! This better be nothing like that!*

It's not, he told himself. This is real. I know what's real and what isn't.

If this *isn't* real, he thought, when did it *stop* being real? Maybe I never got out of my house – the quake brought the place down on top of me and I'm out cold and I never did any of this stuff, none of it, everything's been in my head.

Or maybe I'm still asleep by the pool over at the Benson place – in which case the *early* stuff really happened but this about coming back to Sheila is only a dream, and . . .

'Watch out,' Sheila called. 'There's a guy named Stan. He was just here a few minutes ago. Do you see him?'

He ducked as the three strangers raised their heads and scanned the area.

'We don't see nobody,' one of the men said. 'You included. Where are ya?'

'Make sure Stan isn't around. I don't think he's too stable. He . . . he cut me on purpose. That's why I screamed like I did.'

'Don't look like he stuck around for us,' the same guy said.

'Can't say I blame him,' said the woman who was with the men. 'Where are you?'

'Follow my voice.'

'Keep talking.'

Stanley raised himself enough to see past the side of the pile. The three were walking slowly through the debris, side by side but spread out.

'I'm down through a hole in the floor,' Sheila said.

They were making their way through what was left of Sheila's kitchen, so it wouldn't be long before they found her.

When she sees what they look like, Stanley thought, she'll wish she'd kept her mouth shut in the first place.

The big one looked like a grizzly bear masquerading as an outlaw biker. He wore a black Harley-Davidson T-shirt and sagging blue jeans. A great, hairy loaf of fat hung out below the bottom of his T-shirt.

In spite of his size, hair and filth, however, he didn't seem nearly as strange as his smaller friend. That one was hairless. From what Stanley could see, he didn't even have eyebrows. He wore high, black leather boots and black leather pants. Instead of a belt, he had rusty strands of barbed wire wrapped around his waist. He wore no shirt. His skin was dead white, and his tiny eyes looked pink.

What fucking rock did *he* crawl out from under? Stanley wondered.

While the big one lumbered through the ruins of the house, the smaller one walked lightly and fluidly as if he were performing some sort of slow, weird ballet.

He made Stanley's skin crawl.

The gal looked skinny and mean. She might've been as bald as the spook a few days ago, but now her scalp was a sloping field of black stubble. Her eyebrows looked like black, upturned slashes. Her small eyes seemed to crowd the sides of her nose. Her thin, sneering lips pinched a cigarette. Her chin came to a point.

She's not so bad, Stanley thought, and smiled. Just get rid of the head, she's fine.

Drooping from shoulder straps was a gray tank top that ended at her

233

midriff. She had a good, dark tan. Her breasts weren't much larger than tennis balls, but they had a nice bounce to them when she moved, and Stanley liked how her nipples pushed out against her shirt. The shirt was cut off just below her ribcage. She looked flat and sleek below it. She had a golden ring in her belly button. Her jeans hung very low, and she didn't wear a belt – barbed wire or otherwise.

They'll tug right down, Stanley thought.

He watched her, and she was the one who found Sheila. 'Over here, boys.' Squatting down, she tossed her cigarette aside. 'Fine time to take a bath,' she said. It sounded like a complaint, not a quip. Turning her head, she called, 'You boys are in for a treat.'

They came up on each side of her.

'Hey, now,' the big one said. 'Ain't this a pretty picture?'

'Will you help me get out?' Sheila asked.

Stanley thought she sounded a bit tense.

'That's what we're here for,' the man said. 'Why else'd we be here, if it wasn't to help?'

'Go on and climb down there, Crash,' the woman said. 'Give her a hand.'

'You bet.' Before he could move, the hairless one clapped a hand on his shoulder.

'What's the hurry? Know what I mean?'

'Please,' Sheila said. 'Help me. I can't get out. I've been down here . . . ever since the quake. These two beams . . . I just can't get out from under them.'

'What's your name?' the hairless one asked.

'Sheila. Sheila Banner.'

He squatted by the edge, and grinned down at her. 'Sheila,' he said. 'Sheeee-lah. I'm Eagle. My big buddy here, he's Crash. Our main bitch here, she's Weed.'

Fucking freaks, Stanley thought.

'Nice to meet you,' he heard Sheila say.

'Why are you down there?' Eagle asked her.

'The quake.'

'But *why*?'

'I . . . thought the tub would save me.'

'Did it?'

'Yeah. I think so. I didn't get crushed.'

'But you're trapped.'

'Yes.'

'Why?'

'What do you mean?'

'Delve.'

Sheila was silent for a few moments. Then she said, 'I just need someone to help me get out of here. Please.'

'Is it a punishment?' Eagle asked her.

'What?'

'A punishment being visited upon you.'

'No!'

'It's gotta be,' Weed chimed in. 'Everything happens for a reason.'

'And,' said Eagle, 'the punishment *always* fits the crime.'

'Always,' added Weed. 'It's karma.'

'Okay,' Sheila said. 'This probably *is* a punishment. You're absolutely right.' She sounded wonderfully calm. She's trying to humor them, Stanley thought, and smiled.

'But maybe it's time for my punishment to end,' she suggested. 'I've been down here a long time. I'm . . . really sore. I hurt all over. And look at my leg. Look what he did to it. He did that with his *saw*. Like my leg was a board. You know? That's when I screamed. So don't you think all that's enough, and you can help me get out now?'

'That would all depend,' Eagle said.

'On what?'

'The nature of your offenses.'

'Gotta confess 'em,' Weed said.

'Confess,' Crash said as he sidestepped, probably hoping for a better view. He bent over and picked up the saw that Stanley had left behind for the strangers to find. Then he sat down where Stanley himself had preferred to sit – above the foot of the tub.

Can't see her twat from there, Stanley thought. But she's probably got it covered with a hand, anyhow. Probably has her tits covered, too. She isn't gonna give freebies to these three freaks.

'If I confess,' Sheila asked, 'you'll help me get out?'

'If you're deserving,' Eagle told her.

'What do you want me to say?'

'The truth.'

'You *know* why you're there,' Weed pointed out.

'Sure I know!'

Temper, temper, Stanley thought.

And Sheila shouted, 'The goddamn earth shook like hell and the goddamn house fell down, that's why! Wrong time, wrong place, that's why. It's what I get for living in L.A., that's why.'

'That's not why,' said Eagle. His voice was slick, oily. 'Tell us the truth.'

'Stan!' she suddenly shouted. 'You oughta get over here, Stan! You'll love these jerks – they're as buggy as you are!'

'We're here to save you,' Weed explained.

'Then do it!'

'You haven't confessed yet,' Eagle said.

'If I confess, you'll get me out?'

'If you *don't*, all hope is gone.'

'Okay. Okay. It's gotta be poetic justice, right? Some sort of payback that got me pinned in the tub?'

Eagle's strange, white head bobbed up and down. He continued to squat by the break in the floor, but Weed – on the side of him closer to Stanley – sat down and lowered her legs over the edge. 'Tell us,' she said. 'We're all ears.'

Something about that made Crash chuckle, but he didn't say anything.

'Okay,' Sheila said again.

Stanley wished he could see her, gaze down at her wonderful body, watch her face as she tried to con these three weirdos into helping her. But he couldn't see Sheila at all. From where he crouched, he had a great view of Crash's broad back and maybe half the face – all black, greasy hair and beard.

Over Crash's left shoulder, he could see Weed and Eagle in profile.

He wished he could see them better.

But he liked knowing that they couldn't see him – not without turning their heads.

'I'm trapped,' Sheila said, 'to punish me for being too independent. Okay? I like my freedom too much. I never allow myself to be restrained from . . . doing whatever I want to do. Even if it means . . . going against the wishes of other people . . . people who want to hold me down.'

'You're held down now, aren't you?' Weed said. She was nodding, rocking back and forth, hands on her knees. '*Really* held down.'

'That's right.'

'No good,' Eagle said. 'You don't get punished for being independent.'

'Sure you do,' Weed objected.

His hand flashed sideways. The back of it struck Weed's cheek. Stanley heard the sound of a clap, and saw her flinch.

*Yes!*

'What'd you hit her for?' Sheila demanded.

'You got a problem with it?'

'Yes!'

The back of his hand smacked Weed's face again.

'Damn it!'

'Just shut the fuck up down there,' Weed said. 'I'll jump on ya.'

'Give us something else, Sheee-lah. Tell us why you're being punished.'

She was silent for a few moments. Then she said, 'I wouldn't have the foggiest idea.'

'Betcha *I* know why,' Crash said. He hoisted the saw like a kid eager to be called on in class.

'Don't tell,' Weed said. 'She's gotta figure it out for herself.'

'What's *wrong* with you people?'

'Nothing wrong with us,' Eagle told her. '*You're* the one stuck in a bathtub.'

'You want us to set you free, don't you?' Weed asked.

'My God,' Sheila blasted. 'People are supposed to pull *together* in times of crisis. *Help* each other. All I'm getting are a bunch of sadistic *lunatics!*'

'What goes around comes around,' Eagle told her.

'It's your karma,' Weed added.

'My karma's just fine, thanks. Why don't you all just get out of here and take a flying leap!'

Stanley wanted to laugh, wanted to clap, but he only allowed himself a grin.

'You don't want us to leave,' Weed said.

'I want you to get one of these *beams* off me, but you keep playing your stupid games.'

'We only want the truth from you,' Eagle explained. 'As soon as I hear the truth, I'll let Crash jump down with the saw and set you free.'

'Just confess,' Weed told her.

'Yeah,' said Crash. 'I *wanta* cut ya loose, but you gotta play along.'

'Okay.' A few moments passed. 'Okay,' Sheila said again. 'We're looking for . . . my biggest sin, is that it?'

'Sin has nothing to do with it,' Eagle said. 'Sin is mythical nonsense.'

'You're full of it,' Sheila said.

Eagle grabbed up a handful of debris, stretched out his arm, and let go. As his hand opened, Stanley saw dust, grit, a few chunks of stucco or plaster, and a small triangle of broken glass fall out.

'Hey!' Sheila gasped.

'Confess,' said Eagle.

'What am I *supposed* to confess?' she blurted. 'If it can't be a sin . . .'

'How about if we torture it out of her?' Crash suggested.

'If she won't cooperate . . .'

'Pride!' Sheila cried out. 'My pride! That's what put me here! "Pride goeth before a fall," right?'

'Go on,' Eagle said.

'I . . . take too much pride in my appearance. I tell myself that I'm more attractive than anyone else. That I'm beautiful. And I work on it. When I should be doing other things. When I could be . . . I don't know, doing something useful . . . helping others . . . instead, I concentrate on my body. I run, I work out with weights, I admire myself in mirrors, I pamper my body. Pride. It's too much pride. That's why I'm being punished.'

'Good,' Eagle said. 'Very good. Go on.'

'That's it. What do you . . . ?'

'Explain the justice of your punishment.'

'Isn't that obvious?'

'Tell us.'

'I'm stuck here naked. Where everyone who comes along gets a chance to inspect this body I'm so proud of.'

'Very insightful,' Eagle said.

'And where everyone who comes along gets a chance to *damage* it.'

'Yes?'

'And where all my muscles aren't doing me any good at all, and all my beauty is working against me because every creep who comes down the pike only wants to *mess* with me instead of help. Except maybe for that one guy, Ben, and he pulled a disappearing act.'

'Yes?'

'Isn't that enough?'

While Eagle seemed to be thinking about a response, Crash asked, 'How come you got naked?'

'I don't take baths with my clothes on.'

'Oh. Me neither.'

'You don't *take* baths,' Weed told him.

He laughed, then said, 'Yeah, I do.'

'You don't *smell* like it.'

'How about sawing me out of here, now?' Sheila asked. 'I did what you wanted.'

'What'd you think of her confession, Crash?'

'I liked it. Yeah. I really liked the part where she says how she's so beautiful everybody wants to mess around with her. You know? 'Cause I think it's true. I mean, I know *I* wanta mess with her.'

Nodding, Weed said, 'It wasn't too bad a confession. I've heard worse. But I bet we could get some *good* stuff out of her if we kept at it.'

'I wanta get her out,' Crash said. 'You know?'

'We know,' Weed said.

'Can I?' he asked Eagle.

'Go on down and do it.'

Stanley waited while Crash climbed down, saw in hand, and scooted along the sides of the tub. When the big man bent over the beam, Stanley stood up and hurled a clump of stucco at him. The stucco was the size of a small brick.

He aimed at Crash's head.

And didn't wait for the results.

As he launched the stucco, he charged Weed and Eagle. They both turned their heads and looked surprised. The stucco hit the back of Crash's neck.

Weed, seated with her legs hanging over the edge, started trying to get up.

Stanley swung his board with both hands. It whapped her across the back, just below the shoulders, bashing her forward. She grunted. She flung her arms out. From the look of things, she would land on top of Crash, who'd fallen across the beam and onto Sheila. Stanley didn't have time to watch.

Even as he'd struck Weed, Eagle had leaped up and whirled to face him.

Grinning.

Slowly writhing, swaying, undulating.

Hissing.

Stanley lurched forward, going for Eagle's head with the backstroke of the swing that had knocked Weed from her perch. Eagle seemed to have all the time in the world. He swept downward, bending at the waist and knees. As the board passed above him, he stroked the top of his right boot. His rising hand showed Stanley what it had discovered there – a straight razor. The blade flashed blinding sunlight.

Stanley lurched backward as the razor slashed up. It slit air instead of his belly and chest.

Eagle's odd, white face looked puzzled as if he couldn't believe that he had missed.

Stanley brought the board down from overhead with both hands. It broke in half across the top of Eagle's head. His eyes bulged. For an instant, the dead white skin of his face seemed to jump loose. It was still shimmying when his knees struck the floor in front of Stanley. The straight razor fell. He wavered on his knees, his arms hanging limp by his sides, the pupils of his eyes almost out of sight as if he were inspecting the undersides of his upper lids.

Stanley glanced toward the tub. Weed was trying to climb off Crash.

Nobody there needed urgent attention.

Stanley tossed his broken board aside. As it landed with a clatter in the rubble, he took the scissors from between his teeth. He slipped his thumb into the ring handle, his first two fingers into the bow handle, then opened the scissors until their twin points were about an inch apart and punched them into Eagle's eyes.

He drove them in deep.

He expected a scream, but there wasn't one.

Hope bird-boy ain't too stunned to appreciate this, Stanley thought.

The bridge of Eagle's nose forced the blades farther apart. Stanley kept pushing until the crotch of the scissors met the bridge. Then he shoved hard enough to tumble Eagle away. As the silent body flopped backward, Stanley jerked the scissors out.

*One down, two to go.*

He faced the tub.

Weed had her left knee in Crash's back, her right foot on the edge of the tub, her back to Stanley as she reached up about to grab the floor at the far side of the break. Crash, folded over the beam, was struggling to rise.

Stanley jumped down. He landed with both feet on Crash's back. He heard a grunt from the man, a moan that must've been Sheila. As he flapped his arms, trying to catch his balance, Weed vaulted upward. She seemed to rise in a quick blur of tank top and tan back. Stanley tried for her with the scissors. They stabbed at the faded seat of her jeans. But somehow they missed and suddenly his wrist was pounded upward by her escaping foot. He kept his hold on the scissors. About to fall over backward, he dropped to his knees.

He glimpsed a blur of vanishing boots.

*No!*

*Can't let her get away!*

But he couldn't give chase. Not yet.

The body under Stanley's knees started to rise. Teetering, he reached down fast with his left hand and grabbed a fistful of Crash's thick, greasy hair. He dragged at the hair as he fell. He landed on his side. Elbow digging into Crash's back, he reached out with his right hand and stabbed the scissors as hard as he could into the side of Crash's neck.

Crash shrieked. His body lurched rigid.

Stanley tugged out the scissors and stabbed Crash again and kept on stabbing him, over and over, going for the neck and mostly getting it but knowing from the feel that sometimes he was hitting jaw or teeth or cheek. Crash shrieked and grunted and bellowed while his body shuddered and bucked, and blood flew.

Stanley wanted to stop.

Wanted to leap from Crash's back and chase down Weed.

But kept on stabbing Crash.

*Die die die, you dirty hunk of lard! She's gonna get away!*

At last, the blood stopped shooting and Crash stopped making noises and Stanley realized that the huge body was flinching underneath him only because he was punching it so hard with the scissors.

He was worn out, breathless, dripping. But there was no time to waste. Without pausing for even a moment of rest, Stanley pulled the scissors out of Crash, pushed himself up, and climbed onto the floor. He struggled to his feet.

He blinked, trying to clear his eyes of sweat – and maybe blood.

Then he gazed out over the ruins of Sheila's house, her patio and back yard. Weed had taken off in that direction, but there was no sign of her now.

Was she hiding nearby?

Had she made her way clear of the rubble and run away across the yard?

Had she circled around to the front?

'Weed!' Stanley yelled, trying to make his voice sound gruff. 'Weed, it's Crash! I got the guy! Nailed the sum-bitch! Where'd you go off to? Hey, Weed!'

She didn't answer.

She didn't show herself.

She'd have to be an idiot, he thought, to fall for a gimmick like that.

Probably too far away to hear it, anyway.

'Weed!' he called out, louder than before. 'Weed! It's Crash! Get back here, bitch!'

'Get him off me, Stan – please?' The soft, muffled voice came from behind him, came from Sheila.

He turned around. She was down there somewhere, underneath Crash and the beams and all that blood. But he saw nothing that he could recognize, for sure, as Sheila.

'Stan?' she said again.

'Shut up.'

'You've gotta get him off me. Please.'

'I don't gotta do shit. It's your fault these freaks came and found you in the first place, you and your big fucking mouth. Now I gotta go and find the one that got away.'

'No! Don't leave me here under him! Stan! You can't! He's dead.'

'You'd better just shut up,' Stanley said. 'Unless you wanta have more visitors and get them killed, too. I killed that Ben fella, by the way. Your pal, Ben? There wasn't any girl trapped under any chimney. That was just a story to get him where I wanted him. And then I sawed his head off. Thought you oughta know.'

He wiped the scissors on the side of his pajama shorts, turned around, and began his hunt for Weed.

# THIRTY

The sudden pounding on the bathroom door startled Barbara. She gasped, then asked, 'What?'

'You gonna take all day?' Earl complained. 'What the hell're you doing in there, taking a bath?'

'I've got the trots,' she said.

'Well, shit. Get a move on. We got stiffs out here. It ain't pretty.'

'Wait outside if you want,' she told him.

'Oh yeah, sure. So the neighbors can get a good look at us. Come on, would you? Let's get going.'

'I'll come out as soon as I can.'

'We oughta leave without you.'

'Feel free,' she said, knowing they wouldn't.

'This whole fuckin' mess is your fault.'

'I know, I know. Go away and quit bothering me, or I'm *never* coming out.'

'Leave her alone,' she heard Pete say. His voice was quiet, barely audible. 'I think she's pretty upset about all this.'

Damn right, she thought.

'Yeah, yeah, yeah,' Earl muttered. From the sound of his voice, he was still standing just outside the bathroom door. 'Wipe your butt and get outa there, Banner, or I'm coming in after you.'

'Don't talk to her that way, Earl.'

'I'll talk to her any way I want. What're you gonna do, shoot me?'

'Just be nice, okay?'

'Woos.'

'Quit it, you guys,' Barbara called. 'And no talk about shooting anyone. Calm down. I'll be out in a minute.'

'We don't have all day,' Earl said, then walked off.

I shouldn't have stayed so long, Barbara told herself. Should've just peed and gotten out.

But she'd peed, and stayed.

Maybe it was having her pants down.

Maybe it was the feel of the toilet paper.

*Fuck the guy and we walk out with a gun . . .*

*Lee'd be balling you . . . instead of lying here with his brains on the floor . . .*

About to get up from the toilet, she'd suddenly been pounded by the knowledge that Earl had been right: if she'd agreed to his deal and gone to bed with Lee, she would probably still be with him in the bedroom.

Nobody would've shot anyone.

Lee and Heather would still be alive.

*What's your pussy worth?*

Not their lives.

Nobody's life.

*I should've said, 'Yeah, sure, why not, a gun'll come in handy and what does it matter anyway?' But I didn't, and now he's dead and Heather's dead and it's all my fault . . .*

And then she'd come apart there on the toilet, shuddering and crying, making too much noise. To muffle her noises, she'd reached out and pulled a bath towel off the rod where it was hanging, and she'd buried her face in it.

The towel had been slightly damp.

Still damp, she'd guessed, from a shower or bath that Lee must've taken before the quake.

Back when he'd still been alive.

She'd imagined him rubbing his wet body with it – maybe humming or whistling a cheerful tune – and had cried all the harder.

By the time she'd been able to quit, her throat and lungs had felt tired and achy, and she'd had the familiar, tinny odor behind her face that comes from crying too hard or catching a fist in the nose.

She'd lifted her face, checked the wadded towel for blood, found none, and pushed her face into it again.

I've gotta get up, she'd told herself. Get up and get going. They're gonna think I fell in.

*I'll say I've got the trots.*

Cute, she thought. Real cute.

So, who cares?

What'll Pete think?

Who cares?

*I do.*

The hell with it. Just tell the truth – you fell apart. You got Lee and Heather killed because you wouldn't give up your stupid virginity, and so you fell apart.

*Earl would love that.*

Anyhow, I *didn't* get anyone killed. Not really. That's Earl's big idea, and it's a big damn lie. It was the quake and everything else that made us end up in Lee's apartment, and it was Earl with his stupid plan for getting the gun, and it was the bad luck of having a crazy, jealous lunatic like Heather with us, and it was Lee's own fault for leaving a loaded weapon in her reach.

Not my fault.

Too bad for Lee and Heather, but not my fault.

Just the way the ball bounces.

The way the cookie crumbles.

Any one of a thousand things might've gone differently, and they'd still be alive.

*A couple of 'em had to do with me.*

Yeah. True. And I'll live with it, but I'm not gonna let it ruin me.

*I'll try not to.*

Sitting up straight on the toilet seat, she'd wiped her face a final time with the towel, then taken a deep breath. And flinched, startled by the sudden pounding on the bathroom door.

'What?' she'd gasped.

'You gonna take all day?' Earl had demanded.

Barbara found Pete and Earl waiting in the kitchen. Pete, leaning back against the refrigerator, was holding a can of Pepsi. Lee's forty-five made a big bulge in the right front pocket of his pants, and most of its handle stuck out the top of the pocket. Earl had a beer. The rifle was hanging by its leather strap behind his right shoulder.

'Everything come out okay?' Earl asked.

'Very funny.'

'Are you all right?' Pete asked her.

She saw concern in his eyes. 'I'm okay,' she said. 'It's just, you know . . . what happened.'

'The poop hit the fan,' Earl said.

She turned on him, glaring. 'There are two dead people in the living room, you creep! And *you* killed one of 'em. You think there's something *funny* going on?'

He smirked. 'Give it a break, Banner. I saved your life. The crazy bitch was gonna pop you next.'

'Thanks to you.'

'Let's quit arguing,' Pete said. 'We oughta get going, now.' He asked Barbara, 'Do you want a can of something to take with you?'

'No. Thanks. I'm not taking something that doesn't belong to me.'

'Lee would've let you have whatever you asked for,' Pete told her.

'I guess.'

''Sides which,' Earl said, 'he's dead.'

'I'm not thirsty. Let's just get out of here.'

Earl tipped his head far back to finish off the beer, then stepped across the kitchen and smacked his empty can down on the counter next to a stack of brown paper bags. 'We're wearing these,' he said to Barbara, and picked them up.

He handed one to her, another to Pete, then pulled the last bag over his head. He adjusted it until the side-by-side holes were in front of his eyes.

'We made these while you were in the john,' Pete explained.

'Masks?'

'People might see us leaving.'

'They had plenty of time to see us when we were down at the pool.'

'Not me,' Earl said.

'You think nobody spotted you when you were down there yelling for us?'

'Who knows? But that was before all the shooting. Everyone in the whole joint must've heard that. We're lucky nobody came over. Probably scared to. But you can bet some idiot'll be looking out a window to see who comes outa here.'

Pete nodded. 'I think it's a good idea. Why take chances? Anyway, we can take them off as soon as we get away from the building.'

'You and I didn't do anything wrong,' Barbara said. 'We don't need to hide our faces.'

'Shit on you, Banner!'

'Cut it out!' Pete snapped.

'I go down, you go down.' Earl's breath shook and wobbled the bag. 'Both of you.'

Pete put his bag on, and looked at Barbara through its eye holes. 'It'll be better if you just wear it,' he said.

'Okay. Fine. It's not worth fighting over.' She shook open her bag and slipped it on. It was only slightly larger than her head, and the sides of it rubbed loudly against the rims of her ears. It had a slight musty odor like damp cardboard. Twisting the bag, she found the eye holes. One was lower than the other.

'Is it okay?' Pete asked. 'We had to guess where to put the holes in yours.'

'They're all right.'

'You can see out?'

'Sort of. I'll hang on to you.'

Earl led the way. Pete followed, Barbara behind him with her right hand on his shoulder. She couldn't see much except his back.

Which was fine. There was nothing in the kitchen that she needed to see.

In the living room, she was very glad to have the bag over her head. Some of the bad odors reached her nose, but she didn't catch so much as a glimpse of the dead bodies.

245

She could see them without her eyes – Lee sprawled on the floor, Heather slumped on the sofa – but she watched Pete's back, glad that the tiny eye holes allowed her no fresh view of them.

She heard the door open. A moment later, Pete moved forward beneath her hand and she followed him onto the balcony. The afternoon was so bright that she had to squint. She thought that she could feel the heaviness of the sun's rays pressing down on top of the bag and on her shoulders.

They walked to the left.

'So far so good,' Earl said.

The air inside Barbara's bag grew warmer and began to smell vaguely of smoke. The paper felt hot where it touched her ears and face. Her blouse seemed hot enough to burst into flames.

Don't be ridiculous, she told herself. The sun can't set clothes on fire.

The bag'll go first, she thought.

And pictured it suddenly combusting, saw herself stumbling along the balcony with her head ablaze.

Can't happen, can it?

*If it does, I'll jump in the pool,*

I might wanta do that anyway, she thought.

'We're coming to the stairs,' Earl said.

'Is anybody watching us?' Barbara asked.

'Don't think so,' Earl said.

'It'll be okay,' Pete said, 'as long as they don't try to stop us.'

'Here we go,' said Earl. 'Watch your steps, boys and girls.'

Afraid of stumbling and knocking Pete down the stairs, she let go of his shoulder and found the railing. The painted steel scorched her hand. She released it fast, then glided her hand along the top of the railing as she descended, barely touching it but ready to grab hold if she should start to fall.

Turning her head, she could see the pool below and to the right.

'I'm going in,' she said, speaking softly. 'How about you?'

'In the pool?' Pete asked.

'Yeah. Feel like I'm gonna go up in flames if I don't.'

'I don't know,' Pete said. 'I've got this gun.'

'A little water won't hurt it.'

'Nobody's going in no pool,' Earl said.

'Right,' Barbara said. 'Whatever you say.' The railing ended. As she stepped off the bottom stair, she plucked the bag off her head. Without it, the hot afternoon air felt almost cool against her face. Earl, a few strides beyond Pete, was walking toward the rear gate of the courtyard.

On her way to the pool, Barbara pressed the bag against her belly to flatten it so it wouldn't blow away. Then she folded it in half and dropped it.

At the edge of the pool, she tugged off her shoes. She let them fall. They clumped against the concrete.

'Banner!' Earl yelled.

She dived.

The water was wonderfully, shockingly cold – icy silk sliding over her body as she glided through. She wished she didn't have clothes on. They slowed her down, dragged at her, bound her, came between her skin and the water's caress.

*Some other time, maybe.*

Sneak back here some night, she thought. Me and Pete, slipping into the water naked, long after midnight . . .

*I wouldn't dare.*

*Oh, yeah?*

*Maybe I would, maybe I wouldn't.*

Opening her eyes, she saw the blue tile wall just ahead. She surfaced, snatched a quick breath, flipped, rammed her feet against the wall, shoved off, and submerged.

Earl's gotta be royally pissed, she thought.

Tough toenails. He shouldn't be so bossy.

*Why'd I do it?*

I had to, that's why. The hell with him.

*Yeah, right, we're trying to get away from a double-killing, and I decide it's a nice time for a dip. What's wrong with me?*

I was cooking, that's all.

And he has no right to control my life.

And what're we talking about, anyway – two minutes? Big deal.

Angling upward, she swept her arms back and did one more scissor-kick. Her head broke the surface. She reached up and slapped her hands on the concrete edge of the pool.

'Now!' Earl's voice, loud and rough. 'Right now, bitch!'

Barbara thrust herself up.

Earl had the rifle to his shoulder, had it aimed.

But not at Barbara.

Braced up on stiff arms, she snapped her head sideways and saw a woman standing in the open doorway of a ground level apartment. One of Lee's tenants? A gaudy redhead, probably fifty years old, built like Marilyn Monroe, wearing a shiny black kimono that was sashed shut and only reached halfway down her thighs.

'Where's Lee?' the woman demanded. 'That's all I want to know. What did you do to him?'

'Nothing! Get back inside and shut your door.'

'We'll see about that!' She strutted toward Earl, angry and apparently fearless. 'What'd you do to him? I heard those shots.'

247

What took you so long? Barbara wondered. Had to wait and see who came out?

And *we* look like people you wanta mess with?

The woman's bare feet made slapping sounds on the concrete. She swaggered and bounced so much that her sash loosened. The front of her kimono was flung apart by her leaping breasts, but she didn't seem to care.

Is she totally nuts? Barbara wondered. What does she want to do, take Earl's gun away? Slap his face? Throw him down and make a citizen's arrest?

*She's gonna get killed!*

'Go back!' Earl shouted.

'Not on your life, buster!'

'Don't shoot her!' Barbara yelled.

'Earl!' Pete yelled.

The rifle still at his shoulder, Earl used his firing hand to snatch the paper bag off his head. He let the bag go. As it slowly fell, he returned his hand to the rifle.

'I'm warning you, lady!'

'Don't!' Barbara shouted. Out of the pool and on her knees, she scurried toward Earl, waving an arm at him, yelling, 'Don't shoot! Damn it, don't! Don't do it!'

Earl looked ready.

The woman kept on coming, almost to the corner of the pool, no more than thirty feet from the muzzle of Earl's rifle, marching, swaggering, the black kimono open completely now, hanging from her shoulders, fluttering behind her like a cape.

*Caped crusader.*

*My what big boobs you have – look at 'em go!*

*Is everybody nuts today?*

Barbara hurled herself, shoulder first, against the woman's hip. Even as the collision jolted her, she glimpsed Pete thrusting the forty-five against Earl's temple. She heard Pete say, 'You shoot, I shoot.'

The woman went down sideways, letting out a whimper as she fell.

Barbara landed on her.

The woman went, 'Umph!'

'Watch out with that thing!' Earl yelled.

'I'll blow your head off!'

'Hey! Hey! Take it easy.'

Instead of lying still, the woman rolled onto her back. Barbara had no time to climb off or struggle. The body flopped, and her face went down in a pad of soft hair. With a gasp, she lifted her head. The woman was pushing at the concrete and starting to sit up.

248

'Stay down!' Barbara gasped.

The woman thrashed her legs. Her knee pounded Barbara under the armpit.

'Nail her, Banner!'

She glimpsed Earl and Pete standing side by side, their eyes fixed on the action. Pete's mask was gone. Both the weapons were lowered.

Thank God, she thought.

'Offa me!' the woman gasped, and kneed her again.

'Nail her! What're you waiting for?'

'You can take her,' Pete added.

She didn't know whether to feel proud or betrayed. But she suddenly knew that she wouldn't let this woman get the better of her.

The knee caught her in the breast. This time, it hurt.

*Damn it, all I did was try to save you!*

She drove her forehead down. The woman's belly was soft. Barbara's brow and face sank in, and she heard a huff of breath blow out of the woman. Pushing at the hot concrete, she raised her head.

The woman's eyes were bulging, her mouth wide. She was fighting to suck in a breath. As Barbara watched, her straight arms folded at the elbows. She sank down slowly, then lay flat, gaping at the sky and wheezing.

'Give her another one!' Earl urged her.

Barbara shook her head. She climbed off the woman and stepped clear. She was breathless, dripping. Bending over, she clutched her knees. She knew that her blouse hung open, but she didn't much care.

They've got her to stare at, she thought.

The woman was sprawled there, arms and legs flung out, everything showing. And the guys were both gazing at her.

Maybe this is what she was after, Barbara thought. Who knows? Why the hell did she come out like that? Could've at least gotten dressed.

Earl approached the woman.

Barbara stood up straight and said, 'Leave her alone.'

'She ain't a natural redhead, is she?'

'Do you always have to be such a pig?'

Grinning at Barbara, Earl let out a couple of snorts. Then he cradled his rifle, stepped between the woman's legs, squatted down and ducked his head for a closer look.

'Cut it out,' Pete said.

'Looks like somebody already did.'

'Bastard,' Barbara muttered. Wiping her face with the front of her shirt, she stepped around the woman's head and hurried toward Pete. 'Let's get out of here.'

He nodded. 'Come on, Earl.'

'We ain't finished yet.'

Barbara whirled around. 'We're finished! Come on!'

'She saw our faces. And she knows your name, Banner.'

'So what do you want to do, shoot her?'

'We don't want her telling tales, do we?'

'You idiot. Do you think she's the only one? Lee said there're tenants in four apartments. *Four*. This gal only accounts for one. What do you wanta do, go through the whole building and shoot everyone?'

'It's a thought,' Earl said.

Reaching down by Pete's side, she took hold of the forty-five. He made no attempt to keep hold of it. She pulled it from his hand, raised it, and aimed it at Earl's head.

He looked disgusted with her. 'Gimme a break, Banner.'

'Set the rifle down and stand up.'

'Yeah, sure.'

'Do it!'

'Like you're gonna put a bullet in me. I'm sure.'

'I've had enough. Put the rifle down and stand up.'

'Fuck you.'

She fired. The pistol boomed, leaped in her hand. She'd aimed for a near miss. From Earl's reaction, he must've felt the slug's wind in his hair. He flinched so hard that the rifle hopped out of the crooks of his elbows He bobbled it for a second or two. It started to fall, stock first, between his arms. With his left hand, he caught the sling. He sprang up and turned toward Barbara, the rifle dangling by the strap, a sick look on his face.

'Fine,' she said.

'You stupid fucking bitch!'

'Don't try anything with the rifle, or the next round goes in your chest.'

'Fuck you.'

'Yeah, right. Pete, go up and take the rifle from him.'

'Just try it,' Earl said.

'Just do it,' Barbara said, trying to soften the tone of her voice for him. 'If Earl goes for you, I'll put him down.'

Pete started walking toward Earl.

The woman on her back, head turned, stared at Barbara. She was breathing hard, but looked as if she'd mostly recovered from the blow that had knocked her air out. She also looked terrified.

'It's all right, lady,' Barbara told her. 'Nobody's gonna hurt you.'

The woman didn't seem reassured.

She has every reason to be scared, Barbara realized. I'm the one who flattened her and pounded her. I just fired in her direction. And here I am, all set to empty my pistol at the jerk standing between her knees.

250

As Pete walked closer, the woman started to shove at the concrete with her elbows and heels, started to squirm and scoot her way out of the line of fire. Her breasts were lurching around as if they had minds of their own.

Barbara hoped Pete wasn't watching them – or trying to get a good look between her legs.

She almost warned him to keep his eyes on Earl. Then she realized that she was the one who had better pay attention to Earl and stop worrying about the woman or what Pete might be looking at.

She concentrated on Earl's left arm, on the hand gripping the leather strap, on the rifle swaying by his side.

She held the pistol the way her father had taught her to hold his revolver: right arm bent slightly, left hand supporting her right like a platform, legs apart, knees bent.

The weapon shook quite a lot because she was trembling badly, but for the most part she was able to keep the sights on the center of Earl's chest.

Pete approached him from the right.

Good.

He would be able to take the rifle without getting in the way of a clear shot.

Almost within reach of Earl's weapon, he stopped and looked over his shoulder at Barbara.

Waiting for the go-ahead?

The woman was clear, but making no attempt to get up. She lay flat on her back, gasping for air, gazing at Barbara.

'Earl!' Barbara snapped.

Earl flinched.

'Pretend you're a statue.'

The corners of his mouth twitched. He didn't say anything.

'Get it, Pete.'

Pete hurried forward and grabbed the barrel and pulled. Earl let go of the strap. The rifle swung like a pendulum, and Pete trotted backward with it.

'Earl,' Barbara said, 'put both hands on top of your head and intertwine your fingers.'

'You're really asking for it, Banner.'

'Do it now.'

He did it.

'Lady, we're leaving here now and we're taking him with us. You can go back into your apartment. Everything'll be fine. Only next time, don't stick your nose in. You came damn close to getting yourself killed.'

The woman didn't try to get up.

'Should we tell her about Lee?' Pete asked.

Barbara nodded. 'Lee's dead, lady.' The woman showed no reaction to the news, just lay there gasping for air and gazing at Barbara. 'I'm sorry about that. He seemed like a nice guy. We didn't kill him, though. Heather shot him.'

'Heather?' The woman narrowed her eyes. 'The girl that threw the cat in the water?'

*She watched everything,*

'Yeah, her. She went nuts and shot Lee. Then we had to shoot her in self-defense. They're both up there in his apartment.'

'She shouldn't have done that to a cat,' the woman said.

Barbara frowned. 'Shouldn't have done that to *Lee*.'

'He was no great shakes, anyhow.'

'What's the matter with you, lady?'

'Nothing. None of your business. Why don't you just go away and leave me alone?'

'The National Guard's supposed to show up tomorrow,' Pete told her. 'You oughta stay inside and not get mixed up in anything till then.'

'Let's go, Earl,' Barbara said, 'This way. We'll take the alley.'

# THIRTY-ONE

They'd gotten past the other slide without any trouble at all – simply climbed over the loose mound of dirt and rocks near the right side of the road, where it was only a few feet high, then continued on their way down Laurel Canyon Boulevard.

This slide, scattered with fallen trees, boulders and parts of a house or two, covered the entire road to a height of at least sixty feet.

'Now what?' Mary asked, gazing up at it.

Em hurried back from the right side of the road. 'There's like a gigantic ravine over there,' she said.

Caspar grinned at her. 'First step's a big one, is it?'

'First step's a fatal one, if you get my drift.'

'I guess we'll have to climb straight over the top,' Clint said. He was glad they had nothing left to carry; after using the last of the food and water, they'd gotten rid of everything except the knives. 'It won't be so bad,' he said. 'We'll take it slow.'

Loreen put a hand on Caspar's arm. 'I see trouble, Papa.'

Ah, Clint thought. So, he *is* her father. Thought so.

'Trouble of what sort?' Caspar asked her.

'Hey!' Mary blurted. 'No predictions. That was the rule. We don't want any of that gypsy shit around here.'

'Take it easy,' Clint warned her.

'Sure, take *their* side. You're the one who made the rule – no predictions. What're you gonna do now, just let her say any damn thing that . . .'

'The walking dead woman has a lively mouth,' Loreen said.

'See! See! Did you hear that!'

'We don't want that kind of talk, Loreen,' Clint said. 'Please.'

'She is so skinny and aggravating,' Loreen said.

Caspar chuckled softly.

Mary opened her mouth, then shut it and glared at him. Her lips formed a tight, hard line. Clint supposed she must be thinking about Caspar's threat to cut out her tongue.

'Let's everyone try to be considerate,' Clint said. 'Okay? Fighting among ourselves doesn't solve anything.'

'I need to warn Caspar . . .'

'There she goes again!' Mary blurted.

Clint turned on Mary. 'Would you shut up for half a minute!'

Her eyes widened and her jaw sagged.

'Let the woman finish her sentence!'

'Thank you,' Loreen told him, then squeezed Caspar's arm. 'Papa, you don't want to climb this. You're not young. You're not strong.'

His eyes flashed. He jerked his arm from her grip. 'I'm not young?' he bellowed. 'Not strong? Piss on you!'

She greeted his sudden anger with calm. 'It's a very large hill to be climbing,' she said.

'For you, maybe!'

'I'm not an old man,' she said.

'*I'm* not a fat *cow*!'

Her calm collapsed. 'You're calling me a fat cow?'

'You are what you are.'

'Hey!' Clint said. 'Let's stop . . .'

Loreen's hand swung out and slapped Caspar hard across face. 'You don't call *me* a cow.'

'Cow!' Caspar slapped her.

She slapped him again.

Mary, grinning, began to clap. Clint clutched one of her hands. She quit clapping, quit grinning. She looked at Clint and didn't try to take her hand away from him.

Caspar again smacked Loreen across the face.

Em whistled.

No purse-lipped, mild whistle of amazement or appreciation. Certainly not a tune.

She had her thumb and forefinger jammed in her mouth for this high and ear-blinding shriek.

Clint flinched and gritted his teeth.

'Jesus!' Mary cried out, covering her ears.

Caspar and Loreen seemed to forget all about their slapping contest. Looking shocked, they gaped at Em.

Then came silence like the inside of a vault.

Em, smiling slightly, rubbed her spitty thumb and finger on the front of her T-shirt. 'One of my mom's girlfriends showed me how to do that,' she said. She seemed very pleased with herself. 'It sure hurts the ears, doesn't it? Anyhow, I don't want to make a nuisance out of myself, but I really can't stand this rowdy behavior. I think we should all keep our hands to ourselves, especially when it comes to the slapping department. Does that suit everyone?'

'Loreen struck me first,' Caspar explained. 'I give what I get.'

'You called her a cow,' Em reminded him.

'She insulted me, I insulted her.'

'She was only trying to keep you from climbing the hill and dropping dead from a heart attack. That's because she loves you. You called her a cow because she's worried you'll kill yourself.'

His chest seemed to swell. 'I do what needs to be done.'

'Jeez, her and I thought you were a nice guy. It was cool how you stood up for Loreen when Mary called her a bitch . . . but now you end up treating her worse than Mary did. I think probably you must suffer from what my mom calls "a case of macho bullshit." '

'Stupid child,' Caspar said.

'Oh, that's nice,' Em said, looking rather amused. 'I thought I was supposed to be a charming scamp.'

'Let's stop all this right now,' Clint said. 'Em, quit trying to push him, okay? Caspar, be careful who you call names. You want to treat your daughter like crap, that's your business. Em and Mary are *my* business, so you'll treat them decently.'

'The cow is no daughter of mine,' Caspar said.

'Whatever.'

'Granddaughter,' Mary suggested.

Caspar, growling, lunged at her. With a yelp, she staggered away. Clint shouted, 'Hold it!' He hurled himself in front of Caspar, but was shoved aside. As he stumbled, Mary scurried backward up the steep slope of dirt, Caspar rushing for her.

'Caspar!' Loreen yelled.

One foot planted in the dirt, he leaned toward the slope, reached high, and grabbed Mary's left ankle. Then Em crashed against his side, throwing him over sideways. For a moment, he kept his grip on Mary's ankle. Her leg was jerked out from under her. She sat down hard, then skidded downhill on her rump, skirt climbing her thighs.

Caspar struck the slope with his shoulder and flopped onto his back. As he started to sit up, Clint stepped on his chest. 'Stay put,' Clint said. 'I don't wanta hurt you.'

'Keep him away from me!' Mary cried out. She was on her feet again, now at the bottom of the slide, rubbing her buttocks with both hands.

Em sat in the dirt, her knees up, frowning as she glanced from Mary to Clint and Caspar.

'I don't want any more trouble!' Clint snapped. He kept his foot on Caspar's chest. 'From either one of you! I've had it with you, Caspar. You pushed it one too many times. Mary, you've been nothing but a pain in the ass from the get-go!'

'Fuck you.'

Em frowned up at her. 'Cut it out, would you?'

'Fuck you too, you little twat.'

'Hey!' Clint yelled.

'Fuck all of you!' Mary whirled around. She threw herself at the slope and scurried upward, gasping. The filthy tail of her blouse draped the seat of her skirt. The skirt swished across the backs of her thighs. Her shoes sent down tiny avalanches.

Em stood up, turned around, and watched Mary climb. After a few seconds, she glanced at Clint. 'She's not a very happy camper, is she?'

'She'll probably be back.' He looked down at Caspar. 'Don't even think about going after her. Just stay down till I tell you otherwise.'

'Behave yourself, Caspar,' Loreen said, approaching. 'If you try to sit up, the *cow* will sit on you. That is no prediction, but a promise.'

Clint lifted his foot off the man's chest, and stepped away.

Caspar stayed on his back. He was gasping for breath, but he managed a smile for Loreen. 'I've misbehaved, haven't I?' he asked.

'You've behaved atrociously. These people are our friends – with the exception of Mary. As for Mary, she is to be pitied. Her end will be very bad, very bad.'

'Do you have to say that?' Em asked, wrinkling her nose.

'I only say what I see.'

'Just because you see it, you don't have to say it. For one thing, it gives *me* the creeps. And I don't think you really improved Mary's disposition with all that kind of talk. I've gotta admit she isn't any prize, but that's no reason to tell her horrible things are supposed to happen to her, you know?'

'She gets what she deserves,' Loreen said.

Clint looked over his shoulder and found that Mary was more than halfway to the top. She had apparently stopped for a rest. She was bent over slightly, holding herself steady with one hand on a section of brick chimney that protruded from the soil just to her right.

*Could almost feel sorry for her.*

But she's done all this to herself, he thought. Nobody's been holding a gun to her head and forcing her to act so obnoxious all the time. All she had to do was act decent. What's so hard about that?

'Does she get killed because she isn't with us?' Em asked.

'That's entirely possible,' Loreen said.

'May I get up, now?' Caspar asked.

'Yeah,' Clint told him. 'But behave.'

'He will behave,' Loreen said.

Caspar struggled to sit up.

'Maybe we should tell Mary to wait for us,' Em suggested.

'We're better off without her,' Clint said. 'Anyway, it's her choice. This isn't like before. We didn't force her to go running off like this.'

'But we can't just let her get killed.'

'You don't believe that stuff, do you?'

'I don't know.'

'She is right to believe,' Loreen said.

'Don't give me that,' Clint said, turning to face her. 'You two are just a couple of con artists, and you know it. You make a business out of tricking suckers. So don't fall for it, Em. Loreen doesn't know any more about what's in the future than you and I do.'

'The fellow doth protest too much,' Caspar said. On his feet at last, he brushed off the seat of his jeans and nodded at Clint. 'You believe. Oh, yes, you do indeed. And you're frightened by what she . . .'

Mary cried out, 'Eeeeeeee!'

Clint ripped his gaze away from Caspar and swung around in time to see Mary, arms flapping, stagger backward as if to get away from the horrible *thing* crawling above her on the crest of the hill.

He thought, Shit! It's happening already!

Should've stopped her.

It's my fault.

What the hell is that?

*A person? Not a person!*

He only glimpsed it before his gaze seemed to sheer away from the ragged, crimson creature and find Mary as she lost her footing and toppled backward. Grabbing at the air with her hands, she teetered and fell.

Clint thought of ski jumpers.

How their skis seemed to fly for a long while just above the snowy slope before touching down.

Mary glided downward, head-first and face up, her body stiff and straight except for her waving arms – plunging but not quite touching the ground.

Someone was squeezing his arm.

Em?

Em, by his side, was yelling, 'Marrrry!'

Then Mary touched down, but not with the smooth landing of a ski jumper. Her back slammed the tilted earth – off a bit to the side of the chimney where she'd been resting not so long ago – and her legs bounced up. The impact flung them high. Clint saw a shoe fly off and sail away. Then both her legs were pointed at the sky like a V – tall and slender bare legs, a patch of bright pink fabric where they joined at the bottom. They came forward and down as Mary folded at the waist. Her pink panties turned out to be a thong. Her naked buttocks quivered when her knees pounded the slope.

For a moment, she looked as if she might be kowtowing in homage to the beast at the top of the landslide. Then she raised her head and shoulders.

She was upright on her knees, then tumbling backward again. She hit the slope quicker than before. Her legs swung toward the sky. This time, the V looked a little crooked.

Clint jerked his arm free from Em's grip and charged up the face of the landslide, arms pumping, shoes chunking into the loose soil, eyes on Mary.

Her body had turned. Instead of pitching down the slope heels over head, she was now rolling, flipping over and over. Her limp arms and legs were tossed about in a way that made Clint sure she had no control over them. She was unconscious. Or dead.

And tumbling fast down the hill straight at him.

Just as they were about to collide, he braced himself, twisted his body and rammed his right shoulder forward. It caught Mary in the hip. Her weight slammed into him. He grunted. His feet scooted a few inches, then held. But Mary had already flipped over, flinging herself onto his back and knocking his forehead into the dirt.

He shot his left elbow up. It struck her and almost stopped her, but she began to slip. He realized there was no way to stop her from falling off his back.

So he lowered his elbow.

She rolled off him, striking the slope with one shoulder. As she tumbled onto her back, Clint reached down and grabbed her upper arm.

And stopped her.

He knew he wouldn't be able to hold her for long; his own position was too precarious.

But Em was on the way up.

In a moment, Em was kneeling just below Mary. She leaned forward and pushed against the woman's shoulder and hip.

'Got her?' Clint gasped.

'Yeah.'

He let go, then started to get up. As he raised his head, he tried to spot the thing that had startled Mary into falling.

It was nowhere in sight.

He scurried across the slope until he was clear of Mary's feet, then crawled backward past her sprawled body and made his way over to Em. On his knees beside the girl, he pressed his hands against Mary's hip and thigh.

'What now?' Em asked.

'Depends,' Clint muttered.

'She isn't dead, in case you were wondering. Just *really* messed up.'

She lay sprawled on her back, tilted as if all set to roll down on them the moment they let go. She had lost both her shoes. Her skirt was twisted around the tops of her legs. Her filthy, torn blouse was spread open. The left shoulder strap of her bra had broken. A few inches of the strap, along with the flimsy silken pouch, hung beneath her breast. The breast had a few minor scratches. It had fared better than most of Mary.

From her face down her torso, from her thighs down to her bare feet, she was smudged with dirt, blotchy with ruddy contusions, puffy with welts, scuffed raw with abrasions, striped by bright scratches, bleeding here and there from deeper wounds.

But Clint could see the slow rise and fall of her chest and the throb of a pulse at the side of her neck.

'Mary?' he asked.

She didn't react.

He called her name again, louder this time.

Nothing.

With both hands, Em gently shook her. Mary's body wobbled a little bit, but she didn't wake up.

'What'll we do?' Em asked.

'We can't leave her here,' Clint said. 'I guess that means I'll have to carry her.'

'Too bad we can't just call 911.'

'You're telling me.'

'How is she?' Caspar called from below.

'Out cold,' Clint answered, not looking back. 'We're going on to the top.'

'We're coming, too,' Caspar called. 'Do you need a hand with her?'

'No thanks.'

'I'm sorry she fell.'

Yeah, right, Clint thought. But he didn't answer.

'You go on,' Loreen called. 'Take care.'

Em turned her head toward him. 'What *was* that up there?'

'I don't know.'

'Did you see it?'

'I just caught a glimpse. I couldn't tell what it was. I thought it might be a dog – maybe a mastiff, but . . .'

'It didn't have a snout like a dog or anything,' Em said. 'Maybe some kind of a monkey or . . . I don't know . . . I think it might've been a guy, but it looked so bloody and weird.'

'Guess we'll find out,' Clint said.

'Whatever it was, I sure hope it's gone by the time we get up there.'

'I just hope I *can* get up there.'

'I'll help.'

'Why don't you start by fixing her blouse. I'll hold her.'

With Clint bracing Mary to keep her from rolling, Em leaned forward. She plucked up the blouse where it hung off Mary's far shoulder and lifted it and pulled it toward her until she could reach it with her other hand. Then she held the entire side of the blouse at an angle, taut like the slanting wall of a lean-to.

'Last look at her chooch?' Em asked.

'Her what?'

'Her chooch. You know, her boob.'

'Just go on,' Clint said. 'Twerp.'

'I'm a scamp, not a twerp.' She lowered the side of Mary's blouse and let go.

It settled smoothly on the mound of her breast. The dark of her nipple showed through. Moments later, spots and streaks of blood began to appear here and there on the soiled while fabric.

Em reached down in front of herself for the right side of the blouse. She had to tug it out from under her knees before sweeping it forward over Mary.

'Want me to fasten the buttons?' Em asked.

'Yes.'

'You sure?'

'Quit clowning, okay? I'm not interested in her chooches or anything else.'

'You're not?' Em asked as she started to work on the buttons. 'Really?'

*Not much, anyhow.*

'I'm married,' he said.

'So?'

'Just wait'll you see my wife. It'll be pretty obvious why I can't get all that worked up about Mary. They aren't even in the same league.'

'You talking nautical?'

'Baseball.'

Em smiled. 'I knew that.' She finished with the buttons. 'All set.'

The blouse clung to the wetness of the sweat and blood on Mary's skin.

'Okay,' Clint said. 'Now, let's see if I can pick her up.'

'Want me to take her legs, or something?'

'I guess what you'd better do is stand clear. Just be ready to grab her, maybe . . . in case I drop her.'

Em crawled aside, then moved slightly downslope and got to her feet.

'What're they doing?' Clint asked.

'Just watching,' she said. Then she called, 'Stay down there till we're out of the way, all right?'

'Fine,' Caspar called. 'Don't worry about us.'

Clint stared at Mary.

He didn't like the idea of carrying her to the top of the hill cradled in his arms – all her weight would be in front of him – and it'd be hard to climb fast without nailing her in the back with his knees.

Just sling her over your shoulder, he told himself.

Just?

'Here goes,' he said. He moved sideways a bit, shoved his knee against her hip to keep her from slipping, then reached up with both hands and grabbed her shoulders. He jerked her to a sitting position. As she started slumping forward, he caught her by the sides, just under her armpits.

Lifted her.

Pulled her.

Turned her.

Muscled her up and onto his left shoulder and clamped his left arm across her rump and dug his shoes into the dirt and hurled himself at the slope.

'Yes!' Em yelled.

Go go go go go, his mind shouted as he dashed for the top.

Go go go. Don't stop for anything. Go go go.

Get it done, get it done, get it done!

Go go go!

Get to the top and you can put her down.

We'll roll her down the other side.

The other side of the landslide.

I'm a poet.

My feet show it.

Longfellows?

Go go go!

I think I can, I think I can.

Heart attack, heart attack!

Ha!

Shit!

Go go go!

Don't stop, don't stop!

Almost there!

Go go go go go!

And grunting, dragging air into his hurting lungs as his heart slammed, he gained the crest of the hill.

The thing was sprawled in front of him.

Before he could halt himself, his foot hooked under its shoulder.

He plunged forward.

They almost landed on the body.

They landed just beyond it, instead. Mary's rump hit the ground first, taking the brunt of the impact. Then she flopped forward off Clint's shoulder.

He lay on top of her, too spent to move.

261

* * *

Em had arrived at the top and finished vomiting by the time Clint was able to push himself up. He crawled backward off Mary's unconscious body. On his knees, he looked down at the thing that had tripped him.

'It's a man, isn't it?' Em asked. She sounded very calm. She was standing up straight, but facing away from Clint and the body.

'I'm not sure.' The hips and rump didn't seem to flare out. He supposed this was probably a man, not a woman. But there was no way to be sure without turning it over. 'I guess so.'

'How did he get that way?' Em asked.

'I don't know.'

'Earthquakes . . . they don't scalp people.'

'No,' Clint said. 'They don't.'

'Or skin them alive.'

'No. Earthquakes don't . . . skin people, either.'

'Did humans do that to him?'

'Somebody did.'

'He came up over here. I can see where he . . . he must've crawled up all the way from the road. How could you do that, if you'd been . . . wrecked like that?' ·

'I don't know,' Clint said. 'Willpower, I guess.'

Em's head swiveled slowly from side to side. She seemed to be scanning the area below the landslide – the remains of Laurel Canyon winding down toward Sunset Boulevard. 'Some awfully bad stuff must be going on down there,' she said.

Clint struggled to his feet.

Em looked over her shoulder as he approached her.

He stopped beside her. He reached across her back and gently squeezed her shoulder. 'I don't have any choice about going on, Emerald. I've got to get home to my wife and daughter.'

'I know.'

'You scared?'

'I guess so.' He felt her shrug. 'I'm sure not eager to end up like that guy, if you know what I mean.'

'We'll take care of each other, okay?'

'Okay.'

Letting go of her shoulder, Clint stroked the back of her head. Her short hair was dripping wet. 'Yuck,' he said, and wiped his hand on her T-shirt.

Em turned, put her arms around him and pressed her face against his chest.

He wrapped his arms around her.

262

They were still embracing when Mary called out in a shaky voice, 'Clint?'

He turned slowly, Em in his arms, and saw Mary raise her head off the ground. 'Just lie there and relax,' he called to her. 'You took a bad fall.'

Lowering her head, she shut her eyes and started to cry.

Em squeezed herself harder against Clint. 'Stay with me,' she murmured.

'I will.'

'I'm not . . . too good at being scared.'

'You're doing fine.'

'Stuff doesn't usually get me, you know?'

'This sort of stuff would get anyone.'

After a while, she said, 'Maybe we'd better go and see Mary.'

'There's no hurry,' Clint said.

'Maybe we can stop her so she doesn't see the guy.'

'I guess that'd be a good idea.'

'I'm ever the thoughtful type,' Em said.

That brought a smile to Clint. He eased away from her, gave her shoulders a gentle squeeze, then let go.

As they walked side by side toward the place on the ground where Mary lay quietly sobbing, Caspar and Loreen trudged into sight.

# THIRTY-TWO

Earl walked up the alley with his hands folded on top of his head while Barbara and Pete followed, side by side, about ten paces behind him. They held their weapons pointed in his general direction, but kept their fingers off the triggers.

Earl had been cooperating nicely and without complaint since leaving the apartment complex. But now he stopped and turned around. 'Come on, Banner, my arms are killing me.'

'Tough.'

'Just let me put 'em down, okay? I'm not gonna try nothing. What do you think I wanta do, run back and strangle the old bat? I probably couldn't even *find* that place again.'

Barbara looked at Pete. He shrugged. 'Okay, Earl,' she said. 'You can put your arms down. But stick your hands in your pockets.'

'In my *pockets*?'

'You heard me.'

'It's hotter 'n' a mother-dog, 'n' you're telling me I gotta stick my hands in my pockets? No way!'

'Then keep them on top of your head.'

'Shit!' He spun around and resumed walking. A moment later, he called, 'Okay if I just stick 'em up?' Not waiting for an answer, he raised both his arms straight overhead. 'Don't know what you're so afraid of, anyhow.'

'You with a gun,' Barbara said.

'Yeah, right. I saved your ass, Banner. Don't you forget that.'

'We don't think you're very particular about who you shoot,' Pete explained. 'Not to mention, you threatened Barbara.'

'Did not.'

' "You're really asking for it"? Sounds like a threat, to me.'

'I was pissed. Didn't mean nothing by it. What're you gonna do, keep me covered all the way home?'

'If possible,' Barbara said.

'Yeah? Well, I'm putting my arms down, so go ahead and shoot me.' With that, he lowered them. Barbara felt an urge to fire past him – give him a good scare. But she'd already fired a warning shot, back at the

264

pool. That one had probably been necessary, but a shot now would be a waste of ammo. Stupid, she knew, to fire if you didn't absolutely have to.

*The round you save may save your life.*

So far, they had run into no real trouble except for Earl (and Heather, don't forget poor Heather), but they still had a few miles to go.

If those blood-thirsty marauders were more than just a figment of Heather's imagination . . .

*Sure hope that's all they were.*

Just ahead, most of the alley was blocked by rubble from the collapsed rear of a two-story apartment building. Earl angled to the right and started to go around it. He kept his arms partway up. He kept his head down and seemed to be watching his step until he was past the side of the pile. Then he looked to his left.

And jerked to a quick, rigid stop.

'What?' Pete called.

For a moment, Earl didn't move. Then he grinned back at them. 'Nothing. No problem. Thought I saw a snake. Just a piece of rope. No sweat.'

He walked on, but watched over his shoulder.

There wasn't room to walk side by side past the edge of the debris heap, so Barbara went first. She didn't like the way Earl kept watching her.

*Something's going on.*

Maybe he *had* spotted a real snake. The things were rare in Los Angeles, but the quake might've let a few pet pythons get loose. And she knew there were rattlers in the hills around the city.

*Who knows?*

But it wasn't a snake that had startled Earl. Nor was it a piece of rope.

Stepping carefully past the fan of broken stucco and glass, Barbara turned her head to the left and saw the bodies. She flinched and caught her breath.

'Surprise, surprise,' Earl called out.

She glanced at him. 'Bastard.'

Pete came up behind her. 'Oh, man,' he muttered.

Earl had walked on past the bodies in order to pull the gag on Barbara and Pete. Now that his trick had succeeded, he came wandering back.

'What're you doing?' Pete asked him.

'Just want a closer look. Come on over. They don't bite.'

Barbara suddenly found herself approaching Earl and the bodies. She thought, This is nuts. I don't *want* a closer look.

*Sure you do.*

No big deal, anyway, she told herself. It's not like these are the first of the day, or something. Oughta be pretty used to this stuff, by now.

The three bodies were stretched out on their backs, side by side: two young men, a slender blonde woman between them.

Barbara, standing near the feet of the woman, flanked by Earl and Pete, didn't like the similarities.

*They could almost be our shadows.*

They aren't, she told herself. They're dead people, and it's just a coincidence they're lined up this way and they sort of look like us.

They *do not* look like us.

The guy stretched out at Earl's feet was fat, for one thing. Pete's dead counterpart was very tall, probably six-three, and had a crew cut. The blonde between them was probably ten years older than Barbara, had much bigger breasts that stood up solid with implants, slick bare skin where her pubic hair should've been, and a tan that seemed to have no boundaries.

Also, one side of her head was caved in.

The fat guy's guts showed through a deep slash across his belly.

The tall guy was missing most of his right leg.

'They weren't murdered, were they?' Pete asked, his voice quiet and shaky.

'Nah,' Earl said. 'The quake got 'em. I've seen plenty the same way. Some scavengers probably dragged 'em outa the shit and left 'em here.'

'Stripped them like this?' Pete asked.

'Less maybe the babe was catching some rays on her roof-top when we started to rock 'n' roll. She got one a them all-over tans. See that?'

Pete nodded.

'You got one a them all-over tans, Banner?'

'Knock it off,' she said.

'Betcha this babe's a stripper, or something. Maybe does porno flicks. Look how she's got her pussy shaved. You got your pussy shaved, Banner?'

'Shut up.' This time, the warning came from Pete.

Earl chuckled softly. He bent over and planted his hands on his knees and squinted. 'What do you think, they do her?'

'Earl!' Pete snapped.

'Ah, cool your jets. Just kidding around.'

'Real funny,' Barbara muttered.

'Yeah, well, it happens. Don't think it don't. Not that *I'd* be interested. Not me. I like my babes alive and moaning.' He stepped between the bodies of the fat guy and the woman. Turning toward the woman, he squatted down.

'What do you think you're doing?' Barbara said.

266

Casting an innocent smile at her, Earl squeezed one of the breasts. 'Honk honk.'

'What's the matter with you?' she muttered.

'Silicone job. Yuck. I like the *natural* feel. Don't ever get no silicone job, Banner. Love ya just the way you are.'

Feeling a little sick, she nudged Pete with her elbow.

'Let's get out of here.'

'Hang on, hang on,' Earl said. He reached down to the woman's face.

'Earl!'

'Just wanta check out a little something here. Look how she's bloody around her mouth.' Holding the woman's mouth open by the jaw, he hunched down lower and peered in. He turned her head a bit from side to side. 'Yeah. Shit. Just what I thought.'

'What?' Pete asked.

'She's missing a couple of her pearly whites.'

'What are you talking about?' Barbara asked.

'They been pulled. Outa the back.'

'Maybe they got knocked out by the quake,' Pete suggested.

'Yeah, right.' He turned around and inspected the fat guy's mouth. 'This one's okay – least if you overlook his *obvious* problems.'

Pete stepped forward, crouched, and looked into the mouth of the tall guy. 'This one's got all his teeth.'

'It was just the babe, then,' Earl said. 'What happened, some fucking street-vulture yanked her gold crowns.' Shaking his head, he stood up. 'Not enough, they strip every damn body down to the skin and rip off everything – now they're going for the teeth. Ain't seen that before. Beware of trolls bearing pliers, know what I mean? You got any gold in that mouth-hole of yours, Banner?'

'No.'

'Me, neither,' Pete said.

'Guess I'm the only lucky one.' Earl opened his mouth wide and pointed in. Barbara didn't bother to look. 'Three of 'em. Cost my step-dad a fortune. Bet he never figured he was marrying into no dental disaster.' Earl laughed sharply, then scowled. His eyes shifted from Pete to Barbara. 'Something happens – don't let nobody take my teeth, okay? Shit. I go down, I wanta go down in one piece.'

'Don't worry about it,' Pete said. 'Nobody's going down.'

'Right. That's probably what *they* thought.'

'Let's get going,' Barbara said.

Earl took the lead again, but he neither raised his arms nor kept his hands in his pockets.

Might as well let him do what he wants, Barbara thought. He could've jumped us or made a getaway while we were with the bodies. Would've been a cinch to take us by surprise, grab one of the guns . . .

'I wonder if we should get out of the alleys,' Pete said.

Barbara saw that they were coming up on a street. No cars were going by. The alley on the other side of the street looked much the same as this one and the others – a narrow lane of old, crumbling pavement bordered by dumpsters, parking stalls, fences, occasional hedges, and the rear ends of several apartment buildings.

All the apartment buildings that Barbara could see along the alley were standing. She saw no major damage. She saw no bodies. She saw no scavengers. She saw nobody.

'I don't know,' she told Pete. 'It doesn't look bad up ahead.'

Earl turned around and walked backward. 'Hey, the alleys are better. Believe it. I been in the streets. You don't wanta get mixed up in the looting and shit. Here, all you got're the vultures. And they ain't interested in us till we're toes up, know what I mean? Hell, you don't even see 'em. You seen any? They're like invisible. You only know they're around 'cause you can see what they done to the stiffs. But we go out in the streets, and we're asking for trouble. Some of them looters spot you got guns, they're gonna want 'em. Fact is, you oughta put those babies outa sight till we get across the street. We been lucky so far nobody's spotted 'em and come for us.'

Pete and Barbara looked at each other.

Then Barbara opened her purse. The Colt was too large, but she managed to stuff it in. The purse suddenly felt very heavy against her hip. The strap, slanting down from her shoulder, pulled taut.

No way, she thought.

Grimacing, she removed the pistol from the purse and reached behind her back. She lifted the tail of her blouse and pushed the .45 down under the waistband of her shorts. The shorts became a bit more snug, but not uncomfortable. As she inserted the gun, the muzzle or front sight caught on the top of her panties, shoving them down a few inches. The steel felt thick and slightly cool against the crease of her buttocks.

Not bad, she thought. Beats keeping it in my purse.

'What am I supposed to do with this?' Pete asked, gesturing with the rifle.

'Do like Banner and stick it in your pants,' Earl suggested, grinning.

'Sure,' Pete muttered.

'Just carry it by your side so it isn't so obvious what you've got,' Barbara suggested. 'Nobody's bothered us yet. And you go trying to hide something that big in your clothes, you won't be able to get it out if we need it.'

268

'Want *me* to carry it?' Earl asked.

'Thanks, but no thanks.'

'Your funeral,' Earl said, and walked on out of the alley.

Barbara and Pete followed him, staying close together, the rifle between them, clamped under Pete's arm and pointed downward.

Barbara looked from side to side as they crossed the street.

In both directions, cars and pickups and vans were parked along the curbs. A few were double-parked and seemed to be abandoned.

To her right, she could see a lot of stopped traffic in the distance – no doubt where the street approached one of the main east-west roads. Quite a few people seemed to be milling about. She supposed they were drivers and passengers who'd decided not to leave their vehicles behind. She'd seen such groups a lot.

She'd come to think of them as 'the waiters.'

Not doing anything, just waiting around for the traffic to clear so they could drive on home.

Between the waiters and where she was crossing the road, Barbara saw nobody except a pair of women standing together on the sidewalk in front of an apartment building, chattering and gesturing, probably sharing their quake adventures.

To the left, far off, Barbara could see traffic stopped at another major east-west artery. She could barely make out the tiny shapes of the waiters.

Between those distant waiters and where she walked across the street, she saw nobody.

Nobody at all.

A street of empty vehicles. Sunlit air, yellow, adrift with haze and smoke. A few trees that didn't give much shade. Patches of green here and there, but mostly the gray of concrete and the pastels of painted stucco walls of homes and apartment buildings.

Cracks in walls and pavement.

Crumbled stucco.

Shattered windows.

Fallen chimneys.

But nobody.

No people at all.

Just as well, Barbara thought. The main quake's all over and you got through it without getting your head bashed in, so now all you've got to do is worry about getting killed by the survivors.

She was glad that she and Pete had guns.

She thought about the revolver at home, and hoped that Mom had thought to grab it.

Maybe Dad's home by now, she thought.

269

If only they're home and all right and the house is still in one piece . . . then we'll all be together and fine.

If I can get there.

It felt good to get out of the street and into the alley, where they were not so exposed. Pete quit trying to conceal the rifle. He carried it at port arms, ready. Barbara decided to keep the pistol down her waistband. She liked having her hands empty.

She figured that she could probably pull it out fast enough if trouble started.

From the feel she had in her stomach, she was expecting trouble to come soon.

So do they, she thought. Just look at us.

All three were walking much more slowly than before.

Earl, in the lead, kept swiveling his head. Pete, by Barbara's side, was constantly glancing over his shoulder. Barbara, herself, couldn't stop turning this way and that to make sure nobody was about to creep out from behind a dumpster or pounce on them from the shadows of a car stall.

We look like we're walking into an ambush and know it, she thought. *It's just that we're spooked because of the bodies.*

Hope that's all it is.

On the other side of the alley, a Dodge pickup truck was parked in the car port beneath the second story of an apartment building. Beside it stood a Jeep Wrangler. The Jeep didn't bother her; it was a convertible and she could see that nobody was in it. But the pickup bothered her a lot.

It was a big pickup truck, not one of those sporty little foreign jobs. The bed behind its cab had high metal sides. From where she stood in the middle of the alley, Barbara couldn't see over its tailgate.

'I'm taking a look over there,' she whispered.

'What?' Pete asked.

She nodded toward the pickup. 'Don't want any surprises. Just keep an eye on me, okay?' She stepped past him. As she walked closer to the pickup, she reached under the tail of her shirt and drew the Colt.

When she did that, Pete said, 'Wait for me.'

He hurried to her side.

Earl looked back and frowned. 'What's up?'

'Just checking,' Pete told him.

'For keys?'

Pete shook his head.

'Didn't think so. Couple of weenies.'

With each step, Barbara could see more of the pickup's bed. So far, it seemed to be empty except for a rumpled blue tarp near the cab.

*Doesn't look like anyone's . . .*

'Shit!'

The yelp was high and girlish and didn't sound like Earl. But Barbara whirled and it was Earl back-pedaling, Earl turning around with his eyes wide and his lips skinned back, Earl blurting out, 'Hide!' and breaking into a run.

As he sprinted past them, Barbara snapped her head sideways.

And saw what he'd seen.

A scavenger pushing a shopping cart. Pushing it on the run, the cart bouncing and swerving on the rough alley pavement. Inside the cart sat a naked man. He looked as if he'd been tossed in, rump first. His arms and feet hung over the high edges of the wire basket, and flopped about as the cart bounded along. His head bobbed and swayed.

Running hard behind the cart, shoving it along, was a filthy thing in a huge soiled overcoat and boots. The derelict's hair was long and straight, the color of pewter.

A witch, a hag.

But maybe a guy.

A 'street vulture' for sure – racing along with its cargo of dead man, taking him God-knows-where for some ungodly reason Barbara didn't want to think about.

No wonder Earl had lost his cool and . . .

Barbara suddenly spotted the mob.

She knew, at once, that Earl hadn't lost his cool and lit out and blurted the warning because of the horror pushing the shopping cart.

It was the mob giving chase to the vulture.

One glimpse of it was enough. Barbara elbowed Pete and gasped, 'Here,' and vaulted the tailgate of the pickup truck.

Inside, she dropped flat. Pete sprawled beside her. He was breathing very hard.

'Think they saw us?' Barbara whispered.

'Jeez, I hope not.'

'They were pretty far away.'

Letting go of the pistol, Barbara pushed herself up with both hands. She peered over the corner of the tailgate in time to see a thrown hammer bounce off the back of the derelict's head. He or she lost the shopping cart and flew head-first toward the pavement. The cart went scooting and bouncing forward, then veered aside and tumbled, throwing out the dead man.

The laughing, hooting mob engulfed the derelict.

They seemed to be mostly teenagers, mostly boys. But there were girls, too – girls who seemed no less fierce and gleefully wild than the guys.

271

Barbara sank down beside Pete.

Her heart throbbed as if it were being hammered to pulp.

'Jesus,' she gasped.

'What?'

'They'll tear us up.'

'Not if we blast them.'

'Fifteen or twenty of 'em?'

'We can do it.'

'But they're just kids. Younger than us, some of 'em.'

'Better than letting them . . . Maybe they won't find us, but . . . We could pull the tarp over us . . .'

'Wait. No. I've got it. Get your clothes off.'

'What?'

'They won't kill us if they think we're dead.'

As the mob squealed and laughed and hooted over the scavenger they'd downed fifty or sixty feet away, Barbara and Pete in the bed of the pickup truck stayed low and struggled out of their clothes.

Barbara glanced at Pete a few times. He was making good progress, and he wasn't staring at her.

He kept mumbling, 'Jeez,' and, 'Oh, God,' over and over again.

The stripping seemed to take forever.

'Okay,' Pete finally gasped.

Barbara looked. 'Underwear, too.'

'Oh, man.'

On her back, Barbara tugged her panties down as far as she could without sitting up, then worked them the rest of the way down with her legs. Her foot shoved them under the loose wad of tarp.

She rolled onto her side.

Her purse and most of the clothes were heaped between their bodies.

Pete lay on his side, facing her, holding the rifle against his body, the shoulder stock pressed to his genitals. He looked red and shaky.

'Everything goes under the tarp,' Barbara whispered. 'Except the guns. And this.' She plucked her denim purse away from the pile.

Working together, they shoved the pile of clothes down past their waists, past their thighs. Then they used their knees and feet. Soon, everything was out of sight beneath the tarp.

'Roll over and hide the rifle under you. If the crap hits the fan, we'll open up on 'em. But not unless we have to. I don't wanta kill anyone.'

'Me neither,' Pete said. 'But we'll do it if we have to.'

'Right.'

'I'm not gonna let anyone hurt you.'

She felt her throat thicken. 'Turn over.'

He rolled toward Barbara, lowering his body onto the rifle and resting his forehead on the metal floor of the pickup's bed. His head was turned slightly toward her. The single eye that she could see was gazing at her face.

She pushed herself up on one elbow. For a moment, she thought how smooth and nice he looked. He had a deep tan on his back and legs. His rump was white.

This is so nuts I don't believe it, she thought. Got a mob of crazy weirdos gonna be showing up, and . . .

She looked at his face.

Caught him staring at her breasts.

His eye shifted quickly to her face.

'Sorry,' he whispered.

'It's okay. But turn your head the other way. Get your hands out from under your body. And you're too stiff. Limpen up. Get your legs apart. Bend a knee. You gotta look dead.'

She waited until he had turned his head the other way, then reached into her purse. She found her makeup compact and pulled it out. She popped it open. With a fingernail, she pried the mirror loose. She jammed the compact back into her purse and scooted the denim bag toward the tarp. It stopped short. She shoved it out of sight with her foot.

Still braced up on her left elbow, she held the mirror with both hands and snapped it like a cracker.

'What're you doing?' Pete whispered.

'Taking care of business.'

'You better stop messing around and play dead.'

'I know. Yeah. Almost done.' Holding half the mirror in her right hand, she pressed a corner of its broken edge against the underside of her left forearm. She gritted her teeth and held her breath, determined not to make a sound.

Then she ripped a gash.

In her mind, she cried out, 'YOW!'

But she stayed silent.

Blood flooded from the slit.

Setting down the piece of mirror, she cupped the spilling blood in her right hand. She dumped it over the back of Pete's head. He cringed. The bright red blood matted his hair and dribbled down the nape of his neck.

'What is that?'

'Shh.'

She dumped another handful in the same place.

She wanted to be facedown, herself, but didn't see how she could manage the blood that way. So she turned onto her back. She twisted

273

herself crooked. She swung her left leg sideways and draped it across Pete's buttocks.

Then she tucked the pistol under her body, just above her right hip where she would be able to reach it fast.

Finally, she raised her cut forearm and moved it slowly back and forth, letting blood patter onto her chest and neck and face.

With her right hand, she smeared the blood over her skin.

That oughta do it, she thought.

*Let 'em come.*

From the sounds of laughter and voices and wild outcries of delight, the mob didn't seem to be any nearer than before.

Still messing with the scavenger?

*What the hell could they be doing?*

Don't want to know, she thought.

Turning her head, she looked at Pete. She stretched her arm over him, and bled for a little while onto the back of his neck and shoulders.

'Just hope they don't think the blood looks too fresh,' she whispered.

'You gashed yourself, didn't you?' Pete said without moving.

'Yep.'

'That's what I thought. Jeez.'

'Don't worry, my blood's good and healthy. Won't give you AIDS or anything.' She swung her arm away from Pete, lowered it across herself, and pressed the wound tightly against her belly. 'Now,' she whispered, 'long as I don't bleed to death . . .'

'Whooo-eee! You need a bath!'

Though the stranger's voice came from some distance away, it made Barbara flinch.

'Too hot for this shit,' said a girl who sounded annoyed.

'Find us a pool,' said a different guy.

'Fuck that,' said another guy. 'I wanta rip more ass!'

'You see how I done her?' asked a guy who sounded like a braggart.

'We saw, we saw,' said a girl.

'Gonna have to disin*fect* your sorry ass,' said someone else. A lot of people laughed and hooted at that one.

The voices were getting louder. Barbara could hear the scrape and shuffle of a great many shoes coming closer, closer.

She willed herself to relax. She quit pressing the cut to her belly. She shut her eyes and made her mouth sag open. She slid her right hand nearer to her side until her fingertips were less than an inch from the pistol tucked beneath her back.

*This is it.*

She realized she was shaking.

*Gotta stop, gotta stop.*

She couldn't stop.

*Won't fool anyone! They'll take one look in here and see me shaking like a damn leaf*

Please, she thought. Go away. All of you, just go away. Nobody here but us chickens. Please, please.

# THIRTY-THREE

'Here I am, ready or not.'

Sheila didn't answer, and Stanley couldn't see any part of her body from where he stood over the bathtub. He wasn't worried, though. She had to be down there – under the huge body of Crash and under the beams.

'Snug as a bug in a tub?' he asked.

He sat down and hung his legs over the broken edge of the floor. He still wore only his moccasins and the flimsy, cut-off pants of his pajamas, but he had grabbed a towel while roaming through a house in search of Weed. He used the towel to mop the sweat off his hair and face, his neck and chest. Then he draped it over his shoulders.

Now that he was sitting, he could see Sheila's arms at the far end of the tub. They looked as if they were folded, one on top of the other, above the crown of Crash's bloody head. From elbows to hands, they were sleeved with dark, drying blood. Her face had to be under them, but Stanley couldn't see any of it. All he saw of her head were a few wisps of golden hair above the crossed arms.

'Did you miss me, darling?' he asked.

She didn't answer or move.

'Playing possum?'

Nothing.

'Won't do you any good, you know. I'm not going anywhere. Not till I've got you.'

He supposed that she might've passed out. After all, she had been down there a long time. And for quite a while, she'd been down there with a huge dead guy on top of her.

Crash was slumped over the beam, the top of his head at Sheila's chin. His arms were up as if he'd died trying to protect the back of his neck. They looked like thick, bloody wings spread out to shield as much of Sheila as possible from Stanley's view.

It didn't seem likely that the body was mashing her too badly, or had suffocated her.

'You didn't faint on me, did you?'

Still nothing.

276

'No,' Stanley said. 'Not you. You're a tough one. You just figure to keep your mouth shut for a while and see what happens. Right? You been down there so long, maybe you figure it's high time for the Cavalry to show up and save you. Just stall a while longer, and everything'll work out fine.'

He wondered if she was listening.

'Maybe you're thinking Weed made a getaway and she'll be charging over the horizon at the head of a SWAT team.'

He wondered what had made him say that, of all things.

*Maybe because it's what I'm afraid of.*

'Isn't gonna happen,' he said. 'She almost got away, but she was more interested in trying to jump me. Want to hear what I did to her?'

Sheila didn't answer.

'Maybe I shouldn't tell,' he said. 'I plan on doing the same to you, so this way it'll come as a surprise. You like surprises, Sheila?'

'Did you kill her?' Sheila asked.

'Ah, she speaks.'

'Did you?'

'You bet. Eventually. But we had a lot of fun, first. I did, anyway. Did you hear her screaming?'

'You bastard.'

'Did you *hear* her?'

'No.'

'It was lovely.'

And it would've been lovely, too, he thought – if only I'd caught her.

Over and over again, while roaming through neighborhood yards and ruins and abandoned houses, he'd imagined what he would do to Weed when he caught her. Leave the tank top on her – what there was of it – but hang her by the hands from something so she'd be stretched and the bottom edge of the shirt wouldn't quite reach down enough to cover her breasts. Tug those jeans down off her skinny hips, down her skinny legs.

That would've been for starters.

Just to get her in the best position and looking good for the rest of it.

While searching for Weed, he'd come up with many ideas about what to do with her after that. He'd lived them in his head, excited by them, relishing the images for their own sake but also knowing that sooner or later he would find her and get to make his fantasies come true.

He hadn't found her, though.

She must've either run far away or found herself a terrific hiding place.

Stanley had been very reluctant to give up the search. She *might* go and find help and come back with cops or something, but that wasn't what bothered him most.

It was missing out on her.

She was no Sheila. Nowhere close. Sheila was in a league of her own. But something about that harsh, skinny girl really made him want her. Want her strung up by the wrists and helpless so he could look her over good and feel her up and down and *do* things to her – things to make her writhe and twitch and scream.

After giving up on the search and starting back toward the ruin of Sheila's house, he'd felt a terrible emptiness.

*Would've been so great. Now I'll never get her.*

But I'll have Sheila, he'd told himself. I can do all kinds of things to Sheila. It'll be just as good – better.

*No, it won't! I want Weed!*

That's crazy, he'd thought. There's no comparison.

*God, why did I let her get away!*

He'd realized that he could keep on searching for her; there was no law that said he had to quit and go back to Sheila. Why not give it another hour? And another? And as long as it takes?

*It's hopeless, that's why. I would've found her by now if I was gonna.*

And a bird in the tub, he'd thought, is worth two in the bush.

Nothing so special about Weed, anyway. She's nothing compared to Sheila. A skinny, ugly, vicious witch. Sheila's a goddess, a gorgeous Amazon. Better Sheila any day of the week than Weed.

*And here we go.*

'Are you ready for me?' he asked.

'Just do what you're gonna do,' Sheila said.

'Golly, you used to be so *eager* for me to get you out.'

'Maybe I'm getting used to it down here.'

'Would you like me to go away?'

'I'd like you to drop dead.'

'Gosh, that isn't a very nice thing to say.'

'I'm sick of being your game. I'm everybody's game.'

Stanley laughed, then lowered himself down to the bathtub. He stood on its edges and gazed at Crash's body.

The legs hung against the bottom of the tub. The broad, faded jeans were halfway down Crash's butt. At the hips, he was slumped over the four-by-eight that was pinning Sheila. Some of his weight, Stanley supposed, had to be resting on her left leg, pressing it into the beam.

'How's your leg?' he asked.

'Which one?'

'The one getting mashed.'

'Numb. Thanks for asking.'

'I'm a very considerate guy. Shall we see what I can do?' Stanley set the scissors aside, then bent down and grabbed the back of Crash's jeans.

He remembered how he'd grabbed Judy the same way.

Only this morning, but it sure seemed like a long time ago.

He thought now that he should've checked on her while he was out looking for Weed . . . made sure she hadn't gotten loose. He hadn't even thought about her, or he would've done that.

And maybe taken a few minutes to have some fun with her.

She'd been a real treat, right after he'd hauled her in from her driveway.

Hauled her in by the back of her jeans. Which had been nice, in its own way. He remembered how much he'd enjoyed it. The feel of her rump against his knuckles as he'd stuck his hand down there. The look of her butt and her white panties.

But Crash was a guy. A dead guy, at that. His rump was wide and fat and ugly. The feel of it made Stanley want to wash his knuckles.

When he tugged at the edge of the jeans, Crash didn't budge.

'Hate to say this,' he said, 'but we might have to wait for a crane.'

'Very funny,' Sheila muttered.

He decided that part of the problem was his precarious perch on the rims of the tub. So he stepped down, placing his feet on the porcelain between Crash's ankles.

He crouched and hooked both his hands into the seat pockets of Crash's jeans.

When he pulled, the pockets tore away. He stumbled but managed to stay up.

For his third try, he shoved both hands down between the top of the jeans and Crash's buttocks. He clutched the denim waistband and threw his weight backward. *Pupp, zzzz!* Crash stayed put, but the jeans went loose and seemed to leap toward Stanley. As he fell, they were tugged down almost to Crash's knees.

He landed hard on his rump.

'Shit!'

'What's going on?' Sheila asked.

'I'm having . . . problems.'

'Try getting him from this end. You lift and I push . . .'

'Yeah. Yeah, good idea. If nothing else, there's gotta be a better view.'

He stood up, climbed again onto the edges of the tub, and made his way forward. Just beyond the beam was the saw. It stood upright between Crash's body and the left side of the tub, where the big man must've dropped it after being knocked down by the chunk of stucco Stanley had thrown.

'Guess what I see,' he said.

Sheila didn't answer.

'The answer to our little difficulty.'

Bracing himself with a hand on Crash's back, Stanley bent low, reached down for the saw, and caught a glimpse of Sheila's bare right side. It was gray with shadow. It was way down there, almost blocked from view by Crash's overhanging bulk.

The sight of it dragged a moan out of him.

In his mind, he suddenly saw *all* of her. Crash vanished and there was Sheila on the bottom of the tub, one leg hooked over the beam and one leg under it, her hands folded under her head, all of her body there for Stanley to see – smooth and golden – and his.

She's mine, he thought.

Get this fat slob *off* her!

'It won't be long,' he said.

Keeping his left foot on the rim of the tub, he crouched and planted his right knee in the middle of Crash's back. He set down the saw. Using both hands, he forced Crash's arms down to the sides. The arms had been covering Sheila's breasts, just as he'd thought.

Stanley felt his penis rise stiff and poke out through the slit of his pajama pants.

'Oh, honey,' he muttered.

With his left hand, he lifted Crash's head by the hair. With his right hand, he picked up the saw began to cut through the neck.

'*What're you doing?*' Sheila cried out.

Her hands were suddenly up, gripping the edge of the beam that crossed above her face.

Stanley stopped sawing. He smiled at her.

She looked so lovely. It didn't matter that her face was streaked with sweat and filth and old blood, that her lips were cracked, that her features were twisted with horror and disgust.

'*My God! Stop it! You can't . . . No!*'

'I don't hear him complaining,' Stanley said.

'*Please!*'

'You want out, don't you?'

'*No! You can't . . . do that to him!*'

'Sure I can. Just watch.' He pushed again at the saw, running its blade through the shallow, raw groove on the side of Crash's neck.

'*No!*'

'Shut up! Look what you've already done with that mouth of yours. I wouldn't have to be doing this, at all, if you'd just kept it shut in the first place.'

She gazed up at Stanley, gasping and jerking her head from side to side.

'That's better.' He started sawing again, and grinned when Sheila squeezed her mouth shut. 'Good idea,' he said. 'You wouldn't want to swallow some of this.'

Soon, she covered her face with both arms.

Stanley kept a good grip on Crash's hair. The sawing took a while; he had to keep the angle of the blade just right and use very short strokes to avoid gouging Sheila. At last, however, he severed the spinal column. He pumped the saw a few more times. Then he hoisted the head. A few remaining shreds of tissue were still connected to the stump of the neck. They stretched and wouldn't let go, so he ripped through them with the saw.

He flung the head away. It tumbled high, vanished beyond the broken flooring, and thumped into the debris with a sound like a hurled brick.

'I bet you feel lighter already,' Stanley said.

'You . . . you sick bastard,' Sheila said from underneath her crossed arms.

'Let me just take care of his arms, then we'll see if we can't haul him off you. Sure hope so. If I've gotta saw him off at the waist, we'll have an incredible mess.'

One at a time, he sawed off Crash's arms and flung them away.

'That's got him whittled down pretty good,' he said.

Sheila uncovered her face. She glanced at the remains of Crash, whimpered and shut her eyes tight.

'I did it with my little saw,' Stanley said, and laughed.

Then he made his way forward on the rims of the tub, turned around, and sat on the beam above Sheila's head. Reaching out to set aside the saw, he smiled and lowered the flat of its blade onto the eyeless face of Crash's buddy, Eagle.

Then he bent at the waist and peered through his spread legs. Sheila's face was upside-down. She looked up at him from the shadows.

The pulpy stump of Crash's neck was still leaking onto her, spilling red fluid through the valley between her breasts.

'You *are* a mess,' Stanley said. 'But don't worry, we'll wash you squeaky clean as soon as we've got you out of here. I know where there's a swimming pool. Now, let's see you stick your hands under this boy's chest and shove him up.'

'What if I don't?'

'Do you think I was bluffing when I said I'd cut him in half? I wasn't, you know. You either give me some cooperation here, or I'll saw him off at the waist. You think things are messy *now* . . .'

'Okay,' she muttered. 'Okay. But I won't be able to do much. The leverage is all wrong. Don't think I haven't already tried.'

'Just do your best. That's all that we can ask, isn't it? You shove him up, and I'll do the rest with my feet.'

'Why don't you just come down and *lift* him off me. All you'd need to do is bend over and pick him up by his shoulders. It'd be easy.'

He thought about her suggestion.

After a few moments, he said, 'Nah.'

'Why not?'

'Because I say so.'

'But it'll work.'

'So what? It'll be more fun *my* way. Anyhow, I'm all done with women giving me orders. We do it my way. You gotta push him up, and then I'll shove him off.'

She glared up at Stanley.

'Do it. Now.'

'Okay. Okay.'

Watching her, Stanley saw what she'd meant about the poor leverage. With the tub against her back, she had no way of lowering her elbows far enough; she couldn't simply shove Crash up like a barbell.

Even if she'd had the elbow room, Stanley supposed that the position of Crash's body might've given her trouble. The massive shoulders, just below her breasts, were too low for a straight upward push.

Sheila didn't waste much time with awkward thrusts – just made a few tentative tries to see whether Crash's sudden loss of weight had improved the situation.

Then she brought her arms in close to her sides, elbows bent, fists in front of her own shoulders. She took a few deep breaths. Gritting her teeth, she drove her elbows upward against the front of Crash's shoulders.

The headless torso started to rise.

Stanley didn't care about that, cared only about what was happening to Sheila.

*Oh, look at her! Look at her!*

Bulges of straining arm muscles, shoulder muscles, chest muscles. Breasts so much larger than before, squeezed together by her arms, the valley between them gone, a long sloping crease where they met.

Her skin bloody and sweaty.

And the tremors!

*Look at her shake!*

*Magnificent!*

Her right breast suddenly lurched free as she chopped her forearm down over the top of it and into the space under Crash's chest. Her lips peeled back. Grunting, she thrust at the body and rammed her left arm down beneath it.

Stanley couldn't see her forearms, now. But he knew they must be crossed in the space between her lower ribcage and Crash's upper chest.

And they were *raising* him.

'Thata way!' Stanley blurted.

'Do it!' she gasped through clenched teeth.

'Get him higher.'

She pushed the body higher.

'Do it!'

'Higher.'

There was no need for more height. But Stanley didn't want this to end.

*Sheila the Magnificent.*

Struggling, suffering, sweating, muscles and veins and tendons all there and showing under her shiny skin, and every part of her shuddering, shaking, trembling, quaking.

'Do it!'

'Here goes.'

He raised his feet off the edges of the tub, leaned back and braced himself against the broken floorboards, then bent his knees and shot his feet forward. They slammed the tops of Crash's shoulders. A red gob leaped from the neck stump.

The headless and armless torso teetered backward, rising from the waist. Then it dropped. For a moment, it seemed to be kneeling behind the beam. Then it tumbled away and smashed against the other end of the tub.

'Bravo!' Stanley yelled.

Below him, Sheila panted for air.

'Get . . . me out,' she gasped.

'We still have the small matter of sawing through the wood.'

'Do it.'

He pursed his lips. 'Oooo. Are you telling me what to do?'

'No.'

'Good. We wouldn't want that.'

'Do . . . whatever you want.'

'Thank you. I think I will.'

He brought up his feet, one at a time, and peeled off the moccasins. Then he lowered his bare feet toward Sheila's chest. Before they could touch her, she clutched his ankles.

'What do you think you're doing?' he asked.

'You're not doing that.'

'I do whatever I want.' He grinned. 'You told me I could.'

'I lied.'

'You'd better let go.'

She didn't let go.

Stanley shot his arm out, grabbed the saw by its handle and swept it down between his legs. He jabbed the steel tip into Sheila just below her sternum.

With all the blood down there from Crash, he couldn't tell whether the point broke her skin.

But she flinched.

And tightened her grip on his ankles.

'Let go, damn it!'

She didn't.

And Stanley suddenly imagined Sheila giving his ankles a tug that would drag him off the four-by-eight. He could almost feel the heavy beam scraping the skin off his back as he fell. He would land rump-first on her chest. And there he would be, sitting on her, his back braced up by the beam, his arms nearly useless because she would be under him and so hard to reach.

With her strength . . .

*She could kill me!*

Scared, Stanley shoved the saw. It gouged a shallow furrow down toward her navel.

Crying out, she let go of his ankles and tried to snatch the blade. He jerked it clear. He kicked his legs high as she grabbed for them. She kept trying to catch them as he drew them back, but he battered at her hands and arms with the saw, striking and cutting her, finally planting his heels on the top of the beam, springing up and leaping to safety.

# THIRTY-FOUR

Barbara felt Pete's buttocks flex underneath the calf of her outstretched leg. Neither moving nor opening her eyes, she whispered, 'Lie still.'

'They're gone.'

'Let's give it a little longer.'

'Okay.'

They probably *are* gone, she told herself.

Some time ago, the gang had wandered down the alley, laughing and jabbering and arguing, and gone on by without any mention or inspection of the pickup truck where Barbara and Pete were hiding.

Which had seemed too good to be true.

So Barbara hadn't allowed herself to believe it.

Must be a trick, she'd thought. They know we're here. They're just pretending to leave. Wanta see what happens.

So wait, just wait.

If we think the coast is clear and show ourselves, it'll blow any chance of playing dead. We'll end up dead for real.

Maybe they're sneaking up on us.

They startle us, she'd thought, and we'll probably both jump and that'll be it.

*Not that our little dead act is gonna fool someone, anyhow.*

A long time had gone by since the footsteps and voices of the gang had faded and vanished. It seemed like at least an hour. But Barbara knew how time had a way of stretching, slowing down, when things were bad. It probably hadn't been an hour, at all.

At least *half* an hour, she told herself.

They've gotta be gone by now. They wouldn't have that much patience. They never had any idea we were here and they just kept walking.

We could've kept our clothes on, she realized.

I didn't need to cut myself.

Now we're both naked and bloody and I've got a nice gash on my arm.

And if we stay here long enough, someone *else* might come along.

Earl, for instance.

She wondered what had happened to him. He must've seen the gang come running into the alley on the heels of the scavenger. Either they hadn't spotted him, though, or they hadn't cared. Maybe they *had* seen him, but were more interested in nailing the scavenger.

They'd sure spent a lot of time on her.

On *them*. Don't forget the guy in the shopping cart.

Another good reason to stay here, Barbara told herself. Who wants to see those bodies?

But I sure don't want Earl showing up and finding me like this. Even if he did warn us, he's still a major creep.

Better get a move on.

She opened her eyes. Seven or eight feet above her was the dim, raftered ceiling of the parking stall.

Nothing up there to worry about.

She glanced from side to side. Nobody leered down at her over the truck's side panels.

Raising her head, she checked the rear window of the cab.

Nobody there.

So she tipped her head back. The area above the tailgate was upside-down. She saw no one.

'Maybe it *is* safe by now,' she whispered.

'I think they're long gone.'

'And if they aren't, we've got our guns.'

'Yeah,' Pete whispered.

'Okay.' She looked at him and saw that his head was still turned away from her. 'Stay like that, okay? I'll tell you when to look.'

'Sure.'

'Thanks.' She pulled the Colt out from under her back, then shoved herself up with her elbows and studied their sprawled, naked bodies.

*Maybe we could've passed, after all.*

The back of Pete's head and neck, where she'd dumped a couple of handloads of blood, looked as if he might've suffered some sort of fatal wound. Not much blood lower down, though – and the tan on his back seemed too glowing for a dead guy.

Guess we'll never know, she thought.

Her own body was good and bloody, but she could see hand and fingerprints in the brownish-red smears that might make it pretty obvious she'd spread the blood around, herself. And she'd entirely neglected the area below her waist.

Her legs were wide apart, one draped across Pete's rump. Between them, she'd spread no blood, she had no tan, and her tuft of blond curls was too sparse to hide the skin beneath it.

A sudden heat rushed through her body.

*Thank God nobody saw me like this!*

'What're you doing?' Pete asked. He sounded curious, not annoyed.

'Nothing,' Barbara said.

'Just looking?'

She hesitated.

'You are, aren't you?'

'Sort of.' She raised her leg and swung it away from Pete. It left behind a ruddy hue. 'I just wanted to see if we looked all right. You know, bloody and dead.'

'How *do* we look?'

'Pretty good.'

'Too bad we didn't get a chance to see if it worked.'

'We're really lucky, is what we are.'

'I thought you said we look pretty good.'

'Yeah. We just don't look especially dead.'

Pete laughed a little.

'I guess the whole thing was a dumb idea,' Barbara said.

'It was sure extreme. How's your cut?'

She looked down at the gash on the underside of her forearm. All around it, the skin was stained with dry blood. The wound itself was a raw, dark slit two inches long. 'It isn't bleeding anymore,' she said. 'But it's kind of sore.'

'That was really a brave thing, cutting yourself like that.'

'Naw, just stupid.'

'No, it wasn't. It was heroic. You might've saved our lives, doing that.'

'Might've. Except nobody even looked at us.'

'Including me,' Pete said, and made a soft laugh.

'Including you?'

*He wants to look! Oh, my God!*

'I'm . . . never mind,' he muttered. 'I just thought . . . you know, we're playing dead in the back of a pickup truck. It doesn't, like . . . happen every day.'

'That's for sure.'

'It's all right,' he said. 'I mean, I know I can't look.'

The pounding of Barbara's heart quickened. 'Do you want to?' Her voice sounded shaky.

'Me? No. Jeez!'

Heart pounding very hard, she sank down against the floor. She couldn't believe she was planning to go through with this. And she couldn't believe how much she wanted it. 'Yes, you do,' she said.

'No, really.'

'Wait a second. I'll make it the way it was.' She swung her leg onto

Pete's rump, stuck the Colt beneath her back, and ran through the position in her mind to make sure it was the same as before.

The same except for her head and eyes.

Because she had to watch Pete.

'Okay. You can look now.'

'No, really, I . . .'

'Come on. It's okay. I *want* you to.'

I almost sound sort of calm, she thought. Amazing.

'Like you said,' she went on, 'we don't go around playing dead every day. We've got all this blood on us . . . I don't want you regretting how you blew your chance to see . . . how we looked.'

'Are you kidding?'

'I mean it. Come on.'

She watched Pete raise his head and turn it toward her. He pushed himself up with his elbows. He stared into her eyes. Then his gaze moved slowly down her body. He licked his dry, cracked lips. He blinked a few times. Barbara could see that he was shaking slightly.

She wondered if her own shaking showed.

More than likely.

Bracing himself up with his right elbow, Pete twisted his torso and peered back at her.

*He can see everything!*

She thought about trying to cover up – flinging an arm across her breasts, clapping a hand between her legs.

But she stayed on her back and didn't move her arms and found breathing a very hard thing to do.

'A lot of blood,' he said, his voice quiet and trembling.

'Yeah.'

'You're right, though. We don't look very dead.'

'Not very.' Lifting her head, she looked at Pete. The way he was turned and holding himself up, she could see the red imprint that the rifle had made on his chest and belly. The rifle was on the floor beneath him, its stock pinned down by his left thigh.

*If the rifle wasn't in the way . . .*

Glad it is, she told herself. Who'd wanta see something like that, anyway?

She turned her attention to his face. He almost looked as if he were in pain. His eyes kept jerking this way and that as if he couldn't make up his mind about what he would rather stare at.

'Hey,' Barbara whispered.

He flinched, then met her eyes.

She couldn't help but smile. 'Are you all right?'

'Oh, man.'

She lifted her leg off his rump, then turned onto her side. Facing Pete, she pushed herself up on one elbow. His gaze flicked to her breasts, but quickly returned to her eyes.

'Sorry,' he muttered.

'It's okay.'

'I've never seen . . . you know . . . a *girl* . . . a real one without, you know, clothes on.'

'Do I look okay?'

'Are you kidding? You're . . . God, nobody would believe this!'

'You aren't going to tell anyone, are you?'

'No! No way! I'd never tell *any*one.'

Reaching out with her right hand, Barbara caressed the side of his face. His cheek felt wet and hot. Her fingertips, curled over the edge of his ear, stroked through dripping hair. She slid her hand down the side of his neck, and up over the solid mound of his shoulder.

His eyes never strayed from her face.

'This'll be our secret,' she said.

'Yeah.'

She followed his arm to the wrist, wrapped her fingers around it, and guided his hand to her breast. She gasped when he touched her. She went rigid and moaned when he squeezed.

He let go fast. 'Did I hurt you?'

'No. No, no.'

His hand returned. But it was more gentle this time. His fingertips brushed lightly over her breast. She felt her skin go crawly with goosebumps, felt the nipples of both breasts squirm and rise hard. She shut her eyes.

When the hand went away, she thought it was going to her other breast. Instead, it pressed against her back.

The bed of the pickup wobbled slightly. For a moment, she thought there was an aftershock. Then she realized that the motion came from Pete scooting toward her. The rifle made scraping sounds.

Pete's hand went away again.

'I'll put this behind you,' he whispered.

Not such a hot idea, she thought. The rifle oughta stay between us . . . we oughta keep *something* between us.

It clamored against the floor behind her back.

Then Pete's arm was on her back, his hand curling around the nape of her neck, urging her closer to him.

His lips found her mouth.

Just like in the pool, she thought.

But different.

Very, very different. Because in the pool they'd had clothes on, and now they didn't, and she wasn't ready for this sort of thing, not at all, and it scared her but she wanted it. His mouth was wet, exciting. She didn't want to stop kissing him. She just wished she didn't have to be scared about the rest.

Maybe not *all that* scared, she thought, realizing that she was squirming on her side closer to him. Closer until she felt her breasts push against his chest. Closer until she felt his penis bump against her belly.

The shock of its touch pounded her breath out.

*Oh, my God!*

It felt slippery and smooth and enormous.

With a sudden gasp that was almost a whimper, Pete pushed himself away from her. He flopped over, rolled quickly onto his other side, and curled up.

Barbara gaped at him, stunned.

A little frightened.

*What's going on?*

She waited for a few moments. He seemed to be shuddering.

*Oh, God, he's not crying, is he?*

'Pete?' she asked. 'Are you okay?'

He didn't answer, just kept shaking and gasping for air.

'Pete?' she asked again.

'Uh?'

'What's the matter?'

'Nothing.'

She reached out and caressed the side of his arm. 'Something has to be wrong. You sure got away from me fast.' When he didn't respond, she asked, 'Was it my breath?'

He blurted out a short laugh. 'It wasn't your breath.'

'What did I do?'

'Nothing. Forget about it, okay?'

'Forget about it?'

After a moment, he said, 'It wasn't anything you did.'

'Something I *should've* done?'

'No.'

'I mean, I don't know much about this sort of stuff.'

'You and me both.'

'I just know that I like you an awful lot,' she said, gently rubbing his arm. 'A *real* lot.'

'Same here. I've never . . . liked a girl this much.'

She scooted toward him and gently curled herself against his back. She kissed the nape of his neck, which was a little sticky with her own blood. Then she reached over his side and started to caress his chest.

'I don't think we'd better get started again,' he said.

'I'm not starting anything.'

'I mean it, Barbara. It got . . . so out of control.'

'Okay.' She took her hand away from his chest, and rested it on his arm. 'It did get out of hand awfully fast, didn't it?'

'That's for sure.'

'It was great.'

'It was great, all right,' he said. 'Man.'

'But I guess it's a good thing we stopped . . . *you* stopped. I don't think I could've. I've never . . .' She patted his arm. 'Now what?'

'Why don't you go ahead and get dressed?'

'Okay.' But she didn't move. 'You aren't mad at me or anything, are you?'

'No! Are you kidding?'

'So, it's not like we won't . . . do stuff . . . again sometime.'

'No. I sure hope not.'

'Me, too.'

'Get dressed now, okay?'

'How about a kiss first?'

Pete shook his head.

'You don't want to kiss me?'

'Sure, I want to. Let's just wait till we're dressed. Just so nothing . . . happens again.'

'Okay. Sounds good to me.' She gave the side of his neck a quick nibble that made him cringe and hunch his shoulders. Then she rolled onto her back.

And smiled and filled her lungs.

She felt wonderful. Wonderful and strange. Shivery and warm, empty and full, frightened and very excited.

You'd think we'd *done* it, she thought.

*Yeah, right. How would I know?*

Maybe I'd *really* feel incredible if we'd done it. But who knows? It's supposed to hurt, the first time. And there'd have to be all kinds of guilt, not to mention worries about a few little matters like getting pregnant or . . .

'You don't have AIDS, do you?' she heard herself ask, and couldn't believe that she'd asked.

'No! Jeez!'

'I mean, the way you . . . just stopped everything all of a sudden like that. I mean, you really got away from me fast, like there was a big emergency, or . . .'

'There *was* a big emergency,' he muttered.

'Uh-huh.'

291

'But it didn't have anything to do with AIDS.'

'I'm glad of that.'

'Or any other disease.'

'Okay.'

'It wasn't anything you need to worry about.'

'Okay.'

'It was a guy thing.'

'A *guy* thing?'

'Never mind. Okay? Jeez, I don't wanta get into it. I thought you were gonna get dressed.'

'I'll get dressed,' she said. 'Excellent idea,' she added, and sat up.

She quickly twisted from side to side, looking both ways and behind her.

She saw nobody.

Then she spotted the overturned shopping cart far down the alley to her right. She looked away fast, but not quickly enough to miss a glimpse of the two shapes on the pavement near the cart.

Her stomach went squirmy.

*Why did I have to look?*

'Coast is clear,' she said.

'Good,' Pete said.

She crawled toward the front of the pickup's bed. At the edge of the tarp, she glanced back at Pete. He still lay curled on his side, legs together, knees drawn up. The ruddy imprint of her calf had almost faded from his buttocks.

'You can turn around if you want,' she said.

'That's okay.'

'You'd rather stare at the side of an old pickup truck than at me?'

'I just think it's better this way.'

'Okay.' On her knees, she peeled back the tarp. Her clothes were mixed together with Pete's. 'Toss you your stuff?' she asked.

'I'll get dressed when you're done,' he said. 'Thanks, though.'

'Welcome.'

She looked around to make sure nobody was in sight. Then she stood up. Staying low, shifting from foot to foot, she stepped into her panties and shorts. She sat down to finish.

'Your turn,' she announced. Leaning back, she stretched out an arm and picked up her forty-five.

'Okay,' Pete said. But he didn't move.

'You want me to leave?'

'Maybe you could, like, stand guard in the alley.'

She grinned and shook her head, uncertain whether to be amused or worried by Pete's behavior. All she knew, for sure, was that she didn't want to give him any trouble. So she slipped her purse strap over her shoulder and stood up. She walked past him, climbed over the tailgate, and hopped down.

Standing with her back to the pickup, she lifted the tail of her blouse and slid the Colt down the rear of her shorts. The muzzle shoved her panties down an inch or two. The cool steel felt good.

'I won't look, I promise,' she said. 'But I don't much wanta go out and stand in the middle of the alley, if it's all the same to you.'

'You're fine right there.'

She heard thumps and shuffling behind her back, as if Pete were racing to reach his clothes and get into them before Barbara might change her mind and look at him.

'No big hurry,' she told him. 'Nobody's coming, and I promise not to peek.'

'Fine.'

She dug into the bottom of her purse. A lot of junk down there: crumbs and gum wrappers, an old Bic pen, several paper clips and rubber bands. She came out with two rubber bands. Holding them between her lips, she reached again into her purse. She took out a small packet of facial tissues, tore away their cellophane wrapper, and folded the tissues in half. She placed the thick square against the gash on her arm, then took the rubber bands out of her mouth and slipped them over her hand. They caught and pulled at some hairs as she rolled them up her forearm, but she got them around the makeshift bandage.

That oughta hold it, she thought.

Hearing a thump of shoes, she turned around in time to see Pete swoop down for the rifle. He came up holding it by the leather sling. His shirt was on, but hung open. It billowed behind him as he planted a foot on top of the tailgate, leaped, and dropped. He landed on his feet and took a few rushing steps past Barbara before stopping himself. As he turned to face her, he hooked the sling over his shoulder.

'Ready?' he asked. He was standing in the sunlight, squinting at her.

'Come here,' she said.

'Shouldn't we get going?'

'You owe me a kiss, remember?'

'Sure, I remember.'

'Now that we're dressed.'

'Yeah.'

'So, come and get it.'

Pete suddenly hurried back to her, out of the sunshine and into the shadow of the car port where she waited, smiling.

He slipped his arms around her. He pulled her against him, gently, and kissed her.

She eased her mouth away. 'Got something for you,' she whispered. Stepping back from him slightly, she thrust a hand down a front pocket of her shorts. 'Something,' she said, 'to help you remember about us in the pickup truck on the day of the big quake.'

'I'm not about to forget about it. Are you kidding?'

'Well, I think you should have a souvenir.' She pulled the crumpled wad of fabric out of her pocket and shook it open in front of him.

He glanced at the dangling bra, then stared at her chest. 'Oh, my God,' he muttered.

'Take it.'

'Thanks. Jeez.' He took it, and stuffed it into a front pocket of his trousers. 'You sure it's all right?'

'Huh?'

'You don't . . . you know, need it?'

'Not much. Nobody'll even know it's gone.'

'I sure know.'

'You're supposed to. You'll cherish it, right?'

He grinned.

'Just don't wear it.'

'Barbara!'

'Except on special occasions.'

He laughed.

'What've you got for me?' she asked.

'Uh . . .' He shrugged and looked helpless.

'I need a souvenir, too.'

'What would you like?'

'Oh, maybe . . .'

'Should've given her a twat-load of come when you had the chance, Pizzaman.'

Pete suddenly looked sick.

Stomach coiling tight, Barbara whirled around.

Earl came strolling out from the far side of the Jeep Wrangler that was parked beside the pickup truck. Smirking, he sniffed and rubbed his nose.

'You watched?' Barbara asked.

'Had to. Oooo, Banner. Ooooo.'

Nobody could've been watching! she told herself. I looked! I looked everywhere!

*You glanced around a couple of times, that's all.*

It's like some kind of damn conspiracy, she thought. Lee watched us in the pool, and now Earl . . . Is somebody *always* spying on us?

'Where?' she muttered. 'Where were you?'

'Here, there.' Grinning, he halted a couple of paces in front of her. 'Close enough to touch you most of the time.'

'No, you weren't.'

Pete stepped up to Barbara's side. He held the rifle low by his hip, its muzzle toward Earl. 'Maybe you'd better get out of here.'

'Oh, sure. What're you gonna do, shoot me? Gimme a break. First off, you haven't got the guts to shoot anyone. Second, that old mob would've had your asses except I saw 'em coming and warned you. Not to mention I stuck to the alley and ran off so as not to give you away. You owe me plenty, both of you.'

Grinning, he rubbed his chin and glanced at Barbara's chest. She knew that she'd left the top two buttons of her blouse undone. Without looking, she started to fasten the top one.

'Nothing you gotta hide from me, babe,' Earl said. 'I seen it all.' He raised his hand as if to stop her from protesting. 'But you got no reason to blame me for looking. Shit, I thought you were dead, both of you. I came circling back around, once everything looked safe, and I figured they'd gotten you. I mean, I took a look in back of the pickup, here, and you're both stretched out starkers and bloody. What was I suppose to think?'

'You took us for dead?' Pete asked.

'Sure.'

Pete bumped Barbara softly with his arm. 'Guess it worked.'

'It worked fine,' Earl said, 'till you sorta twitched your ass, and then Banner tells you to stop it. That was a pretty good giveaway.'

'You were here *then*?' Barbara asked.

'Standing right there.' He pointed at the tailgate.

'How come we didn't hear you?' Pete asked.

'I was being quiet, what do you think?'

'Oh God,' Barbara muttered. 'You saw . . . you watched everything?'

'Ooooo, yes.'

'Could you hear us, too?' she asked.

'Every word.' Shaking his head, he laughed. 'You two are a real pair.'

Barbara groaned.

'Hey, don't take it so hard! You oughta be glad it was *me* caught you at it. Could've been a lot worse. A lot. All I did was watch, know what I mean? Didn't join in. Didn't take the guns. Didn't kill you. I was a real gentleman. All I did was enjoy the show.'

'Well,' Pete said, 'the show's over. Now how about getting out of here?'

'No, I don't think so. I'm sticking with you all the way.'

'What the hell for?' Barbara blurted.

He grinned. ''Cause you're such a babe, Banner. And it's a kick to be around a couple of lovebirds like you and Pizzaboy. And you guys have all the guns.'

'Why didn't you take them when you had the chance?' Barbara asked.

'Too busy watching the fun.'

'Sure.'

'You want the honest truth, soon as I found out you two weren't dead, I figured on sticking with you. So I figured why not let you keep on carrying the things?'

'I've got news for you,' Barbara said. 'You *aren't* sticking with us.'

Grinning, Earl glanced from Barbara to Pete, and back to Barbara. 'How would you like your folks to find out all about what you guys were up to? I mean like a blow by blow description, know what I mean?'

A terrible flood of heat surged through Barbara.

'If you tell on us,' Pete said, 'we'll tell on you for shooting Heather.'

'Oooo, I'm scared. Big fucking deal. You tell what you wanta tell, and I'll tell what I wanta tell. No way you could stop me, unless you shoot me, and we already know you aren't about to do that.'

'Don't count on it,' Barbara said.

He laughed.

She thought she might throw up.

It was so easy to imagine Earl telling her parents every little detail of what she'd done with Pete in the back of the pickup truck. And it would sound so bad, so dirty. They wouldn't understand. They'd blame Pete, no matter how much she tried to explain that it had all been her idea. They'd figure it was Pete's fault, and they'd hate him for it.

And Pete's parents would probably figure she was some sort of slut, and hate her.

*Or maybe they all got killed in the quake, so there's nobody for Earl to tell.*

She felt a moment of relief at the thought, then despised herself for it. *I didn't mean it. I want everybody to be fine. Please.*

'Okay,' she said. 'Let's all decide, right here and now, that we'll stick together and keep our mouths shut about everything. Is that how you want it, Earl?'

'You got it.'

'Pete?'

'Yeah. Fine. But what if he tells on us, anyway?'

'I won't,' Earl said. He grinned again. 'I might be an asshole, but I got my principles. I don't never go back on my word, no matter what.'

Pete met Barbara's eyes, and nodded.

'One more thing,' Barbara said to Earl. 'No more cracks about what just happened here. Pretend you never saw us or heard us. Erase it from your memory. This has been a real funny day, and I have a feeling that it wouldn't take much to make me go ahead and shoot you. I know you don't think I'll do it, but *I'm* not so sure.'

Earl started to grin again.

But only one corner of his mouth curled up, and it wouldn't let him look amused.

'Okay,' she said. 'Let's get moving.'

# THIRTY-FIVE

Mary had blubbered and sobbed and whimpered all the way down from the top of the landslide – a trip she'd made like a terrified kid, feet first and scooting on her rump. 'Don't touch me!' she'd blurted when Clint had offered to give her a hand. 'I can't be touched! Nowhere! Nowhere! I hurt! I hurt! Everything hurts!'

Matters had improved once they'd left the landslide behind. On the paved surface of Laurel Canyon Boulevard, Mary had continued to shuffle along, trembling and wincing, but she'd cut out the worst of her crying and complaining.

Clint walked ahead of her, Em by his side. For Mary's sake, he was careful to keep his pace slow.

Very slow.

He tried not to resent it.

Mary and her damn fall.

It wasn't her fault that she'd been startled by 'Mr Gooey' (as Em had taken to calling the poor guy), but she shouldn't have gone stomping up there in a huff ahead of everyone else. Clint was sure that the fall wouldn't have happened if she'd behaved herself.

So much time wasted, because of it. Because she'd refused again and again to get off her back and start moving. Because, when she was finally ready to get up, she'd insisted on someone retrieving her shoes, so Em had gone back down the other side to find them. Then because she'd taken forever sliding down the hill on her rump. And finally because, reaching the road again, she'd been holding them back by hobbling along like an old lady.

I could be home by now, Clint thought.

Maybe not *all* the way there, but close. Except for Mary. She's such a bitch, but I've let her hold me back this way. It isn't right. Sheila or Barbara might be hurt or trapped or something, needing me. I should be there for them!

Still, he wouldn't quicken his pace.

Have to stick with her, he thought. Have to see her through this. God knows why.

I wouldn't have gotten this far without her car, he reminded himself. It gave us a good start, way back at the beginning of it all. Maybe that's why.

Or maybe it's just because she's a woman. If you're a guy, you've gotta take care of the women. It's just part of the deal, no matter what the feminists say. They're the damsels and you're the knight, whether you like it or not.

He could see, just down the road, an intersection with dead traffic lights and lanes leading off to the left.

'We're almost to Sunset,' he said.

'Is that it?' Em asked.

'That's Hollywood Boulevard. See the street sign? Sunset's just a little farther.'

'That little thing is Hollywood Boulevard?'

'Where it starts.'

'Sure doesn't *look* like Hollywood Boulevard.'

'Not much at this end. Just some apartment houses, condos. But you keep going, and you'll run into all the tourist stuff. The Chinese, the Walk of Fame . . .'

'So, how far are we from your house?'

He grimaced. 'Not far. From here, if we walked at a pretty good clip, we could be there in an hour.'

'Hey, that isn't bad!'

'The rate we're going, it'll be more like two or three.'

She gave Clint her nose-wrinkled look as if something smelled vile. Then she glanced over her shoulder.

'What's your problem?' Mary muttered.

Em shrugged and shook her head and returned her gaze to Clint. 'Wanta ditch her?'

'It's crossed my mind. Can't do it, though.'

'Yeah, I know. She might end up *Ms* Gooey.'

'That's right.'

'Course, you could put Caspar and Loreen in charge of her.'

Clint let out a laugh. 'That'd be a sweet thing to do.'

'Serve her right.'

'A lot of stuff might serve her right,' Clint said. 'But she's already paid a pretty high price. I wouldn't want anything else happening to her.'

Em squeezed his hand. 'You're such a *gentleman*. My mom would absolutely despise you.'

'No, she wouldn't.'

'You're right. But she'd *let on* that she did.' The mischief suddenly fled from Em's face. 'I sure hope nothing's happened to her.'

'She's probably fine,' Clint said. 'Everyone's probably fine.'

'Mr Gooey didn't end up so fine.'

'But he's just one person out of . . . what, twelve million? The odds are in our favor. Your mother, my wife and kid . . . They're probably all just fine.'

'Yeah. I guess so.'

'We'll be fine, too.'

'Except maybe for Mary,' she added, and a glint returned to her eyes. 'Who may or may not be dead meat, depending on whether you're a believer, or . . . '

'Loreen doesn't know beans.'

'If Mary *is* going to meet a bad end, I wish it'd happen soon so we can stop all this dawdling.'

Clint scowled down at Em.

She laughed and bumped her shoulder against his side.

'Such a scamp,' Clint said.

'I'm glad *somebody's* enjoying themselves,' Mary called from behind them.

Em let go of Clint's hand and turned around. Walking backward, she said, 'How're you doing?'

'Horrible.'

'Is there anything I can do for you?'

'Yeah, turn around and leave me alone.'

'Well, that's a sweet thing to say.'

'How much longer is this going to take, Clint?'

He looked over his shoulder at her. 'We're almost to Sunset.'

'Oh. Just great. Loreen'll be happy about that.'

Clint saw Loreen and Caspar walking side by side, probably fifty feet behind Mary. They were facing each other, gesturing and moving their mouths.

'Nothing is going to happen at Sunset,' Clint said.

'If you don't count me getting killed.'

'Including that.'

'Like, you're gonna save me.'

'Like, nothing's gonna happen. Stop worrying about it, okay?'

'You'd be worried, too, if some fucking gypsy bitch said you were gonna die at Sunset.'

'Nobody's gonna die at Sunset,' Clint said.

'We'll see about that.'

A few minutes later, Sunset Boulevard came into view. Em tightened her grip on Clint's hand, and halted.

'Let's keep going,' Clint said, trying to keep his voice steady.

Em shook her head. She made a high-pitched humming sound, not quite a moan, not quite a whine.

'It's all right,' he said. But he knew it *wasn't* all right. Not at all. He knew why Em wanted nothing to do with the intersection ahead, and why she was making such a frightened noise. He had a quick urge, himself, to squeal, 'Let's get outa here!' and whirl around and run away.

It was the first major thoroughfare they'd encountered since Ventura Boulevard on the other side of the hills.

Like Ventura, every lane was jammed with traffic.

But the other boulevard had been alive.

Not Sunset.

Here, the vehicles didn't try to inch forward. None moved. Some had been turned onto their sides, others upside-down. Many were smoky, smoldering husks.

No horns honked.

There was nobody to honk them.

Most of the cars and trucks and vans looked abandoned, as if their drivers and passengers had thrown open the doors and run for their lives.

Many hadn't made it.

There were bodies. Fifteen or twenty of them, at least, that Clint saw from where he stood looking down on the scene. Several bodies were slumped across car hoods. Most of the others were sprawled on the pavement, just this side of the traffic, as if they'd been slaughtered while trying to flee toward Laurel Canyon.

Mr Gooey must be the one that got away, Clint thought.

*But he didn't exactly get away, did he? They took what they wanted from him, and let the poor guy go.*

Who the hell could've done all this? Clint wondered.

He saw nobody down there roaming among the cars. Nobody at all who didn't look dead.

Mary staggered to a halt by his side. She didn't say anything. She stared straight forward and trembled.

Soon, Caspar and Loreen arrived.

Everyone stared at Sunset Boulevard.

After a while, Loreen muttered, 'Blood on the face of the day. So much blood. I saw . . .'

'Stop it,' Clint said.

'There's a police car,' Em said, pointing.

Clint nodded. Like the patrol car at the other end of Laurel Canyon, this one had been parked broadside – stationed there to prevent vehicles from turning off Sunset onto the closed boulevard.

Clint remembered the two cops at the other end.

A young man and woman. They'd been friendly and helpful. He hoped they were still all right.

*These* cops were probably not all right.

Probably among the dead.

None of the bodies scattered on the street near the patrol car wore uniforms.

None wore much of anything.

At this distance, the figures seemed to be made of bare skin and blood. Clint could see that some, at least, had been scalped. Several had been dismembered to one extent or another.

'Shoot 'em full of arrows,' he muttered, 'and it'd look like an Indian massacre.'

'We can't go down there,' Mary said.

'I have to,' Clint said.

'Not me.'

Em squeezed Clint's hand. 'I go where you go.'

'Whatever happened,' Clint said, 'it looks like it's over. Whoever did this might be long gone, by now.'

'They're waiting for us,' Loreen said.

Clint scowled. 'Don't say it if you don't mean it.'

'Don't say it, anyway,' Mary told her.

Loreen shrugged her thick shoulders. 'I only tell what I see.'

'Well,' Clint said, 'please don't. Unless you literally *spotted* someone down there. Did you actually *see* someone?'

'With the eye of my mind.'

'Then we don't want to hear about it,' Clint told her.

'When Loreen sees something "with the eye of her mind," ' Caspar said, 'it's usually there. We'd better turn back.'

'No!' Loreen blurted. 'We cannot turn back. Going back is far worse than going forward. This, I know.'

'Terrific,' Mary said. 'We can't go forward, we can't go back, where the fuck are we *supposed* to go? Not that it matters a hell of a lot, far as *I'm* concerned, seeing as how I've been pronounced dead already by this fat tub of . . .' She cut off her words and eyed Caspar. 'This delightful psychic,' she added, then gave Loreen a grin that looked more like a snarl.

'I only tell what . . .'

'Knock it off!' Clint snapped at Loreen. To Mary, he said, 'I know you're scared. We're all scared. I don't wanta go down there any more than you do. But my home is on the other side of Sunset, so I'm going across.'

He reached into a front pocket of his pants and pulled out the paring knife he'd taken from Em's kitchen. 'Time for these,' he told Em. As he drew the blade from its cardboard sheath, the girl lifted the hanging front of her T-shirt and removed two butcher knives from the pockets of her shorts.

'Give me one,' Caspar said.

She shook her head. 'I don't think so.'

'You don't need the both of them.'

'One's for Mary. If she wants it.'

'That makes no sense,' Caspar protested.

'I hate to say this, Mr Blotski, but I'm not sure you're someone I'd trust very much with sharp objects, if you know what I mean.'

'Me?' Eyebrows leaping up in shock, he pounded an open hand against his chest. Shiny waves of red silk rippled the front of his blouse. 'Me?' he blurted again. 'You don't trust *me*?'

'You've made some threats,' Clint explained.

'Besides which,' Em said, 'Mary was with us first. And she's the one Loreen says is in the most trouble around here, so she oughta have something she can use for defending herself just in case things get hairy.' She held one of the knives out toward Mary. 'You can have it if you want it,' she said.

Mary looked from the knife handle to Em's face. 'Thank you,' she murmured. 'You . . . You really . . . want me to have it? After everything . . .'

'Sure.'

Mary's chin trembled. Tears spilled from her eyes and dribbled down her cheeks. 'Thank you.' She took the knife. 'You're so nice to me. I don't deserve . . .'

'You *don't* deserve!' Caspar assured her. Pounding his chest again, he gaped at Clint. 'I am a *man*. I should get a knife!'

'Go find one,' Clint told him.

'This is outrageous! This girl, this *child*, she has no right to decide who gets what! Are you mad?'

'They're her knives,' Clint pointed out, 'so knock it off.'

'Fool!'

'Settle yourself down, Caspar,' Loreen said, and placed a hand on his shoulder. 'Look at you. And you wonder why little Em doesn't want to give you a weapon?'

'She's a child. She knows nothing.'

'Child,' Clint said, 'rip the tape off your blade. You too, Mary. Then try to keep your knives out of sight when we go in. With any luck, you won't need to use them. If you do get attacked, though, don't let your assailant see your knife. Let him *feel* it before he sees it. Shove the blade in as hard as you can, then twist it, rip with it. Do as much damage as you can, as fast as you can.'

Mary nodded and sniffled.

'Where'd be the best place to stab somebody?' Em asked.

'Wherever you can get to. Just get that knife into him as fast and hard as you can. And don't worry . . . either of you. I'll be there to help.'

'What a *mensch*,' said Caspar.

Clint faced him. 'We'll all help each other. There're five of us. We oughta be able to take care of trouble.'

'I go first,' Loreen said.

'What?' Caspar blurted.

'You heard me, Papa. The madness cannot touch me. My aura will act as my shield. Those who would do us harm will be struck numb with awe. Thus will I settle the turbulence and make the passage safe for you who follow.'

Em wrinkled her nose, glanced at Clint and rolled her eyes.

Mary made a snorting sound.

Caspar said, 'I forbid it.'

'No harm will come to me,' Loreen told him, smiling with gentle confidence.

Maybe she knows something I don't, Clint thought. Or maybe she's just nuts.

'No,' Caspar said. 'Let *them* go first, the Three Stooges. We'll wait and see what happens to them. If they get to the other side without . . .'

'My way is best,' Loreen said.

She took a step, and Caspar blocked her way. They both stood motionless. Caspar glared into her eyes, but slowly his fierceness faded and vanished. He moved out of her way, then turned and watched her walk past him. When he started to follow her, she raised her hand. He halted.

She kept on walking, her peasant skirt swishing from side to side with the sweep of her broad rump.

'Loreen!' Caspar called.

Without looking back, she waved him forward.

Caspar hurried after her. He gained on her for a few moments, then slowed his pace. He stayed about twenty feet behind her as they made their way toward Sunset.

'Let's do some catching up,' Clint said. Holding the knife inside his right pocket, he gestured Mary forward with his other hand.

She started to hobble.

With her left hand at her chest, she held her torn blouse shut. She carried the knife in plain sight by her right hip, blade to the rear.

'Better hide the knife,' Clint reminded her.

Without argument, she swept it upward. The knife and the hand that held it disappeared inside the front of her blouse.

'Move it along, now,' Clint said. 'Come on, you can do better than that. Pick it up, pick it up.'

Mary quickened her pace.

'Em, you go now.'

Em hurried past him.

Her right arm, bent at the elbow, hitched up the back of her T-shirt so high that a swath of bare skin showed above the top of her shorts.

Clint felt a sudden ache, glimpsing the skin. Not arousal, exactly. Partly that, but more a strange mix of desire and envy and loss. And a great, awful tenderness.

*Can't let anything happen to her. Can't. No matter what. She's what's best in the world, girls like her and girls like Barbara. Have to take good care of her.*

He had a thickness in his throat, but he smiled about the back of Em's Roadkill T-shirt.

The cloth was so thin and clingy that it took on the shape of her forearm, her fist, and the broad tapering blade that stood upright over her spine. The point of the knife was midway between her shoulder blades.

The knife's almost bigger than she is, he thought.

Such a toughie.

And damn it, she shouldn't have to be going around in this world with a knife in her shirt like some sort of pint-sized Saint Joan.

# THIRTY-SIX

'What're you doing?' Sheila asked.

'Nothing,' Stanley told her. He had exhausted himself earlier by hoisting the remains of Crash out of the tub. Breathless, drenched in sweat, heart slamming, he had sat down in his favorite place beyond the foot of the tub. It had only taken him a few minutes to recover. But he'd stayed where he was, sometimes mopping himself with the towel while he stared at Sheila.

'Are you just going to sit there?' she asked.

'I guess so. It's a nice view. And this way you can't get your hands on me.'

'Sure,' she muttered.

'You look like you're sweating blood. All shiny red, and dripping. Do you want to rub it off?' He raised his towel.

'Please.' She lifted a hand to catch the toss.

But Stanley laughed and draped the towel over his shoulders. 'Nah. You look beautiful just the way you are. You look like a wild woman. A gorgeous, naked, wild woman.'

'You wanta do more than look, Stan. You know it and I know it.'

He grinned. 'But what are we going to *do* about it?' he asked.

'*You* have to finish sawing through this beam.'

'Uh-huh.' He bobbed his head. 'But what happens to me when you're no longer pinned down? There's the rub, so to speak. The sad fact is, you're not only gorgeous but extremely powerful. Muscles, muscles, everywhere. If I set you free, you might try to take me apart.'

She stared up at him. Her face was bloody. In the shade of the beam above it, the whites of her eyes had a pale blue tint.

'Maybe we can make a deal,' she said.

'What sort of a deal?'

'You help me get out of here, and . . . I won't do anything to you. I won't try to hurt you.'

'Will you let me fuck you?'

She pressed her lips into a tight, straight line, and nodded. 'Yeah,' she said. 'Okay. If that's what it takes to get out of here.'

'No fighting? I get full cooperation?'

'Yes.'

'Promise?'

'I promise.'

'Liar, liar, pants on fire! Woops! *What* pants?'

'I'm not lying, Stan. Quit the games. Just let me out of here. I'll do anything you want.'

'Why is it that I don't believe you?'

'Believe me.'

'Maybe if you hadn't grabbed my ankles when all I wanted to do was play a little footsies with your tits . . .'

'I'm sorry. That was a mistake.'

'A big big big mistake.'

'What do you want me to do?'

'There might be something.'

'What? Name it.'

'Because, the thing is, I've got half an inclination to just leave you down there, call it a loss, and wait around to see who else shows up. Maybe your husband, for instance. You've seen how easily I kill people. But do you know who I think is bound to show up sooner or later? Barbara. Wherever she is, I'll bet she's on her way home right now. I've seen her in her bikini. She's got a sweet, young body. Is she a virgin? I'll bet she is. I'll bet she has a . . .'

'You don't want her,' Sheila said. Her dry, husky voice sounded fairly calm, but Stanley heard a tremor in it. 'I'm the one you want. She'd be a lousy substitute, and you know it.'

'But she hasn't got your muscles. If she fights me . . .'

'*I* won't fight you. I'll do anything you say.'

'Will you? We'll see about that.'

'You'll see.'

'At the first sign of resistance, it's over. You're history, and I nail Barbara.'

'I won't resist.'

'And you'll do exactly what I tell you to do.'

'Exactly.'

'Very good. We'll see how it goes.'

With that, Stanley got to his feet. He made his way alongside the hole in the floor and crouched over Eagle's pale, hairless body.

The barbed wire was wound four times around Eagle's waist, its ends twisted together in front.

*Why on earth anyone would wear a barbed wire belt . . .*

Maybe so he'll have some handy, Stanley thought, for occasions like this.

Or maybe it's just a fashion statement.

After untwisting the ends of the wire, Stanley used Eagle's straight razor to slash the belt loops. Then he nudged the ring of wire higher, past the top of the leather pants, so the four loops encircled Eagle's bare waist.

Holding one end, he stood up and stepped to the other side of the body. Then he pulled hard.

By the time all four loops had unwound, Eagle looked as if he wore a frayed, red ribbon around his waist.

Stanley coiled the wire. It was slippery. There were bits of skin on some of its sharp little points.

He stepped over the body and placed the wire on the floor near his saw, scissors and straight razor. Then he climbed down onto the edges of the tub. When he leaned over the middle beam, his leg and back muscles began to tremble.

'Boy,' he said, 'am I ever gonna be sore tomorrow.'

Sheila didn't open her mouth.

'Okay, now let's see if you're as good as your word.'

'I am.'

'Give me your hands.'

She raised her arms from her sides and stretched them toward him.

'Put them together.'

She did, and Stanley watched the way her breasts got squeezed between her upper arms.

'Very nice,' he said. 'Keep them that way.'

He reached out and grabbed the coil of barbed wire. When Sheila saw it, her eyes opened wider. But she said nothing, and held her arms up toward him, hands together.

He began to bind her wrists, winding the wire around them, drawing it between them, bending it, twisting it, pulling it tight. Sheila twitched a few times when barbs dug in, but she never protested or struggled.

Finally, her hands seemed securely bound together and Stanley had his 'lead' – five or six feet of leftover wire that extended from between her wrists.

'So far, so good,' he said.

'You didn't have to do this,' Sheila told him.

'Sure, I did. You may now put your hands down, but be careful where you put them. You don't wanta poke yourself.'

He paid out the lead and watched her. Wrists bound so tightly together with the barbed wire, she had trouble finding a new position for her arms. Finally, she swung them up and rested them against the edge of the overhead beam. Face between the undersides of her arms, she looked as if she were about to perform a high dive.

*Sans diving board.*

*Sans swimsuit.*

*Sans pool.*

Stanley moaned with delight, then set aside his end of the wire and anchored it down with a chunk of plaster.

He picked up the saw. Its blade was smeared with Crash's blood. He shook it. The wide blade shimmied and made whangy sounds.

'Shake for me, Sheila,' he said. 'Shake like the saw.' She pressed her lips together. Keeping her arms up, she shook her body from side to side.

'Harder!' He shook the saw harder. 'Hard as you can!'

She shook so hard that sparkles of bloody sweat skittered over her skin. Her breasts flung off a crimson spray.

'Oooo, beautiful. Beautiful. But that's enough.' He quit shaking the saw.

The rough shudders of Sheila's body ceased. Stanley watched how her breasts continued to sway. Then the only movement came from her hard breathing.

Stanley twisted himself awkwardly to the left and fit the saw blade into the cut of the beam. He worked it into the slit until it would go no deeper, then began to pump the saw back and forth. Wood dust began dribbling down into the narrow space between the wall of the tub and Sheila's right thigh.

He remembered how she had talked him out of making the cut in the middle.

Seemed like years ago.

*Who's giving the orders now?*

He glanced at the old cut. Shallow. Awfully shallow. She had stopped him before he'd made much progress at all.

I could go back to it, anyway, he thought. Just to show her.

*Screw that. I'm almost done.*

But he was winded again, wheezing for breath, sweat spilling down his body. Every muscle in his neck and shoulders and arms, in his back, in his buttocks and legs seemed to be jumping and twitching out of control.

He stopped sawing, climbed down backward into the tub, and stretched. With the towel, he mopped his hair and face. He plucked the clinging seat of his pajama pants away from his rump, but it stuck again the moment he let go.

'Almost done,' he gasped. 'Hot work.'

'I'll bet.'

'But don't worry . . . I'll have you . . . outa there.'

'Looking forward to it,' Sheila muttered.

'Sure you are.' He wiped his face again. 'Tell you something . . . *I* am. Looking forward to it. You've got no idea . . . I've been watching you . . . Never thought I'd . . . get a chance at you, but . . . thanks to the quake . . . my lucky day. Thank God for earthquakes.'

Sheila's right foot suddenly jerked. Her knee shot upward and her thigh slammed the underside of the beam. Stanley flinched at the quick blast of exploding wood. The saw jumped from its slit. As it lifted into the air, the slit spread wide at the top. Sheila's thigh came punching up through the bottom. A spike of splintered wood leaped after the saw.

'No!' Stanley yelled.

Her blow knocked the beam on end. It stood upright between her legs like a two-foot post.

Stanley looked around, trying to spot the saw.

It didn't seem to be in the tub.

With the fists of her wired hands, Sheila rammed the post near its top. It scooted toward Stanley and tumbled. As it fell toward him, he hopped backward. It thudded against the bottom of the tub, skidded and pounded the toes of his left foot through the soft leather of his moccasin.

Yelping in pain, he saw Sheila shove at the overhead beam. She slid forward. The moment her head was clear of the wood, she sat up.

But she can't *stand* up, Stanley told himself.

She drew her legs in, crossing them, leaning forward.

The hell she can't, Stanley thought. Damn it, she'll get up even if she *can't* use her hands.

He thought about leaping onto her.

*That might be just what she wants.*

*Can't tangle with her, she'll destroy me.*

She was suddenly on her knees.

Stanley squatted and grabbed the sawed-off chuck of four-by-eight at each end. He stood up with it. As he raised it overhead, he saw that Sheila already had her feet on the bottom of the tub. She was still crouched, but rising.

She had her eyes on him.

She looked fierce – but wary.

'This'll bust ya!' Stanley yelled.

She froze.

'It'll bust ya good! Don't make me do it!'

'Don't,' Sheila gasped. She shook her head. 'Put it down. Just put it down.'

'I'll bust ya with it!'

'You've got me, Stan. Okay? I'm not going anywhere. You don't have to use that.'

'I'll cave in your head!'

'No. Please.'

'On your knees,' he said.

She sank to her knees and stared up at him.

He hurled the heavy stump of beam.

It crashed into the debris on the floor beyond the far end of the tub.

'Thank you,' Sheila said.

'You're welcome,' said Stanley.

Then he crashed his knee into her forehead. Her head jerked backward. She flopped away from him. The other beam caught her across the back, just below her shoulders. It stopped her with a massive jolt. As she started to slump, Stanley crouched in front of her.

The leftover length of barbed wire dangled from between her hands. He picked it up.

He pulled.

Raising Sheila's arms from where they hung in front of her body.

Tugging them toward him.

She opened her eyes and gave him a lazy look. She hardly seemed aware of what was happening.

He continued to pull.

She toppled forward.

He pulled hard enough to straighten her arms so that she wouldn't be able to break the fall with her elbows. Her torso made a nice moist slapping sound when it landed on the bottom of the tub.

'Are you gonna give me any more trouble?' he asked.

She groaned.

'Is that a yes or a no?'

She didn't answer.

'Who are we kidding?' Stanley asked.

She squirmed a little.

'You'll keep on giving me trouble as long as you've got a breath left in you.'

The sound that came from Sheila was more like a rough growl than a voice. But Stanley was pretty sure of what it said: 'That's right.'

He forced himself to laugh, but he felt an odd little shiver race up his spine and tingle his scalp.

# THIRTY-SEVEN

Clint didn't see Loreen go down.

She'd entered the jam of abandoned vehicles on Sunset with her arms outspread as if ready to embrace all comers. Caspar had followed her in, but stayed well behind her, apparently realizing that his presence might disrupt Loreen's protective aura.

Caspar must've had his eyes on her.

Clint had been sidestepping through a narrow space between two cars, facing a Mazda where the body of a man was sprawled across the hood. The man's throat had been slashed. Not only was he naked and scalped like most of the other bodies, but someone had spray-painted his genitals black.

Em, moments ago, had turned her head away fast after a glimpse of the man.

Clint was wondering if he should say something to her. But what *could* he say? *It's all right?* It's *not* all right, not even close. Some sort of madness happened here, he thought, and we're walking through what's left of it, and maybe it isn't over yet.

*This sort of stuff doesn't happen.*

*Not even in L.A.*

*It's like some kind of . . .*

'Loreen!' Caspar suddenly cried out.

Clint saw him, two lanes ahead, scurrying sideways between a couple of cars, struggling to get through like a man trapped among theater seats and desperate to reach an aisle.

'Answer me, Loreen!'

'What happened?' Mary called, herself in an open area just ahead of Em.

'I don't know!' Caspar shouted. 'Loreen!' He looked back. 'She just went *down*. Maybe fell?'

'Where?' Clint asked.

Caspar pointed, the red silk sleeve of his blouse fluttering in the hot breeze. 'Behind that van.'

The gray van was in the next lane over, and about fifty feet to the left of where Caspar stood.

Though Clint hadn't been paying much attention to Loreen, he supposed she must've gone that way in search of a good passage. Since starting across Sunset, she'd done a lot of meandering to avoid areas where burnt cars still smoldered, or where there was little or no space because of vehicles that were bumper to bumper. They had all followed her lead.

*What the hell happened to her?*

It's my fault, Clint told himself. I should've led the way.

None of this hunting for good places to cross; except for avoiding a few smoky wrecks, he would have taken them straight to the other side of Sunset, simply climbing over hoods or trunks when there were no spaces between vehicles.

Should've done it, Clint thought. Might've been a little rough on Mary and the Blotskis, but we'd be finished with all this by now and nobody'd be missing.

'Loreen!' Caspar called again. Staggering clear of his narrow pathway between the cars, he ran toward the van.

'Wait for us!' Clint shouted.

Caspar paid no attention.

Mary, ahead of Em, had stopped between the lanes and seemed to be watching Caspar's dash for the van.

'Mary!' Clint said. 'Stay put.'

As if sensing the need for quickness, Em leaped out of his way. He stumbled free of the bumpers and caught a glimpse of Caspar's head beyond the next two lanes. 'Follow me,' he gasped at Em and Mary. As he started to give chase, he shouted, 'Caspar! Wait for us!'

Caspar didn't even slow down.

Clint poured on more speed. But didn't get far before Mary called, 'I can't . . . !'

He glanced back. Em was only a stride behind him, arms pumping, the big butcher knife jerking up and down in her right hand.

Mary wasn't keeping up.

No wonder, Clint thought.

Like Em, Mary ran with her knife out. Her other hand was busy clutching the front of her blouse shut. The sodden blouse clung to her. It was torn, soiled with dirt, streaked and stained and blotched with blood from the injuries that it covered. Her torn skirt showed legs that were dirty and scratched and bloody.

Mary's red face was swollen, scratched, dripping sweat, twisted with pain.

*She's a wreck, and I'm making her run like this. She oughta be in a hospital bed.*

Clint stopped running.

He turned forward again and looked for Caspar.

313

Couldn't spot him.

But cars and pickups were in the way. Maybe the old man had simply crouched or bent down.

'Caspar!'

No answer came.

Clint called out again.

'They got him, too?' Em whispered.

'I don't know,' Clint said. 'Just be ready for anything. You, too, Mary.'

Mary sleeved sweat out of her eyes, and nodded.

Clint took the knife from his pocket. He started moving again, but slowly. Every few steps, he glanced back to make sure that Em and Mary were staying close behind him.

All around them, nothing seemed to move.

It's like sneaking through a graveyard, Clint thought. A hot, smoky graveyard. Where mad killers might be lurking, waiting to pounce.

Someone *must* have pounced on Loreen and Caspar. What else could've made them disappear?

Clint tried to think of a good explanation that didn't involve murder. He had no luck.

*And we're heading straight for where it happened.*

Maybe this isn't such a good idea, he thought.

*It's the only way we'll ever know. Besides, what if they aren't dead? Maybe they need help. We can't just run off and forget about them.*

Deciding to approach the van from a different direction than Loreen and Caspar, Clint stayed two lanes away and walked on past its front. Then he climbed onto the hood of a Mustang. He got to his feet and looked for the Blotskis.

No sign of them.

He couldn't see much, though; a large pickup truck blocked most of the van from his view.

Nor could he see down close to the street.

The Mustang wobbled slightly under him. Turning, he watched Em climb onto its hood. He took hold of her arm and helped her up.

Mary came next.

The three stood together atop the Mustang's hood and surveyed the area.

'Caspar?' Clint called again.

'How could they just vanish like this?' Em asked, speaking softly as if afraid there might be strangers trying to listen. 'They never even yelled or anything, you know?'

'It must've been awfully sudden,' Clint said.

'Could they be playing a trick on us?' Mary asked.

'Why would they do a thing like that?'

'They hate me, for one thing.'

'I doubt if it's a trick,' Clint said.

'What *do* you think?'

'Somebody got 'em.'

'Oh, God.'

'Whoever got all these others . . .'

'It was by the van over there?' Em asked, pointing with her knife at the bit of van that showed beyond the pickup.

'Apparently,' Clint said.

'So that's where the killer is . . . or where he was up till a couple of minutes ago, anyway.'

Clint nodded. 'But probably more than one.'

'They're probably watching us right now,' Mary muttered. 'Or coming.'

'Maybe we oughta hide our knives,' Em whispered.

Clint almost smiled. 'Don't worry. When they show up, they'll be on us so fast . . . just keep your knives ready.'

'Aye-aye, sir.'

'Where the hell are the cops when you need them?' Mary asked.

Clint shook his head. Why bother trying to answer? The pair of officers who belonged to the patrol car were either gone or dead. All the other cops were probably scattered over Los Angeles. Many, he supposed, must be fighting to regain some order. Some were certainly dead.

'Where the hell is *anybody*?' Mary added.

'Who knows,' Clint said.

Em smiled. 'There's still us.'

'Not for long,' Mary said. '*I'm* supposed to get killed, remember?'

'You know what I think?' Em asked. 'I think Loreen wasn't much of a fortune-teller, after all. You know? I mean, the way things are starting to look, she's the one who bit it. And Caspar . . .'

'Let's go,' Clint said. He stepped to the edge of the Mustang's hood, glanced both ways, saw nobody, and jumped. Keeping watch, he waited for Em and Mary. Em leaped and landed on her feet with a springy bounce. Mary sat down, then lowered herself to the street like a timid child easing into a swimming pool.

'This way,' Clint whispered.

Unwilling to turn his back on them – afraid that Em or Mary might suddenly vanish like the Blotskis – Clint sidestepped alongside the pickup truck toward its rear. He glanced all around, but never let his vision stray from his companions for more than a few seconds at a time.

They looked scared, but alert, as if they expected an attack but had no idea where it might come from.

The bed of the pickup truck was empty.

Clint thought about climbing in. The bed would make a good observation platform; from the far side of it, they'd be able to look directly at the place behind the van where Loreen and Caspar had apparently gone down. But this was a bruiser of a pickup with big wheels, an elevated chassis, and high side panels. There would be no easy way to climb in. It'd be a major struggle, especially for Mary.

'We going up?' Em asked.

Clint shook his head. 'Too high.'

'It isn't so high.' She stood on tiptoes to peer over the panel. 'I bet we'd have a great view.'

'Let's just go around.'

'I could hop up there for a second, just to see.'

Her suggestion gave Clint a sick feeling. It was a way he had felt watching Barbara, on their vacation in the mountains last summer, when she'd wandered too close to the edge of a cliff.

'No,' he said. 'You're not going up there by yourself. Not a chance. We stick together. And we watch out for each other. Nobody goes anywhere alone.'

Nodding, Em shrugged with one shoulder.

Clint sidestepped the rest of the way to the rear of the pickup. The Porsche behind it had left a good, wide space that led like a corridor to the driver's door of a Mercedes that was stopped behind the van.

He saw no one.

'Stay close,' he whispered, and started through the gap.

'Wait,' Em whispered. She tugged the back of his shirt. 'Just a second.' She stepped around him, dropped to her hands and knees, then bent her elbows and lowered her head to the pavement. She peered underneath the pickup truck.

*A kid on her knees, butt in the air, checking under her bed for boogeymen.*

Clint dearly hoped she wouldn't find any.

He watched her head swivel very slowly, stopping sometimes, then continuing to turn. Soon, she was gazing straight forward at the area under the Mercedes. After a pause, her head resumed its slow movement to the right.

Things must be okay, Clint told himself. She wouldn't still be down there looking around if she'd spotted anything terrible.

At last, she was gazing past her right shoulder at the space beneath the Porsche.

'Anything?' Clint whispered.

Em slowly pushed herself up. When she turned around, Clint felt his stomach sink.

Mary moved in beside him and clutched his arm.

316

They both stared at Em.

'They're under there,' Em whispered.

'Oh, no,' Mary murmured.

Em's lips twitched as if she were making a Bogart face.

'What do you mean?' Clint asked very quickly, very quietly. 'Who's down there? Where? Loreen? Caspar?'

'Not them. I'm pretty sure. People, though, and they're underneath . . .'

'Dead people?' Clint asked.

'I don't think so.'

Mary groaned.

'How many?'

Em raised and dropped her shoulders. 'Nobody under these,' she said, nodding to either side at the pickup truck and the Porsche. 'Nobody under that, either.' She pointed her knife at the Mercedes in front of them. 'But there's like, I think, maybe *four* people under the van. Maybe more. There were tires in the way. I couldn't really tell . . .'

'Did they see you?' Clint asked.

'Maybe. I only saw a couple of actual faces. And it's dark under there. I couldn't tell what they were looking at. Maybe their eyes weren't even open, for all I know.'

'What makes you think they were alive?'

'Some of 'em were moving.'

'Oh, God,' Mary muttered.

'Coming out?' Clint asked.

Em shook her head. 'Just, you know . . . fidgeting, squirming, like that.'

Mary gave Clint's arm a quick tug. 'Maybe they're just hiding! They might be scared, and . . .'

'Then what happened to Loreen and Caspar?'

'I don't know, but . . .'

'These people got 'em,' Em said. 'I'd bet anything. Killed 'em, maybe threw their bodies in the van, or something. This bunch isn't just hiding, I can tell you that. I saw what they look like.'

'You said you *couldn't* see them very well,' Mary pointed out.

'I saw enough.' Em lifted her gaze to Clint and stared into his eyes. 'What're we gonna do?'

Before he could answer, Mary tightened her grip and said, 'We've gotta get out of here.'

'No,' he said. 'We have to get *through* here.'

'They're just waiting for us,' Em said. She looked as if she were trying hard not to cry.

'They won't get us.'

'But I don't think they're the only ones,' she told him.

'What do you mean?'

'It doesn't make any sense, you know? That Loreen just happened to go straight to the only place where a bunch was waiting to grab people. I think maybe . . . they might be all around us. And we've just been lucky so far?'

Mary made a quiet groan.

'It's possible,' Clint muttered.

What the hell isn't? he thought.

All this at Sunset Boulevard seemed like madness. One person, alone, couldn't have committed such slaughter and mutilation; Em had supposedly seen at least four people lying in wait for them. If that many had reverted to savagery, why not twenty? Why not a hundred?

*Or a thousand.*

*A thousand wild savages, banded into tribes.*

*Lurking everywhere.*

Don't even think about something like that, Clint told himself. There can't be that many.

*Can't be that many people so messed up that they'll let a little thing like an earthquake – not even a major quake – knock apart every civilized restraint and turn them into barbarians.*

Not even in Los Angeles, he thought.

And a voice in his mind said, *Oh, yeah?*

'What'll we do?' Em asked.

Clint faced Mary. 'Are you with us?' he asked.

'Have I got any choice?'

'You could go back.'

'By myself?'

'I have to go on ahead,' Clint said. 'You know that. I have to get home.'

'Even if it kills you?'

'It won't.'

Mary smirked. 'Famous last words.' She frowned at Em. 'What about you?'

'I'm sticking with Clint. No matter what.'

'He's already married, you know.'

'It's pretty amazing to me,' Em said, 'that you can find it in yourself at a time like this to still be such a snot.'

'Both of you stop it,' Clint said. 'Are you with us, Mary, or not? That's all I wanta know.'

'I'm supposed to go off by myself . . . ?'

'It's up to you. If you go back, you go back alone.'

'Or plug on ahead with you on your big odyssey home and get myself killed. Some choice.'

318

'It's your choice,' Clint said. 'Now, make it.'

'I'm staying with you.'

'Okay.'

'So, now what?'

'I'm not sure yet.'

'Terrific.'

Em dropped again to her hands and knees, lowered her head and scanned the area underneath the nearby vehicles. A moment later, she sprang up. 'Still there,' she said.

Mary sneered at her. 'What did you think, they'd go away?'

'I was afraid they might be sneaking closer.'

'They're staying put?' Clint asked.

'So far.'

'Just waiting for us to walk by.'

'And then they grab our feet?' Em asked.

'Something like that, I guess.'

'Let's just make a big detour around them,' Mary said.

Clint shook his head.

'*Why not?*'

'A lot of reasons.'

'Name one.'

'We know where these are.'

'So?'

'That makes 'em easier to deal with. I don't wanta waste time making a detour just so we can get jumped somewhere else. Come on.'

They backtracked out of the space, and Clint led them alongside the pickup truck. When he came to the driver's door, he stopped and faced them. 'Okay,' he whispered. 'We need a plan. Any ideas?'

Em raised her eyebrows. 'They're hiding underneath vans and cars and stuff, right? So they can grab us when we go by? It's kind of like this movie I saw, only there was this giant monster worm-thing that came up out of the ground to get you. So what Kevin Bacon did – he and the others? – they like got away from it by *pole*vaulting from boulder to boulder. That way, they stayed off the ground and the thing couldn't get them. *Tremors*, that was the movie.'

Mary said, 'Do you see any *poles* around here?'

'No, but . . .'

'Yes!' Clint blurted. 'That's it! Em, you're brilliant!'

'It was just a movie I saw.'

Scowling, Mary muttered, 'Who knows how to polevault, anyway? Even if we *had* poles, which we don't.'

'We don't need poles,' Clint said. 'Everything's parked so close together, we oughta be able to make it across just by jumping – never have to touch the street at all. We stay high, move fast, and . . .'

'Wait, wait,' Mary said. '*Jump?* You mean like from car to car? From their *roofs*?'

'Roofs, hoods, trunks.'

'I can't do that.'

'Sure you can,' Em said.

'No. No way.'

'It'll be easy.'

'We're wasting time,' Clint said. 'Come, or don't.' He pushed his knife back into its makeshift sheath in the right front pocket of his pants. Then he turned around and climbed onto the hood of the pickup truck. On his feet, he approached the other side. The space between the lanes looked clear. So far, nobody was coming out from under the van or any of the nearby cars.

He waited for Em and Mary to join him on the pickup's hood. Then he stepped up onto the roof of the cab. It seemed to be about the same height as the top of the van.

The two vehicles were separated by a gap that looked about five feet wide.

Not bad, he thought.

Turning around, he offered a hand to Em. She took it, and he gave her a pull as she came up onto the roof. She smiled, squeezed his hand, and stepped out of the way.

Mary halted at the base of the windshield. She glanced over the side, then gazed up at Clint.

He held his arm toward her, and nodded. 'Come on,' he mouthed, not speaking the words.

Looking scared and miserable, Mary stopped clutching her blouse shut. She switched the butcher knife to her left hand, and raised her right toward Clint. They clasped hands. She planted her right foot at the top of the windshield.

Clint pulled.

She bounded up. The left side of her blouse flapped open. Her breast was bare above the flimsy triangle and broken strap of her bra.

Clint glimpsed it, looked away, then felt its firm, warm pressure against his chest as she stumbled into him.

The moment Mary seemed steady on her feet, he stepped back from her. She hadn't covered herself yet. He turned away and faced the gap.

The area below still looked safe.

Maybe they aren't even under there anymore, he thought. Maybe they've moved on, and all this is a waste of time.

*Who you trying to kid? They haven't gone anyplace. Just fall, and see what happens.*

There's no reason to fall, he told himself. Just one good stride and you'll be across. It won't even take a jump. Not a real jump. Just give it a little oomph on the take-off, then try like hell not to let the momentum run you off the other side of the van.

He stepped to the edge of the pickup's roof.

He swung his right leg out over the chasm and shoved off with his left. His stomach dropped away as he went airborne. For a moment, he hung above the gap. Then his right foot landed on top of the van. A couple of quick staggers, and he halted himself.

He turned around.

Em and Mary stood side by side atop the pickup's cab. Em, smiling, gave the blade of her knife a twirl. Mary, knife clamped between her teeth, was using both hands to tuck the bottom of her blouse into her skirt.

Clint gestured for them to come over.

Em mouthed something to Mary that looked like, 'You go first.'

Mary shook her head.

*Let's not dawdle, ladies! Let's move it before the creeps crawl out!*
He beckoned again.

Em nodded. She took a couple of backward steps to give herself a running start. She switched the butcher knife to her left hand, didn't seem to like it there, and returned it to her right hand. She took a deep breath. She wiggled her eyebrows at Clint. Then she rushed toward the edge.

She kicked out over the gap.

As she shoved off, her left foot slipped.

# THIRTY-EIGHT

Clint glimpsed a look of disbelief on Em's face.

In midair, she tilted backward.

*No!*

Her arms thrashed. Her knife waved. For a moment, she looked as if she were trying to slide into base, right foot reaching for the edge of the van's roof.

Clint was going to be there to catch her.

But he knew she wouldn't make it. She was coming in almost horizontal.

Dropping to his knees, he bowed over the edge and reached for her foot.

Caught it!

The sole of her sneaker pounded the van.

Gasping, she bent at the waist and swiped her left hand at Clint. It didn't even come close. She was already dropping.

Clint braced himself.

A moment later, Em's back slammed against the metal side of the van.

Clint didn't let go. He held her right ankle in a solid, double-handed grip.

She hung upsidedown directly beneath his eyes, her free leg waving about as if she didn't know what to do with it, her panties showing through the wide and drooping leg holes of her shorts, her body bare below her shorts, her arms outstretched to the sides, her face hooded by her fallen T-shirt.

Clint strained backward, trying to raise her. 'Somebody's got my hair!' she yelled.

*No!*

Had an arm reached out from under the van? He couldn't see it, but he couldn't see much of anything; the Roadkill T-shirt had flopped down until stopped by Em's armpits. It shrouded her face – her entire head – concealing whatever might be happening between her neck and the street.

*They could scalp her . . .*

*Slash her throat . . .*

*I wouldn't even know it.*

He saw that Em still had hold of her knife.

'Use your knife!' he called.

She started stabbing at the area hidden under the loose tent of her shirt.

Someone cried out as if wounded.

Clint tugged at her ankle. He couldn't raise her at all.

She kept on stabbing. With each jab, her body jerked and twisted.

Clint felt a freezing sickness in his bowels as three people came squirming out from under the van.

They came out on their bellies. The hair on the backs of their heads was matted with blood. Their arms, shoulders and backs were smeared and blotched with it.

*Two men and a woman.*

One of the guys appeared to be a boy, skinny, small enough to be ten or twelve years old. He wore a T-shirt. He held a claw hammer in his right hand as he scurried out from under the van.

The other guy, possibly his father, was much larger. Husky. Like the boy, he wore a T-shirt. He clutched a Bowie knife. Its broad, stained blade was as long as his forearm.

The woman, as bloody as the others, had her hair in a ponytail. She wore some sort of top that left her back bare except for strips of cloth that tied behind her neck and in the middle of her back. In her hand, she held a hunting knife.

Is this the mother? Clint wondered.

We've got a family here?

*The family that kills together, stays together.*

Clint tried again to pull Em up by her ankle.

This time, she started to rise.

*Yes!*

But a pair of red arms suddenly shot out from under the drooping shroud of her T-shirt, swung up off the pavement, reached high and swept down. Their hands hooked into her armpits.

Clint held on.

He knew he could keep holding on.

But he couldn't bring Em up. Not with someone hanging on to her like this.

The man was still squirming out, but the boy and woman were already clear of the undercarriage and getting to their knees.

I can't do her any good up here, Clint thought. I've gotta let go.

*Drop her on her head?*

*I can't!*

*Gotta!*

As he was about to release Em's ankle, he glimpsed a quick plunging movement directly in front of him. Someone leaping down from the other side?

*What, more of them?*

He looked.

Mary!

He couldn't believe it.

Not Mary, leaping down to help Em.

But that was certainly how it looked.

Hair and skirt hoisted high by the wind of her descent, she landed on her feet beside the cab of the pickup truck. Her shoes struck the pavement with a clatter. The impact seemed to jolt her whole body.

She staggered forward, and Clint thought she was falling.

She *was* falling.

She fell to her knees by the head of the man as he tried to shove himself up from the pavement, and slammed her butcher knife into his back.

He squealed.

Mary tugged out the knife and stabbed him again.

The woman and boy started to rise.

Still hanging onto Em's ankle with his right hand, Clint let go with his left. He used his left to brace himself while he bent down fast over the edge of the roof and reached as low as he could.

He opened his right hand.

Em dropped.

As she plummeted down the side of the van, he sprang.

He sprang for the boy, who was just to the left, standing but still bent over.

Both Clint's feet landed on his back, driving him toward the street. He rode the kid down. He knew what he was doing. He hated it, but not enough to leap off.

The boy's face struck the pavement. The sound of it made Clint wince. He stumbled off the kid's back.

The woman, halting her rush at Mary, looked over her shoulder. She glared at the sprawled body. Shrieking, 'Randy!' she whirled around, raised her hunting knife overhead and ran at Clint.

Her top seemed to be made of bandannas. She wore cut-off jeans with slits up their sides.

From her leather belt, several thatches of hair dangled and swayed.

And dripped.

Scalps?

Clint crouched and snatched up the boy's hammer.

She sprang at him, screaming, and her right arm swept down, plunging the knife toward his chest.

He knocked her arm aside.

With the hammer, he smashed the side of her face. Her eye bulged and popped out of its socket. Leaving the hammer embedded in her temple, he turned quickly and plucked the knife from her hand. He jerked its blade across her throat. As blood shot out, he jammed the blade deep into the center of her throat, then hurled her down on top of the boy.

He leaped over them and rushed toward the place were Em had fallen – where two bodies now struggled on the narrow alley of pavement between the van and pickup.

Mary was already there, on her knees and stabbing.

Fresh blood flew up, splattering her face and neck.

The way the bodies were tangled, Clint couldn't tell *who* Mary was driving her knife into with such fury. He couldn't tell one from the other.

'Stop!' he gasped.

Mary stopped. Huffing for air, she backed away on her knees, then rested her knife-hand on her thigh and gazed at the two bodies.

The one on top was completely shirtless and had a dozen gashes in its back. It wore jeans, not shorts. As Clint told himself this couldn't be Em, the body rose, tipped sideways, and tumbled. When it rolled onto its back, he saw that it was a boy.

Randy's brother, he supposed.

The handle of a butcher knife protruded from his side, just below the left armpit.

Em's knife?

Em lay on her back, panting. Knees up, limp arms outspread, she looked like a long-distance runner after the end of a race.

But bloody.

So much blood.

Her hair, skin and shorts were splashed and spattered with it.

Can't be hers, Clint told himself. Not much of it, anyway.

*She's gotta be all right. Gotta be.*

Em raised her head enough to see what she looked like. Without comment, she fumbled at her T-shirt and drew it down to her belly. Then she propped herself up on her elbows. She turned her head toward Clint, then toward Mary. 'We're all still alive?'

'So far,' Clint said. 'Thanks mostly to Mary.'

'Thanks, Mary,' Em said.

Mary raised her bloody face. She stared at Em. She shrugged her shoulders.

'Are either of you hurt?' Clint asked.

Keeping her elbows on the pavement, Em lifted her right hand and wiggled its fingers at him. 'Somebody dropped me,' she said.

'Sorry about that. I had to.'

'I figured. It wasn't so bad, though. Mostly, I ended up on top of the guy. I think I hurt him pretty good. Not as much as when I stabbed him, though. Boy, that sure took the wind out of his sails, the dirty rat.'

Nodding, Clint turned to Mary. 'How are *you* doing?'

'Okay. I guess.'

'You really saved our bacon. I couldn't believe it when you jumped down like that.'

'Neither could I.' She struggled to her feet. 'Are we gonna get going?'

'We'd better.'

'Yeah,' Em said, sitting up. 'Let's am-scray before we have to kill *another* bunch of loonies.'

Clint stepped over to the dead man, crouched and picked up the Bowie knife.

'What do you want *that* for?' Mary asked. 'You didn't use the knife you had.'

He looked at her and saw a smile.

Not a smirk, an actual smile – weary, but friendly.

He waved the Bowie knife at her and said, 'This one's bigger. Want it?'

'No, thanks.'

'The gal has a good hunting knife,' he pointed out.

She shook her head.

Em, squatting and about to pull her butcher knife out of the boy's side, looked up at Clint. 'Yeah?' She stood up and turned around. 'Her?'

'It's in her throat.'

Em walked toward the woman, and abruptly halted. 'Oh my God,' she muttered. 'Her eye.'

'You don't have to study her,' Clint said. 'Just grab the knife.'

Her back to Clint and Mary, Em crouched beside the woman's body. She reached out. Suddenly, her back went rigid. She leaped up and staggered backward.

'What?' Clint asked.

'She's got . . . !' Shaking her head, she continued to back away. Then she turned around. Her face, still painted with blood, was twisted with disgust. 'Did you *see* what she's got?'

'The scalps?'

'Yeah!'

Mary grimaced. 'Scalps?'

'She's got 'em,' Em said. 'Five or six of 'em, anyhow. They're hanging off her belt.'

'God, how sickening.'

'I wonder . . .' Em reversed her direction. She approached the woman's body slowly, knees bent, back hunched, like a kid trying to sneak up on someone.

'What're you doing?' Clint asked.

'I want to see if she's got Caspar's hair. Or Loreen's.' Standing over the body, Em shook her head. 'Doesn't look like it. Looks like she preferred blondes.'

All of a sudden, Em crouched, grabbed the hunting knife by its handle and jerked the blade out of the woman's throat. She hurried backward. Then, turning around, she met Clint's eyes. 'Okay,' she said. 'I'm ready.'

'Okay,' Clint said. 'Let's start by seeing if we can find the Blotskis.'

'Might be in there,' Em said, and nodded toward the van.

'I'd bet on it,' Clint said.

He glanced at the bodies. From the look of things, a family had been massacred here. No one was likely to realize it had been a family of savages.

Not without a close inspection.

A glimpse of the woman's trophy belt should set the record straight.

'Okay,' Clint said.

He led the way to the rear of the van, and stepped behind it. The double doors were shut. Each had a rectangular window near the top, but he could see curtains on the other side of the glass.

Clint switched the Bowie knife to his left hand. With his right, he reached for the door handle.

'Wait,' Em whispered.

For a moment, he thought she might be planning to drop down for another look under the nearby vehicles. But she stayed up, stepped quickly past the corner of the van, and swung her head to the left. She gazed in that direction for a few seconds, then glanced the other way before returning.

'First off,' she whispered, 'nobody's over there. So, you know, it's not like we're about to get attacked. Unless it's by somebody hiding *under* something, if you know what I mean. Anyway, the thing is, I mainly wanted to check on the van. There aren't any windows over on that side. What there is, there's one of those big sliding doors.'

'Is it open?' Clint asked.

'Huh-uh.'

'Guess I'll try this one,' he said.

Mary put a hand on his arm. 'Maybe you shouldn't,' she said. 'What if somebody's in there? Not just Loreen and Caspar. Maybe more of *them*.'

'I don't think so,' Clint said, and pulled open the door.

He was wrong.

# THIRTY-NINE

Barbara had tried not to look at the remains of the scavenger and the body from the grocery cart, but there'd been no way, short of shutting her eyes, to avoid catching peripheral views of the gory messes.

There'd been no way to miss Earl's comments, either.

'Oh, Lordy, look what they done to him. Ouch! Oooo, makes me hurt just looking . . . Watch out there, Banner, don't step in her . . . Ugh, those guys musta been hard up. How'd you like'm doing that to *you*?'

'Hey,' Pete had said, 'shut up.'

'Ha! Sorry, sorry.'

There had been more bodies, later on. Whenever Barbara spotted one in the distance, she fixed her eyes on the pavement at her feet. But she saw enough, and heard enough from Earl, to know that the people had been stripped naked, robbed of everything, and usually mutilated in horrible ways: breasts and genitals had been cut off, eyes gouged, scalps taken, patches of skin peeled off (for the tattoos, Earl had suggested), teeth torn from mouths.

According to Earl, *everybody* had been raped. Men as well as women.

But maybe he was exaggerating, just to make things sound even worse than they really were. After all, he was the only one who went up close to the bodies and studied them. Pete and Barbara stayed together, dodged the remains and never paused to inspect them.

Several times, Earl had said, 'Come on over and look at this,' or, 'You gotta get a load of *this*!' or, 'You don't know what you're missing, folks.'

But they'd refrained.

Though Barbara didn't keep score, she guessed that they had probably walked past at least twelve bodies – and that was *after* leaving the scavenger and shopping cart guy behind.

Earlier in the day, the alleys had seemed like fairly safe havens. Now, she hated them.

But she knew that the streets were much worse.

Each time they came to one, they hid and checked carefully before crossing. At the end of almost every block, the streets were jammed with halted vehicles. Most of the cars and trucks appeared to be

328

abandoned, but a few people always seemed to be sneaking among them.

They saw bodies in the streets, on the sidewalks, on lawns, sometimes dangling from tree limbs or tied to fences. They saw looters hurrying out of houses and apartment buildings with full arms. They saw armed gangs that looked like hunting parties in search of prey.

Not long ago, they'd watched a fat, bald man get surrounded. The gang had closed in on him, and his screams had been joined by wild shouts and laughter.

Though the alleys were awful, the streets were insane.

Barbara dreaded the end of every alley and what she might have to see when she came to the street. But she especially dreaded the sprint to reach the alley on the other side; you just never knew who might spot you dashing across.

Who might come after you.

So far, they'd been lucky.

But she was afraid that the luck wouldn't last.

It doesn't have to last much longer, she told herself. We're almost to the school. Just a few more blocks. Could be home real soon. Half an hour, maybe.

Earl, in the lead, turned around and walked backward. Barbara quickly glanced over her shoulder. Nothing. Just fifty feet of alley, and the street they'd raced across a couple of minutes ago.

'What is it?' she asked.

'Nothing.' He grinned at her. 'Enjoying the view.'

She looked down at herself. Her blouse was untucked, and she hadn't bothered to refasten any of the buttons that had come undone since she'd handed over her bra to Pete. Only the button at her waist remained fastened. Plenty of her skin showed between the blouse's open edges. Not her breasts, though. Nothing showed that should be of much interest to Earl, especially since he'd seen everything when she was in the pickup truck.

'Made ya look,' he said.

'Go to hell.'

He grinned. 'We're there.'

'You're not kidding,' Pete muttered. He was walking close to Barbara's side, the rifle across his back. He looked tired and feverish. He also looked as if he might be getting ready to throw up. 'I don't get it,' he said.

'What?' Barbara asked.

'It's been getting worse. It wasn't like this . . . none of this *really* bad stuff was happening . . . just since . . . about when we were at Lee's.'

'It was pretty bad before,' Barbara said, remembering way back to the kid who'd snatched her purse, who'd shortly afterward been killed for his bicycle.

'It wasn't like this,' Pete told her.

'That's right,' Earl said. 'I'm the living proof. Back in the good ol' days – like this morning – all they did was beat you shitless and steal your clothes.' He grinned. 'I didn't get screwed or killed. I still got my scalp, my teeth and my dick. The difference a few hours makes, you know? I tell ya, we're in hell.'

'Are not,' Barbara said. She didn't like to hear that kind of talk. 'That's bull, and you know it.'

'*Something* is sure going on,' Pete muttered.

'Yeah,' she admitted. 'God knows, I've noticed.'

'It's like they aren't human, any more – the ones doing this stuff.'

'I bet they weren't any great prizes to begin with,' Barbara said.

'They probably didn't go around *butchering* everyone in sight,' Pete said.

'Or bangin' everything that has hole,' Earl added.

Barbara scowled at him, then met Pete's haggard gaze. 'I think what's happened, is that they're just . . . doing what they wanted to be doing all along. Only they just *didn't*, most of them, because there was stuff in the way. But now there's nobody to make them stop. The quake . . . it knocked all the barriers down. You can't exactly dial up the cops, you know? So anything goes. And more and more of them are taking advantage of it. Doing whatever they wanta do, and the hell with everything.'

'Welcome to hell,' Earl said.

'It's *not* hell,' Barbara insisted. 'It's a bunch of your typical everyday assholes doing what comes naturally. The only thing is, now they're running amok because they figure they can get away with it.'

Pete was staring at her. He looked as if his weariness and nausea had receded. He looked almost amused.

'What?' she asked.

He shrugged. 'Where'd you get *that*?'

'Where'd I get what?'

'What he means, Banner, is he's amazed by your analysis of the situation. Like he didn't know you had such depth. Me, I always knew you was deep. You're a regular *hole*.' He laughed.

'Shut up,' Pete snapped at him.

'Relax. I called her a hole, not a twat. Don't you know a *compliment* when you hear one?'

'Just knock it off. And why don't you . . .'

Three quick booms stopped Pete's voice.

Earl flinched. 'Shit! Those were shots!'

They hadn't come from very far away.

330

Barbara whirled around and reached under the back of her blouse. As she pulled the forty-five out of her shorts, Pete unslung his rifle.

Instead of more gunshots, she heard engine noises.

The loud, blatting thunder seemed to come from somewhere up the last street they'd crossed.

When a white car skated sideways and leaped into the alley, Barbara knew it wasn't the source of the thunder. The car was long and low and wide. A Lincoln? After the squeal of its tires, it rushed forward with an urgent but well-muffled roar.

Behind its windshield, a woman gripped the steering wheel with both hands. She was looking back over her right shoulder.

Someone grabbed Barbara's arm and yanked it so hard that she stumbled sideways and almost fell.

But she kept her eyes on the mouth of the alley.

The thunder came.

Bikes.

Fat-wheeled hogs – two of them side by side, three more, two after that – seven choppers kicking up gravel and tilting as they turned, their riders hunched low, some with firearms aimed at the fleeing Lincoln.

Outlaw bikers.

Barbara stumbled sideways, dragged by the hand. But it stopped pulling when a big metal dumpster blocked her view of the action. With a glance, she saw that it was Earl clutching her arm. Pete, his back against a garage door, was sinking down to a squat, scowling fiercely and swinging the muzzle of his rifle toward the alley.

She heard two more gunshots.

She jerked her arm free and rushed forward, halting at the corner of the dumpster and peering around it as the Lincoln came speeding up the middle of the alley.

It'll miss us, Barbara thought, unless the gal swerves in the next second or two . . .

The two bikes at the head of the pack were tight on the Lincoln's tail.

'*Back* here,' Earl gasped, and yanked her by the hair. This time, she did fall. As the Lincoln sped past, she dropped against Earl. He caught her under the armpits, and held her up.

Struggling to stand, she watched the gang blast by.

The lead biker raced up alongside the Lincoln and snapped off two quick shots.

But not at the driver, though she would've made an easy target. At the front tire.

Though the bullets missed, whinging off the alley pavement inches away from the tire, the big car suddenly swung out of control. Brakes shrieking, it cut hard to the left. It skidded sideways, then smashed through

331

an old aluminum trash can and slammed into the corner of a garage. The stucco corner caved in. The front of the car crumpled. The driver lurched forward, then rebounded. Barbara couldn't tell whether she'd hit the steering wheel or been saved by her safety belt. She seemed to be all right, though. She turned her head to glance over her shoulder, made a terrified face at what she saw, then turned her attention to the dash.

Her car must've died, Barbara thought. 'Come on,' she muttered. 'Get it going. Go!'

But the car just sat there as the bikers flanked it and dismounted. When they shut their engines off, the stuttering thunder abruptly stopped. Barbara heard the whinny of the car.

It had died, all right. The woman was trying to start it up again so she could get the hell out of there.

But one of the bikers, the one who'd shot at her tire, was already striding toward her door. He was lean and walked like a cowboy. He wore a shiny, black Nazi helmet. On the back of his denim jacket was a skull-and-crossbones emblem. His jeans hung low on his rump. He held a revolver in his right hand, down by his side.

Barbara felt a dull punch against her upper arm. She looked back.

'Come on,' Earl whispered. 'We're getting outa here.'

Pete, nodding at her, was standing again, his back to the garage door.

'We'll cut through,' Earl said.

He led the way, hunching low, rushing past Pete and apparently heading for a gap on the other side of the garage.

Pete waved her to get moving.

*I'm coming. Just hold your horses. Gotta see what's . . .*

With the other bikers close behind him, blocking some of Barbara's view, the lanky one demolished the side window of the Lincoln. Moments later, the door swung open. The woman was pulled out, screaming, and vanished completely as the pack closed in and took her down.

'Leave her alone!' Barbara yelled.

Yelled as she broke into a run.

Ran because she knew she was too far away, had to get closer to take control and save the woman – near enough to hit what she aimed at if it came to that.

'Barb!' Pete shouted. 'No!'

Yes, she thought.

As she charged at them, she wished she hadn't yelled. The yelling hadn't stopped anything.

At first, she thought that nobody had even heard her. Then a couple of the bikers at the outside of the cluster looked back, saw her, and turned around.

One of them, with a face a lot like the skull on the back of the leader's jacket, grinned at her. He was missing teeth.

The other was fat and bearded, and wore a Viking helmet that looked like a tin bowl with horns. His eyes seemed to light up when he saw Barbara dashing toward him. He rubbed his hands together.

I'm coming at them with a gun, she thought, and they look like they're glad to see me.

*'Cause your shirt's wide open, idiot.*

Just as she thought that they might not try to shoot her – wouldn't want to ruin her looks – the cadaverous one brought up a weapon that looked like a sawed-off shotgun.

Barbara had no time to halt and take aim. Stretching out her arm, she pointed her pistol at him and fired.

And watched the Viking helmet fly off the head of the fat guy.

At least Skull-face was distracted. Looking surprised, he glanced at his fellow biker, who was now stumbling backward into the others, a hole in his forehead.

Barbara skidded to a stop. She braced herself and took aim for another try at Skull-face as he leveled his shotgun at her.

Before she could fire, a sharp *blam* pounded the air.

She pulled her trigger.

*At least I take him with me.*

Waiting to be hit by the blast from the shotgun, she realized the shot had come from behind her. Skull-face fired into the air as he was knocked off his feet.

She risked a quick look back.

And there was Pete by the garage door. He hadn't gone anywhere. What he'd done was shoulder the rifle and join the battle.

A battle that ended very fast.

The other side got off a few shots.

As many as Barbara, maybe.

She had hardly begun to fight when the slide of her Colt locked back and nothing would make it shoot any more. But Pete had Lee's rifle, some sort of military thing that could be fired very fast and held a lot of ammo.

A lot.

The storm of bullets tore down all the remaining bikers very fast. Incredibly fast – before they could do much more than quit brutalizing the woman and turn around to see who was killing them and throw back three or four quick, wild shots.

When it was done, all she could hear was a high-pitched ringing sound as if someone had struck tuning forks and held them to her ears.

Those in front of her were sprawled about in positions that mostly looked awkward and uncomfortable. A few were moving slightly: here, a knee lifted; there, a head turned, a foot kicked; one man, in a fetal position, twitched and jerked. Nobody was crawling or trying to get up.

'You okay?'

She turned. Pete was now standing beside her. She nodded. Looking him up and down, she saw no sign that he'd been injured in the abrupt gunfight. But she asked, 'How about you?'

He shrugged. 'Okay.'

'My God, you sure got 'em.'

He wrinkled his nose and said, 'Yeah. I tried not to hit the woman.'

'We'd better check.'

Pete nodded. He started walking forward, and Barbara stayed at his side. As they stepped between a couple of the Harleys, he muttered, 'I can't believe I did this.'

'You did fine. We couldn't just let them kill her.'

'I couldn't just let them kill *you*. What were you trying to do, commit suicide?'

'I just wanted to stop them.'

'You stopped 'em, all right.'

'There she is.'

The woman, surrounded by the dead or badly wounded bodies of her assailants, was sprawled face-down on the street. Her arms were crossed over the back of her head. A biker had fallen forward across her rump.

Halting near the shotgun dropped by Skull-face, Barbara called, 'Lady?'

The woman didn't move.

'Lady? It's okay, now. We're here to help you.'

Still, she didn't respond.

'Oh, man,' Pete muttered. 'I bet I shot her.'

'I don't think so,' Barbara told him. The back of the woman's cream-colored blouse was spattered with blood, but not sopping. Though a sleeve had been ripped from the blouse's shoulder, Barbara could see no holes.

'Why don't you wait here?' Pete suggested.

'I'll come with you.'

'Some of these guys aren't dead.'

'I know. What'll we do about them?'

'Just make sure they don't try anything, I guess.'

She glanced at the Colt in her hand. 'I'm all out of ammo. How about you?'

Pete shook the rifle slightly as if testing its weight. 'I'm not empty yet.'

'Are you sure?'

'I've got one ready to go, I'm sure of that. It might be the last, but . . .'

'Yo! *Compadres!* My oh my, what *have* you done?'

Glancing back, Barbara saw Earl come striding toward them. She quickly fastened a middle button of her blouse. Then she crouched and picked up the sawed-off shotgun.

'Fine shooting, Pizzaboy.'

'Why didn't you just keep running?' Pete asked. He was watching Earl's approach, so Barbara kept her eyes on the bikers and the woman.

'I *waited* for you, but then I heard all the gunplay so I came back to help out.'

'Yeah, right.'

Earl laughed. 'Not really. Just wanted to see who won. And see who was doing what to who, if you know what I mean. Looks like you sure cleaned house. Hey, Banner.'

She looked at him. He had halted on the other side of Pete. Grinning, he raised a hand in greeting. 'Aren't ya glad I'm back?' he asked.

'Thrilled.'

'Now you guys're killers, just like me. Feels good, don't it?'

'Shut up,' Barbara told him.

'Looks like ya missed a few.'

'They aren't missed,' Pete said.

'Aren't dead, either. Want me to take care of 'em for you?'

'Just leave everyone alone,' Pete told him, and walked in among the bodies.

'Give you a hand,' Earl said, starting after him.

'No,' Barbara said. 'Stay where you are.'

'What's your problem?'

She ignored him. 'Pete, why don't you take all the guns and stuff away from them? I'll keep you covered.'

Nodding, he slung the rifle behind his shoulder. 'What about the woman?'

'She can wait. I don't want you getting killed by a "dead" guy. It happens all the time in the movies.'

He looked back and smiled at Barbara. 'You're some kind of an expert on playing possum, aren't you?'

Though she returned Pete's smile, the reminder of their time in the pickup truck made heat rush to her face. 'Yep, that's me.' In a loud voice, she said, 'Any of you animals can hear me, I'll blast anyone who makes a sudden move. Got it?'

Nobody answered. Nobody moved.

She wondered if all the live ones had either passed out or died in the past couple of minutes.

Not likely.

'Careful,' she said.

335

Wandering slowly among the bikers, stopping over each, Pete crouched again and again to pick up weapons. He only went after those in plain sight: handguns and knives that were still clutched in hands or had fallen to the pavement; knives sheathed on belts. He stuck the guns into the pockets of his trousers, and pitched the knives away.

But he disturbed none of the bodies. He seemed reluctant to touch them at all, much less frisk them or turn them over.

Not exactly a thorough search, Barbara thought.

*I wouldn't wanta touch them, either.*

But, my God, if one of them comes up with a gun . . .

'Do you want to go in and help?' she asked Earl.

'Thought you'd never ask.'

'Turn 'em over, make sure they don't have anything.'

'Never fear, Earl is here.' He pointed at Skull-face. 'Dead.' He pointed at the Viking. 'Dead.'

Pete, now standing above the woman, looked up and asked, 'What's going on?'

'Earl's double-checking things.'

'Maybe dead.' Earl kicked a body in the head.

'Hey!' Barbara yelled.

'My way of checking.' He smiled down at the corpse and pronounced, 'Dead.'

'For the love of God,' Pete said.

'Just turn them over, Earl.'

'If they're dead anyhow, why bother?'

'Stop kicking them in the head!'

'Okay, okay. Don't wet your pants.' The next biker was face down. Unlike the two that Earl had kicked, this one still wore a helmet. The back of the black T-shirt had a few holes in it and looked awfully bloody, but Barbara noticed that one arm was tucked out of sight beneath the body.

'Be careful of that one,' she warned.

She worked the shotgun's pump action, and took aim.

'Okay, turn him over.'

Earl stepped to the other side of the body and glanced at Barbara. 'Make sure you don't shoot *me* with that thing.'

'I'll try not to.'

Crouching, he reached over the body. He grabbed it by the shoulder and hip. Then he pulled. It came up, rolling onto its side.

The hand had a gun in it.

Big surprise, Barbara thought.

She saw the pistol start to come up, muzzle rising toward her.

She yelled, '*No!*'

336

And fired.

Blasting apart the face guard and the face behind it, blowing the helmet off.

The pistol leaped out of the biker's hand. It fell, clattered against the alley pavement, and Earl snatched it up.

Barbara cocked the shotgun. 'Put that down,' she said.

'Yeah, right.'

'Do it,' Pete called. His rifle still hung down the back of his shoulder by its strap, but he'd already pulled a revolver from one of his pockets and pointed it at Earl.

Earl glanced back at him, then faced Barbara and shook his head. 'Hey, this sucks, you know? All this shit going down, and *I'm* not supposed to have a gun?'

'Put it down,' Pete said.

'Come on!' Though keeping his eyes on Barbara, Earl spoke loudly enough to be heard by Pete, too. 'I could've had *yours* back at the pickup, and you know it. I could've taken *both* of 'em and even shot off both your asses if I'd wanted to! But I didn't. 'Cause I'm not the bad guy around here, you know what I mean? I'm on *your* side.'

Pete tilted his head to one side and shrugged at Barbara.

'Okay,' she said. 'We'll let you keep the gun.'

'Thanks. You're a champ, Banner.' He stood up, turned away, and walked to the next biker. 'Dead,' he announced. He stepped around it. Bending over another sprawled body, he said, 'Maybe dead.' He bent lower, shoved the muzzle of the pistol against the nape of the biker's neck, and fired. 'Dead now.'

'Earl!' Barbara cried out.

He grinned. 'Better safe than sorry.'

'Don't *do* that!'

'Okay,' he said. Standing in place, he aimed quickly and fired into another body. The biker flinched and cried out. 'Live one!' Earl yelled.

'Damn it!' Barbara shouted as Earl fired twice more. The body jerked with each impact, then went limp.

Earl lowered the pistol. He grinned at her. 'I won't do it any more. I promise.'

'That was the last of them,' Pete pointed out.

'Ah, then,' Earl said, 'I guess we don't have to worry about any surprises from them, do we?'

'You're such a bastard,' Barbara said.

'Me? A bastard?' Laughing, he shook his head. 'I'm not a bastard. How can you possibly call me a bastard? If I was a bastard, I might do something like *this*.'

His arm came up fast.

Laughing, he shot Barbara and she fired back as he pivoted and shot Pete.

The thunder of the gunshots crashed through the alley. Blood exploded from punched flesh.

All three went down.

# FORTY

'We're almost there,' Stanley said. 'The pool's just on the other side of this fence.'

Sheila didn't respond. She hadn't spoken at all, or resisted in any way, since her small rebellion in the bathtub.

After slamming her down on the bottom of the tub, Stanley had let her rest. He'd needed time, himself, to recuperate before starting the journey to the Bensons' swimming pool.

So he'd stepped around her body and sat on the remaining beam and tried to be patient. The view was nice. This was his first chance for a good, long look at her backside.

Her hair wasn't much to see, the way it was dark and ropy and plastered to her head. Though her skin glistened, it was filthy, stained with blood, sprinkled with dust and crumbs of plaster that had adhered to the moisture. But her *shape* – her shape was lovely. Even with her arms stretched overhead, Stanley could see how broad and strong she was across the shoulders. She tapered down from there, smooth curves of muscle showing where he'd never seen them before on any other woman; not on a flesh-and-blood woman, just on superhero types in comic books, on body-builders pictured in magazines and sometimes on television. Never on an actual woman sprawled in front of him.

And her *ass*.

He'd seen it many times before, full mounds flexing under shorts or sweatpants. He'd seen it in jeans. He'd seen it in little bikinis that didn't cover much at all. But never like this, never naked so he could study the twin, bare globes, linger on them, run his eyes down the curve of their crack.

Near enough to touch.

To kiss.

*Mine. She's mine from head to foot.*

I could go ahead right now and fuck her, he'd realized. She isn't trapped anymore, and she's sure in no condition to fight me. Just step down, spread her legs, and have at her.

'No no no no no.'

*That'd ruin everything.*

His heart was set on taking her to the swimming pool, getting her all washed up so her skin would be shiny, wrestling with her in the cool water . . .

'What are we waiting for?' he'd said.

No answer from Sheila. She lay on the bottom of the tub, and all that moved were her back and ribcage, just barely rising, expanding, lowering, shrinking with the in and out of her breath.

'Sheila? We're leaving, now, so get up.'

Her head had lifted slightly.

'We're leaving right now. I'm taking you to a nice, cool swimming pool where you can wash up and get all squeaky clean. You can even wet your whistle, if you don't mind the chlorine. Any questions?'

She hadn't answered.

But from that moment on, she'd followed every order: climbed out of the tub while he'd watched from below; waited on hands and knees for him to climb out; made no fuss when he'd knelt behind her and steadied himself with a hand on her rump while he ducked down and reached forward between her thighs to find the loose end of the barbed wire. Suddenly hard again, his face so close to her, he'd been tempted to mount her without any more delays.

No no no, he'd told himself. You've waited this long. A few minutes more won't kill you, and you'll be able to have her all clean and wet in the pool. Don't spoil it. There's no hurry. Stick with the plan.

*Why wait for the pool? I can lick her clean.*

'No!'

*Just a little bit, and then I'll stop. What can it hurt?*

So he'd stuck out his tongue and begun moving his head toward her, but then his hand, groping through the rubble under her torso, had found the barbed wire.

Was the timing of the discovery a signal that he should hold off?

In a high-pitched mockery of his mother's voice, Stanley had said, 'No snacking, boy! Do you want to go and spoil your dinner?'

'How about just a little taste?' he'd asked in his own voice.

'You go and do that, boy, you'll shoot your squirt and spoil your appetite same as if you'd whanged her.'

'Hmmm. Good point. No snacking for me.'

With his left hand, he'd picked up the scissors and straight razor. Then he'd pushed at Sheila's rump and raised himself, holding on to the long strand of barbed wire with his right hand.

'Up.'

Offering no objection, Sheila had gotten to her feet.

'Now. A few simple instructions. You're going to walk ahead of me. I'll be holding the other end of this.'

Lifting his hand, he'd pulled the dangling wire up between her legs until it met her flesh. She'd flinched a bit and gone up on her tiptoes. After a moment on tiptoes, however, she must've figured out a better course of action; bending forward at the waist to lower her bound wrists and *her* end of the strand.

'If you give me any trouble,' Stanley'd gone on, 'I'll be forced to give it a yank. Which is bound to hurt, don't you think? I don't care how much you bend over, I give it a good pull and you'll be sorry.'

After the warning, he'd given the wire some slack so Sheila could stop bending over so much.

'Okay. Start walking.'

She had begun to make her way slowly through the ruins, walking ahead of Stanley. She didn't stand up completely straight, but Stanley couldn't blame her for that; the lower her hands, the less chance of catching the wire in sensitive areas. She kept her legs apart to spare them from the barbs. As a result of her precautions, her gait was more a waddle than a walk.

She'd flinched and winced sometimes when she either stepped on something with her bare feet or allowed the barbed wire to scratch or poke her.

It had taken a long time to get through the ruin of her house, but she'd picked up her pace after that. They'd made fairly good time crossing her patio and back yard, but they'd been stopped for a while by the cinderblock wall at the rear of her property.

'How do we get you over this?' Stanley had asked.

She'd simply stood facing the wall, neither speaking nor gesturing.

'It's going to be a problem, since I'm not stupid enough to undo your hands.' Frowning, he'd swept the wire gently from side to side, watching it swing below her buttocks like a wicked jump-rope.

'We can't exactly go around, can we? I suppose we *could*. Take the front way, and we wouldn't have to worry about any walls at all. But I think we'd probably attract a wee bit of attention, I walk you around the block like a dog. What a dog, huh? What a leash! Ho! Can't you just see it? It'd almost be worth a try. But somebody'd come running out of a house, sure as hell, and try to save you. Wouldn't want that. I'd have to kill 'em, and I'm too pooped for any more of that. Gotta save all my energy for you. So I guess we'll have to go *over*.'

He'd let his end of the wire fall to the ground, then shoved her toward the wall. 'Give you a boost.' After setting down the scissors and razor, he'd crouched behind her and cupped his hands. 'Put a foot in the stirrup, my dear.'

Sheila had raised her arms, placed her bound wrists against the upper edge of the wall, and planted her right heel into the cup of his hands.

Then she'd straightened her leg, thrusting herself upward, rising toward the top of the wall. As Stanley had uncrouched, he'd looked up and watched Sheila swing out her left leg and kick it high.

'Oh, look at you,' he'd said.

*Too bad there aren't ten walls between us and the pool. Or a hundred. I could look at that all day!*

As her foot started to rise out of his hands, he gave it a sudden upward thrust that sent Sheila hurling over the top.

'Surprise!'

No complaint had come from Sheila. Just a squeal of alarm as she went head-first over the wall, feet kicking at the sky. Not waiting to hear her land, Stanley had snatched up his scissors and razor, tossed them over, then hurled himself at the wall and clambered up.

From the top, he'd looked down at Sheila.

She had apparently not landed on her head. Perhaps she'd hit the ground arms-first and done some sort of somersault. She was lying on her back, head toward the wall, hands on her belly, knees up.

'You're lucky I cut down the rose bushes,' he had called to her. Then he'd lowered himself to the ground, retrieved his scissors and razor, and squatted beside Sheila to pick up the end of the barbed wire. 'Fall down go boom?' he'd asked in baby-talk.

No answer from Sheila. Just a narrow-eyed glare.

She was gasping very hard for breath, so Stanley had spent a while watching her chest heave, lifting and lowering her breasts. They were shiny with sweat and blood. They were spickled with goosebumps, and the nipples stood erect.

'You turned on? You *can't* be cold. Maybe you like all this. Do you? Do you like *pain*?'

She'd blinked her eyes, then crossed her legs and sat up.

'Ah. You'd rather get going. Scared I'll start on you, I bet.'

The momentum of her quick sit-up had carried Sheila to her knees. From there, she'd gotten to her feet. Instead of bolting, she'd only stood there, her back to Stanley, the wire hanging between her legs to the grass.

At her back, Stanley had ducked and reached between her knees and grabbed the wire. He'd drawn it up behind her.

'Welcome to my back yard. That's my house right there – what's left of it. Of course, it fared better than yours. Mine is only *half* down. Over here is my garage, which fared even worse than my house. Mother's in the house. Deader than shit, as the saying goes. And a good thing, too. She would not approve of my behavior today. Wouldn't approve in the least. The old bat always *did* think I was a pervert.'

Laughing, he'd given the wire a couple of quick upward tugs that made Sheila jump and gasp.

'Giddy-up, horsey.'

Bending over, Sheila had started to hobble forward.

'To the right, to the right. Our next obstacle is the block wall there by my driveway. But I think we'll go around it. Would you like that? You took such a nasty fall at the last wall, so we'll try to spare you, this time. I think we can probably make it to the gate without drawing undue attention to ourselves, don't you? We'll just go down my driveway.'

She'd led the way, and Stanley had kept a sharp watch as they approached the front of his house. Making her wait, he had stepped past her and opened the gate that shut off Judy's side of the cinderblock wall.

Then they'd gone in and made their way alongside her house to her back yard.

'This is the home of my friend, Judy. I don't believe you know her. Me, I've gotten to know her *quite* well since the quake. It was her saw we used to get you out. A lovely woman. Not in your league, of course. *Nobody* is in your league. Perhaps we'll visit with her, later on. You two have a lot in common. Me, for one thing. And guess what – she's *still* in her bathtub. Not that her house fell on her. Her house didn't fall at all, the lucky bitch. But *I* fell on her. Ho! Maybe we'll let her out, later on, and ask her to join us for cocktails and hors d'oeuvres. Why not? It'll be her stuff.'

Stanley had kept the monologue going all the way across Judy's back yard, smiling at Sheila's backside, sometimes chuckling, wondering if she was at all impressed by his wit.

Under the circumstances, he'd thought, I can hardly expect her to be amused.

'We're almost there,' he said. 'The pool's just on the other side of this fence. See where I made a doorway for us? We won't have to climb over this one or go looking for a gate – we can walk straight on through. But watch your head.'

Hunching down, Sheila stepped over the lower crossbeam and slipped through the gap in the redwood fence. On the other side, she halted. Stanley stepped through. He ducked, but not quite enough. The upper beam scraped the top of his head.

'Ow!'

Sheila ignored him.

'I hurt myself.'

She acted as if she were deaf.

'Say you're sorry.'

'I'm not sorry,' she muttered.

'You're not being very nice to me.' Stanley flipped the wire from side to side, switching it against her thighs. 'But why *should* you be? All I did was rescue you.'

She didn't look back, didn't make a comment.

'Get moving.'

She waddled toward the pool.

'Go to the right. We're going to the other end. That's where the water is.'

She followed orders.

As they walked alongside the pool, Stanley said, 'Bet you can't wait to get in. I've been in. Not a whole lot of water down there, but it's plenty good for washing off blood. And it's really quite refreshing. I'm sure we'll both enjoy it. Okay, stop here.'

Sheila stopped.

'Face the pool.'

She turned and looked down.

This is it! Stanley thought. Suddenly, he was trembling.

He could hardly believe that he'd actually freed Sheila from the bathtub and brought her to the swimming pool – that they were finally here, exactly as he'd hoped.

*This is my day! The greatest day ever! And the best of it hasn't even started yet!*

Dreams *can* come true, he told himself. All you've gotta do is reach out for them and not let anything get in your way.

Stanley peeled the clinging remains of his pajama pants away from his rump. He crouched, lowering them to his ankles. While still down, he placed the scissors and razor on the concrete. Then he straightened up. With a few quick, silent movements, he stepped out of his moccasins and the scanty rag that draped his feet.

Sheila seemed to be unaware of what he'd done. 'We can't go in here,' she said.

'Sure we can.' The concrete felt awfully hot under his bare feet. He was glad to be naked, though. He wished Sheila would turn around and look at him.

*See how big I am? It's all because of you.*

Just tell her to turn around.

No no no. I want her right where she is.

'It's too shallow,' she protested.

'This is the *deep* end, moron!'

With that, he used both hands to jerk upward on the wire. Sheila cried out. The barbed steel vanished in the crease of her rump, but she bent down and it came out fast. Still tugging the wire, Stanley took a quick step backward.

The pull made Sheila fold as if broken at the waist. Her bound hands came swinging toward him between her calves. Her elbows struck the inner sides of her knees. Her face appeared, upside-down, hair hanging.

Stanley yanked the wire upward as hard as he could.

Sheila shrieked.

For a moment, Stanley thought he might be able to drag her whole body, arms-first, through her widely spread legs.

*Make her kiss her own ass!*

But suddenly her legs flew up, bare feet almost kicking him as she flipped over. Her back, just below the shoulders, struck the edge of the pool. The blow jolted her body, straightened her out. Stanley strained at the wire as if he hoped to drag her from the brink.

Propped up at only one end, Sheila was stretched out over the pool like the naked and bloody victim of a demented magician more interested in torture than levitation.

The wire lurched in Stanley's hands.

Letting go, he watched his end of the wire leap high.

Sheila's legs dropped out of sight and the fulcrum of the pool's edge seemed to launch her upper body forward.

Stanley rushed to the edge.

At first, he thought she would hit the water flat, a real belly-whomper. At the last instant, however, her body twisted and curled. Her side hit the surface. A geyser of white, sparkling spray shot up and she was submerged in a roil of froth.

The spray sprinkled down.

The froth vanished.

After her impact with the water, Sheila must've rolled over. She was face down, bound hands hanging toward the bottom, legs spread apart. Submerged in water tinged with pink, her body seemed to waver and shimmer.

As Stanley watched, she glided slowly upward.

The surface of the water slid away to make room for her back.

Her back became a slick, clean island that gleamed with sunlight.

But it was the only island.

The rest of Sheila stayed down, a layer of water rippling over her buttocks, the hair on the back of her head rising and swaying.

She's faking it, Stanley told himself. Wants me to think she's drowning so I'll let my guard down. She'll come up for air any second.

But the only movements of her body seemed to be those made by the gentle shifting of the pool water buoying her up.

*What if she's out cold?*

*What if she drowns?*

'Sheila!'

Nothing.

*She can't drown! That'd ruin everything.*

But even as Stanley leaped from the edge, he wondered if this was exactly what she wanted him to do.

345

He was on his way down when he realized that his hands were empty. He'd set down the scissors and razor . . .

'Shit!' he yelled.

His feet slapped the water. A moment later, they struck the bottom of the pool and he felt as if his legs were being rammed up through his hips. His knees folded. He tumbled forward through the rising spray of his splash and slammed onto Sheila's back.

He drove her down.

He felt a slight jolt when she hit the bottom of the pool.

No struggle came from under him.

No good, he thought. No good at all.

*What if she drowns?*

He knew he should act quickly to save her, but he wanted to savor the moment – the silence, the mild and heavy coolness of the water, the slick feel of Sheila's skin against his chest and belly, the way he was pressed against her rump with his penis snug between her buttocks.

Why they call 'em buns, he thought.

*Could do her right now. Go just a little lower, and shove it in . . .*

And she'll drown for sure, he warned himself. Don't want that. She's gotta be alive and kicking, or it won't be any good at all.

So he clutched her just below the armpits and slid himself backward. On his knees, he leaned away from her and pulled. She glided up with him. As her body rose, her arms descended and slid over the backs of his hands, pressing them against her sides.

Their heads lifted out of the water.

Stanley gasped for air.

Sheila didn't. She hung limp in his arms, her head drooping.

Stanley shook her. 'Hey!'

Nothing.

He stopped shaking her.

She didn't seem to be breathing.

Doesn't mean anything, Stanley told himself. Maybe she's just holding her breath.

From his position at her back, hands clamped to her sides, he couldn't tell whether she had a heartbeat. So he shoved his hands forward, forcing them through the tight spaces under her arms.

When they came out the other side, they met her breasts.

Which ended his quest for her heartbeat.

He filled his hands. The breasts were wet and slippery, heavy. He squeezed them. They were soft, firm, springy. He swirled his hands around them. The nipples under his moving palms were stiff, rubbery nubs.

Breathless, he grew so hard that he ached.

'Can you feel it?' he whispered, pushing against her.

She didn't respond.

'Answer me.'

She didn't.

'This is a test,' he whispered. He clamped both her nipples between his thumbs and forefingers. 'Tell me when it hurts.' He squeezed.

Not gently.

She didn't flinch rigid and scream with pain, as Stanley thought she might. But she did moan. She did squirm slightly. As if disturbed in her sleep. Then she started to cough. A wet, rattling cough.

Stanley cupped her breasts loosely so he could feel them lurch and bounce, slapping against his hands as she was wracked with spasms of coughing.

*Don't wait till she stops! Get her now while she's screwed up!*

Clutching her breasts, he pulled her backward until she was tight against him, then put his feet on the bottom and stood up, lifting her. The water was almost waist-high. He glanced over his shoulder and spotted the chrome ladder fixed on the side of the pool, near the corner. It didn't extend down very far – was intended for use when the pool was full. He wondered if he would be able to reach the lowest rung. Hoped so.

Wading backward, he dragged Sheila toward the ladder. She twisted and writhed, and couldn't stop coughing.

At the corner of the pool, he swung her around and shoved her at the wall. She didn't bring up her arms in time to stop the collision. Her body made a wet, smacking sound when it hit the tiles. Her forehead thumped. Stanley's hands felt pleasantly trapped between the wall and her breasts. He kept them there while Sheila coughed a few more times. Then he slipped them free.

He stepped away from her back, grabbed her upper arms, and spun her around to face him. She tried to push him away. The effort was feeble.

So much for our Amazon, Stanley thought. Bash her around enough, she ain't so tough.

He thrust her bound arms high.

Her wrists reached almost to the ladder's lowest rung.

Pinning them to the wall with his left hand, he caught the dangling strand of barbed wire with his right. Though he jabbed himself a few times, he drew the wire up and wound it around the side rail and bottom rung of the ladder. With a few twists, it was secure.

He stepped back.

'Fabulous,' he muttered.

In his wildest fantasies, perhaps Sheila had almost looked like this.

But perhaps not quite so beautiful, so vulnerable, so ready for him.

Most of the filth and blood had been washed away. Except for a few

347

bright red trickles sliding down her forearms from fresh wounds on her wrists, her skin looked clean and glossy. It ran with streamers of silver water. It dripped diamonds.

Arms raised high, she stood straight and tall, her head tipped back.

Each time she coughed, her body shook. Between coughs, she panted for air. The shaking and panting did wonderful things to her breasts.

The ruffled surface of the water encircled Sheila's waist like a fluid, transparent skirt, vaguely pink. Just below it, the fine curls of her pubic hair sparkled like gold. Stanley could see through them as if they weren't there.

Her legs seemed to blush in the sunlit, blood-tinted water. Stanley knew they weren't moving, but they appeared to undulate.

My Sheila, Stanley thought. Just the way I always dreamed, only better.

While he was gazing at her, she lowered her head. She grimaced at him, eyes squeezed almost shut, teeth bared. She coughed a couple more times, then sniffed.

'Are you all right?' Stanley asked.

She didn't answer.

'You *look* spectacular.'

He moved closer. He dipped his hands into the water by her hips, then slid them up her sides to the smooth hollows of her armpits. Then he explored the sleek muscles of her upraised arms before sliding his hands down to her breasts.

He watched her breasts as he fondled them, hefted them, pressed them together, squeezed them. Sometimes, Sheila moaned.

She likes it, Stanley thought.

She squirmed and made quiet wincing sounds when he pinched her nipples. When he pulled and twisted them, her back seemed to stiffen and she hissed through her teeth.

He caught one of her nipples between his lips. He flicked and wiggled it with his tongue, then opened wide and sucked in her breast until his mouth was full of the slippery, cool flesh. He tested its springiness with the edges of his teeth.

*What if I bite it?*

*Bite it off and eat it?*

*She wouldn't look so great afterwards, but imagine the scream! And the taste! And she'd turn into part of me, flesh of my flesh . . .*

Sheila attacked him with her knee.

Stanley felt it thrust in and slide up between his thighs.

A groin shot – sapped of its power by the weight of the water.

*If we hadn't been in the pool . . .*

*But we are! Yes yes!*

As the knee rushed upward, Stanley shut his legs to trap it. But the water slowed him. By the time he clamped his thighs against the sides of Sheila's knee, it was already touching his scrotum.

Instead of crashing into his testicles, her knee simply stopped, barely touching him, and hoisted Stanley upward. His feet lifted from the bottom of the pool. His mouth lost hold of her breast, which popped out with a squelchy, sucking noise.

Rising out of the water, he saw the fierce look on her face.

The agony.

And despair, because she could obviously see that her attack had failed. Stanley was riding her knee like a pony, grinning, pointing at her with his stout penis.

He didn't even fall off.

He simply rode her knee up, and rode it down.

'Wanta try again?' he asked.

She glared at him.

'You could've hurt me, you know. You could've ruined everything.'

'That was the point,' she said.

'I know.'

Stanley punched her in the stomach. There was no water in the way to slow down his fist, so it landed good and solid just above her navel. It sounded like smacking wet meat. Her breasts jumped nicely. Her legs jerked upward as if she wanted to double over but couldn't. Her breath blasted out and she was smashed backward against the side of the pool.

Stanley punched her once more in the same place.

Not only did her breasts bounce like before, but this time her eyes bulged wildly and her knees broke the surface of the water so that she hung there by the barbed wire around her wrists. Hung there and squeaked as she tried to haul air into her lungs.

*Fabulous!*

Stanley shoved his hands into the creases behind her knees. Clutching her there, he pulled the knees wider apart and drew them toward him and stepped between them.

As he lifted them above his hips, her dripping cleft came up out of the water and tilted toward him.

He plunged into her.

He thrust up hard, rising on his tiptoes to reach high and deep, staggered by her tight, gripping slickness.

It had never been like this for him.

Not even close.

This was better than he'd thought possible.

*I'm in her! Sheila! I'm fucking her! Yes!*

Sliding his hands up the backs of her thighs, he clutched the solid globes of her buttocks. He clung to them and tried not to move.

349

Don't move a muscle, he told himself. Don't, or you'll lose it. Hang on. You're in her. In her as in as it gets. Hang on. Make it last. Try to think of something else.

*That'd be a neat trick.*

Suddenly, the hug of Sheila around his shaft was too much.

Or maybe the knowledge that he was inside her, inside Sheila, finally, was more than he could stand.

He felt himself swelling tight with a massive urgency. Even if he didn't move, he was past being able to stop. Even if he tried to think of something else.

No use holding back.

*Go for it!*

Gripping her ass, he quickly slid almost all the way out. When only his tip was still embedded, he rammed hard into her again. He felt as if he were being clutched and sucked up.

Torn from his throat was a noise he'd never made before.

*'RAWWWWWAHHH!'*

And he was pounding inside her, throbbing, pumping, grabbing her by the hips and trying to shove himself higher and deeper, jolting her so hard that he had trouble hanging on.

*Slam it to her, slam it to her, slam it to her!*

*Yes yes yes!*

'Stop it! Leave her alone!'

He heard the shout – a woman's voice from somewhere close behind him.

But the voice couldn't stop him. He kept thrusting, kept squirting.

'Get away from her right now!'

Someone I know, he thought. But who?

*Judy! Sounds just like her.*

*How the hell did Judy get loose?*

'Get away from her or I'll shoot!'

*Shoot?*

He quit thrusting. He was done with Sheila, anyway – at least for now.

'I'll stop!' he gasped. 'Don't shoot!'

'Put your hands up!'

He let go of Sheila's hips and raised his arms. Though no longer supported by his hands, she stayed against him, still impaled.

'Judy?' Stanley asked, not looking back.

'You better believe it.'

'Don't shoot.' He took a few quick breaths. 'I give up.'

'Get away from the woman.'

He nodded. Then he tried a couple more thrusts. *Look, Ma, no hands!*

He watched how the thrusts made Sheila jiggle. Great. But not nearly as great as how she felt on him.

*I could do her all over again.*

'You fucking bastard!' Judy cried out.

And a new voice said, 'Here, give it. *I'll* shoot him.'

He pulled out fast and turned around.

When he'd last seen Judy, she had been naked at the bottom of her bathtub, feet bound to the faucets, a chair on her chest, her arms wired together with a hanger.

Now, she stood directly across from him, looking down on him from the edge, only the width of the pool away. She wore cut-off jeans and an old blue workshirt with rolled sleeves. They looked like the clothes she'd been wearing that morning.

Her arms were straight out in front of her. She was using both hands to hold the revolver that was aimed at his chest.

The revolver was big and shiny. It looked like something Dirty Harry might use.

Standing by Judy's side, tugging the sleeve of her shirt, was Weed. 'Give it to me,' Weed said. 'I'll blow his fucking head off.'

Judy shook her head. 'Don't do that.'

Weed. She looked exactly the same as Stanley remembered her: skinny and mean, her scalp hairless except for black stubble like a two-day growth of whiskers, her eyebrows pointed, her eyes tiny, her chin sharp. She still wore the gray tank top that was cut off just below her ribcage. The golden ring in her navel glinted sunlight. Her jeans looked ready to drop from her lean hips.

She held a butcher knife in her left hand.

Stanley'd had big plans for her. If only he could've found her.

Seeing Weed with Judy, a lot of things suddenly made sense.

He *hadn't* searched for her in Judy's house. But that was obviously where she'd gone to hide from him. And while there, she must've found Judy in the bathtub and set her free.

Two of his victims, joining forces.

And coming for him.

*Shouldn't have cut through Judy's back yard.*

*Shouldn't have made Sheila scream so much.*

*Tipped 'em off, and now they're here like a couple of fucking harpies.*

It's like some kind of a nightmare, Stanley thought.

*Maybe it is a nightmare. Maybe none of this is real, and I'm asleep. Or in a coma. Maybe I never even got out of my house this morning, and I'm trapped there under . . .*

Bullshit, he thought. Forget the 'Owlcreek Bridge' bullshit, this is real. It better be real, or I was only dreaming I fucked Sheila.

It's real, he told himself. So deal with it.

'I surrender,' he called. 'Don't shoot. You don't wanta hit Sheila. I mean, that's a *big* gun. It'd shoot right through me and right through her, too. You don't wanta kill her, do you?'

'Of course not,' Judy said. 'Just you.'

'I give up. See?' He raised his hands even higher. 'I won't try anything. I promise. Just tell me what you want me to do.'

With the barrel of the revolver, Judy gestured to her right. 'Move that way.'

He looked back at Sheila. She was still panting for air, but her head was upright between her raised arms. She was watching him, her eyes narrow.

He faced Judy again. 'She won't be in the line of fire if I move over there. What's to stop you from shooting me?'

'I could shoot you where you stand.'

'And kill Sheila.'

Hand on Judy's arm, Weed leaned closer to her and spoke softly. Stanley heard the murmur of her voice, but couldn't make out any of the words.

Judy nodded. Keeping the revolver aimed at Stanley, she sidestepped to the corner of the pool and started walking toward him.

Oh, no, he thought.

Then he gasped, 'Shit!' as Weed, straight in front of him, leaped off the edge.

She dropped toward the water, the bottom of her tank top gliding up. Her breasts were tanned as dark as her belly. They had wonderful nipples that stuck out, and Stanley wanted to feel them in his mouth.

She vanished for a moment in the middle of a splash. When Stanley could see her again, she was soaking wet, her tanned skin gleaming, her tank top clinging to her breasts. She waded toward him. The water was high enough, on Weed, to cover the ring in her belly button.

The blade of the knife in her left hand was at least twelve inches long.

Should've kept after her, Stanley thought.

Stupid, stupid, stupid. Could've taken her down and had her. And taken her out of the picture.

Now she's gonna kill me.

If she doesn't, Judy will.

As Weed sloshed closer, he looked over his shoulder. Judy stood at *his* corner of the pool, not far from the shiny chrome arches of the ladder's rails. From there, she had a clear line of fire at him; her bullet would pass high over Sheila's head.

'I could've *killed* you!' he shouted at Judy. 'I spared your life! You owe me!'

Her upper lip twitched. 'I owe you dick,' she said.

'I saved your life!'

'You raped the shit out of me!' she yelled. With the thumb of her right hand, she hooked back the revolver's hammer.

*SNICK-CLACK*

The black tunnel of the muzzle pointed at Stanley's face.

*Oh, God, I'm dead.*

He didn't want to see the gun go off, so he turned his face.

And found himself looking at Weed. A stride away, she swung the butcher knife at his neck with a hard sideways sweep as if she planned to lop his head off.

The earth shook.

# FORTY-ONE

The afternoon roared, and the alley shuddered under Barbara's back. Startled out of a dream, she thought, *Christ, a quake!*

She thought she was at home, so she tried to hold on to the mattress of her bed. Her groping hands met pavement.

She jerked open her eyes.

Sky above her. A lurching, shimmying garage to the left, nothing nearby on the right.

*Nothing to fall on me. I'll be okay. It's the stuff that falls on you . . .*

Suddenly, the roar faded. The earth stopped jolting and pounding her, but seemed to continue swaying slightly.

An aftershock, she told herself. That's all it was.

All? Had to be better than a six-point.

But not like the big one, not even close.

Now that it was over, Barbara realized that she was hurt. From the feel of things, something had clobbered the back of her head. The alley, maybe. Had the quake knocked her down? She couldn't remember, but it seemed likely. Her head felt as if it had been smacked a good one.

Grimacing, she raised her arms to clutch her head. And let out a cry as the movement stoked a fire in her left side.

The starkness of the pain frightened her.

*What happened to me?*

She suddenly remembered the gunfight.

Pete!

She'd seen Pete go down, shot by Earl. She'd been hit first, herself, but she'd stayed on her feet long enough to shoot Earl while he'd been spinning around to fire at Pete. He'd gotten off his shot at about the same moment that Pete had fired at him – an instant before the blast from Barbara's shotgun had slammed into his back. While Earl was going down, so was Pete.

Then me, Barbara thought. I stayed up long enough to watch them both get shot. Probably bashed my head when I fell.

The pains tore a cry out of her as she shoved herself up on her elbows.

Below her left breast, her blouse clung to her side like a sodden, red rag.

That's where he shot me, she thought. Jesus H. Christ. Shot. I'm actually shot.

*Forget it. It didn't kill me. Worry about it some other time.*

She quickly checked for other wounds. Her blouse was open a few inches, and the bare skin between its edges looked okay. The right side of her blouse wasn't too bloody. She looked okay from the waist down.

So she raised her eyes and tried to spot Pete.

*Maybe he's alive. Maybe he was only wounded, like me.*

Beyond her outstretched body, she saw motorcycles and bodies. A couple of the bikes had fallen over, but most of them still stood upright. Something didn't look . . .

The Lincoln.

The huge, white car was gone.

Explains how the bikes got knocked over.

Who drove off? she wondered. The woman? Some scavenger? Not Earl, that's for sure. That's him, there.

The guy on his back.

*How'd he get on his back?*

Doesn't matter, she told herself. Where's Pete?

She couldn't see him. But a lot of dead bikers were sprawled and piled in the alley. Pete had been standing beyond most of them at the time of the shootout.

*I just can't see him 'cause of all the bodies in the way.*

'Pete!' she yelled.

No answer came.

She decided not to call out again. The wrong sort of person might hear her.

As gingerly as possible, she sat up. The effort made her tremble, and the pain filled her eyes with tears. Blinking to clear them, she looked about for the shotgun.

Gone.

'Hell with it,' she muttered.

Then she struggled to stand, whimpering, flinching at times with sudden stabs of pain. When she was up, she swayed and almost fell. Spreading her feet, she kept her balance. Her side felt as if it had been scorched with a white-hot rod.

She wiped tears from her eyes.

She began staggering toward the bodies.

They hadn't been stripped.

What's with the vultures? Barbara wondered. They don't like biker duds?

Just haven't gotten here yet, more than likely.

She changed her mind, however, when she halted above Earl's body.

355

Maybe he'd still been alive after she'd blown him off his feet and he'd made a face-first dive at the pavement. She supposed it was possible that he'd turned over by himself. More likely, though, he'd been rolled onto his back by someone else.

Someone wanting to get at his mouth.

His mouth, wide open, brimmed with blood.

Using her foot, Barbara pushed against his cheekbone. His head turned sideways, the blood dumping out. With the edge of her sneaker against his ear, she managed to tilt his face upright again.

She peered into his mouth.

Gory in there, but she couldn't see well enough to tell whether or not his gold crowns had been removed. To do that, she would need to hunker down over him and take a long, hard look.

The way her head ached and the way her wounded side throbbed with pain, she didn't want to do that.

Doesn't matter anyway, she told herself.

*I promised him I wouldn't let any damn scavenger yank his teeth.*

So what.

He shot me. He shot Pete. We killed him. Some asshole took his teeth, tough tacos.

She glanced around, searching for his pistol. It was nowhere near his body, nowhere to be seen.

Gone, just like Barbara's shotgun.

Looks like somebody took the guns, she thought.

She moved on, walking in among the bodies. Several had bloody mouths.

Someone had been at them with pliers, she was sure of it.

Didn't take their clothes, scalps, tattoos or motorcycles. Maybe stole their wallets; she had no intention of checking.

Scavenger specialists.

*Not my field, honey. I deal only in guns and crowns.*

*How about knives and bridges?*

*Never touch 'em, sweets.*

I'm losing my mind, Barbara thought.

She tongued her own teeth.

And wondered if some filthy, jibbering vulture had searched her mouth while she was out cold. Stuck fingers in. Poked around with pliers.

She began to feel as if she might throw up.

But forgot her nausea when she saw that the woman who'd been dragged out of her car was gone, for sure. Here was the biker who'd fallen across her rump. And here was the sleeve of her cream-colored blouse.

Pete apparently hadn't shot her, after all.

*A possum player, same as me.*

After all the gunplay, she'd simply gotten to her feet, climbed back into her car, and driven away.

Maybe.

Or maybe someone took her.

Threw her in the car and raced off with her.

None of the bikers could've done that; all of them had been dead before the final gunfight.

Maybe a scavenger snatched her.

*Guns and crowns and ladies.*

Then how come he didn't take me?

Thought I was dead?

Quit stalling, she told herself. You've gotta find Pete.

She moved her gaze to the bodies that she hadn't yet studied – that she'd been avoiding, knowing Pete would be among them and not wanting to see him dead. So long as she didn't see him, she could keep her hope that he'd survived the gunshot.

Just turn around and walk away, she thought.

Don't look. You don't want to see him dead.

If you don't see him, you can remember him the way he looked when he was alive.

How he looked in the pickup truck.

How he felt.

Sobbing, she wiped her tears away.

If you don't see him, you can pretend he's still alive and you'll meet again someday, and he isn't gone forever, and you'll kiss him again, and you can go off somewhere secret in the moonlight and make love all night long.


Clint heard the approaching roar. Before he could say anything, the road began to jump and shake under his feet.

'Holy Samolie!' Em yelled.

Mary cried out, 'Oh, God!'

Tugged from both sides, Clint stumbled and capered about like a blind man at a square dance, torn between two partners.

'Aftershock!' Em shouted. Was there triumph in her voice? She'd been predicting a big aftershock, and here it was.

Clint hated that he couldn't see. He knew that they were somewhere on Crescent Heights, and they'd crossed Wilshire a while ago. But he couldn't see what buildings might be near enough to collapse on them, couldn't see what might be overhead about to fall and crush them, couldn't see anything at all except for the blackness.

As he pranced sideways, Mary cried 'Wah!' and his right arm was suddenly dragged downward. He stumbled and fell, not knowing whether he would land on hard pavement or soft Mary.

He landed on Mary.

Em, still gripping his left arm, was pulled down on top of him.

The quake stopped.

From the feel of things, Clint supposed that his fall had been cushioned by Mary's chest. She was gasping for air as if she'd just finished a sprint.

Em seemed to be pressing down against Clint's left side, straddling his hip as if it were a saddle. He felt her chest working like a bellows against his upper arm, her breath brushing the side of his neck.

After a few moments, she said, 'That was a good one.'

'Are we okay?' Clint asked.

'Bet it was a six-point-five. Maybe better.'

'Can everybody climb off me, now?' Mary asked.

'Nothing's going to fall on us?' Clint asked.

'Nope,' Em said. She squirmed and pushed. Her weight went away from him. 'We're in the middle of the street.'

'Is anything coming?'

'Nope. No cars. No nothing. Give you a pull?'

'Maybe you'd better let go.'

Em let go, and Clint suddenly felt as if she had vanished.

'Don't go anywhere,' he said.

'Right here.'

As he tried to climb off Mary, she helped by pushing at him and rolling. He seemed to skid across her body. When she was out from under him, the hard flatness of the pavement pressed against his back. He started to rise, but was held down by a hand on his chest.

'Don't.' It was Mary's voice. 'Don't move. We gotta rest. I'm dying.'

'You're long overdue,' Em said. 'You were supposed to bite it at Sunset.'

'So much for predictions,' Mary said. She sounded grim.

'God almighty,' Em muttered.

Clint wondered if she was thinking about Loreen. The fortune-teller had sure predicted death at Sunset, but she'd missed by a mile on who would die.

The single advantage of losing his eyesight: he hadn't been able to see the remains of Loreen and Caspar. By the time the big battle was over and Clint had gotten around to opening the rear door of the van, the guy inside had apparently already stripped off their clothes, scalped them both and gotten into some sort of vile, intimate surgery that Em and Mary had refused to give details about.

The guy had greeted Clint with a can of spray paint – a blast of black paint full in the face.

Full in the eyes.

Clint remembered hearing giggles through his own outcry.

But the giggles had stopped very fast.

Must have been a nasty surprise for the guy: taking out the big tough man who had the Bowie knife, only to be killed within seconds by two women.

A real 'team effort,' according to Em.

While Clint had stumbled backward away from the door, Em had hurled her hunting knife. 'Got him right in the throat,' she'd bragged.

'Sure,' Mary'd said. 'With the hilt.'

'But it knocked him down, didn't it? I had it planned that way, so you could get all the glory.'

'So I could get the dirty work, you mean.'

They'd sounded mighty cheerful for two gals talking about how they'd subdued a man and slashed his throat. But Clint supposed they had every right to feel proud of themselves. They'd done a hell of a job.

If they hadn't found the bodies of Loreen and Caspar, they probably would've started a party right there in the rear of the van.

With water she'd found inside the van, Mary had washed out Clint's eyes. The water had taken away some of the burning sting, but hadn't restored his vision. Em had tied a cloth around his head – a blindfold to protect his eyes from the sunlight.

Then they'd each taken one of his arms and guided him across lane after lane, weaving through a tangle of stopped vehicles until they reached the other side.

'Guess what,' Em had said, shaking his arm. 'We made it. We got all the way across Sunset. And Mary's still alive.'

'Maybe that *was* the only bunch of killers,' Clint had suggested.

'Maybe,' Em had said. 'But maybe what happened, the other gangs, they saw how we totally demolished that bunch of weirdos and so they figured us for *bad news* and hid when they saw us coming.'

Mary had made a quiet chuckle. 'That's us, bad news. Two babes and a blind guy.'

'You know what, Mary?'

'You're gonna tell me, Em.'

'Looks to me like adversity agrees with you. You were a major sort of pain in the old rumpazoid a few hours ago, and now you're almost human. Why do you think that is?'

'Better not look a gift horse in the mouth.'

'Yeah. Good point. Maybe you just like killing people.'

'I think it might be the other way around,' Clint had said. 'She likes *saving* people. And she's been doing a damn good job of it, too.'

After that, they'd continued on their way. Em on one of his arms,

359

Mary on the other. Guiding him around obstacles, describing what they saw: the collapsed buildings, the fissures in the pavement, the abandoned vehicles, an occasional small group of people digging through rubble in search of those buried or trapped beneath fallen walls.

There seemed to be few people wandering about. Though Mary and Em reported seeing no roving gangs, they found plenty of dead bodies. Most of the bodies had been stripped and maimed.

Clint wasn't able to see them, which was fine with him.

He was glad that he couldn't look at the bad stuff, but he hated not being able to keep watch for trouble. He felt as if he'd betrayed Em and Mary. He was supposed to be their guardian. How could he protect them when he couldn't see the dangers?

What if I don't get better? he wondered. How can I take care of Sheila and Barbara . . . ?

*Maybe they're dead.*

No!

It occurred to him, lying there on the street with Em and Mary beside him, that he might already have found himself a replacement family.

*Don't want replacements! I want Sheila and Barbara!*

He elbowed the pavement and sat up. 'We've gotta get going. I have to get home.'

He raised his arms. He reached out to each side.

Mary clutched his right hand and said, 'I'm ready.'

His left hand, searching for Em, found her face. She didn't say anything, or move. He felt her forehead and eyebrows under his fingers, her nose pressing against his palm, her lips soft near the heel of his hand.

They kissed him.

Wouldn't mind keeping you around, he thought. If your mother didn't make it . . .

Stop it.

He gave Em's nose a gentle twist. Then she took hold of his hand. 'We better hit the trail,' she said. 'Time's a-wastin'.'

Instead of chopping into the side of Stanley's neck, the butcher knife only nicked his throat as the quake shoved Weed backward. She staggered away from him through the pitching, raging water.

Mixed in with the hurricane roar of the quake was the crash of a gunshot.

Stanley, thrown off his feet and falling, didn't feel a hit. He twisted around.

For a moment before the water blurred his sight, he glimpsed Judy above the corner of the pool. She looked like a terrified sailor dancing the Hornpipe, her revolver jabbing at the sky.

Water closed down over Stanley's head.

360

He was tossed, shoved, rolled over.

*Gonna drown!*

*Shit!*

It rushed through his mind that the aftershock had come like a miracle, just in time to save him from Weed's knife and Judy's .357 magnum or whatever it was – but it had been a big joke, a false save, a dirty trick. It had saved him from the harpies only to drown him.

Gonna drown in three feet of water.

*Should've fucked Sheila in her safe, dry tub.*

But the vicious currents of the pool suddenly loosened their grip on Stanley. He splashed and thrust his face into the sunlit air. His feet found the bottom. He stood up.

Judy was no longer standing at the corner of the pool.

Had she fallen in?

*If she's in, I'll take her. Get that gun . . .*

But he could've spotted her easily if she had fallen into the pool; the water was only waist-deep and almost clear.

She wasn't in it.

She must've fallen backward.

He glanced at Sheila. She still hung from the bottom rung of the ladder. She looked freshly splashed, glossy, gorgeous.

*I'll nail you again after I get rid of these two . . .*

Judy came stumbling to the edge of the pool, looming high above him, the revolver in her hand.

Stanley glanced at Weed.

Out of reach, still submerged.

*Try and get to her, use her for a shield?*

*She'd probably cut my balls off.*

*Do something quick!*

Stanley flung himself sideways, splashed down, kicked and battered his way through the shallow water until the bottom slanted up under him. He scurried along, leaving the water behind, racing over the slick tiles toward the stairs at the end of the pool.

*Gonna catch one in the back.*

'Stop!' Judy shouted from behind him. 'Stop or I'll shoot!'

'Don't shoot!' Stanley yelled, and kept on running.

'Stop!'

'Don't shoot!'

She fired.

Off to Stanley's right, a blue tile exploded. A flying chip from it slashed his calf.

He bounded up the pool stairs.

Judy fired again.

# FORTY-TWO

Dad's old blue Ford wasn't in the driveway. It wasn't parked out front by the curb, either. It was nowhere to be seen.

Beat him home, Barbara thought.

Then she saw that the house was down.

She muttered, 'Oh, my God,' but could hardly hear her voice over the rumble of the Harley's engine.

She steered into the driveway, coasted to a stop, and put down her feet to hold the huge motorcycle steady. The vibrations of the bike made the house seem to shake.

She shut off the engine and dismounted.

She stared at the ruins.

*If Mom was in there when it fell down like that ...*

She's gotta be all right, Barbara told herself. Gotta be. I made it, didn't I? Mom made it, too. Somehow. Please. We've all gotta be all right – Mom and Dad – Pete, too, wherever he is.

Standing in the driveway, she yelled, 'Mom! Mom?'

She listened for an answer.

None came.

She knew that she would have to enter the demolished house and search for her.

*Gonna find her crushed.*

No! She's fine.

Barbara felt a sick reluctance to start the search.

She decided to fix her bandage.

Back in the alley, after checking all the bodies and not finding Pete, she had pulled the T-shirt off the biker who'd worn the Viking helmet. Somehow, his shirt had escaped most of the blood from his shot head. She'd folded it into a long pad, placed it against the raw furrow on her side, then strapped it in place with the guy's wide, leather belt.

The makeshift bandage had worked fine for a block or two, but then the rough vibrations of the motorcycle had started shaking it down her ribcage. She'd caught the T-shirt in time to save it, and tucked it under the front of the belt.

Now, the belt drooped around her waist, the T-shirt hanging from it like a loincloth.

She started to take off her blouse, then changed her mind.

This wasn't some alley far from home; this was the driveway in front of her house. Neighbors might be watching.

Her back to the street, she peeled the sticky blouse away from her side. She slipped the T-shirt underneath, placed it gently against her wound, and strapped it secure with the belt.

Then she fastened a couple of buttons to hold her blouse shut.

She took a deep breath. It made her lungs ache the way they usually ached when she got home from the family's annual visit to the L.A. County Fair in Pomona – a day of breathing badly polluted air. She guessed that the ache, now, came from too much smoke and dust.

She wondered if she would ever again go to the Fair with her mom and dad.

Wondered if she would ever again see them alive.

She swallowed. Her mouth and throat felt very dry.

Go on and get it over with, she told herself. Stalling won't make it any better. And what if Mom needs help?

She decided to check around, one more time, before starting into the house.

So she turned slowly and scanned the neighborhood. Near the far corner, a house had burned down. A couple of other homes had been destroyed, some had major damage, and a few looked almost unharmed. She saw no one.

No one at all, dead or alive.

If a gang had come through, she told herself, there'd be a lot of bodies around.

That's good news, at least. But where is everyone?

At work, she supposed. Or at school. Or staying inside their houses – cleaning up the messes, or hiding.

She wondered if any of her neighbors had turned wild.

Turned wild and gone on a rampage.

Some must've, she thought.

Damn near everyone she'd encountered had been nuts, one way or the other. As if the quake had released a virus buried in the depths of the earth – a virus that turned people into savages.

Barbara doubted that anything like that had happened, though.

Nobody'd gone nuts because of a virus or a gas or space invaders.

It seemed to be more like everyone had a drooling, wild-eyed lunatic walled up inside, eager to get free, and the quake had broken apart the walls holding them in.

*Everyone but me and Pete.*

363

*Pretty much.*

*Maybe we went nuts, too, and just didn't happen to notice.*

*Who knows, who knows, who knows?*

*Quit stalling.*

She wished she still had a gun. Or a knife. Or any weapon at all. She had nothing.

Doesn't matter, she told herself. Nobody's around.

Not yet, anyway.

She started walking toward the remains of her home.

She was only vaguely aware that she no longer had a house to live in, that everything she owned was probably broken or ruined, that her life would never be the same as it had been before the earthquake.

She supposed that, later, such things might really hurt.

For now, though, all she really cared about was the safety of her mother and father.

If they're okay, she thought, everything else'll turn out all right.

And if Pete's okay, too.

But she'd seen Pete go down, shot. He might've crawled off, she supposed. But why would he do that? Maybe the woman had driven him away in her Lincoln. Or his body could've been rushed off in a shopping cart by some filthy scavenger who wanted him for reasons too awful to think about.

*Just don't think about him.*

Barbara climbed the front stoop.

The house looked like a bombed-out ruin.

I've never *seen* a bombed-out ruin, she reminded herself. Well, in documentaries.

But she'd seen something that reminded her . . . Places burnt during the L.A. riot of '92.

Those places had been black, though – smoked and charred. No fires, here. Just everything torn apart, shattered, busted, smashed, splintered, crushed.

'Mom?' she called out. 'Mom! Are you here? Mom?'

She stood motionless and held her breath. Nearby, everything seemed very quiet. The only sounds came from far off: sirens, car engines, bangs that were probably gunshots, shouts, helicopters.

The activity was elsewhere.

Los Angeles was a place of troubles, but her own neighborhood had always been spared – a tranquil island surrounded by raging seas and sharks.

It was tranquil now.

Tranquil, but devastated.

'Mom?' she called again. 'Where are you? Can you hear me?' She listened again.

And heard a groan from somewhere in the debris.

It seemed to come from her left, from someplace near the area where the kitchen used to be.

'Hello?' she called. 'Mom?'

'Buh – Barrrr?' It was barely a murmur, but she heard it.

'Yes!' she cried out, tears flooding her eyes. 'It's me, Mom! It's me! I'm home! Where are you? Talk to me. I'm on my way.'

She started trudging through the rubble, stepping carefully to avoid nails and broken glass.

'I'm okay,' she explained. 'Basically. I got shot a little bit, but I'm okay. We got stuck downtown 'cause Mr Wellen went nuts. The driver's ed teacher? He flipped out . . . who didn't, though? God, you're lucky you were here. It was like a horror movie downtown, you wouldn't believe it. Are you okay? Could you say something?'

She went silent and halted.

Heard nothing.

'Mom?'

'Baaa . . . bath . . .'

'You're in the bathroom?'

'Tub.'

'You're in the tub? Great! I'll find you. That's probably what saved you, the tub. I saw what the house looked like, and I figured you . . . I just hoped you weren't in it, that's all. I hope Dad's all right. He's probably stuck in traffic somewhere. You wouldn't believe how crazy it is out there. Everyone went nuts. People are getting murdered right and left . . . The good news is, the National Guard's supposed to get here tomorrow. That's what I hear. Won't be a minute too soon, if you ask . . .'

The head stopped her voice.

It was staring up at her from the cluttered floor behind the refrigerator.

A head of tangled black hair and shaggy beard and blood and plaster crumbs.

Its neck, near Barbara's foot, was an ugly raw stump.

She took a quick step backward to get away from it.

'Mom? Who's this?'

No answer came.

'There's a head over here.'

She was answered by a groan from somewhere not far beyond the half-buried stove.

Approximately where the bathroom should be.

She hurried toward it.

When she got past the stove, she found a body stretched out alongside a place where the floor was missing. A man.

All his clothes were gone.

He had his head, though.

*A gang got here, after all. Scavengers, too. But they missed Mom.*

Barbara stepped past the head of the naked man and peered down into the hole in the floor where she expected to find the tub.

The tub was there.

But not her mother.

The body at the bottom of the tub was a man, a skinny little guy in black leather pants and boots. He had no shirt, but he had his head. It was hairless. He didn't even have eyebrows.

He didn't even have eyes.

His sockets were dark, gooey pits.

Barbara jerked her gaze away from them and raised her head. Turning, she scanned the broken remains of the house.

'Mom?'

She glimpsed a pair of feet sticking out from behind a nearby pile of rubble, but the feet wore black boots.

'*MOM!*' Barbara shrieked. '*MOM, WHERE ARE YOU? WHAT'S GOING ON?*'

'Here I am, dearie.'

She flinched. The voice came from just behind her, and sounded like a man mimicking an old lady.

She turned around fast.

The dead man she'd found stretched out naked on the floor wasn't dead.

He was no longer stretched out.

He was squatting, leering up at her.

'Surprise,' he said.

Barbara felt chilly prickles on the back of her neck.

I was right, she thought. One of the neighbors *did* go wild.

He didn't have on a stitch of clothes. His eyes were as wild as any she had ever seen. From the fiery redness of his skin, he must've been out in the sun all day. Hands on his wide-apart knees, he made no attempt to hide his erection; it looked as if it were pointing at Barbara's face.

'Hi, Mr Banks,' she said.

His leer slipped. 'You know me?'

'You live behind us. Over there.' She dipped her head in the direction of his house. 'With your mother.'

He frowned. 'How do you know that?'

'We've gotten your mail by mistake. I've walked it over to your house a few times. And I've seen you around. Are you all right?'

*Good one, Banner. Sure he's all right. Slipped a few cogs, that's all. And any second he's gonna pounce on your sorry ass and do God only knows what to you.*

'I'm hunky-dory,' he said. 'And you?'

*What'd he do to Mom?*

*Ask?*

*I don't think so.*

'It hasn't been the best day ever,' Barbara said. 'For one thing, I got shot.'

His eyes widened. He suddenly looked eager and gleeful. 'Shot? Is that so?'

'Do you want to see?'

His gaze latched on the bloody side of her blouse. 'Under there?'

'Yes.'

'Show me.'

Hands trembling, she started to unfasten the two buttons that kept her blouse shut. 'That was a good trick,' she said. 'Playing dead? I've used it myself.'

*Shouldn't have fallen for it.*

She opened her blouse.

Banks nibbled his lower lip. He was still squatting, hands on knees, but now his lower end was swaying a little from side to side. 'What's that?' he asked.

'A belt.' She reached for the buckle that was just beneath her right breast, and started to unfasten it. 'I took it off a dead biker. It's what holds my bandage on.'

'Ah.'

'You want the bandage off, don't you?'

'Sure. I want *everything* off.'

She tugged, and the belt went loose around her chest. The rag against her wound started to slip. She pulled some more, and the belt fell out from under her blouse. She kept hold of its buckle. As the leather strap swayed by the side of her leg, she shook herself slightly. The sodden T-shirt still stuck to her wound for a moment, then let go. It dropped and landed by her foot.

'It's sure bloody,' she said.

'That's all right.'

'Do you want it?'

'Show me where you were shot.'

'Okay.'

He gazed at the bloody side of her blouse. 'Show,' he said. 'Off with the blouse.' He wiped his mouth with the back of a hand.

'First, you have to tell me where my mother is.'

He grinned. 'Dead. Deader than shit. Like all good mothers.'

The words made a sick, cold hardness grow in the center of Barbara, somewhere just below her chest.

'I fucked her to death,' Banks said. Rolling his eyes upward and hanging his tongue out, he made quick thrusting motions with his pelvis.

Barbara whipped the belt at him. He jerked his hands up to block it, but wasn't quick enough. He cried out as the leather strap smacked the side of his face.

Barbara leaped away from him, twisted around, and ran.

'You're dead!' Banks yelled.

She glanced back. He was already up, already chasing her. He flapped his big arms and brought his knees up high like a crazed man charging through surf.

Barbara had a good headstart.

She knew that she would be fine if she could make it as far as the patio. Clear of the debris, she would be able to pour on the speed. Banks wouldn't stand a chance of catching her.

Not far from the remains of the rear wall, she glanced back again.

He was huffing along, staggering, farther behind than before.

*Not gonna get me!*

She leaped over a small pile of debris, right leg stretching out, foot pounding down.

Driving a spike of pain up the middle of her foot.

She squealed.

Looking down, she saw the point of a nail come up through the top of her sneaker.

*Oh, my God!*

She didn't stop running.

Her left leg stretched out and went down and landed on nothing horrible, but the pain in her right foot turned to ripping agony. Looking over her shoulder, she saw it kicking up behind her, a plank attached to the bottom of her shoe like a short wooden ski.

The toe of the plank stubbed a block of plaster.

Barbara fell headlong.


Stanley hooked his right hand under the waistband of her shorts and lifted her out of the rubble where she'd fallen.

She swung her arms, kicked, squirmed and squealed.

A few strides, and Stanley was clear of the ruined house. He hauled her across the patio.

Barbara squirmed and twisted so much that she started to come out of her shorts. When they were halfway down her rump, Stanley lowered her to the concrete and let go.

She tried to scuttle away.

Crouching, he caught her shorts by their sides and yanked them down to her knees. Her panties went down with them. Though they hobbled her, she kept on crawling.

Stanley grabbed them and tugged them the rest of the way off. They took a shoe with them. He glimpsed the bloody bottom of her right sock.

And stomped on it.

Barbara shrieked.

The pain seemed to freeze her on her hands and knees.

Stanley grabbed the back of her collar. He jammed his other hand between her legs. With both hands, he picked her up. He carried her to the lounger.

The lounger where she liked to stretch out and sunbathe.

Where Sheila did, too.

Both of them nearly naked in their bikinis – their bodies long and tawny and gleaming.

He swung Barbara into position above the faded green pad, and let go. She dropped onto it. He peeled the blouse off her shoulders and down her back. He flung it away.

She was facedown on the pad, naked except for her socks, one sneaker, and a pad of tissues attached with rubber bands to one of her forearms.

Good enough, Stanley said.

He spread her legs.

*No no no no! Turn her over. The best stuff's on the other side! You haven't even seen her tits yet!*

Standing by the side of the lounger, he bent and reached across her body. He grabbed her upper left arm and hip, then pulled. The lounger suddenly tipped toward him.

Barbara was holding on to the aluminum frame under the pad.

'Let go!' Stanley yelled.

'No!'

He released her hip and jammed his thumb into the pulpy groove of her bullet wound. Her body jerked rigid and the blast of a gunshot crashed through the noise of her scream.

Stanley jumped.

He stood up straight.

Judy again.

Standing atop the cinderblock wall at the rear of the yard, her revolver pointed at the sky.

Weed stood on one side of her, Sheila on the other.

The three women looked the same as before, except that Sheila wasn't naked anymore. She wore a shiny, royal blue kimono that probably belonged to Judy. It was much too small for her. It wouldn't shut all the way, in front, and reached only a few inches down her thighs. Its sleeves barely reached to her elbows.

Both of Sheila's wrists were wrapped with broad, white bandages.

'Don't move a muscle!' Judy called.

Stanley shook his head.

This'd be funny, he thought, if it wasn't such a pain in the ass.

*She thinks she can hit me! She couldn't hit me at the pool, and this is three times the distance. At least!*

But he didn't see how he could enjoy a good time with Barbara – not with them here.

Why the hell hadn't the bitches stayed away?

For a while after escaping from them, he'd thought they would try to hunt him down. He'd hidden in the ruins of Sheila's house and waited, frightened but eager, planning to take them by surprise when they came looking.

*Take 'em by surprise and take 'em down.*

*Have myself a ball.*

But they hadn't come.

Barbara had showed up, instead.

He glanced down at her.

Her head was raised. She was looking toward the three women on the wall.

Probably surprised to see her mother there, alive after all.

'Get away from her,' Judy called. 'Get away and walk toward us.'

'Go ahead and see if you can hit me!'

She took aim at him.

'Sure thing,' he called.

With a laugh, he bent over, grabbed Barbara and flipped her onto her back. The noise of a gunshot made him flinch. But he didn't bother looking up, because he knew that Judy wouldn't have risked hitting the girl.

He gazed at Barbara's slick body.

Not in Sheila's league, he thought. But close. Close enough to make him ache to have her.

He squeezed her breasts. They were smaller than Sheila's. Very hot and slippery and firm. The nipples felt like tongues probing the palms of his hands.

Judy fired again.

*You're hurting my ears, you bitch. I'll drive nails into your ears, when I catch you.*

*Forget about Judy, you've got Barbara.*

*A bird in the hands.*

*Birds. A couple of tits.*

She was gasping for air, gazing up at him with very wide eyes.

Scared to death, hurting bad.

Turned on?

370

'Love it!' Stanley blurted.

And thought, maybe I *have* got time. Just a quick one. In and out. Once, maybe twice.

The way he felt, just once should be enough.

*I'll blow the roof off the joint!*

It could get me killed, he thought.

And laughed, and jerked her legs apart and climbed onto the pad and knelt between them. The lounger wobbled, but held.

Another gunshot.

Was it nearer than before?

*If Judy's off the wall, running . . . She gets close enough, I'm dead.*

He looked at the wall.

Judy was still on top of it, and Weed still stood at her side.

But Sheila was in midair, dropping toward the ground. The breeze of her fall lifted the bottom of her kimono and spread it open to the sash at her waist.

My honey, Stanley thought. Come to me!

Her feet hit the ground. Her legs bent. She did a very fast somersault and came out of it sprinting over the grass straight toward Stanley.

He glanced down at Barbara.

*Do it! One quick one!*

But he couldn't stop his eyes from being pulled back to Sheila. The sash of her kimono had come loose. The silken blue robe shimmered and flowed behind her like a cape.

She raced toward him, long legs striding out, arms pumping hard, fists clenched. Her legs gleamed, alive with shifting curves of muscle under their sunburn and scrapes and welts. She had a long white bandage high on her thigh where Stanley had cut her with the saw. Except for the bandage, her legs were bare all the way up to her wispy tuft of golden curls.

Her breasts lurched and jumped with the rough motion of her running.

Stanley had always hoped to see her running without a bra on.

Getting my wish, he thought. At last, at last.

*No wonder she always wore one!*

*Look at 'em go!*

They looked splendid.

*She* looked splendid.

Not just her body, but her face. As weathered and battered as it was, it still looked glorious to Stanley. At once smooth and hard, delicate and powerful, silk and granite, innocent and sophisticated. But altogether beautiful, the face of a movie queen and a warrior goddess melded into one stunning, incredible Sheila Banner.

*My naked, caped crusader.*

*Wonder Woman.*

*Super Sheila.*

*MIGHTY MOM COMING TO SAVE HER KID AND SHE'S UNCHAINED, UNWIRED, ON THE LOOSE, COMING FOR ME – SHIT!!!*

Suddenly, watching Sheila dash toward him, Stanley was scared.

Scared to death.

*Gotta get the fuck outa here!*

He was kneeling between Barbara's legs.

He started to scoot backward.

Barbara reached out fast and grabbed him, one hand wrapping tight around his penis.

'Let go!' he shrieked.

She tightened her grip.

'No!'

He jerked his head sideways.

Sheila, dashing full speed, bare feet smacking loud on the concrete of the patio, stretched out her arms and took to the air.

She dived into Stanley.

Hugged him.

Tore him down sideways off the lounger – from the feel of things, Barbara held on too long – and smashed him against the concrete.

He had Sheila on top of him.

Sitting on his belly.

He was in agony, too breathless to scream.

But he could feel the slippery heat of Sheila's buttocks against his skin. The tickle of her bush. The sharp iron blows of her fists against his face. He watched how her breasts bounced and jerked as she punched him. He watched her face, too.

She had such fury in her eyes.

Banner, Barbara
English 11A
September 23

## THE QUAKE AND I

I guess that a subject like 'what I did on my summer vacation' would make a fairly lame assignment, considering that we all went through such an incredibly bad earthquake just before the end of last semester.

It turned out to really be the end of last semester.

Anyway, I am glad to be back in school, even though I'm not exactly filled with joy about having to write about the earthquake.

It was like Charles Dickens said: 'It was the best of times; it was the worst of times.'

I was out on the streets in the driver's education car with the teacher and three other students when the earthquake struck. Mr Wellen took over driving, and took us on a detour to downtown, where we ended up getting stranded. We had quite an adventure trying to get back home.

When I finally did get home, I discovered that our house had been completely knocked down by the earthquake. My mother, inside the house at the time of the collapse, lived through it by jumping into our bathtub. The bathtub saved her life.

My father was at work in the Valley when the quake struck. Like me, he had all sorts of adventures trying to get home. He arrived about an hour after I did, and had a couple of strangers with him. The strangers were a grownup woman named Mary, and a thirteen-year-old named Em, short for Emerald. Dad was blind when he arrived home, having been injured by getting some paint in his eyes. It was a good thing he had Mary and Em with him, because they are the ones who led him home. Fortunately, Dad has since regained his eyesight.

As our house was destroyed, we all lived in the home of our neighbors, Judy and Herb. All of us stayed there together for about a week – and what a week it was! Judy and Herb were really neat people. Mary got to be very annoying, but Em and I became very good friends. We've gotten together quite a number of times since then, and we always have a fine time. Em's mother is a real character, and sort of fun.

Anyway, my parents and I found ourselves an apartment and are living there while our new house is being built, which is supposed to take about a year.

The worst thing about the quake is that so many people got injured and killed. Stuff fell on some of them. A lot of people, however, slaughtered each other during that first day, before the National Guard showed up. People can be so horrible when they think they can get away with things.

The best part about the quake is that I learned a lot about things such as courage and loyalty and love.

I just hope that when the next major earthquake hits Los Angeles, I am out of town on a vacation.

the end

'Jeez, you left out a few things.'

'Yeah? Like what?'

'Like me.'

'Oh, you want me to tell what we did in the back of the pickup truck? That'd be cute. I'm sure Mr Kling would *love* that.'

'You could write about how we saved the woman from the bikers, and how she drove me to the hospital and saved *my* life.'

'I don't wanta write about that. I mean, it's great that she saved you, but . . . I sure wish she'd left me a note, or something.'

'She thought you were dead.'

'I know, I know. A very observant lady. But I spent like *weeks* thinking about all the awful things that might've happened to you. I figured maybe one of those street-vultures had probably eaten your pancreas for dinner.'

'Can someone eat a pancreas?'

'If someone's hungry enough. Sure. Why not?'

'Anyway, you're just gonna leave everything out of your paper?'

'I didn't leave *everything* out.'

'Almost everything. And all of the bad stuff.'

'If I put all *that* in, my report'd be like hundreds of pages long and I'd never get it done. Besides which, I'm not about to go telling some teacher about that nut trying to rape me. And God knows, I don't want to incriminate anyone. It isn't as if we didn't kill quite a bunch of people, you know?'

'It was in self-defense.'

'Yeah, but you don't go around admitting to that sort of thing in an English paper.'

'Your mom really *beat* that guy to death?'

'With her fists.'

'God. It's hard to imagine her doing something like that. I mean, she's so . . .'

'Beautiful?'

'Well, you know, yeah. But *nice*, too. I mean, she's one of the nicest people I've ever known.'

'Just don't get her mad at you.'

'Great.'

'And my dad can be even worse.'

'You're sure they know I'm here?'

'*Why?* Are you worried? I mean, we're just doing our *homework* together, right?'

'Yeah, I guess so.'

'My homework's done. How about yours?'

'As if I had any.'

'What do you want to do, now?'

'I don't know.'

'The apartment house across the street has a pool in its courtyard.'

'It does?'

'I've never seen anyone using it, either. I bet we could sneak in and have it all to ourselves.'

'What if we get caught?'

'What're they gonna do, *shoot* us?'

'What time are your parents supposed to get home?'

'The movie gets out at ten, so we've got almost a whole hour. And by the way, they *don't* know you're here.'

'I could sure go for a swim, about now.'